About the Author

Ian Wishart is an award-winning journalist and author, with a 30 year career in radio, television and magazines, a #1 talk radio show and five #1 bestselling books to his credit. Together with his wife Heidi, they edit and publish the news magazine *Investigate* and the news website www.investigatedaily.com.

Winston
The Story Of A Political Phenomenon

Ian Wishart

HOWLING AT THE MOON PUBLISHING LTD

Howling At The Moon Publishing Ltd

First edition published 2014
by Howling At The Moon Publishing Ltd
PO Box 188, Kaukapakapa
Auckland 0843, NEW ZEALAND

Email: editorial@investigatemagazine.com
Web: http://www.ianwishart.com

Copyright © Ian Wishart, 2014
Copyright © Howling At The Moon Publishing Ltd, 2014

The moral rights of the author have been asserted.

Winston is copyright. Except for the purpose of fair reviewing, no part of this publication may be copied, reproduced or transmitted in any form or by any means, including via technology either already in existence or developed subsequent to publication, without the express written permission of the publisher and authors. All rights reserved.

ISBN 978-0-9941064-1-4

Cover photo by Ian Wishart
Typeset in Adobe Garamond Pro and Chronicle Display
Cover concept: Heidi and Ian Wishart
Book design: Bozidar Jokanovic

Contents

Introduction 6
Humble Beginnings 8
Ngati Luigi 16
A Fuse Is Lit 25
We All Live On A Yellow Submarine 33
Vladimir Putin Lived In Karori 53
The Maori Loans Affair 59
When In Rome 72
Battle Of The Bolger 84
Sickly White Liberals 90
How To Win Friends 104
The Years Of Living Dangerously 115
Enter The Gladiator 124
Mutually Assured Destruction 138
The Sarah Neems Mystery 158
Conspiracy Fact 165
It's 2am, It Must Be Winston 183
A Funny Thing Happened On The Way To The Poll 201
The Battle Of Black Stump 208
Winston On The Witness Stand 232
Winston's Secret Deal With Ratana Church 248
Great Expectations 260
Crash And Burn: 1997–1999 276
And They Got Up Again 296
The Price Of Politics 306
Keeping The Bastards Honest: Snapshots 319

Introduction

Let's assume you've just arrived from Planet Mars to New Zealand, and know nothing of a politician named Winston Peters. Why should you care, what's to know?

This book is intended to shake you out of that faulty assumption. Love him or loathe him (and there are few people to be found in the middle ground), Winston Peters has been a driving force, a Colossus, of New Zealand politics for nigh on four decades.

Although he's constantly dismissed as a "conspiracy theorist" or a "populist" or a "racist" – or sometimes all three – by his foes, it is easy to fall into the trap of being beguiled by popular opinion, of following the dogwhistle that sharp political operators employ when trying to manipulate public opinion.

Of course, some would say Winston Peters is just as good at dogwhistling himself.

There has been a previous attempt at a biography – 1995's *Winston First* by Martin Hames, a former Ruth Richardson staffer. Unfortunately Hames' book contained no bibliography and no footnotes, so proving the accuracy of the claims made in that book was difficult if not impossible for scholars.

Those who paid real cash for *Winston First* generally loved it, if only because Hames was preaching to a choir who loathed Peters with a passion. However, in a scathing review of *Winston First*, political historian Barry Gustafson wrote:[1]

---

1 "Book Review: Martin Hames, Winston First", by Dr Barry Gustafson, *Political Science* December 1995

"Unfortunately Martin Hames' version is a sustained and at times almost hysterical partisan polemic with little if any pretence at academic objectivity or balance…According to Hames, everyone that Peters ever criticised was a blameless victim and there was never any justification for a public inquiry into the activities of the BNZ, Fay Richwhite or European Pacific's Cook Islands tax avoidance schemes.

"There is an interesting little essay on populism, as part of an attempt to use a psychobiographical approach to portray Peters as a Narcissistic Populist pandering to popular prejudice in an obsessive drive to be Prime Minister. But Hames, who worked as an advisor for five years in the offices of Peters' two most bitter critics, Jim Bolger and Ruth Richardson, is unconvincing in trying to explain why Peters sacrificed that objective by refusing to play by the rules," wrote Gustafson.

In other words, if Peters was really the megalomaniac Hames was claiming, why did he give up his chance at absolute power by refusing to work within the system?

It is easy, with highly charged subjects like Winston Peters, to go all one-dimensional – 'it's either black, or its white, choose the biography colour that suits your view of the man!'

Somewhere in between those books, between *Winston First* at one extreme and *Winston Walks On Water* at the fictional other extreme, you'll find a more accurate telling of the Peters story, the story of how one man and his beliefs and policies have impacted a generation and changed the course of New Zealand history in ways you may never have realised.

This is not an exhaustive political biography covering every meeting or minor dispute in intense detail. Rather, it's a 'greatest hits and misses' package that covers the things that had a lasting impact on Peters and NZ First, helping determine the identity and direction of the man, and the party as it stands today.

It's an entertaining, at times hilarious, account spiced with things the media never bothered to report or in many cases never even knew.

1

Humble Beginnings

> *"The bulk of better reporting consists of information that does not meet the courtroom standards of proof. Journalism is not a court of law; it is a process of weaving together, often from necessarily anonymous sources, the strands of history. If legal standards were applied to news reporting, the public would have learned nothing of the Watergate scandal and President Nixon would not have resigned in disgrace"*
>
> – **William Pinwill, National Times on Sunday, 1988**

The voice down the end of the phone sounds almost pained: "I can't be interviewed for this book, I'm in the middle of preparing for an election campaign!" All politicians are addicted to publicity, and there's no doubt Winston Raymond Peters is a consummate politician. One gets the feeling that asking him to be interviewed under these particular circumstances is like offering chocolates to a Jenny Craig member, or the squirrel-rat character 'Scrat' in the *Ice Age* cartoons desperately trying to choose between the tempting acorn or avoiding the avalanche hurtling toward him, eyes darting as he struggles to make a decision between desire and necessity. On this day, Winston Peters is that squirrel-rat.

"When you've got 58 boxes of documents in storage to back up what you've said, it takes time to go through them. I've got to concentrate on this election."

Vintage Peters. Always on the go, always on the case, living for now and the future, not the past, but with the ever-present hint that he's capable of dropping a ton of evidence on someone, even after nearly four decades in politics.

An official biographer, sometime, will undoubtedly revel in the contents of Winston's treasure chest, but it will probably have to be posthumously and even then the spectre of a gnarled, skeletal hand punching through the turf and clamping itself around the wrist of anyone reaching for those documents cannot be ruled out. That's one thing about Winston Peters, he may be down from time to time but "out" is another matter entirely.

To truly understand the phenomenon of Winston Peters, one has to put aside the prejudices – one way or the other – and simply listen to the story unfold.

Born April 11, 1945 in Whangarei hospital, home was the tiny rural coastal settlement of Whananaki, 50km north east of Whangarei. Winston Raymond Peters (his birth was actually registered as 'Wynston'[2]) was a baby-boomer, the sixth of 11 children, with six brothers and four sisters. His parents Len and Joan (*née* McInnes) farmed the area and, like all rural kids in that time, young Winston was expected to help with the chores as he grew up. As he once told the *Herald*, as a boy he wasn't usually finished "milking the cows" until around 8.45pm.[3]

Father Len Peters was of Ngati Wai iwi with a measure of Ngati Hine and Ngapuhi – "his family had lived there for hundreds and hundreds of years," says Winston[4] – while Joan, as her maiden name suggests, was Scottish. Many have made the comparison between Scottish clan structure and Maori iwi and hapu, and when Joan passed away in 2008 in her late nineties, those paying tribute included Maori Party leader Pita Sharples:[5]

"Joan was such a driving force in the Far North, you'd never know she was not Maori. But her clear moral values, her hard work and thrift, and her ethic of selfless service is very much part of her Scottish background as well," he told journalists.

Mana Party leader Hone Harawira was another remarking at the impact of Joan Peters and her family on New Zealand:[6]

---

2 The 1945 microfiche index of births spells it "Wynston". "The registrar thought the spellings were interchangeable," says Peters.
3 "Dining with Winston Peters," by Jonathan Milne, NZ Herald, 21 August 2005
4 Interview with Mark Sainsbury, RadioLive, 29 June 2014
5 "Winston Peters' mother dies on eve of party conference," NZPA, 18 July 2008
6 Ibid

"Among Joan's 11 children, Jim was a school principal and chaired the regional council before becoming an MP, Marie has been involved in tribal history and research, Wayne's a well-known lawyer, David has managed the farm, Lynette has managed hauora services and chairs the Northland DHB, Heather's the director of the Auckland University Teacher's College Campus in Whangarei, Ian is a former MP, Winston needs no introduction – the list of achievements and Joan's legacy goes on," Harawira told NZPA.

"My mother died when she was 97," Peters recalls, "my father when he was 85 and possibly would have gone much longer but he wouldn't go to hospital. He could be pretty stubborn and the last thing he wanted to do was die in a hospital."

To an outsider, life in Whananaki might seem idyllic. Nestled at the mouth of the Whananaki Inlet where the Te Wairahi stream drifts lazily, emptying itself into the azure Pacific, Whananaki is redolent of long, languid summers and kids playing in the shallows, catching flounder for the evening meal and kina in the rock pools.

Asked what he learned from his parents in such a big family, Peters remembered a childhood ruled by a work ethic.

"One needs to work to eat," he told the *Herald*.[7] "The Little Red Hen story was often a parental parable. Saving leads to realisable dreams. Waste not, want not, which is why one becomes a bit of a hoarder. Timeless lessons."

He added that his parents had the same aspirations for their children as many others of their generation:

"That we would all be successful and happy, safe and healthy. The greatest parent-taught ambition was that if we deserved it, we could be whatever we aspired to be; and never give up."

In Maori, the word "whananaki" means "kicking", and the village supposedly earned the moniker from no less a personage than the ancestral Ngapuhi chief Puhi, leader of the Mataatua canoe, on account of the restless night he spent at Whananaki being chewed on by mosquitos.

Evidently the mosquitos were no worse than anywhere else, because people stayed and have lived there for eight or nine centuries now. Today, the heart of this village is its school.

Founded in 1887 with an initial roll of just 23 children, Whananaki

---

[7] "Twelve Questions: Winston Peters", by Sarah Stuart, NZ Herald, 18 April 2013

School is – like its most famous pupil – a survivor. Bucking the trend of rural school closures as a result of falling rolls, Whananaki found a novel solution when the threat of extinction raised its head:

"When faced with this dire possibility in the early 1970s," Winston Peters told the school's 125th Jubilee in 2012,[8] "the local people thought 'outside the box' and placed an advert in the *New Zealand Herald* newspaper published in Auckland, for solo mothers with children to come and live here rent free."

The concept of a rural community luring new blood to their settlement by offering rent-free accommodation to mothers in need resulted not just in an advertisement but a front page story in the *Herald*.

"The Whananaki people had spruced up empty houses and set its mind to raising the school roll and keep the school open," remembered Peters. "That has been the spirit of this school, teachers, dental and district nurses, and the local school board, parents and students.

"This place and this school is part of who we are. Or rather this school is the better part of who we are."

As I said, to understand the man, you first have to understand his story. Winston was never a city kid; he was a country boy with old-fashioned values forged in a crucible of clan and iwi culture – a place where everyone had the right to get themselves a feed from their own hard work, and better themselves. It was a place where people helped each other – even strangers – as the solo-mums influx shows. Even so, it still had its boundaries:

"This of course was a most unusual community," recalled Peters at the jubilee, "comprised of Maori and European, a significant number of which were members of the Exclusive Brethren Church, in which case most of us, whether Maori or European, had our noses pressed against the window because for this Church, the rest of us were all outsiders!

"We all remember that for many of us, our early days here were a time of significant hardship and economic deprivation, of rowing across the estuary or riding horses to school. But we all believed that tomorrow would be better, and it was."

Horses were a mainstay back in the day; Winston was riding while still

---

8 "Whananaki School – 125th Anniversary", Winston Peters speech notes, 20 October 2012, http://nzfirst.org.nz/speech/whananaki-primary-school-125th-anniversary

a toddler.⁹ Former pupils at the jubilee had equally fond memories:

"We had to ride our horse Snowball to school and we would come down through the river and catch flounder on the way," Suie Rata (*née* Waetford) told the *Herald*.¹⁰ On one occasion they even gave some of the catch to the teacher, but rather than 'thanks for tea' received a "growling" for being late. In those days the footbridge that now crosses the estuary to link both sides of Whananaki did not exist, and it was up to the school principal to row kids across the inlet.

Some of Winston Peters' whiter-skinned opponents, particularly those of a more liberal, Ponsonby, bent, have scorned the fact that Peters is not fluent in Maori – implying he's not authentic. The reason for that is simple: Winston was born at a time when speaking Maori was discouraged.

"I have Maori children in my care who can hardly speak a word of their native tongue," said a Wanganui school teacher in the 1930s.¹¹ "When I question them on the subject they say that their parents will not allow them to speak it. It is a great pity that some Maori parents are ashamed of their language, and I would emphasise the need of introducing the teaching of Maori into our education curriculum in some way if the native tongue is not to die out altogether."

Maori parents had demanded that schools should allow conversations only in English, in order to bring their children up to Pakeha literacy standards as rapidly as possible, and many Pakeha were aghast, as this letter writer to a newspaper in 1935 demonstrates:¹²

"During a recent visit to Rotorua I was appalled to find that no effort at all is made in the native school at Whakarewarewa to teach the Maori children their own language, and what is more, they are actually punished if they speak Maori in the school or school grounds."

Whananaki School, likewise, had a policy – endorsed by its community – that children were not allowed to speak Maori at school.¹³

Clearly, the Peters children have become high achievers. Some would

---

9 "The man who would be king" by Helen Bain, New Zealand Herald, 25 May 1996, p 16
10 "Whananaki School in the most magnificent setting", by Kristin Edge, NZ Herald, 23 October 2012
11 The Maori Language, New Zealand Herald, Volume LXIX, Issue 21311, 12 October 1932, Page 12
http://paperspast.natlib.govt.nz/cgi-bin/paperspast?a=d&cl=search&d=NZH19321012.2.125
12 The Maori Language, New Zealand Herald, Volume LXXII, Issue 22052, 7 March 1935, Page 13
http://paperspast.natlib.govt.nz/cgi-bin/paperspast?a=d&cl=search&d=NZH19350307.2.149.7
13 "Whananaki School in the most magnificent setting", by Kristin Edge, NZ Herald, 23 October 2012

say they did so because of their parents' and community's desire to look outward, rather than inward. With a Scottish mother and a Maori father, Winston Peters was to some extent the epitome of Captain William Hobson's Waitangi promise, "He iwi tahi tatou" – we are now one people. The language around the hearth was English, for fairly obvious reasons – it was the native tongue of Winston's mother.

He is also, says former NZ First colleague Doug Woolerton, "almost Victorian" in his manners. "For instance, he hates my swearing."[14] Woolerton told the *Herald* how he and Winston had seen a dusty old ute with a sign saying "I wish my wife was as dirty as this ute".

"He was shocked by that. He thought that was just disgusting."

From his country school Winston spent a year at Whangarei Boys High before transferring to Dargaville High School for his fourth form year. Gail Matich (nee Bruce) remembers him well.

"He was the only boy in our class and the girls used to give him what for!," Matich laughs.[15] It was a "Commercial" class as they called it back then, with lessons in typing, book-keeping and the like. "He was a nice bloke, all the girls got on with him – as a friend," she adds quickly. "He was quiet and played a good game of rugby."

Matich initially suspected her classmate was more of a Labour voter than a National one:

"We used to have a few little political arguments in the library sometimes, my parents were National and Winston and I often disagreed, so I wonder if he started off more of a Labour person – I don't know."

Matich says she still sees Winston occasionally.

"I remember going down to parliament years ago when my kids were little, sitting up in the gallery. He was there and I waved. I could see him looking, wondering, 'who is that person?', and he'd look up again and I'd wave, and then next thing he was up behind me in the gallery: 'Gail Bruce! I knew that would have to be you!'."

Many have wondered when Peters found his political mojo. His family, he says, were farmers and mostly voted National, and the impact of the Great Depression was a constant reminder.

"If you had come through the Great Depression you were seriously

---

14 "Winston's first fifteen" by Audrey Young, NZ Herald, 12 July 2008
15 Interview with author

political…the Depression did not stop in the far north in 1938, it went on in some parts of the country into the 1950s. My mother always had a serious grasp of history, she was a public nurse. If you get an interest in history inculcated in you, there's a very small divide between history and politics."

By 1966, 21 year old Winston Peters was a teacher himself, in charge of a class of 11 year olds at Te Atatu Intermediate School. In the words of one song from the era, he was a dedicated follower of fashion, even then:

"He was a great teacher," remembers pupil Sandy Senk (nee Archibald), "very firm, but he was very good, and he always wore a brown corduroy jacket."

"He was a character," recalls John Gardiner, now living in Australia. "He did some odd things – I didn't get a very good report from him from memory, probably because I was a little bit of a smartass back then, but he was a different sort of a teacher, more of the new generation who wanted to get on with you and be your friend and that.

"He used to have this corduroy jacket and a big pair of boots, we used to stir him up about his boots, I remember that, they were pretty flash boots."

Gardiner moved to Australia in the mid-seventies, and discovered later that his teacher had become a high profile politician. "I've seen him on TV, even recently, on the New Zealand parliament channel which they have over here."

Another pupil to end up across the ditch was Susanne Laird, nowadays a muscle-car collector in Queensland. Back in 1966 she was a precocious tweenager raising hell on the first day of class:

"He was very nervous, and we weren't very nice to him," she laughs, "we made him cry."

The exact details of the event that brought the mighty dragon-slayer of Winebox fame to his knees are now dim in the memories of those involved, 48 years after it happened, but the end result remains indelibly etched. 'Everybody screamed, when I dissed the teacher…'

It was Peters who eventually ran screaming from the room – abandoning the teaching profession at the end of that first year in favour of life in the lucky country. Jobs at BHP as a blast furnace worker in Newcastle, and a tunneller in the Snowy Mountains project beckoned. For Winston, this was solid working class toil. It gave him a further appreciation, if it were needed as a former farm boy from a large family, of the values of hard work.

Returning to New Zealand at the end of 1970, Winston enrolled at

Auckland University, majoring in history, politics and law. Like the rest of his brothers, rugby was a passion for Winston as well, and he captained the Auckland Maori Rugby Team.

Money was tight, and the future politician added to his working class credentials by working on the Auckland wharves and in the freezing works to help pay his living expenses while studying. Graduating in 1973 with a BA and LLB, Peters married sweetheart Louise and joined prestige law firm Russell McVeagh, ironic given events that would later transpire, working there from 1974 to 78. It was law school, however, that set off another pathway that was to shake the country.

2

Ngati Luigi

> *"One had to be careful in pronouncing 'wh' in Maori. It was not 'f', and when it was sounded that way it was as a concession to the weakness of the pakeha, who had difficulty in pronouncing it"*
> – **Maori language expert H W Williams, 1928**

In his book *The Demon Profession* former NZ First strategist Michael Laws writes dismissively of Winston's Maori heritage:[16]

"Winston [had] only a scattered understanding of Maori issues at best. He had, instinctively, opposed the amendment to the Treaty of Waitangi Tribunal Act allowing Maori claims prior to 1984, supported Muldoon in opposition to the Bastion Point settlement, and privately regarded the Treaty itself as a chimera that distracted Maori from focusing on more immediate concerns. One detected an unease within Winston over all things Maori.

"Others within Parliament were less charitable, suggesting that he was embarrassed by his Maori background and had attempted to pass himself off as a swarthy Italian in his university days. This discomfort was exemplified by his inability to speak the language and thus feel relaxed on the marae."

It's not clear whether Laws has ever lived in Ponsonby but he did do a talkback show for a station based there once. The question is, was it true?

---

16 "The Demon Profession" by Michael Laws, HarperCollins 1998, p84

Was Winston out of touch with Maori as the latte set imply, or was there a deeper resonance that his foes were blind to?

The truth is important, because the claims have repeatedly been bandied around by critics of Winston Peters.

One who practically chokes on his flat white when he hears the words of Michael Laws is former NZ First MP Ron Mark, now the mayor of Carterton in the Wairarapa.[17]

"That has to be the most stupid comment! I have watched Winston, he is absolutely mindblowing. The guy is like a damned encyclopaedia. He remembers so much detail and times and dates and names. I have been with him in Invercargill, and Wanganui, and Whakatane, and the far north, and he's met someone who is Maori and he has asked them their name and tested where they are from, then he's connected the dots and told them who this relative was and who that relative was, and 'your dad must have known this person', and I just sit there with my mouth open, absolutely gobsmacked. How the hell do you know so much about Maori people?

"And when you go to Ratana, what, Ratana doesn't think Winston knows much about Maori people? Give me a life, good heavens, give me a second life because I could use it! I'd spend all that time teaching Michael Laws. Go and talk to Api Mahuika, leader of Ngati Porou, about what Winston did up there for them."

The educated, enlightened and conservative Maori, says Ron Mark – now a lead negotiator for Ngati Kahungungu in the Wairarapa region treaty settlements – "agree with Winston actually, and they are all well-informed enough to know that he has done more for Maori quietly, without fuss or fanfare, than most Maori under the age of 40 will ever know.

"Whether it's the claims up in Northland, or getting Hikurangi handed back to Ngati Porou, there are a range of issues. Simple things like allocating funding for the Maori Women's Welfare League, which still goes on today, funding for the national Kapa Haka, which had never happened until Winston got there, funding for the Maori Wardens. In his own quiet way, without blowing his own trumpet, at the end of the day Winston is Maori. And just like all Maori, we all have varying political views and varying philosophies – some of it depends on which tribe you come from or which part of the country you come from.

---

17 Ron Mark interview with author

"His family has philosophies that they live by and it is pretty much reflected in everything he's done, but he is still Maori and don't you ever forget it. He understands more than any, the impacts of deprivation and confiscation that occurred in the 1840s-70s and still goes on to this very bloody day."

Further proof, however, that Michael Laws' urban liberal critique of Peters lacked any nuanced depth can also be found in the history books. Would someone "embarrassed" by their Maori heritage have stepped forward to conspicuously captain the Auckland *Maori* rugby side?

Then there's the story of Dame Whina[18] Cooper. Few people know it, but it was Winston Peters' work on a Maori land claim for his Ngati Wai iwi that inspired Cooper to lead her now famous hikoi from the far north to Wellington in 1975, known to history now as "the Land March".

The Labour government of Norman Kirk/Bill Rowling had proposed turning coastal areas into public reserves. The Ngati Wai, who'd enjoyed their ancestral coastland for centuries, turned to their new Russell McVeagh legal beagle, Winston Peters, who mounted a legal challenge that forced the government to back down. Dame Whina Cooper joined the effort and was so taken with it she decided to march on parliament, as retiring Labour MP Shane Jones noted in his valedictory speech:[19]

"It is a rite of passage to be a Māori politician in the north and to have a burst of that activism. In 1975 Winston Peters was leader of the Ngāti Wai Land Retention Committee with Dame Whina Cooper," noted Jones.

It was this event, says Peters, that pushed him into politics:[20]

"I never thought about becoming a politician until 1974 when the then Labour Government decided they were going to – through the Tourism Ministry and in concert with the Whangarei County Council – designate a whole lot of rural coastal land for public utility purposes, for reserves and parks and what have you – in short, just taking it all off us.

"So myself and another young lawyer decided we were going to take these guys on. We acted for hundreds and hundreds of Maori, and even a number of European owners, we took the council on and after 16 years we won nearly everywhere."

---

18 Pronounced Finna, not Feena
19 Shane Jones, Hansard, 21 May 2014, http://www.parliament.nz/en-nz/pb/debates/debates/50HansD_20140521_00000020/valedictory-statements
20 Peters interview with Mark Sainsbury, RadioLive, 29 June 2014

Again, regardless of one's personal views about the Peters phenomenon, is it really credible to suggest he had only "a scattered understanding of Maori issues", or that he was "embarrassed" to be seen as Maori? Is it credible to suggest he did not understand marae protocol, despite his work for his iwi?

"E te taonga o te motu, takoto mai I runga I te atamira oo matua tupuna," Peters eulogised in Parliament on learning of her death in 1994; "Oh treasure of the land, lie upon the platform of your ancestors."[21]

"I got to know Whina in the 1970s. She had been brought from Auckland to meet the Ngati Wai land retention committee, for which I acted as legal counsel. It is not really true to say that Whina started the land protest movement; rather it should be said that she was seen by younger Maori in Auckland as having the credibility and the respectability that European people deemed necessary if they were to negotiate with Maori on cultural matters.

"The protest movement had already started, but Whina's backing gave it impetus at a national level at a critical time, and thus the land march was born. In fact, a number of us remember the very night that she said, in response to hearing about the problem at Pataua: 'I know what I will do. I will lead a march to Parliament'. And she did. The land march was designed to halt the alienation of Maori land, and the catchcry was, 'no more land to be taken'."

In fact, as others have noted, Dame Whina's view of the Treaty was fairly similar to Winston Peters', as she explained at the opening of the Auckland Commonwealth Games in 1990, urging people to remember: "that the Treaty was signed so that we could all live as one nation in Aotearoa."[22]

One nation. It's a wonder no one has thought of using that as a political slogan. ;)

"The greatness of Whina Cooper lay in her perception of what life ought to be and what it ought to hold for all humanity," remarked Peters, "regardless of gender or race. She yearned to see a state of peace and harmony between Maori and European in New Zealand, and she expected people to work to create that climate."

Nonetheless, the politician agreed, Whina also expected people to

---

21 Hansard, Obituary, 29 March 1994
22 http://www.nzhistory.net.nz/people/dame-whina-cooper

respect New Zealand's Maori culture and heritage because this is the only country in the world where it is found. "Hence her symbolic gesture of driving the pouwhenua into the ground while saying, 'This is our land'."

As her biographer Michael King noted, Whina Cooper's message didn't go down so well with modern Maori activists:

"No Maori leader has attracted more public praise from Pakeha (European) people and more public criticism from sectors of Maoridom than Whina."

In its obituary on Dame Whina's death in 1994, Britain's *Independent* newspaper wrote:[23]

"Many young Maoris, impatient for results, favoured more aggressive action and established a makeshift camp on the steps of Parliament in defiance of her orders. Their resulting arrest aggravated differences between the conservative approach of Cooper, who devoted her life to creating harmony between the races and finding peaceful solutions to differences, and the more militant forces of Maoridom."

The reason for this divergence between Dame Whina's conservatism on the one hand, and the modern Maori renaissance on the other, was a massive re-think on the part of the latter about what the Treaty of Waitangi actually meant, and this goes to the very heart of the treaty debate and race relations in New Zealand. It also goes to the very heart of understanding Winston Peters' and New Zealand First's views on treaty issues, and will allow readers to see in context why urban liberals like Michael Laws did not fully understand the big picture themselves.

Dame Whina was born in 1895, and her perception of the Treaty of Waitangi was very much coloured by Maori and European understanding at the time which, essentially, was this:

The treaty was a compact between two peoples to unite as one under a common sovereign – the Queen of England – and build a new nation together. The treaty guaranteed Maori communal property rights over the lands and territories each iwi possessed, but provided a mechanism for tribes to sell land to the Crown if they wished. This clause was inserted to head off private land speculators who'd been doing deals for vast tracts of land at peppercorn rates prior to the treaty.

---

23 "Obituary: Dame Whina Cooper", Independent, 28 March 1994, http://www.independent.co.uk/news/people/obituary-dame-whina-cooper-1432167.html

In effect, the agreement cancelled existing land purchases subject to their ratification by the Crown, to ensure Maori were not being cheated, and required Maori in turn to only deal with the Crown in regard to future land sales.

As noted, the treaty recognised and preserved the traditional Maori practice of communal ownership and control of land.

This worked well for the first few years after the treaty, but for one inconvenient truth. The treaty had guaranteed Maori all the rights and privileges of British citizens, and this included the right to hold title to their own piece of land – not communal title but individual freehold, just as we enjoy today.

Enterprising Maori realised that their communal model of tribal land ownership was preventing them from carving off pieces of land and having their own sections that they could develop and sell. In essence, many iwi came to the realisation that communal land ownership, like grass skirts and kiwi feather cloaks, was not as profitable or useful to them as freehold European titles, warm European clothes or solid timber housing.

Pressure began to build from within Maoridom for the government to grant Maori the right to carve up their land and have European title to it. The government, conscious of its promises under the treaty to protect the old system, didn't wish to see the remaining tracts of tribal land broken up into lifestyle blocks.

The chiefs, however, saw the restriction as unfair. Their Pakeha brothers could buy and sell land as they liked, but iwi could not:

"This is about the land. It is, in accordance with my opinion that it should be divided that each man should have a certain number of acres, that he may be able to sell his portion to the Europeans without creating confusion," chief Matenga of Tarawera told the massive national hui at Kohimarama in 1860.[24]

Wiremu Tamihana agreed: "Let me state my grievance. It is this. Our lands are not secured to us by Crown Grant. Every man is not allowed to get a Crown Grant to his land."

When the government relented and put in place a procedure allowing Maori to break up tribal land and individualise it, the move created a flashpoint that led to the Taranaki land wars.

---

24 Speeches from the Kohimarama hui of 1860 can be found in "The Great Divide" by Ian Wishart, Howling At The Moon Publishing, 2012. These ones are on p196

In the aftermath, massive land confiscations for the rebellion, which even inadvertently swept up some of the non-rebellious iwi, caused problems leading to the treaty settlements process we know and love today.[25]

However, the other key point to emerge was that the majority of Maori in the 1860s and beyond continued to view the treaty as a unifier, not a divider. They continued to swear utter allegiance to the Crown as the only sovereign of New Zealand.

Now the land wars had also been about the Maori King movement. The King movement decided that Maori mana would be enhanced if New Zealand were to have two rulers – a British sovereign to rule over the European settlers, and a Maori sovereign to unite and govern Maoridom. This was the emergence of what we now see as the modern Maori activist movement, or tino rangatiratanga – self government.

Although it was soundly defeated by an alliance of Government forces and friendly Maori iwi, the seed that germinated within the King movement had been planted, and with the right conditions (government breaches in regard to land, education and health) it would sprout in fertile ground over the century that followed.

Which is a shame, because here is how most chiefs saw the Maori sovereignty movement back in 1860:

"I am grieved about this new thing. I mean this new name – the Maori King. Its tendency is to cause division and ill feeling between the Maories and the Europeans. Its tendency is to lower both Pakehas and Maories. I say let this movement be suppressed…and let the Pakehas and the Maories live together as brethren. Let the Queen be Queen for both England and New Zealand, It was not without good ground that the title of Queen of England and of New Zealand was assumed."

The person who uttered those words was no mug – it was Tamihana Te Rauparaha, high chief of Ngatitoa.[26]

"I say, let our views be clear. Let it not be supposed the Pakehas wish to enslave (oppress) the Maories. It is not so. The Pakeha wishes to raise the Maori. I am therefore very much grieved on account of this move-

---

25 Ironically, the Waitangi Tribunal would later rewrite history and say the government had never asked iwi whether they wanted individual freehold title, and therefore that the Crown had breached the treaty by creating such titles without iwi consent.
26 The Great Divide, p190

ment. Our old Maori customs are at the bottom of it, and it has been set up to attract our younger brothers. What has changed our clothing, and caused the dog-skin mat to be laid aside? This new name will lead to our debasement; therefore, I say, let it be suppressed.

"Let this King be put down. We are becoming divided amongst ourselves by means of this King. It therefore appears to me we shall be of this opinion, Chiefs of the Conference, that we must support the Governor, and that we should avail ourselves of advantages offered to us and thus share in; the superiority of the Pakehas.

"Let us abandon Maori customs. Look at the superior condition of the Pakeha! This is not slavery. Let this title of King be put down. Even though the King's flag has been hoisted at our place Otaki it shall be cast down, it shall never be allowed to stand. It is calculated to produce ill-will and division, and if the Maori is separated from the Pakeha, he (the Maori) will find himself wrong. The Queen's shall be our only flag. We will hold our lands under the protection of the Queen."

All of which brings us back to Dame Whina Cooper and Winston Peters' understanding of the Treaty of Waitangi. Like their illustrious forebears, both knew the Treaty guaranteed Maori property rights, but was never about joint sovereignty; 'treaty partners' did not mean co-rulers in a land divided according to race.

Unfortunately, however, that's exactly how the Maori renaissance movement of the 1970s and 80s was pitching it. In universities and news media opinion columns, the idea gradually took hold that the Treaty had guaranteed Maori 'tino rangatiratanga' as a self governing people, and that Pakeha New Zealanders were merely 'manuhiri', or 'guests' whose continued right to live in Aotearoa was entirely at the mercy of Maori whim.

This, as you have now seen, bore no resemblance to what the rangatira who actually signed the Treaty had understood or wanted, but a century down the track, on the back of the cultural revolution of the sixties, that seed planted by the renegade king movement back in the 1860s suddenly sprang into bloom.

Amongst the intelligentsia, many saw their struggle against the establishment in semi-Marxist terms, 'my enemy's enemy must therefore be my friend', and it became fashionable to support virtually any cause that threatened the status quo, under the banner of 'inclusivity'. Maori sovereignty was one of those issues quickly adopted by urban liberals, leading to lashings of what Peters would later call "sickly white liberal guilt" – a condition where one is supposedly so ashamed at the actions of one's Pakeha forebears that one throws one's entire lot in with the Maori renaissance to atone for the ancestral guilt. The Grey Lynn version of Stockholm Syndrome, if you like. The doctrine of 'Tolerance' decreed that all anti-establishment viewpoints were valid without question, but establishment views were not to be tolerated.

Winston Peters, Dame Whina Cooper and others were smart enough to differentiate between genuine treaty land grievances, and the wider aims of Maori sovereignty, which they did not regard as authentic. Urban liberals, however, never understood the nuances because they'd grown up only hearing the modern interpretations of the Treaty, not the real version.

In describing Peters as having a "scattered understanding" of treaty issues, Michael Laws was only advocating what many liberal New Zealanders still genuinely but mistakenly believe.

Little did Peters know in 1975 when, as a young lawyer, he nailed home his Ngati Wai tribe's land rights in the face of a government land grab – and little did Dame Whina know as she enhanced Winston's efforts and established the 1975 land march – that they were uncorking a genie that Winston would spend the next few decades trying to put back in the bottle.

3

A Fuse Is Lit

> *"Fifty years ago the noble but savage Maori was undisputed owner of the wild but fertile lands where now prosperous and growing cities, towns and villages stand"*
>
> – *Evening Post*, January 1890

Many things happened in 1975. Bill Rowling's Labour Government was tipped out of office in the landslide that brought Robert 'Piggy' Muldoon and his National Party to power, but Rowling's most enduring work had already been done – cementing in place the Treaty of Waitangi Act on 10 October 1975. This piece of legislation was the first since 1840 to actually give the Treaty a basis in law, and it was the first to use the phrase "principles of the Treaty", as its introductory paragraph shows:

"An Act to provide for the observance, and confirmation, of the principles of the Treaty of Waitangi by establishing a Tribunal to make recommendations on claims relating to the practical application of the Treaty and to determine whether certain matters are inconsistent with the principles of the Treaty."[27]

No 'principles' are actually spelt out in the Treaty itself, and no one has therefore ever been able to truly say what the 'principles' actually are. Although the Act restricted claimants to matters arising after 1975, its

---

27 Treaty of Waitangi Act 1975, http://www.legislation.govt.nz/act/public/1975/0114/latest/DLM435368.html

loose language made it a legal timebomb. More on that in due course.

Two years earlier, in 1973, Prime Minister Norman Kirk had passed the New Zealand Day Act, to create a national holiday on February 6. Although ceremonies had been held at Waitangi – sporadically prior to 1940 but increasing after World War 2 ended – New Zealand had never celebrated the day as such. It had been a manifesto policy for Labour in 1957, and Labour MP Matiu Rata raised it again with a private members Bill in 1971. It was Rata's work that led to the New Zealand Day Act.

It may seem hard to believe, but 6 February 1974 was the first time in history that the New Zealand flag had ever flown from the main pole at Waitangi. Up until then the ceremonies had used the British Union Jack. It was also the first time the entire country had been given a day off to reflect on Waitangi. Labour added to its Maori policy by making Maori an official language alongside English, for the first time – this amid fears that te reo was dying out along with the last vestiges of tribal culture.

If the Kirk/Rowling years are remembered for nothing else, they will be remembered for the Treaty of Waitangi Act, but not for the New Zealand Day Act. When the National Government came to power, new Prime Minister Rob Muldoon changed the name of the holiday to "Waitangi Day". Many Maori felt Labour's "New Zealand Day" was demeaning of the treaty, and Muldoon agreed with them. Waitangi Day better suited the subject matter, he felt.

One of those intimately aware of the Waitangi Day debate was Winston Peters. Hard on the heels of his legal fight against Labour's coastal land grab, he stood for National in the Northern Maori electorate at the 1975 election.

"When I have the privilege to represent the Maori people in parliament, he told *Thursday* magazine in 1975 before the election, "I shall expend every effort for the retention of Maori land in Maori hands. I will do anything to see that any Maori who wishes to return to his land is provided with the opportunity and the incentive to do so."

In one of his election campaign pamphlets, Peters had written, "A vote for me next Saturday will guarantee that no Maori will ever march again for the retention of Maori land. I am a landowner at Whananaki, and with you I stand on the land issue."

One could argue it wasn't a serious tilt at a parliamentary career, given that no National MP has won the Maori seats, but nonetheless Winston strapped on the pads and stepped up to the crease, scoring a creditable

1873 votes against Labour's Mat Rata. The respectable performance owed a lot to the Ngati Wai legal work and the publicity surrounding it.

Muldoon was impressed, so much so that when Peters stood again – this time on the general roll for the Hunua seat in 1978, Winston was used in National's TV "Lightning Years" advertising campaign as the 'interviewer' of Prime Minister Muldoon. The telegenic Peters was in his element, although surprisingly unsuccessful on the night despite having his face plastered all over TV – or perhaps because of it: the ads coming across as patsy political in-house efforts, which of course they were.

Although he failed to unseat Labour incumbent Malcolm Douglas (Sir Roger's brother) on election night, the result was close enough to force a recount and, when that failed, a legal challenge based on whether some of the votes were invalid. Many candidates, faced with a loss after the recount, would have given up and simply walked away. Not Winston. He is the archetype of the cartoon frog that's been swallowed by a pelican, but the arms are still visible reaching out from inside the beak and strangling the bird with the words, "never say die".

Peters' determination and legal knowledge paid off. He won the legal challenge, with the Supreme Court[28] ruling on 11 May 1979 that enough votes were invalid to unseat Douglas in favour of Peters. The boy from the far north was in, the Maori in the general seat had made his mother proud.

Winston spent two years on National's backbenches but he couldn't avoid the growing backlash against the increasingly erratic Muldoon administration. The 1981 Springbok Tour divided the nation as never before and National paid the price at the 1981 election. What had been a 10 seat majority in 1978 turned into a hung parliament on the night in 1981, with National on 46, Labour 44, and Social Credit holding the balance of power with two seats. After recounts National regained Gisborne from Labour and ended up with a fragile two seat majority. Among the casualties, Winston Raymond Peters, dumped by the marginal Hunua electorate in favour of Labour's Colin Moyle, who'd been forced to endure homosexual slurs from Muldoon six years earlier after being caught following men by police on a street in Wellington at 11pm one night in 1975 while he was still Minister of Fisheries. The area was a known gay haunt.

Moyle initially told police he was waiting for a friend to come out of

---

28   In the 1970s, the Supreme Court was the equivalent of the High Court as we know it now.

the library, although that story fell apart when police explained the library had already been closed for two hours. Deciding that valour was the better part of discretion, the Labour MP took the metaphorical spade being handed to him by detectives and continued to dig a hole furiously. Sorry, he muttered, my mistake, "I thought you might be a cat-burglar", he told the constable he'd been following. The next morning he told the Chief Superintendent he was meeting homosexuals for 'research purposes' in regard to a forthcoming parliamentary debate, and Moyle later changed his story again telling an official inquiry he was meeting someone about a "security leak".

Either way, when Moyle later tried to question the Prime Minister's business dealings after Muldoon's 1975 election win, Muldoon hit back with the tragic story of the Labour minister caught on the street with no lawful excuse.

Moyle's eventual resignation from parliament opened the door for an unknown candidate named David Lange to replace him – further proof that history can change on a dime. Nonetheless, having served six years in the political wilderness Moyle was resurrected by the Hunua voters at the same time they dumped Peters.

In hindsight, Winston probably counts his blessings at not being part of the final Muldoon administration between 81 and 84. These were the years of the wage and price freeze – the former proving less prone to melt than the latter, a period when "the amazing Dr Muldoon", as the 1978 campaign badges had pitched him, seemed to have run out of economic medicine and ideas.

When junior National MP Marilyn Waring announced she was quitting the Government in June 1984 Muldoon, after one too many drinks, decided he couldn't be bothered relying on Social Credit's two votes for the remainder of the year and called a snap election. The old warhorse evidently reasoned that voters would admire his toughness in taking stern action in the face of a challenge; he misread the mood of the country badly – voters had been wanting out for ages and they simply sprinted for the door Muldoon had opened for them.

National was given a good old fashioned spanking by New Zealanders and Muldoon was out on his ear. While Labour took the credit and basked in the glory, everyone knew that you could have put a garden gnome up and it still would have beaten Muldoon at the polls in 1984.

Once again, as in 1981 when Social Credit scored nearly 21% of the vote and secured two seats in the first past the post system, third-party protest votes played a big role in 1984 as well. For this election, it was the New Zealand Party led by Bob Jones and Janie Pearce that stormed in from the sidelines capturing nearly 13% of the vote – mostly from National. In many electorates the NZ Party actually polled second.

Winston Peters – who'd been cooling his heels setting up a legal practice in the Auckland suburb of Howick – decided to return to politics in 1984. He replaced retiring and, as it turned out, terminally ill National MP Keith Allen in the Tauranga electorate and actually managed to more than double National's majority in the seat from 2232 to 4912, despite the massive swing against National nationwide. It was a sign, he'd found his spiritual home amongst the good citizens of the Bay of Plenty provincial capital.

Tauranga was a city founded by missionaries and with more churches per capita than most towns. Winston cottoned on that spending a Sunday morning in worship with a hundred or so parishioners, with the added bonus of tea and scones and a meet and greet after the service, was actually a highly effective form of canvassing without all the legwork. He began turning up at places like the Wesleyan Methodist Church at Otumoetai.

"We'd see Winnie four weeks in a row," remembers one parishioner, "then nothing," she added cynically. What she didn't appreciate at the time, of course, was that Winston was caught by practicalities: so many churches, so little time. A month of Sundays turned out not to be as long as the cliché implied.

Winston's mentor Sir Robert Muldoon didn't escape the night of the long knives after his disastrous election defeat and subsequent King Canute effort to stop the incoming Labour Government from devaluing the New Zealand dollar. There had been rumblings for years within National about Muldoon's autocratic leadership, with Cabinet Minister Derek Quigley ditched for daring to question his leader during the 81-84 term. In 1983 Muldoon had been knighted with a GCMG[29] honour – one of the top ranks in the British honours system; there'd been a standing joke arising from the *Yes, Minister* TV show that CMG honours allowed recipients to boast, "Call Me God". This time, the pundits teased, Muldoon's title stood for "God Calls Me God". The knighthood couldn't save him from

---

29 The Grand Cross of Michael and George

his former lieutenants however. Any number of them were lining up to play 'Brutus' to Muldoon's 'Caesar'.

Winston Peters tried to persuade his colleagues they were making a massive strategic error. Whilst even he could see the writing on the wall for Muldoon, he argued that with the election only just in the rear view mirror and no new poll until 1987, it was better to leave Sir Robert in the job with a view to a dignified retirement later and an orderly transition to new leadership. "If you stab him in the back now, he's not going to go quietly and the party will suffer," was the essence of Winston's warning. In short, Muldoon was bound to squeal like a stuck piggy.

Winston's words fell on deaf ears.

Muldoon himself, as early as the week after the election in July 1984, accepted that the leadership would have to be reviewed.[30] His pick was early 1985 and he told caucus he was "unlikely" to be a candidate. A group led by Jim Bolger were impatient, they wanted a leadership vote now. Another group including Peters and Philip Burdon, were arguing for an orderly transition down the track.

For his part, Muldoon's reluctance to go early was partly because he didn't think his would-be replacements had the right stuff for leadership. He felt Jim McLay, for example, was emotionally weak, in the sense that he was too cautious and therefore indecisive under pressure. Additionally, McLay lacked any experience in Opposition.

The Peters-Burdon faction argued that the caucus, and particularly the eight new MPs, needed at least six months to familiarise themselves with the various leadership contenders and see how they performed in an Opposition environment. Many of these guys, they noted, had never been in Opposition and still had the 'born to rule' mentality of cabinet ministers.

If caucus had been unified on delaying the leadership tumble, the matter might have ended there, but the Bolger-Gair faction remained defiant, supported by the leadership of the National Party's organisational wing who labelled caucus "gutless" for failing to use their blades. Electorate officials were reported publically calling Muldoon a "megalomaniac".[31]

Muldoon began digging his heels in, releasing counter-statements blam-

---

30 "His Way: A Biography Of Robert Muldoon" by Barry Gustafson, AUP, chap. 23
31 Comment made by Roy Johnston to the Wellington Divisional Conference of the National Party, 23 October 1984

ing dissension within caucus as the reason for the election loss, rather than his own errors. Suddenly it looked like he might not stand aside in early 1985 after all.

The tensions erupted to the surface in November 1984 when the caucus decided to bring forward the scheduled February encounter to a pre-Christmas one in early December. Muldoon was now furious, and refused to step aside – not because he expected to win but because, as his biographer Barry Gustafson wrote, he "preferred to go down fighting". Lined up against him were Jim Bolger and former Deputy Prime Minister Jim McLay – the latter reluctantly at this point because he'd accepted the Peters-Burdon argument about an orderly transition.

A TVNZ *Eyewitness*/Heylen poll showed Muldoon still had immense public support. Although McLay was the public's preference as the new leader at 39%, Muldoon was second on 23%, with George Gair on 19%, Bolger on 8% and Bill Birch bringing up the rear on 4%. When drilled down further, National Party voters still preferred Muldoon, on 43%, ahead of anyone else. Muldoon told *Eyewitness* that while he might lose because caucus wanted a change, "I'll go down with my flag flying."[32]

Faced with events moving so rapidly, and having seen the poll results the night before, it was Winston Peters and Philip Burdon who pushed the battle to the precipice, arguing that the leadership vote should be decided "now", on 29 November. The boil had to be lanced.

McLay eventually carried the day, winning leadership on the first ballot, leaving the old warhorse to clear his desk.

Columnist and cartoonist Tom Scott, who'd been banned from Muldoon's press conferences for a time, was there as Muldoon returned to that desk and a barrage of waiting media. "The man who for 24 years maintained the impression, at least for public consumption, that he was constructed of granite with a surface coating of rhino hide, abandoned all pretence and wept openly, burying his face in a white hanky. Most who bore witness to these rare, unprecedented scenes could not help but be shocked and affected by it all."[33]

Muldoon soon regained his composure and later invited Winston Peters, Paul East, Don McKinnon and Philip Burdon for a final drink in his office.

---

32 Eyewitness News, TVNZ, 28 November 1984
33 Tom Scott column, Evening Post, 1 December 1984

McLay was an urban liberal, hoping to take the National Party away from the conservative Muldoonist policies. Perhaps his biggest mistake was not giving Muldoon some dignity. Whereas Bolger had assured Muldoon of a place in any future cabinet, McLay refused to keep Muldoon on the front bench. Muldoon rejected a second-row position, opting instead for the backbenches. In the opinion polls, by mid 1985, Muldoon was still rating above 20 as preferred Prime Minister, while McLay had dropped to 4%.

In early 1986 McLay was rolled by the more centrist Jim Bolger, putting in place the leader who would come to play such an instrumental role in the rise of Winston Peters.

4

We All Live On A Yellow Submarine

> *"Listen, I'm a politician which means I'm a cheat and a liar, and when I'm not kissing babies I'm stealing their lollipops. But it also means I keep my options open"*
> – ***The Hunt For Red October,*** **1990**

In his first term as Hunua MP up to 1981, Winston Peters had been almost invisible; just another backbench wannabe given the patsy questions to make the boss look good at question time in parliament.

While even his critics acknowledge Winston can be an effective minister, it's his work on the opposition benches that truly sets the man alight. It wasn't until his return to parliament as the member for Tauranga in 1984 that Peters began to step up a gear, developing a nose for scandal.

In politics, it's all about scoring points, about making the other side look dim-witted and slothlike; incompetent or corrupt. You're either too incompetent to be in government and should be thrown out now, or you're so incompetent that sensible voters should never let you and your mates anywhere near the Treasury benches. Flip a coin, the strategy works no matter where you sit in parliament. It's a lot like being a lawyer, trying to argue the other side are wrong or lying. Little wonder that Russell McVeagh-trained Winston Peters took to politics like a duck to water.

In fact, it was water, or things in it, that gave him his first mini-scandals in the public eye, and for which the Labour government labelled him a conspiracy theorist.

The first was a series of allegations that Russian submarines had been seen between Auckland and Great Barrier Island. Peters is still teased about that to this day:

"What about those Russian submarines, Winston?" mocked National's Nick Smith during a 2014 parliamentary debate. What about them indeed.

"Where is the evidence for the Russian submarines seen off the coast?" teased Labour's Michael Cullen, then in opposition, in 1997, during a Treasury debate of all things.[34]

The media too, have joined in the sport of Peters-baiting, accusing him of "making wild allegations of conspiracy theories.

"Over the years Russian submarines have charted local waters, the Government has covered up a ferry running aground, and the IRD and SFO have been wound up in a criminal conspiracy," jibed the *Herald on Sunday* in what they thought was Winston's political obituary after the NZ First party's 2008 election defeat.[35]

Political commentator Bryce Edwards, in his mini-biographical "New Zealand First party history" published online, accuses Peters of taking up "political positions and populist campaigns with little apparent caution or strong ideological principle.[36]

"Examples of ill-informed Peters campaigns included allegations about the interisland ferry becoming grounded, [and] bizarre conspiracy theories about the sinking of the Russian cruiseliner, the *Mikhail Lermontov*, in the Marlborough Sounds."

Clearly Peters' credibility takes a dent every time someone says he got it wrong, but no media and certainly none of his political rivals have ever been interested in doing any hard work to prove or disprove the allegations.

So what was the story behind the Russian submarines? The allegations broke in 1984 and 1985. According to Peters, defence forces had been placed on alert amid sightings of Russian submarines off the New Zealand coast. He speculated they were charting New Zealand's seabed for military purposes.

The new Labour government had just enforced its new anti-nuclear policy, and the implication was that we were endangering the ANZUS defence alliance at the same time as hostile submarines were patrolling

---

34 "Treasurer, Statutory References Bill, second reading," Hansard, 8 May 1997
35 "Winston Peters' last stand is a lost battle", NZ Herald, 9 November 2008
36 "NZ First party history – part one" by Bryce Edwards, 17 November 2008

New Zealand waters. Winston's purpose in raising the issue was clearly to create political embarrassment for Labour and put some runs on the board for an embattled National Party in opposition.

It's actually hard to understand the Press Gallery's problem with the Russian submarines story. Possibly it's because the parliamentary journalists get their talking points from political spin doctors, and the gallery is therefore often one step removed from real newsgathering and far too prone to take at face value assurances from so-called authority figures. Take the free ride the gallery gave Prime Minister Helen Clark in 2001 when she justified not spending $568 million on updating our anti-submarine capabilities by telling the gallery defence forces had never found a submarine in 35 years of searching:[37]

"We would be most unlikely to spend on the antisubmarine warfare capability," she said. "We were being asked to spend more than half a billion dollars to spot vessels which aren't there and haven't been found to be there in the entire time we've been trying to spot them."

The men who fly the RNZAF Orions just about choked on their Weetbix when they read the morning papers. Why? Because the Royal New Zealand Air Force had actually photographed a Soviet Foxtrot-class sub, the *Regul*, in December 1982 en route to the South Island. As Stuff.co.nz reports, "the Soviets said they were doing oceanographic work."[38] 'Oceanographic' is seabed mapping, and they were not likely to be charting New Zealand's sea floor for trade purposes. Squadron Leader Tony Medcalf told a *Herald* journalist the military submarine was most likely looking to map deep trenches the nuclear submarine fleet could hide in, or areas of warm/cold water convection which would throw off the detection abilities of submarine-hunting ships and aircraft.[39]

The former head of the Whenuapai Airbase Orion squadron, Wing Commander and submarine-tracker Gordon Ragg, explained there had been numerous detections of submarines and that New Zealand's east coast is a "well known route" for nuclear submarines to travel on their way to the Indian Ocean.[40]

---

37 "Sub-hunters say PM out of her depth over claims", NZ Herald 15 March 2001
38 "Russian submarines heading to NZ waters," by Michael Field, 19 June 2013, Stuff.co.nz
39 "Sub-hunters say PM out of her depth over claims", NZ Herald 15 March 2001
40 "Sub-hunters say PM out of her depth over claims", NZ Herald 15 March 2001

"There were all kinds of submarines at times, and we were quite effective at finding them," Ragg explained. "At times we found submarines that weren't meant to be there."

The Wing Commander's tenure in the job ended in 1985, so it covered the period Winston Peters had talked about. But hey, Helen Clark said the submarines weren't there and had never been found there, so it must be true, right?

Let's remind ourselves again of what the media say about the submarine allegations:

"The allegations earned headlines but frequently failed to withstand scrutiny. Even so, that didn't seem to matter," wrote the *Christchurch Press*. "Memorables include the Maori loans affair, allegations that a Soviet submarine was plotting Cook Strait, that the sunken *Mikhail Lermontov* was a cover for Russian spies..."[41]

Again, we've seen that press gallery "scrutiny" usually means a quick one-on-one interview with the nearest mirror, and we've seen what armchair journalism can do, but what happens when you actually go out and track down the story? The truth about submarines around the New Zealand coastline is more surprising than you'd imagine. Fiordland is at the heart of it.

"To most of us," *Investigate* magazine revealed in April 2000, "Fiordland is a wilderness far, far away, from a time long, long ago. The ancient, dark and brooding forest that probably once rumbled to the tread of flesh-tearing dinosaurs, is an expanse too vast for the average New Zealander to even bother comprehending – nearly 13,000 square kilometres at last count. The area is also officially one of the wettest on Earth, with average annual rainfall of up to seven metres in some remote corners. It is a place to easily get lost in and never be found.

"A storm has whipped the already volatile Tasman sea into a fury. Four metre waves lash the rocks at the entrance to Doubtful Sound with a surge so powerful that even on the sea bed 90 metres below the sand is being stirred up by each wave.

"A southerly gale, carrying the breath of Antarctic ice, heralds an early winter, and the two fishermen on their small lobster boat shrink deeper into the warmth of the cabin and the glow of the stove as a billy boils tea.

---

41 "He's back: Winston Part 4", Press, 10 December 1999, p5

"Although their own craft is some four kilometres inside Doubtful Sound, sheltered by an island, the sea is still running a good two metre swell out in the channel. But as one of the men gazes across the inlet his attention is suddenly captured – a black mass breaks through the waves less than a hundred metres away, seawater draining from it like waterfalls. Even in the dusky twilight, the outline of a submarine is obvious to the fishermen.

"It is not the first time they've seen a submarine at Fiordland, and it probably won't be the last, but with the news media full of reports of fishermen getting ridiculed after claiming to have seen submarines around New Zealand, these men are bright enough not to bother calling it in – not to the daily media at any rate.

"Within 90 seconds, the underwater ship has gone – sinking back into the inky depths of Doubtful Sound that plunge from 90 metres at the entrance to a staggering 421 metres deep (1400 feet) within the Sound itself.

"Such reports have become part of local folklore in Fiordland…"

Why Fiordland, you may well be asking. Let me enlighten you. As the story extract reveals, the Sounds are up to half a kilometre deep. They are a fantastic place for a nuclear submarine to hide from pesky surveillance, as Squadron Leader Tony Medcalf noted earlier in regard to Russian oceanographic mapping around New Zealand. There are a couple of other factors, however, that make Fiordland the French Riviera for nuclear subs.

One is the rainfall. Much of Fiordland measures its annual rainfall not in inches but in metres. Up to seven metres in places. All that fresh water falling from the sky has to go somewhere, and it does – tumbling down the forested hillsides into the fiords themselves. But there's a twist:

"Formed by massive glaciers of ice some 15,000 years ago, the fiords are effectively mountain ranges that were swamped by the sea when the last iceberg melted. The entrance, or sill, to each of the Sounds, where the sea comes in, is relatively shallow – the deepest entrance is only 90 metres – but if you'd been a cave dweller standing on the crest of the sill looking inland, you would have seen a deep rocky valley dropping hundreds of metres even further, well below sea-level, like the dip in a spoon if you were standing on the edge.

"On the seaward side of the sill, looking out towards Australia, is a massive underwater cliff. If the sea were removed, a cave dweller who decided to jump would plummet several kilometres before smashing to a stop at the bottom of the Tasman sea-bed. It is only at the southernmost fiords that a continental shelf extends out from the sill, and then only for a few hundred metres.

"Most of the fiords are still fed by glacial rivers that pump millions of litres of fresh water into them every day, and it's that fresh water that creates a unique marine environment. Depending on how much rain there's been, a layer of fresh water up to 10 metres deep sits on the surface of the fiords."

What is the one thing you cannot easily get access to in a nuclear submarine on a six month voyage? Fresh water. That's the "twist". Popping into the Sounds allows subs to take in fresh water without even needing to fully surface, because they can suck it in from the fresh water layer. There are few places in the southern hemisphere which allow fresh water access to massive submarines. Especially somewhere close enough to the South Pole. Why the South Pole? Because that's a crossover point for subs.

"Because of the Earth's strong magnetic fields over the poles, spy satellites are unable to "see" the nuclear submarines in those areas," reported *Investigate* in 2000, "which is why the US and Russian subs spend time in both the Arctic and Antarctic circles. In addition, orbiting the poles provides the submarines with easy rapid deployment if required to any ocean."

Although Antarctica, as a result of a 1959 treaty, is a demilitarised zone now, the law of the sea allows transitional passage by military craft through international waters surrounding Antarctica and arguably within the 12 mile limit.

To most New Zealanders, America's Harewood air force base at Christchurch airport is just another section of tarmac where Operation Deep Freeze flights to the Antarctic are based. The truth is a little more complex. Harewood has been the only major metropolitan US airbase in Australasia for decades, it is sovereign US territory – not New Zealand territory. It carries air traffic to and from the Pine Gap eavesdropping centre in Australia, and it provides supplies to the apparently scientific research going on at McMurdo Station in Antarctica.[42]

US defence intelligence sources indicated to *Investigate* that McMurdo is essential to the nuclear submarine patrols, and indeed the establishment of the base coincided with the deployment of long range strategic missile submarines in the 1950s and sixties.

Think about it for a moment. McMurdo base is home to up to a thou-

---

42 http://www.converge.org.nz/abc/otherbases.html

sand people. It is a military installation and has been fully staffed since the 1960s when it was initially powered by a nuclear reactor.[43] It is run jointly by the US military and private defence contractor Raytheon which, as one of its former staff notes, is "paranoid" about security at McMurdo:

"Here's a story about working in Antarctica," explains the former Raytheon employee.[44] "Raytheon is an extremely paranoid company, especially when it comes to their image. They made it very clear to everyone on base that a) they'd read all of our emails, and b) that we weren't allowed to say anything negative about the company, the base, or base personnel at all. You actually sign a contract to this effect prior to deployment. I also learned that Raytheon has a team of folks who do pretty much nothing other than try to track down posts/blogs that talk about them, and punish any employee who dares to besmirch their name.

"While I was down there I made a few videos with my 'spy sunglasses' for family and friends to show them what the base was like. I uploaded these videos to my server back home and told my friends/family to take a look. They did and a couple of days later I deleted the videos because I no longer had a use for them. Didn't seem like a big deal to me at the time.

"A day after that my server started screaming about an attack taking place – and lo and behold, someone was indeed trying to break into it. First they specifically tried to access the direct links to the videos (which no longer existed), and then they tried to crack the server itself so they could run through the files on it.

"They weren't very good at their jobs, though, and I was able to track back their IP address. It turns it that the attack was actually coming from McMurdo. I thought it might be a fellow employee, but I managed to isolate the computer i.d. – and it turned out to be coming from a company laptop being used by some of the visiting members of the security team.

"I confronted (politely, although I wanted to do something much less polite at the time) the guys about this and asked what they thought they were doing. They rambled on about 'company security' and whatnot, at which point I reminded them that company policy didn't mean that they could try to hack privately owned servers based in the States. I also pointed out that just the attempt was a felony and could land the entire lot of them in jail.

---

43 http://www.southpolestation.com/env/env1.html
44 http://www.reddit.com/r/IAmA/comments/j4q42/iama_techie_who_worked_at_mcmurdo_base_in/

"They didn't try to hack my servers after that. Still, I thought the sense of entitlement they exhibited was appalling (i.e. "we're Raytheon and we can do what we want"). It only went away when I made it clear that I knew the law and what they were doing was illegal, and there'd be some serious repercussions if they ever touched my server again. They seemed to be surprised that I'd even known about the attempted breach, which was really stupid given that just checking my resume should've shown them that trying to get into my server was a fairly bad idea."

Other Raytheon staff contributing to the discussion confirmed that the extra high security contract provisions only applied to the Antarctic division operation.

Peace researcher Owen Wilkes worked at Antarctica back in the early 1960s, as friend and fellow campaigner Murray Horton noted in Wilkes' 2006 obituary:[45]

"He lived and worked with the Americans at McMurdo Sound, getting $US500 per month and duty free booze. He got on very well with the Americans, but became aware of the military nature of the whole Deep Freeze programme, with Antarctica being used as a gigantic military training ground. Owen, however, was not politicised, and not yet disturbed enough to do anything about it."

America had, in fact, treated Antarctica as a militarised zone since the end of World War 2, and in the summer of 1946/47, the US deployed some 12 warships and 4,700 troops to the Ross Shelf for polar combat training. The exercise was known as "Operation Highjump", and its purpose was to prepare US forces to fight a war in polar conditions with the Soviets if it came to pass.[46]

Unaware of the allegations that US nuclear submarines are tied in to the McMurdo programme, another Fiordland charter boat operator tells of a retired US Navy commander who'd hired their boat for a tour of the sounds.

"His job in the Navy was tracking submarines," the charter operator says, helpfully, "and basically. If you saw the movie *The Hunt For Red*

---

[45] http://www.converge.org.nz/abc/pr31-119.html
[46] "Hitler's Antarctic base: the myth and the reality", Colin Summerhayes, Scott Polar Research Institute, University of Cambridge, Polar Record 43 (224): 1–21 (2007). Printed in the United Kingdom. doi:10.1017/S003224740600578X, https://wikileaks.org/gifiles/attach/49/49783_.pdf

October, his job was the one portrayed by Denzel Washington. But during our trip he remarked that the American Trident submarines hide just off the Fiordland coast, because there's a major anomaly in the magnetic field there, and a bloody deep hole that the spy satellites can't penetrate."

The area he's talking about is just south of Preservation Inlet, the bottommost of the fiords, and covers an area out to the Solander Islands further southeast. On marine charts, skippers are warned that they cannot trust their compasses in that area because of a magnetic field "discrepancy".

The revelations about US nuclear submarines routinely tracking through New Zealand waters prompted a former SAS boat squadron soldier, now in the private sector, to make contact[47] and shed further light on why submarines are sometimes seen in the Hauraki Gulf.

"I have personally been on American submarines off Great Barrier Island on a number of occasions," he told *Investigate*. "The Yanks don't come in as often as the Aussies, but they like to test their anti-detection systems against the New Zealand and Australian airforces, so there's something in it for everyone."

One of Winston Peters' parliamentary allegations had raised the issue of Russian submarines mapping the Cook Strait seabed. While that's possible, there might have been another more technical reason, according to the former SAS boat squadron soldier, based on his own first hand experience in the Auckland region. The submarines, he says, "use the big electric power cable that runs out to Tiri [island, opposite the Army Bay restricted defence area on Auckland's Whangaparaoa Peninsula]. Now the average Joe on the street probably thinks it's just a power cable, but it does a lot more than that.

"The electric field thrown out by that particular cable is used by submarines for de-gaussing their hulls. One of the methods used by satellites and Orions to detect submarines is to look for their magnetic footprint. So what the subs do when they come past Auckland is to de-gauss themselves over the Tiri lighthouse power cable."

The Cook Strait power cables are much bigger again and, at a depth of only 128 metres, easily accessible to any submarine going through the strait.

This then is one reason for submarine activity around the New Zealand

---

47 I know who he is and we have stayed in touch from time to time over the past 14 years. I have not identified him because of the work that he does. The story is carried in "Busted!" Investigate, June 2000 issue

coastline. We are not a mere irrelevant blip, but an important hiding place, de-gaussing area and water replenishing station.[48] The press gallery may have chortled over their lattés about the submarine conspiracy theory, but there are good reasons for both Russian and American submarines to have been lurking here in the 1980s.

There's another good reason that Winston's claim probably stacks up, however. The French.

When the Greenpeace vessel *Rainbow Warrior* was blown up in Auckland harbour in 1985, huge amounts of pre-planning by the French military had gone into that operation. One of their agents had even been working in the Greenpeace Auckland office for a considerable time prior to the bombing. But, importantly for this particular story, it also involved the use of a French submarine which rendezvoused with the getaway yacht *Ouvea* and spirited most of the special forces team away who'd been involved in the Greenpeace attack. Of course, New Zealand police did manage to nab Captain Dominique Prieur and Major Alain Mafart, four other members of the French unit were never caught.[49]

For a while, there were serious fears that the French were planning a military raid on the Auckland prison where the French agents were held, as one of the former police inspectors involved in the security operation, Ross Meurant, later revealed:

"Prieur's detention presented another problem to a French Government under threat at the polls. Her return to France from New Zealand was vital.[50]

"On Monday 16 September 1985 a submarine was sighted off the west coast of New Zealand. Another submarine sighting had been made a week earlier.

"On 19 September, Inspector Ashley Edwards, Officer-in-Charge

---

48 We're also involved in US naval research into submarine detection, Project TESPEX. "The first experiment took place off the East Coast of New Zealand" says a US military report, noting it was now "possible to detect locate and track" submarines in shallow water, something too difficult back in the 1980s because of unwanted sonar reflections from objects on the sea floor. The NZ defence official assigned to TESPEX was Dr Ralph Marrett. The suggestion that there are no submarines in NZ waters can safely be dismissed as laughable.
49 Well, three of them were arrested by Australian police on Norfolk Island but they couldn't be held and were released, sailing away in the *Ouvea*. The yacht subsequently transferred the trio to the *Rubis*, and the submarine then sank the *Ouvea* without trace.
50 The Beat to the Beehive by Ross Meurant, Harlen Press, 1999 http://www.rossmeurant.co.nz/books.html

Auckland Armed Offenders and Auckland Anti-Terrorist Squad issued an interim operational order named 'Operation Rainbow' – dealing with the security of French prisoner, Dominique Prieur.

"As I was briefed, Christchurch women's prison where Prieur was being held was considered 'insecure' and the belief was that Paremoremo prison, four minutes' run from the head of an estuary on the Waitemata Harbour, and Mt Eden prison only slightly further from the harbour, were both considered vulnerable to an attack by French commandos who would be put ashore, probably by zodiac, from a French submarine (which had been sighted in and around the New Zealand coast) anchoring in the Rangitoto Channel. It would be a simple matter for commandos to 'blow' their way in and shoot their way out of these institutions, with nothing more than a dozen or so police to stop them. Any police who were armed with the standard issue .38-revolver would be no match for heavily armed elite troops, trained to kill.

"As a precaution Prieur was moved to the military corrective establishment, 50 minutes' run at best (even to Peter Snell) from the nearest harbour estuary, and right next door to the Papakura Army camp where New Zealand's own elite killing group, the SAS (and even better, the Counter Terrorist Team) was stationed. The CTT are the elite of the SAS.

"My task as a duty inspector for nightshift during the period the operation was on, was to visit the scene to acquaint myself with the layout and topography, and to return to the scene and take charge if the French did come ashore and the CTT/SAS got amongst them.

"That night I really polished up my .38-Smith & Wesson revolver," Meurant writes.

On his website he publishes an extract from the book, including a transcript of the actual security order issued by police describing the spectre of a commando attack from the French submarine *Rubis* and what police and the Army needed to do.

"Intelligence suggests there is a real threat that an outside agency may attempt to free the prisoner," the order decrees. One of the aims is to "Take necessary action and co-ordinate Police and Army action to apprehend Offender(s) and prisoner."

The French submarine in question was seen in New Zealand waters close to Auckland at the time of the threat alert. In typical Gallic defiance of New Zealand sovereignty and Labour's policy, the *Rubis* was a new generation *nuclear* attack submarine [both armed and powered], weighing 2,600 tonnes and nearly 80 metres in length.

It was this sub that had provided logistical support to the French DGSE marine commando team assigned to bomb the Warrior, and it had probably been in our waters for some months while the agents scoped out their plan. If it wasn't a 'Russian' submarine that Winston Peters had warned of, it will have been either an American one or, even more likely, the *Rubis* doing some early reconnaissance work.

Nearly thirty years after first warning Parliament about the presence of Russian submarines, Winston Peters still feels the effects – his recent attacks on National's Judith Collins blunted a little by the past:

"I say that Judith Collins is withholding the truth and so are her colleagues, because they know the consequence. The trouble is that there is, Mr Brownlee, more to come."[51]

"Well," boomed National's Gerry Brownlee, "I would have to say that the catchcry of Winston Peters' political career has always been: 'There is more to come'."

"And there was!," retorted Peters.

"And there was -" began Brownlee again before an interjection from his colleague Nick Smith:

"What about those Russian subs?"

Brownlee grinned and continued, "—but for one of those moments when the propeller hit the bottom of the Cook Strait, the Russian subs came in, the surveillance device was on the *Mikhail Lermontov*, there was not cash in the brown paper bag at the Kermadec restaurant, and when he said no, he did not know what he was saying. But there was always more to come."

As you can see, it wasn't just Russian submarines creating early parliamentary headlines for Winston Peters. New Zealand became the only Western country in the cold war to have sunk a Russian ship, the cruise liner *Mikhail Lermontov*. It sank in the Marlborough Sounds on 16 February 1986, with the loss of only one life, a Russian crew member.

Everyone who was still there in the final moments remembered them well:[52]

"The noise was deafening when the *Mikhail Lermontov* sank to the

---

51 Hansard, 06 May 2014. Volume:698;Page:17491.
52 http://www.nzmaritime.co.nz/lermontov.htm

bottom of Port Gore, 35 miles from Picton. As the bow gradually sank down in the sea the stern rose higher. The bow hit the seabed, the stern settled and she rolled on her side beneath the surface. Bubbles more than six feet high belched from the sea, and anything loose on the ship shot to the surface, leapt into the air and then smacked down on the surface of the water. The haunting sounds reverberating from the bowels of the ship were never forgotten."

The vessel, which became the largest cruise liner to sink since the *Titanic* in 1912, was carrying mostly-elderly Australian passengers on a voyage around New Zealand. It was navigating out of the Sounds under the skills of harbour pilot Don Jamison, who decided to take the ship through a rocky passage despite not having accurate charts to hand, according to the official preliminary inquiry.

Precise details have always been murky, however. Evidence from some eyewitnesses was ignored and parts were sealed. Yet there was evidence from Royal New Zealand Navy Lieutenant Peter Batcheler, who captained the rescue patrol board *HMNZS Taupo*, that the Russian lifeboats were so rotten passengers had put their feet through the bottom of one. He explained that some of the lifeboat motors didn't start, only one boat had a radio, and the life jackets were in poor condition. Some of the inflatable liferafts had perished and couldn't be inflated.

"If the sinking had been out at sea, they would not have got back alive with that equipment, I am quite convinced of that," Lieutenant Batcheler told journalists.[53]

Captain Reedman, helming an oil tanker carrying 33 tonnes of highly explosive LPG, steamed at full speed to the scene despite the Lermontov indicating it did not want assistance. The scene was chaotic when they arrived in the dark.

"One lifeboat ran out of fuel and we topped him up so he could go back and get more people – another boat, a fully enclosed one, came alongside with smoke pouring out of it – we thought it was on fire – but it was caused by the exhaust pipe falling off the motor. The poor buggers were half asphyxiated. They had us worried – the last thing we wanted was a fire alongside us – it could've blown the whole place sky high."[54]

---

53 "Remove sunken ship, Soviets told," Sydney Morning Herald, 19 February 1986, p1
54 Interview by maritime journalist Lindsay Wright

Australian newspaper journalists covering the hearing in Wellington reported that the Russians were alleging pilot Jamison was responsible, and that the maps did not list the reef, while "the New Zealand version was that Captain Jamison had handed over the helm well before the ship struck a plainly marked reef."

The Navy's chief hydrographer at the time, Ken Robertson, rejected the Soviet complaint saying the reef was on the charts and the charts were "more than adequate".

The Russians repeatedly kept refusing offers of assistance, telling Wellington's two tug boats, *Kupe* and *Toia*, to stand down, and cancelling Mayday calls that Captain Jamison had sent. Instead, the Soviet crew did radio a Russian base in Vladivostok, more than 10,000 kilometres away, asking for a salvage tug to urgently be dispatched from there.

Again, all this effort to avoid the presence of New Zealand maritime authorities on the ship raised eyebrows, although a police and navy dive team was permitted to briefly search the wreck for the missing Russian crewman. They found that watertight doors that the Russians had sworn were sealed were wide open. They did not find the crewman's body.

Adding further intrigue to proceedings, Jamison was in the custody of two Soviet guards, quite possibly KGB – not New Zealand Police, and then the New Zealand Government began to swing in behind the Soviets. Despite newspaper photos of seriously dodgy liferafts and equipment, Maritime New Zealand issued a statement saying the cruise liner's gear had been inspected and was in good order. Then the Royal New Zealand Navy issued a statement denying that HMNZS Taupo commander, Lieutenant Batcheler, had ever given the interview blasting the Russian safety equipment. It never happened, they said. This despite the journalist from the *Evening Post* having copious notes.

Picton's Deputy Harbourmaster, Captain Neill, recalled having discussions with Batcheler at the Picton wharf on the night of the sinking, where the naval officer had repeated his assertions that the lifesaving gear was shocking. When they next caught up, Batcheler told Neill he'd been ordered to keep his mouth shut.

Something strange was going on.

Despite hearing that evidence, mysteriously, the report of the inquiry made three main findings:

- The sinking was the fault of Captain Jamison who was at the helm
- The Russian crew were to be praised for their efforts at saving the passengers
- The life saving equipment was adequate for a cruise liner

Captain Jamison has never spoken about what happened, and his testimony to the inquiry was suppressed and given in a closed hearing – and some of the evidence remains suppressed to this day – raising further suspicions about whether New Zealand rolled over under pressure from the Soviets.

Transport Minister Richard Prebble went so far as to issue a statement saying, "allegations made subsequently, concerning deficiencies in the *Mikhail Lermontov's* lifesaving appliances, have not been borne out by the evidence presented to the inquiry."

Again, this flat denial despite media photos of faulty equipment. Prebble refused to order a formal inquiry because he received instructions that the Soviet Union was taking over the formal investigation, and to this day allegations continue to swirl from investigators that Prebble ordered papers relevant to the sinking to be deposited in the National Archives:

"The answer to the mystery may be contained in papers of the then-Transport Minister, Richard Prebble, which have been deposited with the National Archives and cannot be opened until after Mr Prebble's death," reported the *Herald*[55]. Prebble denies there's a secret stash of documents,[56] and for his part has previously levelled the same allegation at Winston Peters.

"When the member was in Opposition he said that he had a safe full of documents that would prove the Maori loans scandal, and that when he revealed them the Government of the time would fall. He lost the key to that safe full of documents. The documents did not ever appear. He said that he had a safe full of documents that showed that there were Russian submarines in Cook Strait; that the *Mikhail Lermontov* was a spy ship; that a ferry had gone aground--the list of accusations was very wide. Members opposite enjoyed the exposure of those accusations, and used them in order to win office."[57]

---

55 "Documentary missed secrets of Lermontov sinking, says critic," NZ Herald, 29 March 2000
56 "Lermontov sinking still lures conspiracy buffs", NZ Herald 16 February 2006
57 Hansard, 7 October 1992

As other commentators have noted, "As a young National MP in the 1980s during the chilly last years of the Cold War, Peters was fond of 'reds under the beds' rhetoric. In 1986 he bemused parliament and the media by claiming that the *Mikhail Lermontov*, the Russian cruise ship which ran aground and sunk in the Marlborough Sounds, had been on a secret KGB mission."[58]

"Reds under the beds" rhetoric maybe, but the Lange administration wasn't averse to the concept either. In 1988 it politely declined a Russian request for the missile tracking ship *Kosmonaut Georgy Dobrovolsky*[59] to refuel in Wellington Harbour, sending it instead to Bluff where there was less chance of eavesdropping. "For reasons of national security I am not able to give the details," cabinet minister Colin Moyle told parliament in response to a question from National leader Jim Bolger.[60] So clearly they knew Russian vessels could pose a threat; it just suited Labour and later even National to paint Peters as an idiot for suggesting the massive cruise liner could be one.

The *Lermontov*, built 1972, was originally a regular on the New York run from the Baltic port of Leningrad. On its first US visit in 1973, officials with America's NSA reported expectations that the ship would contain intelligence gathering staff and equipment, "as do virtually all Soviet missions".[61]

When President Reagan banned Russian ships from American ports in 1980 as a sanction for invading Afghanistan, the Soviets re-tasked the *Lermontov* on European and eventually Pacific voyages.

The idea that the Soviet Union would *not* be gathering intelligence through its commercial fleet was naïve in the extreme. The Cold War

---

58 http://readingthemaps.blogspot.co.nz/2011/11/winson-takes-deng-xiaoping-for-drive.html
59 Named after one of the three Soyuz 11 cosmonauts found dead in their capsule when it re-entered the atmosphere and landed at the end of June 1971. During their 23 day space flight the crew had docked with a Russian space station and sent televised messages back to earth, one of which from mission commander Lt. Col. Dobrovolsky was full of praise: "The ship steers very well – very well. It responds well. Thank the planners for a successful design." Sadly, just after he flipped the switch to bring Soyuz 11 back home to earth, a valve inside the capsule opened and the air supply gushed away during the few minutes it took to hurtle back through the atmosphere. When recovery crews opened the door of Soyuz, all three men were dead.
60 Hansard, Questions on Notice, 11 October 1988
61 "Soviet Spy Ring Active Across US", by Victor Riesel, Beaver County Times, 4 June 1973, p4

marked the height of spookery – humble New Zealand even had its own SIS agent in Albania monitoring military movements in Eastern Europe. The new American Embassy built in Moscow was so full of KGB bugs they actually outnumbered the cockroaches – it had to be vacated and torn down in the ultimate form of electronic pest control.

As I wrote in *Totalitaria*, where I cover the intelligence community in more detail, it's not as if the Russians had no prior form. In 1946 the Russians presented the US ambassador to Moscow with a copy of the US "Great Seal" to hang in the American embassy. For seven years until it was discovered, the Ruskies were able to eavesdrop on embassy conversations using a special bugging device they had planted in the Seal. Of course, the dastardly plan all hinged on where the Ambassador chose to hang the Seal, but the Russians probably figured it was a safe bet the prestigious icon wasn't going to be displayed by the men's urinal.

More recently, China purchased a brand spanking new Boeing from America to become China's Air Force One, only to discover 27 bugging devices. As a consequence, they ripped the interior of the new Boeing to shreds looking for the rest of the devices they hadn't yet found. It's rumoured they were laughing so loud and hi-fiving so hard at CIA HQ in Langley, Virginia you could hear the guffaws from as far away as Beijing.

Like I said, the espionage game was a running gag; each country was out to maximise its surveillance capabilities by whatever route they could. In New York in 1973, President Nixon was shocked to discover the majority of Russia's 816 UN diplomats were KGB agents, and of course who can forget "The Amerikans" – the deep sleeper cells where KGB agents posed as American families for decades until they were discovered? The CIA created its own airline, Air America, and in the early 1990s tried to buy into Royal Tongan Airlines to create a legitimate cover for espionage. The Soviets were just as crafty, and the Chinese are pulling similar stunts today.

Across the ditch the Australian intelligence agency ASIO had long recognised that the perils of Soviet cruise ships extended beyond the normal horrors that cruise liners are known for, as one former agent recounted to author and university professor David McKnight:[62]

---

62 "The New Left and the Old Moles," by David McKnight, 9 July 2006 Chapter 19, 'Australia's Spies and Their Secrets' (David McKnight, Allen & Unwin, 1994), http://www.davidmcknight.com.au/archives/2006/07/new-left-and-old-moles

"The cruise ships caused us on the KGB desk a lot of concern because ... they were ideal place for compromising someone [by photographing illicit sexual activities]. More importantly, it was a perfect meeting place for a long term debriefing of an existing informant.... The [Soviet] case officer could be part of the crews. It made us shudder. 'We had people on the ships from time to time. You didn't know who the operators were. You didn't know who the KGB people were. ... Another thing that used to worry us was [an agent] meeting a Soviet submarine at sea. The person on the cruise ship would go out past the Sydney Heads, the agent would go over the side onto a Soviet submarine and then go in the sub to somewhere else for the duration of the cruise and then go back on the ship just outside the heads at night. [Agents] could go off, be specially trained; illegals could be brought onto the ships, people being substituted. Your mind ... could just run rampant with it -- and it did -- but what the hell could we do about it?"

ASIO, MI6, the CIA and presumably New Zealand's SIS swapped details on passenger lists and tried to screen the Soviet ships for known KGB agents, but it was like looking for a needle in a haystack while blindfolded, with the added pressure that once Russia sussed out what the Aussies were up to, they made the haystack bigger, increasing the number of cruise ship visits so as to overload Western intelligence with work.

"There were so many bloody cruises that you have just described an unsolvable problem," the agent told McKnight. In the end everyone gave up and tried not to think about it.

Did the *Mikhail Lermontov* carry KGB agents and electronic eavesdropping gear? Possibly. We will never know for sure. The Russians salvaged what they could from the wreck and undertook the formal inquiry back in Russia, not New Zealand. Much of that evidence was sealed as well.

Another incident sprung up the month after the *Lermontov* sinking that continues to haunt Peters as well. The Cook Strait ferry grounding was a classic of its time. On 28 March 1986 one of the ferries was en route to Picton through the Marlborough Sounds. On the bridge the senior crew were diverted by the Dustin Hoffman movie "Tootsie" playing on the ship's VHS entertainment channel. Suddenly they realised they were heading towards another of the Cook Strait ferries coming the other way from Picton to Wellington. Naturally, they took evasive action but in doing so accidentally scraped the ferry on the seabed in the sounds.

The incident was serious enough for Railways Corporation to send divers into the water at Picton to assess the damage, and the ship was later sent to dry dock for examination.

Winston Peters received a tip-off, but Transport Minister Richard Prebble denied the story as did Railways Corporation. It had happened soon after the *Mikhail Lermontov* sinking so transport safety was a sensitive issue and Prebble and his officials had already been prepared to seal evidence in the earlier case.

"The captain who drove the boat into dry dock was a Master Anderson," says Peters, "and he wasn't going to wear this damage on his record so he compiled a report on the damage. Someone leaked it to me."[63]

Peters says he gave the leaked report and the story to the *Dominion's* Richard Long, who wrote a front page story on the grounding. TV1 news later followed it up and Peters laughs as he recalls, "TV1 even had an interview with a couple of men who'd been fishing and literally had to swim for their lives to get out of the way of the off-course ferry bearing down on their boat."

But for 28 years, he sighs, Prebble has denied it and it later suited his former colleagues in the National Party to ridicule him as well, despite Master Anderson's report.

Peters says it was an issue of passenger safety and in his view minister Prebble was playing fast and loose with the truth. A sobering illustration of why there needs to be accountability on public transport systems came with a later event involving the Cook Strait ferry Aratere. Here's how the *Christchurch Press* reported it after obtained a leaked maritime safety report:[64]

An Interislander ferry came "extremely close to capsizing" after its skipper showed poor judgment during a stormy Cook Strait crossing, a highly critical safety report has found.

Had it failed to right itself, "most persons on board would have been trapped inside the vessel and previous examples of roll-on, roll-off vessel casualties indicate a heavy loss of life would have resulted," the report said.

The Aratere was carrying 391 people at the time.

The draft Maritime New Zealand report into the sailing, leaked before its

---

63 Interview with author
64 "Aratere almost capsized: report", Christchurch Press, 11 November 2006

official release next month, makes a string of safety recommendations, including the introduction of rough weather sailing guidelines and stricter controls on cargo lashings on ferries.

The Aratere broached and heeled over 50 degrees on two separate occasions in heavy seas, and rolled by up to 30 degrees for three minutes after the ferry stalled when the skipper tried to change course, the report into the March 3 sailing said.

"In the opinion of the investigators Aratere was extremely close to capsizing, particularly on the second broach, and that, if more cargo had shifted and/or down-flooding had commenced, she would have done so."

Such a capsize would have been rapid, leaving little time for passengers or crew to don lifejackets.

It seems maritime scandals have hung, perhaps undeservedly when the evidence is objectively considered, around the neck of Winston Peters like an albatross well-past its best-before date.

It appears, however, that when Winston Peters alleged KGB involvement with the *Mikhail Lermontov*, he didn't realise the full extent of the story he was actually sitting on, and far from allowing Richard Prebble to tease him mercilessly for the next three decades, if he had known what you will read over the page, he might have brought down the Lange government in a spy scandal then and there.

5

Vladimir Putin Lived In Karori

> *"Mr. Ambassador, you have nearly a hundred naval vessels operating in the North Atlantic right now. Your aircraft has dropped enough sonar buoys so that a man could walk from Greenland to Iceland to Scotland without getting his feet wet. Now, shall we dispense with the bull?"*
>
> – ***The Hunt For Red October*, 1990**

There is a grainy black and white photo circulating on the internet of *Lermontov* captain Vladislav Vorobyev entering the preliminary hearing in New Zealand flanked by two men from the Soviet embassy in Wellington.

Vorobyev is in the centre of the picture – the guy looking directly at the camera in a very apprehensive fashion. The man on the left, however, appears to be Russian President Vladimir Putin.

"No wayyy!", I can hear you saying.

Yes, way.

On page 102 there is another clearer photo of the same man entering the inquiry on another morning with a ship's officer and a lawyer. Notice how short the Putin character is?

Vladimir Vladimirovich Putin was born 7 October 1952, making him 61 years old today. In February 1986 he was aged 33. He joined the KGB in 1975, specialising initially in monitoring foreigners and diplomatic officials.

His official biography states he was assigned to East Germany in 1985. "During that time, Putin was assigned to Directorate S, the illegal intelligence-gathering unit (the KGB's classification for agents who used falsified identities) where he was given cover as a translator and interpreter."[65]

Now, here's the punchline. Our mystery man in the photograph is listed as a translator and "interpreter" for the Soviet embassy in Wellington. He was the official "interpreter" at the New Zealand inquiry. He is named, and was identified at the inquiry, as "Boris Ashikhmin". Despite database searches, I have been unable to find a man of that name fitting that description or age online. That's not to say he doesn't exist, but there is no digital footprint for him, lending weight to the suspicion that it was a false identity – something Putin's Directorate S specialised in.

Of course, the President of the second most powerful nation in the world is not going to bother taking questions about specific previous clandestine missions for the KGB, so we will never be able to prove "Boris" was actually Vladimir unless the SIS chooses to release its classified files. Expect hell to freeze over first. Assuming of course they realised Boris was a spy. They may not have.

There are more points of corroboration, however. Apart from the striking facial resemblance to the Russian President, the "translator and interpreter" Boris is also short, like Vladimir Putin who stands only 5'6, or 1.7m, just over the height of an average woman.

Applying the now famous "duck" test, if it looks like a Putin, if it walks like a Putin, if it is doing the same job that was Putin's official cover at the time, then it's most probably a Putin.

Of course, although a senior KGB spy in the 1980s operating under the cover of "interpreter", nobody then knew what the future had in store for Vladimir Putin, so it has become a bigger story in hindsight than people would have appreciated at the time. What is more fascinating is that Putin appears to have lived in Wellington for a while, probably shopped for groceries at the Karori supermarket, drank at a local bar, listened to parliamentary broadcasts of Winston Peters being ridiculed for alleging KGB involvement, and he probably chuckled softly to himself all the way home.

Challenged as to why the inquiry had used a Soviet embassy interpreter to be the official translator at the sinking of a Soviet government liner, Transport Minister Richard Prebble said "Boris" was available at short

---

65 "The Man Without a Face: The Unlikely Rise of Vladimir Putin," by Masha Gessen, Riverhead Publishing, New York 2012, p60

notice because he'd been involved in interpreting for joint venture fishing deals between New Zealand and the USSR.[66] Clearly Putin could not have flown down from Europe specially for the hearing, because the hearing began only 36 hours after the sinking. He had to have already been in the country, and it is clear Prebble or his officials were familiar with him based on his interaction with New Zealand government departments. Putin's involvement was signed off by Transport Minister Richard Prebble.

Other Russian interpreters offered their services to the inquiry but were told they wouldn't be needed.

So we end up with the bizarre situation that a ship Winston Peters claimed was linked to a KGB operation is the subject of a New Zealand investigation where a senior KGB operative attached to the USSR embassy in Wellington is the sole gatekeeper of the entire inquiry. After all, none of the New Zealand officials could speak Russian. They had no idea what Putin was really saying to the Russian witnesses, or whether he was truthfully reporting their answers.

Peters merely 'believed' the ship had some kind of KGB link. If he had *known* the government's own preliminary inquiry was apparently under the total effective control of the KGB, he'd have been able to bring the Lange government down in the ensuing spy scandal.

Peters certainly suspected some jiggery-pokery had gone on because of the Soviet government interpreter, and demanded to know from Prebble in parliament why the proceedings of the inquiry were not recorded on tape so the evidence could be verified later? It was too hard, was essentially the response. The inquiry did not feel it necessary.

Certainly veteran *National Business Review* journalist and espionage expert Graeme Hunt made the same connection in his 2007 book *Spies and Revolutionaries*. Hunt found evidence indicating Putin was here when Soviet diplomat Sergei Budnik was expelled for spying in 1987, and he was also up to speed on Putin's suspected appearance as a 'translator' assisting the captain at the hearing into the sinking:[67]

"A man bearing a striking resemblance to [Mr Putin] was in New Zealand in 1986 for the inquiry into the sinking of the Russian cruise ship *Mikhail Lermontov* in the Marlborough Sounds."

---

66 The USSR was one of only three nations permitted to fish inside NZ's exclusive economic zone
67 "Did Putin visit New Zealand for the KGB?" NZ Herald, 3 August 2007

Skepticism around foreign espionage in New Zealand is common, usually based on the assumption, "who'd be interested in us?". The Soviets, as their American sleeper cells showed, were not looking for state secrets in these kind of operations, but for opportunities; opportunities to cultivate contacts in influential positions, or apply pressure on them at a later date.

"It was the sort of information the Russians routinely collected," wrote Hunt, "not just from New Zealand but right around the world, which they could use for blackmail purposes, to influence people in high places, to provide a dossier of information which could be used at some time in the future."

Richard Prebble, whose official dossier on the sinking is sealed, went on to lead the Act Party, and one of his favourite political weapons over the years was to take the 'Mikhail' out of Peters at every opportunity.

"Where's the evidence?" Prebble would chide.

"In your safe!" Peters would shout back.

"Some days he has me in tears of laughter," said New Zealand First's Ron Mark after one Prebble speech in 2000 about the need for openness and transparency,[68] "and other days I think he is just crying crocodile tears, because it seems rather ironic that the same man who was responsible for locking up all the documents relating to the *Mikhail Lermontov* –"

"No I'm not," interjected Prebble before boasting, "I have got every single document".

Ron Mark looked him in the eye. "The documents are locked up from the public so that the public cannot see them."

"I do not speak much Russian," admitted Peters one evening during a debate on Act's bill improving public access to official information,[69] "but I know two Russian words that have a great relevance to this debate, and they are the *Mikhail Lermontov*. The leader of the Act Party put a 50-year embargo on the documents from that investigation. Act members believe in transparency, they say. Here is their bill, the Access to Official Information Bill.

"Well I ask Mr Prebble this: how about taking off the embargo for the next 50 years…and letting us all see them? [Interruption] Do members see what I mean? The very member of the Act Party who five minutes ago

---

68 Hansard, 'Appointment – Ombudsman', 24 February 2000
69 Hansard, 'Access to Official Information Bill', 14 March 2001

told me that that party believed in transparency and information across the board now does not want us to know."

As Peters told the House, there had been 31 inquiries into marine accidents in New Zealand, "and for the biggest accident ever, we had no inquiry at all. Guess who handled it? None other than Richard Prebble."

The extremely unusual circumstance of New Zealand not holding an official inquiry into a fatal maritime disaster – when such inquiries had been held both before and after this into foreign-owned vessels running aground in NZ – fuelled conspiracy theory. What would the Russians have to hide? Why did they spirit the crew back to Moscow as rapidly as possible? Why did New Zealand surrender its sovereignty? As critics noted, it would be like inviting France to take the lead role in investigating the Rainbow Warrior bombing.

Two significant footnotes exist to this historical incident. In his epic book on the history of Soviet intelligence, *The KGB: The Eyes of Russia* published in 1983, author and historian Harry Rositzke notes that the USSR had a New Zealand Labour cabinet minister spying for them at one point or, as the KGB preferred to call it, "an agent of influence". Obviously the publication date precludes the Lange administration which came to power a year after the book, but it could have been Kirk's 72-75 government or the Nash administration in the late 1950s.

Of more immediate confirmation, former Army territorial force intelligence staffer Ben Vidgen claimed in his book *State Secrets* that the 1987 expulsion of Sergei Budnik as a KGB operative in NZ was because he'd blackmailed a member of Lange's Labour caucus to spy for the Soviets: "Budnik had for two years been running an agent placed within the Labour Government's own caucus – a person with cabinet access," he writes. "It is alleged the MP was involved in an illicit affair, and the Soviets found out about it."[70]

Vidgen sourced the story to his former military intelligence colleagues and an SIS officer, saying he'd been told this in 1991 during Operation Ivanhoe in the South Island. For his part, David Lange denied the blackmail story or, more accurately, skirted around without actually denying:

"What you have to remember is that a great deal of intelligence people and former intelligence people are mentally unstable on both sides of the

---

70 State Secrets by Ben Vidgen, Howling At The Moon, 1999, p276

divide," Lange told Vidgen, "or suffering from over active imaginations."

If the story is true, however, it's little wonder Labour wanted Peters discredited on anything to do with Russian "conspiracy theories".

Winston Peters, as you've seen, was unable to get too much traction surrounding the *Mikhail Lermontov*, despite the fact the ship most likely had an espionage role, but as 1986 wore on, he hit the political mother-lode.

6

The Maori Loans Affair

> *"The story had the lot: con artists, Hawaiian middlemen and shady Middle Eastern financiers"*
> – Prime Minister David Lange

With National still recovering from its own identity crisis as Labour's Lange/Douglas administration outflanked it on the right, and the aftermath of the leadership bloodletting that had taken the political lives of Rob Muldoon and then Jim McLay, it wasn't until the end of 1986 that National really began to recover its mojo. Unsurprisingly, in hindsight, it was the Member for Tauranga who landed the first real big hit on the Lange administration.

Labour's decision to ban nuclear warships from New Zealand ports, and to do so publicly, had put the American government on edge. Brinksmanship between Washington and Moscow was underway at the time, of a kind so delicate that New Zealand didn't really have a clue what was at stake. President Reagan and Britain's Margaret Thatcher, with occasional input from Pope John Paul II, were manipulating world events and public opinion about the Soviet Union with the aim of sparking reform in the Communist bloc of Eastern Europe.

The end result of their finely-balanced chess game was a nuclear missile reduction treaty, a declaration of "glasnost" (openness) and "perestroika" (reform) by Soviet leader Mikhail Gorbachev, followed later by the collapse of the Berlin Wall and then freedom – first for the Soviet satellite territories like Romania and Poland, and later for the USSR itself. All that, of course, was still in the future when New Zealand told America to keep its ships away, but those were the stakes of the game. US Secretary of State George Schultz was "most displeased" at New Zealand causing a rift in what should have been a solid western alliance. In this international game of chicken between the US eagle and the Russian bear, it was the bloody kiwis, happening to cross the road, who blinked first.

America had dealt with dissent like this from its minor treaty partners in the past. Across the ditch in Australia to be exact. In 1975, Gough Whitlam's Labor government had dared to question US authority over the satellite eavesdropping base at Pine Gap – part of the network now used to listen to all our phone calls and read every email and web page we browse. Next thing Whitlam knew his government was suddenly embroiled in a fake Arab loans scandal and Labor was turfed out of power by Australia's Governor General and replaced by a more US-friendly conservative government under Malcolm Fraser.

The suggestion that the two events were linked might remain as conspiracy theory, were it not for the embarrassing revelations that America's CIA set up a black operations merchant bank, Nugan Hand Pty Ltd, in Australia. The director of Nugan Hand Australia was William Colby, the former head of the CIA itself. In his autobiography[71] Colby writes that one of the biggest crises of his tenure in the CIA was the election "of a left wing and possibly antagonistic Government in Australia."

Let that sink in for a moment. The Vietnam War had been raging, the Cold War was at its height, and the biggest threat facing the USA and its intelligence operations was Gough Whitlam's Australian Labor government. It was, said Colby, at the same risk level as Soviet intervention in the 1973 Arab/Israeli war. Go figure.

The Americans sucker-punched Whitlam by sending an Arab by the name of Khemlani to Australia with a bunch of fake documents purporting to provide US$4 billion worth of funding for energy projects. Australia's Minister of Energy was forced to resign as news of the scam was leaked to the media in late 1975, leading Whitlam into open warfare with the CIA, naming and shaming four suspected CIA operatives in the country. Whitlam also sacked one of his own intelligence bosses for failing to follow orders.

---

71   *Honorable Men: My Life In The CIA* by William Colby, Simon & Schuster, 1978

Years later, a former top CIA official, Chief of Counter-Intelligence James Angleton revealed his agency had indeed been working with Aussie spy agencies against Whitlam:[72]

"I will put it this way very bluntly. No one in the Agency would ever believe that I would ever subscribe to any activity that was not coordinated with the chief of the Australian internal security."

Ray Cline, another CIA supremo associated with the Nugan Hand Bank told Australia's *National Times* newspaper:

"The CIA would go so far as to provide information to people who would bring it to the surface in Australia...if we provided a particular piece of information to the Australian intelligence services, they would make use of it."

Nugan Hand, incidentally, provided banking services to the Mr Asia heroin ring. One of the bank's CIA associates, Ted Shackley, had land holdings in New Zealand but stepped into the fray on 8 November 1975 by sending a memo to the Deputy Director of ASIO, the Australian intelligence service. That memo warned that if Whitlam didn't back off, the CIA couldn't see "how our mutually beneficial relationships are going to continue."

Within three days, Whitlam was gone. For those who are conspiracy-minded, the man who sacked Whitlam, Aussie Governor-General Sir John Kerr, had been seconded during World War 2 to America's Office of Strategic Services – the department that became the Central Intelligence Agency.

So if Australia's revolt over the Pine Gap listening post in 1975 was as big a threat to the US as the Soviets attacking Israel, where might New Zealand's raspberry to nuclear deterrence – just as Reagan and Gorbachev were about to test each other's mettle – fit in the great scheme of things ten years later?

Winston Peters was about to find out. You just had to know how to read the signs. One of the first indicators for those in the know that the US might be up to something came in a front page story in the *New Zealand Times* Sunday newspaper in November 1984. The article revealed the former US Secretary of State Henry Kissinger and former CIA Deputy Director Ray Cline (yes, the same Cline who featured in Whitlam's 1975 downfall) had joined forces to establish the Centre for Strategic and International

---

72 All references to the Nugan Hand CIA pressure on Australia can be found in my book *The Paradise Conspiracy*, chapter 9

Studies at Georgetown University in Washington DC. The purpose of the "think tank", they said, was to analyse the potential impacts of New Zealand's anti-nuclear position. A think tank at Georgetown established by Kissinger and Cline and devoted to New Zealand policy? Seriously?

The highly-placed Mr Cline then visited New Zealand in 1986, in his new role as an economics and political studies professor, and talked of meeting "some friends" down here. In August 1986, 58 year old former CIA operative Ralph W McGeHee turned up in New Zealand on a whistle-blowing expedition. McGeHee and the CIA had parted ways some years back and he was an early version of Edward Snowden, warning the public what the spy agency was getting up to. The former secret agent told journalists all the signs were pointing to a US attempt to destabilise the Lange administration sometime before the 1987 election.

"Unless I'm very much mistaken," he told the *Herald*, there'll be "a deliberate CIA operation to destabilise or displace a Labour Government with [its] anti-nuclear policies. I can see the early signs of such an operation. And I've seen – and been involved in – too many such operations to be in much doubt about it.

What signs?, asked the paper.

"Well, these can range from recent visits from some pretty prominent and hawkish Americans to infiltration and destabilisation of organisations such as labour unions.

"You've recently been visited by such people as Ray S Cline, now a prominent American academic but formerly a Deputy Director of the CIA. Under his academic guise of clean, ideological inquiry, such a man is in an excellent position to push official American policy."

Unbeknownst to the media, in June 1986, details began to emerge in New Zealand hush-hush government circles of an approach by two foreign businessmen, Hawaiian Michael Gisondi and West German Max Raepple, offering a US$300 million loan package (about NZ$600 million at the time) to the Maori Affairs Department, now called Te Puni Kokiri. It was illegal for New Zealand government agencies to obtain funding from anywhere except Treasury under proper parliamentary procedures. That, after all, is what the Budget is all about each year.

But mere legalities didn't appear to worry the wide boys running Maori Affairs. Nor did they worry Maori Affairs Minister Koro Wetere, who gave it the big tick. The money was allegedly part of a US$10 billion fund provided by a Kuwaiti Arab royal named Ahmed Omar for the purposes of countering Soviet financial influence in the Pacific.

Sound familiar?

Maori Affairs wanted to use the US$300 million to create a subsidiary company making prefabricated houses for export, using Maori labour.

One of the go betweens in the deal was Maori businessman Rocky Cribb, a former bankrupt who leaked information to one Winston Raymond Peters. Another source was Edwin Perry, later to become an NZ First MP, and Peters had also obtained documents from inside the office of Maori Affairs Minister Koro Wetere.

While the media, courtesy of Winston Peters, didn't find out about the plot until mid-December 1986, secret diplomatic cable traffic as early as late-November indicates New Zealand intelligence agencies were already trying to find out who was behind it.

Stamped "CONFIDENTIAL", marked "priority" and sent to the Governments of Tonga, the Cook Islands, the United States and Britain, a diplomatic transmission was fired out by the Ministry of Foreign Affairs in Wellington on November 26, 1986.

"The Department of Maori Affairs has been approached by an Hawaiian group with an offer of a low interest loan (4 percent for 25 years) of USDLRS 300 million. The loan is envisaged as a source of funding for the proposed Maori Resource Development Corporation.

"The Department has been in communication with Hawaiian-based Michael Gisondi, who claims to have acted as an adviser to the Kingdom of Tonga (making reference to the Hon L L Kavaliku and Hon J C Cocker).

"There are also claims that investments have been made in Tonga and the Cook Islands, using the same source of funds.

"We have been told that Gisondi acts on behalf of Max Raepple based in West Germany who in turn is the agent for the original source of the funds in Kuwait. The purpose of the funds is reported to be to counter Soviet influence in the South Pacific, and the total sum for this purpose was thought to be USDLRS 10 billion.

"As far as the Department of Maori Affairs knows the Kuwaiti Government is not involved. Could you please check on Gisondi's activities in Tonga and the Cook Islands, and the validity of the claim that investments have been made. He describes himself as a certified financial planner, and appears to have experience in insurance.

"If London or Washington have any leads on Gisondi, Raepple or the source of funds, please let us know. Reedy from Maori Affairs will be travelling to Hawaii on Sunday 30 November where he will meet with Gisondi and Raepple, so we would appreciate a response by our Friday."

The news wasn't good. A Kuwaiti royal allegedly fronting the cash, Ahmed Omar, did not exist. Hawaiian Michael Gisondi had US military connections, as did Stephen Thomas – one of five men involved in the pitch, reported to have been a CIA station chief. Gisondi and Raepple also claimed to be working for ousted Filipino dictator Ferdinand Marcos. Another of the five, Robert C. Allen, was identified in FBI files as a CIA agent connected to a CIA front company called Bishop Baldwin Rewald Dillingham Wong Ltd, based in Hawaii but which had recently opened an office in Auckland. A character named Eldon William Morris of Hawaii was tied up with Gisondi, and Morris was pitched as "a retired General". In fact, he was a retired Lieutenant-Colonel and he died only a few years back in Hawaii.

The appearance of the Bishop Baldwin group in Auckland is fascinating. Company president Ron Rewald testified at his Hawaii criminal trial for embezzlement that his business had taken over Nugan Hand's CIA work in the Pacific and Asia after the Australian bank's director Frank Nugan was found with his head blown off in a parked Mercedes near Sydney. One of the first signs for Australian police that they were dealing with something 'spooky' in that case was that Nugan's pocket contained a business card of CIA director William Colby. The second clue that all was not as it seemed: there were no fingerprints on the rifle found beside Nugan's body. How does a dead man commit suicide and then wipe his fingerprints off the gun?, police wondered. Obviously he doesn't, at least not in a genuine suicide.

Of Robert C. Allen's role, author Rodney Stich writes:[73]

"Both Allen and [James] Hannah[74] have been described as being on the CIA payroll by lawyers in the 1985 trial of Ron Rewald, who operated a CIA front corporation called Bishop Baldwin Rewald Dillingham and Wong. BBRDW was involved in money laundering, gun running, intelligence gathering and providing commercial cover [business aliases] for various

---

73 Explosive Secrets Of Covert CIA Companies, by Rodney Stich, Silverpeak, 2006
74 Another involved in the Maori loans affair

CIA agents and operations. The CIA admits they used the company for cover, but deny they used it for money laundering.

"After the swindle was revealed, and Rewald attempted suicide, Allen, Hannah and a third person Angelo Cancel were employed by the CIA to go to the BBRDW office and recover records of foreign bank accounts used for laundering CIA dirty money. These records were sealed permanently by court order, and Allen was prevented by the CIA from being subpoenaed as a witness in the Rewald trial on 'national security' grounds."

Ronald Reagan's vice president at the time was George Bush senior, himself a former CIA director. Ron Rewald says he was invited to meet Vice President Bush when the CIA was setting the mission for BBRDW. Intriguingly, New Zealand was mentioned in dispatches:

"Taiwan, Singapore, Australia, New Zealand, Hong Kong, the whole [Pacific] rim is going through big changes now," Bush told Rewald.[75]

That's the background. These were some of the characters tied up with the men offering fake Arab loans to the Maori Affairs Department, in what looked like a copycat version of the scandal that tipped Whitlam over. The first inkling of trouble broke in the New Zealand press courtesy of Winston Peters and a parliamentary question on 16 December 1986. As Michael Laws, later to become Winston's parliamentary researcher, writes:[76]

"One of the disgruntled parties in this ill-fated adventure had taken umbrage and deposited various papers and documents with Winston Peters. In turn, Peters provided fragments of this dossier to the media, outlining a sorry saga of foolishness and suggesting a New Zealand Watergate. When shadowy CIA operatives were rumoured to be involved, a surreal character overtook the whole affair."

Newspapers in New Zealand and Australia told of a "rowdy" parliamentary debate sparked by Winston Peters producing "a letter" detailing a loan offer from Michael Gisondi, and accepted by head of Maori Affairs Tamati Reedy.

Foreign Affairs Minister and Prime Minister David Lange told parliament he was completely in the dark: "The first I knew anything about this matter was today on my return from Great Barrier Island."[77]

---

75   Stich, supra
76   "The Demon Profession," Michael Laws, HarperCollins 1998, p73
77   Hansard, Urgent Debate, 17 December 1986

Peters could have had a field day with that answer if he'd had access to the confidential MFAT diplomatic cable traffic that later ended up in my clutches, because the smoking gun was the November 26 cable stamped "CONFIDENTIAL" in capital letters and "PRIORITY" and sent from the Ministry of Foreign Affairs – David Lange's own department for which he had ministerial responsibility. Three weeks after his own officials had sent out an APB – All Points Bulletin – to governments around the world, their own minister claimed not to know?

Once again, almost alone among opposition MPs, Winston Peters had come so close to blowing up the Labour Government without even realising. As Michael Laws quipped, it was like a political game of *Battleship*, call out a co-ordinate number and hope like hell you'd hear a 'boom'. First Prebble and now Lange had watched a Winston torpedo whizz past their bows.

If Lange didn't know his department was investigating a fake loan scandal for three weeks prior, then he ran his department incompetently. If he did know, then his reported outrage towards Maori Affairs minister Koro Wetere had a 'faux' ring to it and Lange was as guilty as his minister for not acting decisively. Here's how Lange tells the story in his autobiography:

"The year ended in farce. Officers of the Maori Affairs Department attempted to raise an unauthorised loan of NZ$600 million overseas. The story had the lot: con artists, Hawaiian middlemen and shady Middle Eastern financiers. Official inquiries followed the disclosure of the scheme in parliament but the critical question for the government was the degree of involvement of the minister.

"Investigations found nothing conclusive and the minister himself denied all knowledge of the loan. It looked bad; if the minister was not a liar he was hopelessly incompetent," writes Lange.

The reason the "investigations found nothing conclusive" however, is because Lange was running interference or, as he puts it, "I started 1987 by inventing defences for the minister".

Elaborate and cunning defences they were, too:

"I can remember the night the matter first broke in the House," thundered Winston Peters one afternoon in parliament.[78] "It was the present Prime Minister [Geoffrey Palmer] who was up there with the Minister of

---

78   Hansard, 'Maori Affairs Restructuring Bill', 7 September 1989

Maori Affairs [Wetere] and the Secretary for Maori Affairs [Reedy] who were trying to cover their backsides."

The Government's solution was to announce a *Yes, Minister* style inquiry, to be carried out by the State Services Commission. Peters called it a 'whitewash'.

"All the witnesses who came before the inquiry were required to give evidence on oath, with the exception of two – the Minister of Maori Affairs and the Minister of Finance. Everyone was required to be recorded, with the exception of the Minister of Maori Affairs."

Instead of his evidence being on oath and recorded on tape, Koro Wetere gave an informal verbal briefing to the inquiry and was allowed to write a formal statement – presumably on his lawyer's advice – later.

"Can anyone believe that?" growled Peters as he looked around the House before fixing Geoffrey Palmer in his gaze.

"The Minister of Justice of the time set up the inquiry and then had the audacity in his book *Unbridled Power*...to try to excuse that kind of behaviour.

"He wrote that the minister was guilty of no impropriety whatsoever."

"Quite right!" exclaimed Palmer, trying to defend his conclusion.

But if that's the case, Peters shot back, why did the minister offer his resignation on 3 February 1987? Lange in his book says it was because Wetere was "formally responsible" as minister, although that definition would make Lange himself "formally responsible" for his own department's involvement as well.

Lange's denial of any knowledge rings even hollower when you consider that not just Foreign Affairs but the Reserve Bank, Police and the intelligence agencies were all tasked with investigating the scam – and Lange was minister in charge of the intelligence agencies. He even offered an SIS briefing to the National Party leader. Gerald Hensley, the man running the Prime Minister's Department, called the plot "a convoluted rat-run of money-launderers, criminals and snake oil salesmen."[79]

In fact, Peters was a little too hard on the State Services Commission inquiry headed by Roderick Deane. Deane's report went as far as he could within his limited terms of reference, and he found that "some ministers" – plural – knew about the loan deal in advance and did nothing to stop it. Koro Wetere claimed to have got the green light for the loan from Finance

---

79 "Final Approaches: A Memoir" by Gerald Hensley, AUP, 2006, pp 292-293

Minister Roger Douglas, who told the inquiry he couldn't remember. Wetere was a protégé of Douglas, and the rift between the Prime Minister and his Finance Minister that eventually blew the Labour Government apart began there, with Winston Peters' Maori Loans scandal, according to Douglas.[80] Peters' strike on the government didn't kill it instantly, and not even at the next election, but the wound turned out to be mortal nonetheless, more like a cancer than a bullet.

Revenue Minister Trevor de Cleene tried to leap to Wetere's defence on that first day, telling the debating chamber, "If there is incompetence anywhere, it lies heavily in the head of the Department of Maori Affairs."

De Cleene tried to divert National MPs away from comparing it to the Australian loans that brought Whitlam down, insisting instead that the Maori Affairs Department must have tapped into the Marcos millions:

"I have got a suspicion where that stupid loan offer was made from... it was not coincidental that that international criminal Marcos lives in Hawaii and it is alleged that he has got a lot of money to launder."[81]

It wasn't the exiled and ailing Filipino dictator. Even Marcos wasn't stupid enough to give NZ$600 million to a New Zealand make-work scheme at a rate of only 4% locked in for 25 years at a time when mortgage interest rates were close to 20% and you could earn 14% on deposit in the bank.

The public and political uproar was huge. In fact, it drowned out the other piece of news that broke that day – the tabling of a Royal Commission report on proposed changes to the New Zealand electoral system. The report recommended extending parliament out to 120 seats with half to be voted in on the party list. Winston Peters had managed to eclipse the very electoral reform he would later come to rely on.

According to Laws, Lange, who could normally handle the embarrassment, "had worked his emotions into a state well beyond embarrassment – Lange was livid. Not only had one of his ministers attempted to contravene the law of the land, but Wetere's behaviour had allowed the Opposition to score its only palpable hit during the entire first parliamentary term. There were tense and secret meetings, first to discuss damage control, and then resignation."[82]

---

80 "Hostilities started with the Maori Loans affair," NZ Herald, 16 December 1988, p3
81 Hansard, 17 December 1986
82 The Demon Profession by Michael Laws, p74

Except Lange rejected Koro Wetere's resignation. The former Prime Minister says while the Ratana Church agreed it was scandalous, Wetere had to be supported by Lange, not held to account. With Ratana's support deal with Labour clearly in play, Lange felt he had no choice but to pony up and take the punishment being dished by Peters. It was better, perhaps than the alternative:

"I convened a meeting of Maori leaders and something close to a fist fight broke out in front of me, and the deputy prime minister [Palmer] who had asked me to convene the meeting, handed me a note which said 'I am not of this planet' and left the room."[83]

It's a criticism that had often been levelled at the lofty, awkward Palmer by unkind critics, and perhaps a gag line you'd expect to see on TV's *Miranda*, but it was unusual to read those stark words in the deputy PM's own handwriting. Was Geoffrey Palmer confessing to being a David Icke-style reptilian shape-shifter? Or was he simply getting out of there in fear for his safety, making the assumption the angry leaders wouldn't hit a portly and bespectacled Lange? Imagine what Winston Peters could have done with *that* note.

Michael Bassett, Lange's former Health Minister and a noted historian, says his boss is being a little evasive about Wetere, that Lange's book doesn't tell the whole story. It turns out that while Ratana did not want Wetere sacked, Lange came back and told Wetere they did, which resulted in a formal offer of resignation from the minister. Lange took it to Cabinet but only four MPs, including himself, supported sacking Wetere.

Bassett says Lange then wanted the officials in Maori Affairs sacked, "but he resiled when Deane pointed out that if foolishness were to be the benchmark for sackings, then the minister would need to go too."[84]

It was a Catch-22. When TVNZ broadcast its current affairs programme linking the whole thing to the CIA, David Lange poured all the opprobrium he could onto the five principals and their hangers-on. In return, rather than fleeing the glare, West German Max Raepple turned up in New Zealand demanding a public apology from Lange.

Even the Australian newspapers were running stories about Lange refusing to meet Raepple.

---

83 My Life by David Lange, final page
84 Working With David: Inside The Lange Cabinet by Michael Bassett, Hachette, 2008

For Winston Peters this was political manna from heaven, the gift that kept on giving. One of the men, Steve Thomas, threatened to sue Lange.

"Steve Thomas is thought to be the new CIA station chief for Honolulu, operating under a commercial cover," reported the left wing *Peace* magazine.[85] "Thomas has been feeding information to the New Zealand media about the negotiations, and has made statements that opposition politician Winston Peters does indeed have evidence that the Cabinet knew of the negotiations."

National's leader Jim Bolger had actually tried to muzzle Peters over the Maori Loans affair in early February 1987, according to Labour's Michael Bassett.

"We soon discovered that Wetere had an ally in Jim Bolger, who was becoming sick of the grandstanding by his unruly colleague. When the House resumed on 3 February 1987 Bolger vetoed any questions from Peters."

Bassett was probably making a little political hay while the sun shone there. Bolger had some pet questions of his own on contract work schemes that he wanted to ask, and Peters was back in full flight the following day, with the release of the full report by Rod Deane of the State Services Commission.

Lange would later complain that journalists were spending too much time listening to Peters, and that there existed "a holy alliance of leakers, spivs, scabs and scandalisers" all plotting to send the Lange government into extinction.

Although it was a slow-burning fuse inside the government, the scandal didn't do any long-term electoral damage to Labour in the public eye; the inquiry had seen to that. Labour's support was being cannibalised from right wing former National Party voters anyway, but the publicity over the Maori Loans affair did put Winston Peters on the map as far as the public were concerned.

For his part, even if David Lange and Geoffrey Palmer refused to publicly concede they were the victims of an American plot, Lange appears to have realised he was on notice:

"In 1987 the cabinet agreed to build an electronic interception facility

---

85   Peace Magazine Aug-Sep 1987, page 21.

at Waihopai," he writes in his autobiography.⁸⁶ Waihopai would mimic the activities of Australia's infamous Pine Gap interception facility, thus bringing the bizarre parallel lines of the two loan scandals on both sides of the Tasman full circle. When Labor in Australia threatened US access to Pine Gap it was removed from power by the CIA. The same kind of scare in NZ brought our Labour Government back into line.⁸⁷

"I thought we should build the base because it seemed unwise at the time to further upset the Americans, who were the chief beneficiaries of the information it provided."

As his personal poll ratings started to rise, so too did the heat in the National Party caucus. Peters was promoted to the front bench of the Opposition when parliament resumed after the 1987 election. Finally he was being taken seriously, or so he thought.

It was the beginning of the rest of Winston Peters' life.

---

86 *My Life*, supra, Kindle location 2522, Chapter 14

87 Much has been written – and still is today amid claims that New Zealand was only fully invited back into the electronic eavesdropping 'Five Eyes' agreement in 2009 – that this country's defence and intelligence ties to the US were cut outright as a result of our nuclear policy. It just isn't true. In June 2000, Investigate magazine stumbled across some de-classified military documents that disclosed New Zealand military involvement in an alliance known as AUSCANNZUKUS, reflecting the five powers Australia, Canada, NZ, UK, US behind the Echelon/Five Eyes system. The magazine became the first media outlet to reveal details of secret military exercises and research and intelligence sharing between America and New Zealand. It quickly became apparent that while 'above the line' military cooperation like port visits and the like had certainly been cut, there was a level that remained untouched. I have referred to NZ special forces meeting up with US submarines earlier – that's an example of AUSCANNZUKUS links. Once again it shows the parliamentary press gallery can sometimes be misled by spin doctors, and the mythology about New Zealand being out in the cold continues to run 14 years after we broke the story that disproved the myth. The full story is here http://www.investigatemagazine.com/june00subs.htm

7

When In Rome

> *"Are you not entertained? ARE YOU NOT ENTERTAINED?!?! Is this not why you're here?!"*
> – **Maximus shouts to the crowd after killing a foe in the ring**, *Gladiator*

Ancient Rome has a lot to teach us about modern politics. The archetypal image of Caesar and his fawning minions gathered at the Coliseum, feasting on wine and women while the real gladiators battle it out in the circus below, isn't far removed from Winston's relationship with the National Party during its second term on the opposition benches.

Conscious of his warrior's growing reputation, party leader Jim Bolger installed Peters at number eight on the front bench with responsibilities for Employment, Maori Affairs and Race Relations – close enough to really mess up the enemy, not close enough to be part of the inner sanctum at the feasting. He might get thrown the occasional bone, but every time he wanted to join the masters at the top table the chain kept coming up short.

Joining Peters this election cycle was Michael Laws, an impish character whose facial look back in the 80s was perhaps best described as "Richard Simmons with a moustache". And eyeliner. At least, that was the wide speculation within the community for a long time. Others put it down to a recessive racoon gene left over during the evolutionary process in the distant past. Either way, Laws was to politics what Simmons was to fitness – a guru prone to fizz at the bung when some exciting new moves were in play.

"Laws, I'll do you a deal," he remembers the chain-puffing Peters saying from somewhere within a cloud of smoke when they first teamed up as politico and research assistant. "You look after me and I'll look after you. You find the issues – and I'll put them on the front page."[88]

It was probably as close as Laws will ever get to knowing how Moses felt talking to a burning bush, but the relationship was similar. As part of National's parliamentary research unit, it was Michael Laws' task to choose the weapons and ammunition for each weekly duel. Laws was 'Steve Williams' to Peters' 'Tiger Woods', although critics – and there were many even within National – came to see Laws more as Dr Jekyll to Peters' Mr Hyde. Laws, perhaps understandably, saw their relationship in a slightly different hue, saying Peters knew his junior's Achilles heel, a "craven and pathetic need" for a masterful pat on the head. "I had a nagging image of Mephistopheles and Faustus," Laws writes.

It wouldn't be the last time someone compared Winston Peters to the Prince of Darkness but coming from Laws it was a tad ironic.

Political spin was in its infancy in 1987/88 compared to now. Under governments leading up to and including Muldoon's final administration, only the administration in power had press secretaries, and then only 1 or 2, usually seconded from the Tourist and Publicity Department. That changed with Labour in 1984.

The Lange administration brought with it some lessons from the US presidential campaigns – in fact when I was head-hunted to become a "contract" press secretary for Overseas Trade and Tourism Minister Mike Moore at the start of 1986 I was given a book to read on how the US spinmeisters had done it.

My own appointment ruffled more than a few feathers within the Tourist and Publicity Department and became the subject of parliamentary debate: why was Labour bringing in professional media advisors like Bevan Burgess and Patrick Smellie in Roger Douglas' office, Ross Vintiner and Trish Green in Lange's office, or Graeme Colman and Ian Wishart in Mike Moore's office, when Tourist and Publicity writers were available at much lower cost.

The reality was that journalists and PR strategists from the private sector better understood how the news media worked than career writers for a government department. Colman and I for Moore simply got down to

---

88 The Demon Profession, Laws, p82

the task in 1986 of ensuring our man got as much favourable news coverage as possible, by writing tight news releases that stayed on message, and making our minister as accessible as possible.

On trade missions, for example, that meant Colman waking me in the middle of the night by phone from somewhere deep in the Himalayas or similar with a recorded interview he'd done himself with Mike Moore on a walkman cassette deck whilst ensconced on the furry haunches of a Nepalese yak. As a former broadcaster, he knew how to dismantle a phone and hotwire it to send audio, and as a radio journalist at the other end, I knew how to record that audio from my own hacked phone and release it to the press gallery on a slow news day.

Sometimes the job had its hazards, like pulling the wool over the eyes of TVNZ's Bill Ralston as a massive trade deal New Zealand needed looked like it was hitting the rocks because of the Rainbow Warrior bombing complications. Colman used to say to me, "Never lie, never ever tell a lie for the Government, but avoid giving the media as much of the truth as you can manage!"

TV's *Yes, Minister* was compulsory viewing in Mike Moore's office. I dealt with Sir Humphrey on a daily basis.

Of course, once the Opposition realised spin had entered a new era, they looked for ways to equalise and gain funding for extra staff themselves. Although Michael Laws wasn't a journalist he was an excellent researcher who had twigged to the secrets of successful spin, and by 1988 was parliament was certainly feeling the force of the Peters/Law combo.

As Laws notes, "My spinning role for Winston was unique within the Opposition of the late 1980s." He's dead right, it was. And that's why they got noticed.

Some of Winston's biggest hits during this time were on future Prime Minister Helen Clark, then Labour's Health Minister. The Batman and Robin duo had found out that a lucrative health publicity contract had gone to a company staffed by former Labour party advisors, and which also handled publicity for a tobacco giant.

Peters was particularly pleased to discover this, because the terms of the tender offer were that no company with tobacco links could apply. He told parliament the matter "reeks of corruption, of cronyism, and of party political preference that go all the way to the Prime Minister and the Deputy Prime Minister – the Minister of Health."[89]

The trail went like this: a $638,000 Ministry of Health publicity campaign encouraging people to vote in upcoming area health board elections was awarded to DDB Needham New Zealand Ltd, Peters said, "the same firm that prepared [Labour's] controversial 'Mrs Mop' tax advertisements."

Suggesting this smelt "so fishy that even the Koreans would be interested", Peters then let rip with the allegations. In early May 1989, a group of Wellington PR firms had been asked to pitch for the contract. "There was a special factor," said Peters. "Firms that had clients dealing in tobacco or alcohol were expressly excluded from entering the selection process."

Despite that, on 26 June 1989 Needham Consulting Group was awarded the contract, despite its parent company DDB Needham representing WD and HO Wills New Zealand Ltd. To add further smoke to the fire, insult to injury and other such clichés, DDB's latest advertising campaign for Peter Jackson cigarettes was running in daily newspapers with the catchy slogan "Go for it!".

This breach was brought to the attention of Health officials and their minister Helen Clark, who told Parliament that Needham Consulting Group and DDB Needham New Zealand Ltd were separate companies.

Peters whipped out a *National Business Review* article[90] where DDB's David Birrell confirmed Needham Consulting was indeed part of the advertising agency. How could Helen Clark be telling the truth, Peters wondered aloud, reading from another newspaper article[91] where DDB Needham revealed not only had it taken control of Needham Consulting but, said Peters triumphantly, "it boasted that it had Ross Vintiner – the former Prime Minister's chief press secretary – and that it had Carolyn Rennie, formerly a top parliamentary speech writer and researcher for the present Prime Minister [Geoffrey Palmer].

"Those linkages," roared Peters, "reek of corruption, cronyism and the very worst political preference. What of the free market, when everybody else who complied with the criteria missing out?" The public, he said, deserved answers from Helen Clark.

DDB Needham's past directors, he revealed, included Labour Party

---

89   Hansard, General Debate, 16 August 1989
90   NBR, 28 February 1989
91   The Dominion, 27 February 1989

man James Belich and party activist Stephen Richardson who would be working on the 1990 re-election campaign. How could an agency staffed by Labour Party hacks, claimed Peters, and with a tobacco giant in its pocket, have won a $638,000 public contract from Helen Clark's ministry in clear conflict with the tender rules?

In a thundering 10 minute speech, Winston Peters described how DDB had won "millions" in other lucrative government advertising contracts and Helen Clark, he said, had been explicitly warned about the tobacco giant in the closet but ignored the warning.

"I want, in the House today, an explanation from that Minister about why she should still occupy her job. It stinks. It has all the elements of corruption…how else can members explain why the other 15 companies did not get a fair go and did not get the contract?"

Labour's Helen Clark, as you might expect, hit back the next day.[92]

"The Department of Health received written confirmation from Needham Consulting Group that it was a separate company," Clark told Parliament, stating "that it has not had and will not have connections with tobacco companies."

Clark's assurances were not true.

That was on 17 August 1989, two months after the contract had been awarded. However the evidence now shows the Health Department allowed Clark to mislead parliament. Companies Office official records show Needham Consulting Group Ltd was not incorporated as a company until 8 September 1989,[93] three weeks after her assurance above that it was "a separate company". It cannot have been a separate company – it did not exist as one when the contract was awarded or even when Peters was asking questions.

Winston then discovered that Eugenie Sage, Helen Clark's chief press secretary, sat on the panel that decided to award the contract. He found out that the majority of the panel had actually chosen a pitch from a different agency, Ogilvy and Mather, which had offered to run the campaign for $580,000 – saving taxpayers $58,000 off the higher Needham price.

How was it, Winston wondered, that the selection panel had actually chosen a cheaper pitch from a company with no alcohol or tobacco links,

---

92 Hansard, Questions of the Day #3, 17 August 1989
93 Companies Office website search, http://www.business.govt.nz/companies/

but the contract had mysteriously gone to an agency with Labour connections at a higher cost to the taxpayer.

It turned out that Helen Clark had assembled a second selection panel to reassess the bids. Describing Peters' direct hits as "an elaborate smear", Clark accused Peters of seeing "something sinister" in the fact that a second panel had taken over.[94]

"Two companies stood out. The price for each came within a reasonable range. The documents that have been tabled show that I was concerned to ensure that the cost was kept low. As a responsible minister, I determined at that point that a further panel should hear the two companies [pitches]… My desire was to ensure that the campaign was entirely non-political."

By now, Peters knew he had Clark on the ropes. Low cost, he probed? The Ross Vintiner/Needham pitch was $58,000 more expensive, and it did not include TV advertising, whereas the Ogilvy Mather pitch did include TV at the cheaper price. Clark's response, she preferred to run a "low key" awareness campaign without TV. Her answer only made it seem more like a pay-off to mates than it already did: who runs a "low key" election awareness campaign? It seemed to be an oxymoron.

Clark had released correspondence confirming that DDB Needham New Zealand Ltd and the Needham consulting group were "legally separate". It came in the form of a letter dated 30 June 1989 from Ross Vintiner. Peters had a copy of the letter Clark had released to the media, and promptly accused Clark of "doctoring" the letter fraudulently:

"I have here the letter that her office released…Members should look very carefully at the bottom of it, because it is blank. The one that her office received, the one I am holding up, has the full letterhead on the bottom.

"Why did she doctor the letter? She did so because stated at the bottom are the words 'part of DDB Needham New Zealand Ltd…the Minister's office doctored the letter, and nobody in the press gallery or anybody else knew about it until we got hold of the original letter she had received.

"The Minister knew that Needham Consulting Group was not a separate company, but she did not want members of the press, the public or parliament to know that."

In other words, argued Peters, Deputy Prime Minister Helen Clark was a liar, prepared to produce false documents to back up her spin. This was

---

94 Hansard, General Debate, 11 October 1989

a decade and a half before a Prime Minister Clark became a party to art fraud, but it shows a predilection to deceive: the woman now seeking the UN's top job was not above giving false testimony in parliament when it suited her purposes.

Not only had Clark presented falsified documents, alleged Peters, but she had also failed to fully disclose the documents in her possession under the Official Information Act. "She held back four files". Those files included a report commissioned by the first panel that recommended the cheaper Ogilvy and Mather pitch rather than Needhams. Although Helen Clark denied that her department had a policy of banning alcohol and tobacco ad agencies, Peters tabled a document showing the Director-General of Health had "agreed" to exactly that policy.

Helen Clark decided attack was the better part of defence, raising the old favourites – the *Mikhail Lermontov*, Cook Strait ferry and the submarines:

"He makes grandiose claims of scandal and corruption; he usually neglects to substantiate them with any evidence...his comments are entirely consistent with his calls in June 1986 for a formally inquiry into the alleged grounding of the Cook Strait ferry. He refused ever to supply his so-called reliable evidence of that time... In the middle of 1986 the member made repeated calls for an inquiry into the sinking of the ship, and alleged that there had been collusion between New Zealand and the Soviet Union to cover up details of the sinking.

"During the 1984 election campaign the member claimed that he had evidence that Soviet submarines were plotting the geography of the sea-bed in Cook Strait. In October 1985 he claimed that he had every reason to believe that a submarine had been sighted off Great Barrier Island[95]...his whole history has been one of personal attack, smear, innuendo, claims of dramatic evidence, and of tenuous links..."

Regardless of Clark's protestations, the New Zealand public had long since stopped listening to Labour. The stench Peters had talked of – that Labour was prepared to sell its principles on smokefree policy in favour of looking after its mates financially, was something Peters milked for National all the way to the following year's election.

---

95 Quite possibly the French nuclear sub *Rubis* which had acted in a support role for the Rainbow Warrior bombers, and which the police were worried a commando attack would be launched from in Auckland harbour

The recipe for success wasn't hard. By the end of 1987 when Lange cancelled Finance Minister Roger Douglas' flat tax package and called for "a cup of tea", the wheels had begun to fall off Labour. It literally happened the moment they won re-election in 1987 for their second term. As voters who had drained away from National to Labour since 1984 realised that their political honeymoon was ending in parallel with KZ7's loss in the America's Cup semis at Fremantle that summer, they started to look for reasons to return to National. By constantly attacking Labour's credibility, Winston Peters gave them those reasons.

One of the easiest targets for Peters in 1988 was the employment data. Record numbers of New Zealanders were unemployed because of state sector restructuring and bankruptcy on many farms. In turn, Labour had introduced make-work schemes like Access and Maori Access – supposedly work training schemes designed to upskill the unemployed.

Labour's employment minister Phil Goff took the brunt of it:[96]

"The Minister said that the Access programme was not designed as a single path to employment," Peters told parliament. "Why did the Government run a campaign immediately before the election under the heading, 'Access, a pathway to a job', that cost the taxpayers $1 million?"

"That's right, there's no contradiction there!" shouted back Goff, apparently reading from a dictionary definition of "contradiction" sourced from an alternate universe.

"It was a lie then, and it is a lie now," retorted Peters. Goff, he said, had promised that Access would place 18,000 New Zealanders:

"Place them in what? Not jobs, because the Minister has instituted karate courses, scone-making courses, and ballroom dancing courses."

One of the courses was "rabbit breeding".

"After three years the Minister's rabbit breeding programme has produced 25 rabbits. I telephoned the Department of Scientific and Industrial Research and asked how many rabbits could be bred in three years from two rabbits, and the answer was 1.8 billion[97] rabbits," teased Peters with his trademark wall to wall grin.

"After three years, the Minister's programme with his rabbits – called

---

96 Hansard, Access Training Scheme Bill, 28 June
97 Believe it or not, mathematician Fibonacci worked out that in ideal conditions and unlimited food supply and space, you could have seven billion rabbits from one original breeding pair within four years.

'Goffies' – has produced 25 rabbits from 10. What a disgrace, what a rip-off of taxpayer's money!"

Winston may have had the debating chamber in stitches, but if current Prime Minister John Key is the smiling assassin, then Peters is the laughing executioner – the deadliest blows were often delivered in good humour.

"I want to hear about the *Mikhail Lermontov*," interjected Labour's Annette King, hoping to change the subject. She didn't. Instead, observers of that day's gladiatorial sport went home shaking their heads; Labour, Laughing stock, Losers. The take-home message from this attack was that Labour was so incompetent they couldn't even breed rabbits successfully at a time when Central Otago was plagued with them.

Of course, if the rabbit breeding programme had created millions of rabbits, Peters would have beaten them around the ears with that too. Such is politics.

When Labour went to the polls in 1987 it had largely increased its vote nationwide. One of the exceptions to this was the Wairarapa electorate. Labour's Reg Boorman had won the seat in 1984 by defeating National cabinet minister Ben Couch. In the 1987 poll, facing a strong challenge from National candidate Wyatt Creech, Boorman avoided defeat by a squeak – holding Wairarapa by a one vote majority after a recount. The margin was so close that Boorman's Labour colleagues nicknamed him "Landslide".

Winston Peters was a mate of Creech and advised him not to give up – to instead follow what Peters himself had done in Hunua nine years earlier and challenge Boorman's win in the courts.

Peters and Creech found Boorman had massively exceeded the limits of campaign advertising spending per candidate, which were then set at $5,000. If proven, that would make Labour's candidate guilty of an electoral "corrupt practice" and force a by-election. Peters and Creech also scrutinised the validity of votes cast. With more than 20,000 voters and only a one vote margin, if any of the nearly ten thousand Labour votes were found to be invalid, Creech would win the seat.

In mid July 1988 the Court ruled Boorman had substantially overspent his campaign allowance, but didn't disclose exactly how much. In Parliament Labour MPs rushed to the defence of Boorman suggesting it was only a total of $5,600, the difference being human error over whether the 10% GST component should have been included.

"Members of Parliament had received information from the Department of Justice that the $5,000 limit was exclusive of goods and services tax... the court found differently," exclaimed Labour's Clive Matthewson. Nearly every MP had made the same "mistake" said Matthewson, and it was unfair to single out "Landslide" Boorman.[98]

Winston Peters, waving Boorman's electoral spending document, told parliament "Landslide" had a funny way of calculating GST:

"I have it here. He knew when he signed it that a petition had been lodged alleging corrupt practice and alleging that he had overspent. But he still signed it. Not only did he overspend by twice the amount allowed, but, worse still, in that budget he listed an item of $1,000 and the invoice for that item is not for $1,000 – it is for $1,530. The return did not even repeat the amount the invoice stated. That in itself is a corrupt practice, let alone spending his total amount. He was on notice."[99]

Creech told the Court Boorman's total spending was close to $28,000.

Although media reports over the years have glossed over the case by saying Creech won the seat because of Boorman's overspend, in fact the court recount of valid votes changed Labour's one vote majority to a 34 vote loss in favour of Creech. It turned out Creech had won the seat anyway, thanks to Peters' insistence on checking vote validity.

Labour's Internal Affairs Minister Michael Bassett was highly critical of that as well, saying National MPs appeared to have cast invalid votes and even naming their home addresses:[100]

"What about the Leader of the Opposition? He lives at 109 Churchill Drive, Crofton Downs, and his wife voted in the King Country electorate."

National leader Jim Bolger leapt to his feet. "The Minister is starting to mention the position of my wife and I. I voted strictly in accordance with the Electoral Act. It states the way in which I can vote, and I will not have that miserable member saying that I voted illegally.

"It is proper for me and other members to point out that the Minister is alleging something that is criminal. He is wrong. He alleged that

---

98 Peters later revealed he got himself offside with National's Remuera MP Doug Graham who, he said: "came to me and my lawyers in 1987 and said: 'Don't run the electoral costs' argument, because we've overspent.' The present member for Panmure knows full well how scared the present Minister was. He was spending money like it was going out of fashion." – Hansard, Law Reform Bill, 21 June 1994
99 Hansard, General Debate, 13 July 1988
100 Ibid

Opposition members – specifically, my wife and I – engaged in a criminal act. The Electoral Act states specifically that members of Parliament and their spouses are exempted from the provision. It is improper for the Minister to continue in that way, which will lead to disorder in the House. He must be asked to desist."

Nor was Peters himself immune from a sideswipe:

"He is…on the Tauranga roll," said Bassett. "He spends most of his time outside his electorate. If he is not actually in Wellington he is under a hair dryer – everybody knows that! The member for Whangarei [John Banks] is in the same category."

Peters told the House[101] how he'd won the recount in Hunua, where he discovered more than 200 people who claimed to be living in state rental housing – "the only problem was that they had been living in those houses about 5 or 6 years before the election, but at the time of the election they were living somewhere else. Six people from Tiedmont, California, who had been in New Zealand for 6 years had been gaily registered by a Labour Party enthusiast. Consequently they were casting votes and sending yours truly down the tube on election night," Peters explained.

"The National Party had a few blokes the same, with beach houses in Taupo," muttered Labour's Trevor de Cleene, referring to the recount National had nonetheless won there.

Peters just stared at de Cleene incredulously. Labour were continuously sniping about this, but they'd never taken the matter to court. "If there were a few blokes the same with beach houses in Taupo the Labour Party had months in court to prove it. The only point about Labour Party members is that they do not show the evidence to the court; they keep it covert and secret; they come along and show Parliament. I do not know the logic of that. It might have saved their man in Wairarapa or in Taupo, but apparently there is some ingenious scheme that states: 'Don't show the court; show Parliament, instead'."

Winston Peters was feeling good. His continued successes in parliamentary debates and ambushes were being rewarded with a massive increase in media exposure.

He leapt from around two percent in the preferred Prime Minister stakes to sixteen percent by mid 1988. For journalists, Peters was a gift

---

101 Hansard, Electoral Reform Bill, 6 March 1990

from God. Not only was he effective against the Labour Government, but clearly there was a *frisson* of something between Peters and his own party as well – leader Jim Bolger in particular. Indirectly, his leader was taking hits as a result of Winston's work on the Wairarapa challenge and other hot-button issues.

Calling Peters a "rising young star, and heir to a thousand years of British history", Labour's Social Welfare minister Michael Cullen quoted from a Christchurch Press article.[102]

"That member said that he is not courting popularity as a result of his going up in the opinion polls. In his wonderful praising with faint damns he said of his leader: 'I think he has got potential.' He said that in an interview about his rise in the opinion polls."

The Press article also revealed Peters was refusing to attend "lectures" each week for National MPs given by the party's finance spokeswoman Ruth Richardson.

"One can just imagine it!," chuckled Cullen. "One can just see the member for Tamaki [Sir Robert Muldoon] sitting in the hall every week with his feet up on the desk, listening to an economic briefing from the member for Selwyn about the virtues of a free-floating exchange rate and a tight monetary policy. Meanwhile he is sitting there thinking: 'How do I rid myself of this awful burden on our front bench, and get my mate Winston into the leadership?' "

It was shaping up, said Cullen, as a battle for the future of the National Party; between the New Right forces of Ruth Richardson, and the more conservative faction including Winston Peters, Phillip Burdon and Muldoon.

Cullen had put his finger on it. Winston Peters clearly had leadership qualities, but National was in a state of turmoil. Winston's public popularity but lack of a major support base within the post-Muldoon National Party eerily foreshadowed the Shane Jones leadership aspirations within Labour three decades later. Both were Maori, both men were charismatic, both men were leaders, but in both cases they were leaders without parties, warriors increasingly without warhorses.

As Michael Laws reports, the relationship between the Winston Peters and Jim Bolger was rapidly becoming toxic, even then. Bolger might not have liked Richardson, but he didn't like Winston Peters even more.

---

102 Hansard, Adjournment debate, 19 July 1988

8

Battle Of The Bolger

> "The hyena from Tauranga is laughing because even he looks better. The one contribution the Leader of the Opposition makes to his party is to make the other lightweights look slightly better"
> – Mike Moore, 1988

Labour had taken New Zealand anti-nuclear in 1984, crystallising in the ships ban of 1985. Much has been written of the fact that Prime Minister David Lange did not support the ban initially, and it is common knowledge that National leader Jim Bolger was stridently opposed to the neutering of the ANZUS defence alliance as well.

Bolger's attitude changed, however, and it was Winston Peters, says Laws, who forced the change on National. Realising that the anti-nuclear stand had resonated with the public as a symbol of kiwi independence, and that National would find it difficult to win if it did not acknowledge the mood of the people, Peters tried to persuade National's caucus to stop campaigning on a return to ANZUS.

"His efforts were batted away as an irritant," writes Laws, and the batting was executed in such scornful fashion by "senior National MPs, including the leader", that Winston decided to teach them a lesson. He asked Laws to draft a speech along the lines of "Time has marched on… the people have spoken…the National Party should democratically accept the new consensus".

Bolger, according to Laws, hit the roof:[103]

"Bolger was upset. No, he was more than that. He appeared to me to be at the very edge of his self-control and I had the misfortune to encounter his rage directly."

What followed is recounted in highly entertaining fashion in Laws' book, suffice to say that Winston's Rasputin-like muse spent several days looking for his missing testicles after Bolger had finished with him. The National leader blamed Laws on the basis that Peters had never had an original thought in his life; Laws blamed Peters saying, regardless of Bolger's suspicions, the idea was driven by Winston on this occasion.

"The member for Tauranga said," Labour's Peter Dunne told parliament,[104] "that he had the solution to the ANZUS question. However, he was clipped on the back by his leader for making that statement...the member for Tauranga also criticised the Anzac frigate deal as being crazy and looney, in direct contradiction to the Leader of the Opposition and the Deputy Leader."

It didn't matter how much Bolger ranted and hissed, however; Peters had lit the fuse like Roadrunner outsmarting Wyllie Coyote and quicker than you could say "Beep Beep" the debate within the party began to simmer, gain traction with the party membership then boil over with Caucus voting for a policy reversal, much to Labour's amusement:[105]

"I take it that since Thursday the Leader of the Opposition has wrestled with his conscience and has decided, after due consideration, for the first time, to support his caucus decision," taunted Labour's Mike Moore in parliament.

"I confirm, and do not deny, that the position of the National Party on nuclear weapons has changed," admitted Bolger through clenched teeth.

"Only days ago the Leader of the Opposition 'stood firm on nuke ship policy'. Only a matter of months ago he said that he had told the Prime Minister of the United Kingdom that he was for ANZUS and that he would accept his responsibilities. The issue is more than nuclear; it is one of credibility, integrity, and honour," teased Moore. "What has changed? The numbers have changed."

---

103 The Demon Profession, Laws, p120
104 Hansard, General Debate, 16 November 1988
105 Hansard, General Debate, 14 March 1990

"The whole world has changed," piped up National's defence spokesman Doug Kidd, acknowledging the realpolitik that Winston Peters had forced on them.

Remuera MP Doug Graham, National's shadow Disarmament spokesman, was next in Moore's sights:

"The member for Remuera sought divine guidance on the way he should vote. I respect that. However, he could not have been listening, because the list we received shows that he voted against change. Did you vote against a change in the policy?"

"Yes."

And yet, asked Moore, "you still believe you could be the Minister for Disarmament and Arms Control?"

"Yes."

"Well, you are a fool, and you should resign. The member for Remuera does not support the National Party's nuclear policy, but he is the disarmament man."

It was an open secret that Winston Peters was waiting to be shoulder-tapped into the National leader's job by his colleagues, and Labour played on the Tauranga MP's ambitions on every occasion they could.

"The hyena from Tauranga is laughing because even he looks better. The one contribution the Leader of the Opposition makes to his party is to make the other lightweights look slightly better," scoffed Mike Moore.[106]

Not that Winston wasn't above scoring some own goals here and there. One such was a trip to the United States in November 1988. One night on the phone he let slip to Laws that he might be meeting US president Ronald Reagan. Within minutes the Press Gallery was abuzz with the rumour. The significance of Winston Peters being the first kiwi politician to meet the big guy since the nuclear stand-off was obvious.

Peters has never spoken about the incident since, but the circumstantial evidence suggests it would have been – had it occurred – merely a handshake opportunity at a Republican party fundraiser. The USA was in the final stages of an election campaign, Reagan was stepping down and his vice president George Bush was the Republican nominee.

It's a fair bet the boy from Whananaki never got to press the flesh with Ron, perhaps because the entry fee to fundraisers was high. The political

---

106   Hansard, General Debate, 20 April 1988

fallout from his refusal to answer questions about it was higher:

"Why would he not answer a question on television last night about whether he had met the President of the United States of America?" probed Labour's Peter Dunne.[107] "He allowed people to believe that he did, but when Mr Perigo put a frank question to him last night he played Cupid, went coy and refused to answer."

Annette King watched the same interview, and was more intrigued by Winston's apparent refusal to endorse Jim Bolger.

"In that interview, which was very revealing, the member was asked whether he would give the Leader of the Opposition unqualified support. Did he look straight at the camera? Did he say, 'Yes, I give the Leader of the Opposition my unqualified support'? No, he did not.[108]

"His body language said it all. The eyebrows went up, the secretive little smile crossed his lips, his shoulders shrugged ever so slightly, and he said, 'The question does not arise'...

"The covert grab for the leadership by the member for Tauranga is over. It is now open warfare, open slather, and already the numbers are being done."

King laid out a bit of background to justify her claim that a coup was on. Bolger, she said, had told the party conference "I don't want anyone with personal agendas or personal egos getting in the way of victory". Bolger had also seconded Laws to work for him instead of Peters, and just before Winston had jetted off for America Bolger took responsibility for Maori Affairs.

"A few months ago that spokesmanship could not be given away," claimed King, "but the Leader of the Opposition took it for himself, in the hope that some of the popularity of the member for Tauranga would rub off on him."

Bolger had also stripped Peters of his employment spokesmanship and given it to Bill Birch, making it a Bolger/Birch 'dream team', but "neither of them is half the person that the member for Tauranga is," exclaimed King. She said she "admired" Winston's response to Bolger's action "by saying that he would continue to speak on those matters from overseas."

King said Peters rubbed Bolger's nose in it by deciding whilst overseas

---

107   Hansard, General Debate, 16 November 1988
108   Ibid

"that he would speak not only for his portfolios but for the responsibilities of the Leader of the Opposition as well."

Winston went on to have discussions about ANZUS and, snorted King, "poor hapless" Bolger was left "running around in circles and trying to shore up the problems. He said, 'I'm as well briefed as anybody on ANZUS'."

Australia's *Bulletin* magazine had highlighted the apparent rift, and Bolger was asked at a news conference about the article. "He was told," said King, "that the article quoted the member for Tauranga as saying that he would be the next Prime Minister of New Zealand."

"He will not be the next Prime Minister," snapped Bolger to journalists, "I will be."

"The long knives are out," intoned the Labour MPs as they stared across the debating chamber with barely concealed glee. National's leadership troubles were a welcome distraction from David Lange's implosion resulting in the eventual demotions of Roger Douglas, Richard Prebble and Trevor de Cleene.

In April 1988 Winston was two percent in the polls, while Bolger was on 15%. By June Winston had shot to 17% and Bolger was down to 12%. The most recent poll, October's, had given Winston 19% support as preferred prime minister while Bolger had dropped to nine percent.

Prime Minister David Lange wasn't slow to wade into the National Party's clear discomfort either, saying Roger Douglas' support of him was clearly better than Bolger enjoyed from Winston.

"In respect of the support from the Minister of Finance at this point in time, that is a 100 percent stronger affirmation of loyalty than that given to the Leader of the Opposition by the member for Tauranga, who would not commit himself at any point in time. He spent the rest of the time wondering whether he had shaken hands with President Reagan."

"Did he shake hands, or not?" jeered government MPs.

"Those members will find out," retorted Peters.

"If the credibility of the member for Tauranga was put to the test it would show that no one believes him. He does not know whether or not he shook hands with President Reagan."[109]

It was rare for Winston Peters to be caught in a mousetrap that he himself

---

109 Hansard Questions of the Day # 2, 22 November 1988

had baited, but at the same time an indication that he was human after all. When you perform as a heavy-hitter and nearly always hit the target, your near-misses and complete misses are noticed all the more because expectations of performance are higher.

"I was reminded yet again of my partner's proclivity to talk up a story before it was even alive," lamented Laws, concluding that Winston's hint about Reagan "was just being mischievous".[110]

With Winston refusing to confirm or deny the story, says Laws, "the irony was lost on no one and the Leader's office had great sport with me, openly wondering who Winston might not be meeting tomorrow – the UN Secretary-General, Mikhail Gorbachev, Nelson Mandela?"

Peters did receive support from one unexpected corner.

"I believe that one should hit the ball, not necessarily the opposite player," Labour's de Cleene told the House, "because one should never score off another player. My old hockey coach used to tell me when I grizzled about it, 'Trevor, they can never score as long as they're hitting you. They've got to put a ball into the net'."[111]

Whilst acknowledging Peters as "a mate…a friend" and his clear popularity in the polls, de Cleene told his fellow Labour MPs they were dreaming if they thought Peters "has the slightest chance of getting a seconder in his caucus to ditch the Leader of the Opposition." Anyone who believed it possible "would be better to stick to *Empire Rose* or *Poetic Prince* – at least I tip racehorses with a little more accuracy."

Winston, he said "is in cloud cuckoo-land" if he believed he had a chance of leading National into the 1990 election.

Several defining themes were beginning to emerge however. Winston Peters had proven he was an exceptionally effective opposition politician; he was developing a reputation as a watch-dog. His growing distrust of Ruth Richardson's economic vision for New Zealand, his distrust of her supporters, and his position on the Treaty of Waitangi, would, over the course of the next four years, bring Peters to the brink.

---

110 The Demon Profession, Laws, p123
111 Hansard, General Debate, 16 November 1988

9

Sickly White Liberals

> *"The pakeha are riffraff, the flotsam and jetsam of British culture... go back where they came from"*
> — Atareta Poananga, Te Ahi Kaa, 1985

A seismic shift occurred in race relations in New Zealand in the 1980s. You knew it had happened because even *Auckland Metro*, that hotbed of right-wing fundamentalism, was reporting it[112]. We were collectively introduced in 1985 to Atareta Poananga, leader of a radical Maori independence movement calling itself Te Ahi Kaa – keepers of the flame.[113] Her uncle, Major-General Brian Poananga headed the New Zealand Army, but Atareta saw herself as a different kind of warrior.

"The pakeha," she boldly proclaimed in 85, "are riffraff, the flotsam and jetsam of British culture." It was time, she said, for whites in New Zealand to hand back the keys to the rightful owners of the country – the 12% who identified as Maori, or "go back where they came from."

Her comments were so provocative they even made the *New York Times*.[114]

---

112 "Atareta Poananga and Te Ahi Kaa: What Do Maori Nationalists Want?", Nicola Legat, Metro, March 1986
113 The name chosen is fascinating for the following reason: Ahi Kaa referred to the customary practice of determining who 'owned' or had rights to a specific area or resource. If a chief let his flame, his cooking fires, go out on a piece of land for any length of time, it was said that he and his iwi had lost rights to it. Over the past century and a half many ancient Maori fires have been extinguished, never to be rekindled.
114 The Maori Rights Furor: A Question Of Ancestry, By Seth Mydans, Special to the New York Times, October 29, 1985, http://www.nytimes.com/1985/10/29/world/the-maori-rights-furor-a-question-of-ancestry.html

Among those supporting her were Eastern Maori MP and Labour's Internal Affairs Minister Peter Tapsell:

"New Zealand Europeans, and I am not saying this in a bitter way, are peasants," he told the *Times*. "That is how it is. What we have here is aristocratic Maoris and peasant Europeans. Really, that's the problem."[115]

Pakeha New Zealanders were outraged at the apparent snobbery and venom and complained to the Race Relations Conciliator, to little effect. One of Atareta's contemporaries, Hana Te Hemara (formerly Jackson) turned up the heat even further in early 1988 with comments from a hui at Auckland University reported by the *Sunday Star* newspaper as "Kill a white before you die and become a hero".

Again, the Race Relations office determined the University marae was a "private" place not within its jurisdiction. For her part, Te Hemara said she was only issuing a warning, not an instruction, and her remarks were thus being taken out of their strict context. Regardless, it is fair to say race relations were at rock bottom in the mid 1980s.

The dominant thinking of the Maori nationalist groups was centred on the new and utterly erroneous[116] idea that Maori had not surrendered sovereignty at Waitangi, and that the country should at least be run in two halves – by separate Maori and Pakeha governments.

This later became Maori Party policy[117] – not surprising as Poananga was a Maori Party candidate before being disbarred as a lawyer on four counts of forging documents relating to Waitangi Tribunal claims.[118]

Into this heady mix of pent-up fury came the Lange administration and

---

115 With the greatest of respect, Tapsell was dreaming. Both treaty populations were equally peasant-like, and it took time for Maori tikanga customs relating to slavery and cannibalism to be abandoned in favour of more modern practices. A fairer way of putting it is that early Maori converted to Christianity and became in many cases better Christians than many of the new migrants and the politicians who those migrants elected. Thus Maori felt betrayed when successive governments broke their word.
116 Erroneous because that is not what Maori who signed the Treaty wanted, or thought they were getting. For a full rebuttal of the modernist Treaty interpretations, see *The Great Divide* by Ian Wishart, Howling At The Moon Pub. 2012
117 "The Maori Party wants constitutional change so Maori and the Crown can share governance of the country. Ikaroa-Rawhiti candidate Atareta Poananga launched its Treaty of Waitangi policy at Awatoto yesterday, where she called for the treaty to provide the base for constitutional change." Read more in "Time for Constitutional Change", by Jonathan Dow, Hawkes Bay Today, 1 September 2005, http://www.nzherald.co.nz/hawkes-bay-today/news/article.cfm?c_id=1503462&objectid=10928926
118 "Lawyer struck off for forgery" Gisborne Herald, 11 June 2012

a well-meaning plan to allow historic Treaty of Waitangi land grievances to be settled. It seemed like a good idea at the time, and it was, but its execution has ripped New Zealand apart.

In 1986, Labour passed the State Owned Enterprises Act paving the way for corporatisation – placing the various government entities on a commercial footing under either state or eventual private ownership. The Act required the government to adhere to 'the principles of the Treaty of Waitangi' – a seemingly insipid Grey Lynn feel-good phrase that made it sound like the Government cared about the Treaty. Specifically, section nine said "Nothing in this Act shall permit the Crown to act in a manner that is inconsistent with the principles of the Treaty of Waitangi."

Attorney-General Geoffrey Palmer was the man widely fingered by his Labour colleagues for inserting the phrase, but the Government had also recently passed the Treaty of Waitangi Amendment Act of 1985 which allowed, for the first time, the Waitangi Tribunal to hear claims dating back to 1840.

These two pieces of government legislation were immediately on a collision course. Many of the government departments, like Railways, or Forestry had built infrastructure on disputed Maori land. Suddenly Maori not only had a review panel capable of hearing their ancient claims, but they had an Act transferring assets to the new SOEs but which required the deals to be consistent with the "principles" of the Treaty.

Lawyers around the country rubbed their hands together with barely concealed glee. The first test case was brought by New Zealand Maori Council chair Sir Graham Latimer, himself a senior vice president of the National Party. In June 1987, barely six months after the State Owned Enterprises Act had passed, the Maori Council obtained a landmark ruling from the Court of Appeal, placing land transfers to the new SOEs on hold until Treaty claims had been determined. Court President Sir Robin Cooke[119] said it was the "principles" of the Treaty that had to be followed, not the text of the Treaty. Among those "principles" that he suspected existed was "partnership", whereby the Crown and Maori became two partners in a complicated new constitutional arrangement to run the country.

The Treaty, he ruled, "should be interpreted widely and effectively and is a living instrument taking account of the subsequent developments of international human rights norms; and that the court will not ascribe to

---

119 New Zealand Maori Council v Attorney-General [1987] 1 NZLR 641

Parliament an intention to permit conduct inconsistent with the principles of the Treaty."

Backing him up was Sir Ivor Richardson, another respected jurist, who cast the Treaty adrift from its textual anchor and said it should be free to mean whatever each new generation thought it should mean:

"Whatever legal route is followed the Treaty must be interpreted according to principles suitable to its particular character. Its history, its form and its place in our social order clearly require a broad interpretation and one which recognises that the Treaty must be capable of adaptation to new and changing circumstances as they arise".

These judges and their compadres on the bench were no intellectual slugs, but commentators have joked that their good honours must have been high on 'shrooms when they deliberated. Think of your employer 're-imagining' your employment contract, or a bank 're-imagining' your mortgage agreement because it suited them, or a retailer coming back five years after you had purchased a product asking for another $100 because that's what the price of those products has increased to now.

The Treaty of Waitangi in the form it was signed and understood by Maori in 1840, and 1860 when it was re-ratified at the massive Kohimarama hui, is a good document, giving property rights to Maori and Pakeha alike, but the 1987 Court of Appeal verdict took it beyond what it meant and allowed new meanings to be created, and to continue being created.

The "partnership" principle is like a ticking bomb stuck inside a teddy bear. The language used implies inclusiveness and consensus, but it was never part of the original Treaty. Maori tribes had just endured nearly thirty years of war and massacre between each other. In fact, they'd been at each other's throats for centuries, but the purchase of modern weapons from traders tipped the balance and made war a whole lot more devastating.

There was no "partnership" between Maori and the Crown, because a Maori nation did not exist. A Ngapuhi nation did, and a Tainui nation, and so on down the line, but one of the big reasons they wanted the Treaty was so that Queen Victoria could rule over all of them and impose British law and customs in place of utu.

While the Court of Appeal was going all warm and fuzzy on the question of two sovereign Treaty partners, Labour politicians were muttering darkly about the genie they'd unleashed.

"I am not an expert in Victorian history, but I do not believe for one moment the Queen ever thought her loyal servants were signing her up to a partnership with 400 thumb prints," David Lange told Chapman Tripp law partner and Act MP Stephen Franks at one point.[120]

Meanwhile, those driving the treaty process were jubilant:

"The Treaty is moving in as surely as the tide. In the statutes of our Parliament, in bureaucratic operations, in the level of the administration of the courts and in local authority planning, the Treaty is now well known. You know when we stand at the foreshore we do not always see the movement of the tide. We see no more than the regular breaking of the waves, as if no painful inch is gained. But look back to the creeks and inlets. There, silently, it is plain to see the tide running at full flow ..." (Edward Taihakurei Durie, 1989, Chief Judge of the Maori Land Court and Chairman of the Waitangi Tribunal).

Initially, Winston Peters was delighted to revel in Labour's disarray. He described the June 1987 Court of Appeal ruling as "momentous", and congratulated the New Zealand Maori Council in holding the government to account. When Labour introduced an amendment to give the Waitangi Tribunal more power following the court ruling, Peters ridiculed Justice Minister Geoffrey Palmer for his sudden desire to praise clause 9 of the State Owned Enterprises Act – the one invoking the principles of the Treaty, when he'd utterly failed to mention it in previous speeches:[121]

"He did not mention it because he thought it was of no great significance. What was of significance was that the New Zealand Maori Council took him to court, and when he was beaten he turned round and said that he was pleased that he had been beaten.

"Opposition members and the Maori people will not swallow that. The Bill represents the final sorry chapter in an exercise in deception that ultimately failed because of the vigilance of the New Zealand Maori Council. I say again that the Maori Council has my unreserved congratulations on having done that."

Peters pointed out that Geoffrey Palmer and Labour had only themselves to blame. They had, he said, voted down a proposed Winston Peters amendment to the SOE Act that would have protected Maori and removed the need for a Court of Appeal case before it even arose.

---

120 http://samuelgriffith.org.au/docs/vol14/v14chap11.pdf
121 Hansard

Palmer, a former law professor, had told parliament back in 1986 in response to Peters that his Bill didn't need the amendment because "the rights of people to make claims under the Treaty of Waitangi Act are in no way prejudiced".[122]

As it turned out, he was wrong.

"On 11 December 1986 he and his 36 colleagues voted against my amendment. Within 3 months they faced the biggest land case the country has ever seen," crowed Peters.

While the Maori Council took justifiable action to protect the rights it always had, he said, Labour was now introducing a new Bill "that has magnified those rights – not in relation to its claims, but in relation to the Waitangi Tribunal and its powers...every New Zealander – no matter of what race – should be concerned," he warned.

Peters was worried about the Minister's power to appoint Waitangi Tribunal members, a requirement that the majority be Maori, and that the decisions they made in regard to public land were final with no rights of appeal:

"The Minister has given those people the power of the Law Lords in relation to land that is of immense financial value. I did not believe that such a recommendation could be made to Parliament in such a cavalier fashion."

Peters warned that if race relations were to improve New Zealanders had to have faith in the Treaty process, "people must have confidence in it. Half of the Minister's colleagues are talking about abandoning the Treaty of Waitangi and renegotiating it.

"The tribunal's powers in relation to the Bill are binding. Before the Bill the tribunal only had a recommendatory role...How can it be that less than 10 percent of the population should have a majority of binding powers?"

Another deeply worried about giving the Waitangi Tribunal new powers was National MP Doug Graham:

"The court or tribunal that it sets up and empowers is not impartial. It has a majority of Maori people on it. It has the power to accept evidence that is not normally admissible. The legislation requires and entitles the tribunal to find as fact historical events that are almost incapable of proof.

"What about alternative points of view? They are denied. Only one party can appear before the tribunal to put its case – the claimant – as well as the Minister of Maori Affairs or any other Minister who may have an interest. But if the land has been sold by the State-owned enterprise to

---

122   Hansard, State Owned Enterprises Bill, 11 December 1986

an innocent third party subject to the caveat, the only Minister who can be involved is the Minister of Maori Affairs. Not even an amicus curiae is appointed to represent opposing views. Therefore the justice of the case fails on that ground, too. What about the appeal? There is none."

Labour's Richard Prebble, the minister for State Owned Enterprises, tried to deflect criticism by returning to what he said was the fundamental issue: if it was Maori land, government corporations had no right to it.

"A process has to be gone through to determine the ownership, but the principle is quite clear: the Crown does not believe that it has any moral right to occupy, or exercise ownership over, land that it does not own. It does not matter when the Crown took over the rights of ownership of the land; the question is, does it own the land or not? If it does not, it should be returned to the rightful owners. One either believes in the rule of law in relation to ownership of land or one does not. The Government believes in the rule of law and it does not want to exercise the rights of ownership over land that it does not own."

Yes, agreed his critics, we believe in the rule of law and property rights as well, but the "process" has to be transparent. Peters, Doug Graham and others wanted to make sure that the Waitangi Tribunal process didn't just become a rubber-stamp for plundering taxpayers' land reserves on the spurious evidence that someone's pet seagull once flew over it. Hard on the heels of the Maori Loans Affair, and the "kill a white" controversy, you could see why people were edgy.

Justice Minister Geoffrey Palmer admitted New Zealand was heading into uncharted waters:

"The Bill is unique, as there has never been such a Bill in the history of Parliament. It is extraordinary."

Winston Peters ended up on a seven person select committee reviewing the legislation. Like most things governments do when they don't want public interference it was done in a hurry. The committee opened public submissions on 8 December 1987, just as parliament shut for summer. Submissions closed 29 January 1988.

Of only 51 submissions received, seven were from state owned enterprises, 11 were from Maori organisations, and 26 private individuals in a country of three million bothered to write in.

What was supremely worrying, Peters would later tell Parliament, is that the taking of public submissions turned out to be a sham, because

Labour had done a deal with the Maori Council behind closed doors that left the Bill intact:[123]

"The committee knew that it was being asked to rubber-stamp a decision made outside Parliament. It was very clear to Opposition members that, no matter what any party around the country might suggest, Government members would not change the Bill at all – in any way, shape, or form."

If this was a taste of things to come with the Waitangi Tribunal, he said, New Zealanders had reason to be very afraid:

"Why is it that the tribunal will have the power to make a decision, and, unlike the position with any other court, nobody can appeal against it? It is a decision of a tribunal with less status than the High Court, yet nobody can appeal against it.

"This is not a Maori or a European issue. It is a New Zealand issue. Most people in this country are entitled to have a proper system of law, and this simply will not do. There will be a tremendous delay in the hearings, and there will be much strife among the people, if the Bill proceeds in its present form."

"It has the power to rewrite history," agreed National's Warren Kyd.

The biggest immediate problem with the Bill, however, was what National MP Ian Mclean called the 'heightened expectations" of Maori that suddenly every land issue was going to be resolved. Radical elements, he said, were going even further at a select committee hearing in Auckland:

"At those hearings a Mr Syd Jackson presented a submission containing obscene language. He accused the committee of being racist. He submitted that his objective was to gain control of New Zealand, not only of the land, but also of the Government," warned Mclean.

Labour's Bill Dillon wondered if Peters had a hand in that:

"The only photograph that appeared in a newspaper as a result of the meeting in Auckland was a photograph of the member for Tauranga meeting – and grinning with – the extremists who had broken up the meeting."

Labour's Whetu Tirakatene Sullivan was taking credit for the wording of the clause that changed the future:

"Were it not for section 9 being put into the original State-Owned Enterprises Act 1986 by the Government, the New Zealand Maori Council

---

123 5 May 1988, 42nd Parliament, 1st Session, Hansard Vol 488, pp3970-3982 Treaty of Waitangi (State Enterprises) Bill (Report of Committee on Bill)

would not have had a successful case. Victory hung on that clause, with which I have been very familiar for many years, and I included it in a private member's Bill of my own. Nothing in the legislation permits the Crown to act in a manner that is inconsistent with the principles of the Treaty of Waitangi. The words in the clause go back to what was called a Ratana/Labour alliance, so I have a particular and specific awareness of it."

All the heat that Winston Peters and the National opposition were bringing to bear on the Government began to have an effect. The Minister of Maori Affairs, Koro Wetere, was forced to announce Labour was removing the requirement for the Waitangi Tribunal to have a Maori majority.[124] Public anger was growing, and steam had to be let off somewhere if Labour wanted to push the rest of the legislation through.

"What is going on in the Government? Can it not get the matter right?" railed Peters in a speech that was to signal his future vision for the country.

"At the end of the day the Government cannot understand that we are all New Zealanders; that is what we are when we travel overseas. New Zealand is three million people against the world. We are not Maori, Asian, Scots, or Irish; we are New Zealanders of different backgrounds, different beliefs, and different races. However, we are all New Zealanders and we are the only three million people that New Zealand has.

"The Government cannot get past its ethnic, liberal, guilt conscience that tries to solve problems of the past. I come from a farming family, and one thing I learnt was that one cannot plough a field going backwards. The same applies to race relations. We must look forward in race relations and the future development of New Zealand."

"That's leadership stuff!" interjected Labour's Eastern Maori MP Peter Tapsell.

"It is not," grinned Peters, glancing at his boss Jim Bolger, "none of us have pretensions. We are behind the man who is the best and most honest leader that is offered to New Zealand – on this side of the House. [Interruption.] He has not sold out his principles and beliefs as the member for Hamilton West has done."

"Order!," bellowed Parliament's speaker. "I invite the member to talk about the Bill."

"I am trying to talk about the Bill in a global and futuristic sense. I am sure that the people from the West Coast believe that, because they are

---

124 Ministerial news release, 22 March 1988

among the hundreds of thousands of New Zealanders – whom I call silent New Zealanders – who have no say in what goes on. They do not have a say because of the oppression of a liberal, urban minority in Cabinet that does not care what anyone thinks. The Government listens to academics; however, no one speaks for the ordinary people who are the backbone of New Zealand and who should be represented by the Bill," challenged Peters.

Anne Fraser, the Labour MP for East Cape, accused Peters of inflaming tension.

Why would I want that? barked Winston, "What does the member for East Cape know about the way Maori people feel – apart from moving round her electorate before an election and telling a whole tissue of fabrications about why they should vote for her – whilst the dole queues grow longer and longer day by day and while there is unmitigated violence in her electorate. This morning, a man had half his farm property burnt down."

New Zealand, in the late 80s, was indeed a powderkeg. Justice Minister Geoffrey Palmer was becoming increasingly aware of that:

"I am certain that if New Zealand is to enjoy racial harmony, peace, and tranquillity, Parliament must consider ways in which Maori grievances can be dealt with. If the Government does not provide the means by which those claims can be examined, the Maori people will harbour a sense of injustice. The Bill is designed to alleviate that sense of injustice, and to provide an outlet, through peaceful means, by which decent claims can be examined, and recommendations can be made to the Government. It is important to do that well."

Just how much of a powderkeg was whispered about in police briefings everywhere. Syd Jackson and others were visiting Libya to catch up with Colonel Muammar Gaddafi,[125] and the lead-up to the 1990 Commonwealth Games in Auckland was peppered with police swoops trying to locate an RPG-7 rocket grenade launcher – it was never found and never used, but Tame Iti's Tuhoe "terrorist" camps apparently had a pedigree.

"I do not want to see bloodshed on the streets of New Zealand," exclaimed Peters.[126]

Jim Bolger, meanwhile, had visions of virtually New Zealand's entire fishing industry being controlled by Maori:

---

125 TVNZ 'Marae', 25 January 2008
126 Hansard, Questions for Oral Answer, 22 September 1988

"There are now suggestions that Maori canoes could have been taken out 200 miles and beyond to fish, and therefore that all the fish inside New Zealand's 200-mile exclusive fishing zone belong to the Maori people. There are extravagant claims everywhere and they all have to be handled and determined, not in the interests of one particular sector or group, but in the interests of New Zealand."[127]

Bolger appealed to an iconic Maori leader, Sir Apirana Ngata, who had once famously defined what the Treaty of Waitangi had done for Maori.

"The treaty created Parliament to make laws," Ngata had said.

"The treaty has given us the Maori Land Court with all its activities. The treaty confirmed Government purchases of land and it also confirmed past confiscations."

Bolger looked around Parliament's debating chamber to see if the point was sinking in. The Treaty, according to Ngata, had confirmed that land confiscations were legal. Of course it may not have crossed Bolger's mind that not all confiscations were created equal. Some innocents lost their tribal land as part of a vengeful Crown swoop on rebels at the time of the land wars.

"The treaty sanctioned the levying of rates and taxes on Maori land. It made one law for the Maori and the pakeha. If you think those things are wrong and bad then blame our ancestors who gave away their rights in the days when they were powerful," concluded the Ngata passage Bolger was reading from.

"A different interpretation of the treaty has emerged tonight," Bolger intoned. "It is a definition that is removed from that extended by Sir Apirana Ngata in 1922. It is not for me to say which interpretation is right, but it is for me to say that we should not believe that some of the more flamboyant or extravagant presentations about what the Treaty of Waitangi meant in 1840 are necessarily correct."

As debate that May 1988 evening drew to a close in parliament, Labour's Northern Maori MP Bruce Gregory tried to bridge the gap, pointing out that we were all, increasingly, becoming Maori now:

"The Leader of the Opposition highlighted the issue of cultural mix and of race. The Treaty of Waitangi in 1840 was between Maori chiefs

---

[127] The 1992 Sealord deal struck by Bolger's National Government was worth only $170 million and took Maori control of commercial fisheries to about 20% of the industry.

and Lieutenant-Governor Hobson, representing the British Crown. All of the other groups at the time would have come within the jurisdiction of the British Crown and would have been responsible to the Crown but not necessarily to our people, the Maori people, who were the other signatories to the document."

Gregory wasn't entirely correct on that – the Europeans living in NZ prior to the Treaty were not under British jurisdiction – they were free, out of reach of Her Majesty's justice except to the extent Britain could leverage physical force and abduct a miscreant onto a British ship, where its justice did apply.

In that sense, then, these two or three thousand Pakeha, the so called "riff raff" and "flotsam", were the "all New Zealanders" in addition to Maori that the Treaty purported to cover.

"The injustices are between the Crown and the Maori people," continued Gregory. "For all of the other races that have come to New Zealand and have intermarried with Maori and European people the result can only be in one direction. For example, if a Scot – and I am part Scottish – a Chinese, or a Samoan should marry a Maori, that person becomes part of the Maori race.

"The issue is the part of Maoridom that resides within each individual, and if an injustice has been done as a result of the treaty, that injustice must still be dealt with. The other part of the person is not affected, except perhaps when the person questions why the Maori half is not being treated as well. In a sense, that position may cause a form of cultural schizophrenia. However, whatever the cultural mix, the important issue is the redress of injustice between the Crown and that part-Maori person who is part of the debate."

Anyone who marries a part Maori becomes Maori, said the Northern Maori MP, for treaty claim purposes.

For Winston Peters, the die had been cast. This new interpretation of the Treaty was clearly taking hold in the political arena, and he saw the new wave as divisive and separatist. In Rhodesia and South Africa, separate development was called "apartheid" and Peters wanted none of it in New Zealand. Genuine Treaty grievances must be addressed, but the process had to be consistent with the framework of one law for all, not one law for special people. This would become a fundamental bottom line but, as we are about to see, it was also a ticket to a new level of political influence.

TOP: A picture from the National Archives taken by photojournalist Ian Mackley. The short man on the left is listed as "Boris Ashikhmin", an "interpreter" with the Soviet Embassy. He was the sole translator for the entire inquiry, requested by the Russians. **BELOW LEFT:** The short man in the middle is Vladimir Putin, President of Russia. His biography discloses he was working as a KGB intelligence agent in 1986, under the cover of "an interpreter".
BELOW RIGHT: A grainy photo taken inside the Lermontov inquiry, the man on the left is "Boris Ashikhmin", the man in the middle is the Captain of the *Lermontov*

TOP: They made the teacher cry. Winston Peters in the corduroy jacket with his Form 1 class at Te Atatu Intermediate School in 1966. **BELOW:** Nearly 50 years later, Peters' clothing tastes have improved

10

How To Win Friends...

> *"I think that we are all pleased to see the Member for Tauranga back in the House. I think that we have missed him. For my part at least, I am always pleased to see another member in the House dressed in a suit rather than a scraggly shirt or sports coat."*
> — Peter Tapsell, Labour cabinet minister, 1988

Winston Peters' poll ratings shot up in mid 1988 as a result of his "we are all New Zealanders" speech. It resonated with a community seeking a common way forward when it seemed the Labour Government was hell-bent not just on disrupting the country economically but socially as well. It was also the start of a disconnect between urban liberals and Winston Peters, however.

The enormous upheaval of the Lange years and the rollout of the Rogernomics hidden agenda had destabilised traditional political boundaries. Labour had traditionally been a party of the working class, of socialists and feminists and a range of other lower profile 'ists', but its new economic policies were gaining support from traditional National voters.

Douglas and Lange had hoped that while Labour voters may not like Rogernomics, the financial benefits would soon be apparent and that Labour could keep its core if it maintained its social vision as well.

Winston Peters confused the urban liberals. On the one hand he wasn't above giving Rogernomics a kicking, which appealed to them, but he was now attacking 'Maori rights'. For Labour supporters who'd grown up with activist messages like "no nukes" and "Honour the Treaty", seeing Winston Peters resisting the Treaty as they perceived it, sent mixed messages, especially as he was Maori himself.

Michael Laws' comment, "only a scattered understanding of Maori issues" is reflective of this. It presumes the liberal is 'enlightened' and that one who doesn't think the same is badly informed or sub-par intellectually. The possibility that Winston was tapping into older and better history – or what CS Lewis liked to call 'older, deeper magic' did not occur to them. If you weren't supporting the consensus slogans, then you were part of the problem, not the solution.

Labour's Graham Kelly reminded Peters of his earlier work on the Ngati Wai claim in 1975 and contrasted that with a recent Peters interview:

"We must never hobble the development of this country by freezing New Zealand in a time warp," Peters had said. "As a constitutional device the treaty may well have served its time."[128]

"Is the member reducing the Treaty of Waitangi to the rubbish tin?" bawled Kelly.

But while Peters continued to hammer race relations, Labour's secret agenda to sell state assets after 1988 became his other fertile stomping ground. Not only was it "selling the family silver", it was also putting masses of people out of work.

"When you go back to the fifties and sixties," Peters remarked recently[129], "the halcyon years of the National Party under Holyoake, they had a seriously strong economic policy but a seriously strong social conscience as well. They used to take great pride in the fact that the total number of unemployed was 29. Not 29 thousand. Twenty-nine!"

By March 1989, unemployment was at record levels since the Depression. Peters pilloried "a Labour Government that has allowed unemployment to increase not by 20,000 or 50,000 but by more than a hundred thousand in the short time of four years."

Pointing out that 182,000 people were now unemployed or on job train-

---

128 Peters interview with Dominion Sunday Times, 7 August 1988, quoted in Hansard, General Debate, 5 October 1988
129 Peters interview with Mark Sainsbury, RadioLive 29 June 2014

ing schemes[130], Peters asked what Labour was doing wrong:[131]

"In Gisborne, the rate of unemployment is 22.29 percent...Whangarei has 20% of its population unemployed. Rotorua – the tourism Mecca of New Zealand – has an unemployment rate of 19%."

Labour's Anne Fraser again learnt the hard way not to interject against an armed opponent.

"Government members should hold their heads in shame," said Peters, eyeballing Fraser. "The member for East Cape prissies herself around Parliament. She should tell the House about the position in East Cape. Some areas in her electorate have an unemployment rate of 45%, and for Maori people it is 75% in little hamlets on the East Cape."

It wasn't hard for Peters to locate discontent, as rumours about Labours links to big business continued to grow. When Labour had come to power after ousting Muldoon in 1984, NZ's total public debt was $12 billion. A year later under Rogernomics and the devaluation it had leapt to $18.5 billion, and by 1987 it was a staggering $29 billion. The "Think Big" debt that Labour had ridiculed National over accounted for just $7 billion of the total.

In September 1986, Labour's Richard Prebble had promised not to sell state assets, saying "Government members are opposed to selling the assets."

"No Government has the right to sell off state trading enterprises to its cronies," said Prebble. "Government members are willing to make it an election issue. The assets belong to the people."[132]

Look how that promise turned out.

There are two schools of thought when it comes to state assets. One is that assets can and should be sold off to pay the bills if necessary, or to invest in new infrastructure elsewhere. Usually overlaid on this is an ideological belief that the state should not own such assets, taxpayers should not have to "fund" such assets, and that the assets would run more efficiently under private control.

The other school of thought says that assets like rail infrastructure, power and communications companies and the like, have been built up

---

130 According to government figures, unemployment finally peaked at 189,000 in 1991, under National. It currently sits under 150,000 but our population is now 4.5 million, not three million as it was.
131 Hansard, General Debate, 1 March 1989
132 Hansard, 30 September 1986

over the years with huge public investment, and no "market" sale price is going to ever reflect their true value. A country, for example, might sell its roading network to private toll operators on the grounds that taxpayers are paying millions fixing potholes and the money could be better spent elsewhere. The real value of the roads – the actual cost of building the entire network from scratch – would never be reflected in the sale price because one private company buying today could never afford to really pay the price for 100 years of investment.

Nor does the second school of thought buy into the "taxpayers shouldn't have to invest in this" argument. A dollar invested in a private company that owns a power station makes a return on its investment, the same way that a dollar invested in a state run power network generates a return for taxpayers. These enterprises are structured as businesses, regardless of who owns them. If they are generating revenue streams for the Government, that puts less pressure on taxpayers to fill the government coffers.

The argument that you should sell off an asset generating income, and put the capital that's released into schools or hospitals, sounds noble, but it's a short term gain as you are reinvesting in non-income producing infrastructure. If you end up with less income to pay your bills down the line, because you have sold a revenue earner, how do you pay your bills then?

First school of thoughters counter some of these fears by pointing out that state assets are like a box of chocolates, you never know precisely what you are going to get. Some get sold for a song and make their new owners millions, some get sold high and promptly bankrupt their new owners. What might be considered an "asset" today could turn out to be a turkey tomorrow when, if it had been sold at the right time, it could have been someone else's problem.

Winston Peters is a second school of thought guy. As he got his head around the state asset sales programme in the late eighties, and listened to his colleague Ruth Richardson extol the virtues of privatisation, he wondered if there wasn't some better middle ground. What about a compulsory national savings scheme that could invest in New Zealand business assets and infrastructure? Doing it that way would provide a pool of investment and allow New Zealand income-generating assets to stay in New Zealand control. It was a thought he would chew on for most of the next decade.

To understand what was happening inside National in 1989, you just had to look at Labour. The Government, quite literally, was falling apart.

"My back is so scar-tissued," quipped David Lange to an Australian journalist after narrowly surviving a second coup attempt, "you couldn't find a place to stick a knife."[133]

Racked by division over economic direction and social policy, Lange had sacked Richard Prebble as State-Owned Enterprises minister in late 1988, and by early 1989 Finance Minister Roger Douglas and Revenue Minister Trevor De Cleene had walked the plank. Leadership battles were being fought in broad daylight, but still Lange hung in there.

"To give six months of your life to knocking me off and fail, it must be distressing," he taunted.[134]

The polls were appalling; Labour was so unpopular under David Lange that the McGillicuddy Serious Party could have won by a landslide in comparison.

"The Labour Party has the lowest popularity rating of any Government in the history of New Zealand," intoned the *Sydney Morning Herald*.[135] "The National Party Opposition, with a popularity rating of 58% (despite its unpopular leader, Mr Jim Bolger, and its lack of policies) is poised to sweep back into office at next year's election."

Within National, the certainty of an election win in 1990, or even sooner if the government collapsed, caused a heightened state of excitement within National's deep factions. Ruth Richardson led one of those, and Peters was a quasi spiritual leader of the second faction, although too much of a lone wolf to draw others into a real pack. Both factions sensed they were close to government, and both factions wanted to lead National to victory.

The incumbent leader, Jim Bolger, didn't earn his nickname, "the Great Helmsman" for nothing. He knew that if he steered a careful course and played the factions off against each other, he'd probably be safe. It was a job that needed nerves of steel, when even the Australian newspapers were speculating on his imminent demise at the knife of Peters:

"Mr Peters, a Maori," said the *Sydney Morning Herald*, "is an ambitious National Party MP who is expected to mount a challenge for the leadership of the party within the next few months."[136]

---

133 "Lange heads for defeat at the polls," by Michael Grealy, Sydney Morning Herald, 30 July 1989, p16
134 Ibid
135 "Lange plays a wild card," Sydney Morning Herald, 27 April 1989, p14
136 Ibid

Sitting on 19% as the most preferred prime minister, ahead of actual prime minister David Lange on 14%, Peters felt it was only a matter of time before caucus came begging. Michael Laws writes that Peters was putting too much faith in commonsense, and overlooking the harsh reality that in a country known for tall poppy syndrome, talent scares people:

"You can be too successful in this business; perhaps that was Winston's true crime in the eyes of his colleagues. He showed them up for the rank amateurs they were and they loathed him for it. They expected the man to play 'the team game', to be mediocre and mealy-mouthed just like them. Jim Bolger was thus their natural leader."[137]

Team player?, thought Peters, 'I can be a team player!' Laws had written a speech on the need for national leadership in these trying times when Labour was sinking. Winston tweaked it just a little until it became a speech about the need for National leadership. He proceeded to tell his audience that his party was not yet providing the kind of leadership it was capable of, and he rattled off the names of a number of his caucus colleagues that he would assemble as the party's front bench if he were leader.

Except, of course, he wasn't. Nor were the old guard like Bill Birch and Don McKinnon impressed that they'd missed the cut. Sucker-punching Bolger was one thing, and something of an open sport in National, but ignoring the other potential power brokers was playing with fire.

"Look at the leader of the Opposition," laughed Labour's Peter Tapsell. "He has looked a little more uncomfortable in the past day or two. The member for Tauranga says that he has done nothing, but is he not the member who has more certainly than any other Opposition member successively dug right around the leader of the Opposition?[138]

"Is he not the member who said that his leader 'showed promise'? Is he not the member who said...that the Leader of the Opposition is off a farm, and that he does not have a degree, and cannot be very cerebral? Can members think of any more skilful or deliberate way to dig around one's leader than that? I do not think that in the next two years the member will be able to resist digging the trench a little deeper.

"Other Opposition front-bench members look uncomfortable...those members realise that the member for Tauranga is creeping up behind

---

137 The Demon Profession, Laws, p150
138 Hansard, General Debate, 16 November 1988

them very quietly, and very deliberately, and at the end the result will be that, like a set of dominoes, they will fall, one by one."

It was an entertaining speech from Tapsell, who went on to call Winston's researcher Michael Laws "Luigi's ferret" and to compare the faces of the National front bench – singling out Birch and Richardson as they contemplated their fate under Winston – with a person "trying to suppress an imminent and explosive bowel motion. They all look like they could do with a dose of castor oil." Winston, he said, was "about as shallow as a waka huia".

Peters could muster the support of nine caucus colleagues – seven of whom he'd outed by naming them to his 'shadow' shadow front bench. Ruth Richardson had nine in her pen as well. The Mexican stand-off continued, and Richardson was delighted when Bolger reshuffled his front bench and Winston fell off the end, from place eight to 13. His employment portfolio was stripped from him "for disciplinary reasons". Apparently offering jobs to his caucus supporters wasn't seen as part of his role.

For a Government in waiting, they were actually going stir-crazy, much to the amusement of Labour which was desperate to shift attention from its own woes. National's 1989 party conference provided evidence for any who wanted to see.

"That must come as an awful shock to Opposition members, who had a miserable weekend in Dunedin," teased Labour's Annette King. "When they watch the videotape of the conference, and see the Deputy Leader of the Opposition crawling about in nappies with a bottle in his mouth, they will wonder what the emphasis of that conference was.

"Where was the unity, the fight, and the spark of life? I saw it in only one person – the member for Tauranga. He was the only member who had enough courage to say what he thought about the conference. He said that it was a public relations flop, and, once again, I agree with him. The member for Tauranga knows a public relations flop when he sees one. He will say that he very seldom becomes mixed up in one. Opposition members should take note of that member. They should look across the House to the Government's leadership, and the team it is putting up for the l990s, and examine their own team. I put odds on the member for Tauranga having a great future.[139]

---

139 Hansard, General Debate, 16 August 1989

Peters just grinned across the chamber.

Following his demotion from Bolger's shadow front bench, Winston Peters obtained revenge in his usual way – upstaging his boss. The opportunity came with the arrival of new US ambassador Della Newman. Normally ambassadors don't meet politicians until they have formally presented their credentials, but in this case MPs of all political hues were all over Newman as she arrived. Literally as she arrived.

Deputy Opposition leader Don McKinnon scored a seat alongside for her first flight from Auckland to Wellington. Evidently word of this reached the Beehive because Newman's news conference at Wellington Airport had no sooner begun than new Prime Minister Geoffrey Palmer gate-crashed it with Labour's Foreign Minister Russell Marshall, gushing about how nice it was to meet.

Sensing he was in with a grin, Winston Peters quietly arranged lunch with the new ambassador and let the media know. More accurately, Michael Laws let the media know and tipped them off Peters would be discussing ANZUS. The story, including the fact that Laws had hyped it up to the press gallery, made the TV news that night, and prompted Bolger to sack Laws from National's Research Unit.[140]

"The leader of the Opposition, Mr Jim Bolger, said he would probably discipline Mr Peters for placing the ambassador 'in an awkward position'," reported the *Melbourne Age*. "Mr Peters merely smiled and headed off to Britain, while Mrs Newman coyly told the media that lunch with Mr Peters had been 'delicious'. Nobody is quite sure where that leaves the angry Mr Bolger."[141]

Labour enjoyed the Newman fallout, and when they couldn't find something real to beat the Opposition around the ears with, they made it up. It wasn't unheard of for MPs to interview their typewriters, or purloin the work of someone who had, in order to score a point. On one occasion Labour's Clive Matthewson quoted from a document containing fake statements from National MPs Ruth Richardson and Winston Peters. Peters objected, asking the speaker to rule the quotes out of order as they were fraudulent. Quick as a flash, Labour's Mike Moore was on his feet: "Because something is fraudulent it does not mean that it cannot be

---

140 The Demon Profession, Laws, p157
141 "Politicians vie to grab US diplomat's olive branch" by John Kennedy, The Age, 29 October 1989

quoted. If that were so members could never discuss any of the National Party promises."[142]

Back in 89, Peters, despite ranking only #13 now, gained international news coverage for his progressive views on Asia:

"Mr Winston Peters...who is seen as a potential party leader, said that he saw the development of an Asian-Pacific common market as inevitable and desirable," reported the Sydney papers.[143]

Winston was making headlines where Bolger could not. In a massive feature article about the disintegration of the Lange Government, the *Sydney Morning Herald* talked briefly about "uninspiring dairy farmer Jim Bolger" leading National, quickly pointing out that Bolger couldn't even personally out-poll Labour's most unpopular leader in decades.

"While Bolger is the choice for Prime Minister of only 10pc in the latest Heylen poll, the man who led Lange from April to June and peaked at 20pc is Winston Peters."[144]

What, they asked Peters, did New Zealand need to do?

"Peters, seated in his Tauranga electorate office, told the *Sun Herald* that Labour had taken New Zealand down a segregationist path." Winston explained that the Treaty of Waitangi genie had been let out of the bottle, and that separate sets of rules for Maori and Pakeha were emerging, along with a sense of special entitlement.

"It's proving to be a disaster. The right path out of this racial demise is to concentrate on the fundamental issues that affect all humanity in the modern developed world – education and equality of careers. If we follow that path, we will be more cohesive as a nation and we will give ourselves the only chance we have of ensuring our economic and social survival. There are far too many Maori faces in the dole queues."

What about calls by Wellington lawyer Moana Jackson for a separate Maori justice system?, asked the paper.

"Cultural nonsense," snorted Peters. "The people who are making these calls could not fill a phone booth with their supporters."

The newspaper looked at what Peters would call "sickly white liberal guilt", and gave an example co-written by Kevin Hague – now a Green

---

142 Hansard, General Debate, 26 July 1989
143 "Hawke backed on Asia-Pacific bloc," Sydney Morning Herald, 26 May 1989, p4
144 "Lange heads for defeat at the polls," by Michael Grealy, Sydney Morning Herald, 30 July 1989

Party MP. Hague was a participant in a new book, "Honouring The Treaty, An Introduction For Pakeha To The Treaty of Waitangi, which called the treaty a "contract" between Maori and the Crown:
"We Pakeha are way behind in our obligations. What is worse, we have hijacked the shop we bought from, deposed the proprietors and fixed the courts so we can't be charged with these crimes. Our options are to catch up with out 'repayments' or to have rights given to us by the treaty 'repossessed'."[145]

The book pushed the line that Maori had to co-govern New Zealand, in what Professor Ranginui Walker called Maori "self-determination".

Of course, it was another example of treaty mythology, because it was never about co-governorship or separate development. As you've read earlier, the massive hui at Kohimarama in 1860 not only re-ratified the Treaty, it confirmed sovereignty had transferred to the British for all time, and the Maori were better off with one British crown than they ever had been warring amongst themselves.

The co-governance idea was taking hold, however, and the newspaper feature made special mention of 'liberal-in-chief' Geoffrey Palmer:

"Palmer, who at one time wanted to make the treaty the country's supreme law, has put the brakes on and belatedly released five principles for government action on treaty claims."

And therein lies the beginnings of the so-called "principles of the Treaty" – a Geoffrey Palmer invention that Peters would spend forever trying to neutralise.

Within two weeks of the feature's publication, David Lange had finally fallen on his sword and quit as Labour Prime Minister in favour of Palmer. The Australians couldn't resist taking a poke at Palmer, and catching Bolger in the cross-fire. In an editorial, they compared the "dour" visage of Palmer to "one of the Easter Island face statues", and wondered how his "dull image" would help turn the Labour ship around. [146]

Remarking again on Winston Peters meteoric polling, they wrote that National leader Jim Bolger "has a similar plodding political style to that of Mr Palmer. The Nationals now have to decide if the more colourful and controversial Mr Peters would be a better choice of leader to highlight Mr Palmer's pedestrian political manner."

---

145 Honouring The Treaty, by Kevin Hague, Helen Yensen and Tim McCreanor, Penguin 1989
146 "Editorial: Palmer – a vote for stability", Sydney Morning Herald, 9 August 1989 p14

Little wonder Bolger was sick of Winston Peters. He couldn't even open up a newspaper in Sydney without finding an article praising his black sheep virtually every other week.

There wasn't a leadership challenge from Winston, of course. The polls showed a goat with a blue ribbon around its neck could lead the rag-tag factionalised National to victory, and in 1990 that date with destiny duly arrived. Palmer had by now passed the poisoned leadership chalice to Mike Moore, but even the heavyweight couldn't save his party. It was National's turn to govern, and on day one they received a hell of a shock.

11

The Years Of Living Dangerously

> *"The Minister and his Government, in their typical, arrogant, socialist, paternalistic, sickly white liberal way – are going to 'pardon' the Ngati Awa? What a cheek!"*
> – **Winston Peters, 1988**

It was late spring when New Zealand went to the polls and signed Labour's death warrant. Under Geoffrey 'Easter Island' Palmer they'd faced a public stoning, with polls suggesting Labour might drop to as few as 15 seats in the 97 seat parliament. Moore was Prime Minister for six weeks, but he turned that massacre around.

On election night 28 Labour MPs were left standing, against 68 National MPs and Jim Anderton's New Labour seat of Sydenham. It was a big change from the 56 seats Labour had the day before.

But National's new crop barely had their seats under the table when bureaucrats dropped a bombshell. The majority government-owned Bank of New Zealand, which had already had a $300 million bailout back in June 1989, had gone bang again and hundreds of millions more were needed to stave off a financial crisis. To make matters worse, Labour had known for months and decided to keep it a secret.

It had the effect of destroying many of the manifesto promises National had campaigned on. It would also become one of the defining issues of Winston Peters' career.

If you ask some of Winston Peters' critics who he is, they fling around words like "populist", and say that his ambition to be Prime Minister clouds his judgement.

When National won the 1990 election landslide, even though Bolger hated Peters he gave him a cabinet position as Minister of Maori Affairs. Say what you like about Bolger, he had a touch of Corleone's political instincts in *The Godfather: Part II*: "keep your friends close and your enemies closer."

In what should have been an early lesson about the dangers of political kryptonite, the gloss came off the popular Winston Peters as the collective cabinet decisions of one of the most unpopular governments of the modern era began to taint him. Peters was trapped in a political straitjacket having to take the rap for policy decisions he disagreed. As more and more of arch-rival Ruth Richardson's policies were rubber-stamped by Cabinet, Peters regarded the 'All for one and one for all' mentality as Three Mouseketeers stuff, and he had a gnawing feeling Bolger was enjoying taking the Mickey.

Having said that, Peters approached his role seriously, wanting to concentrate on policies that delivered a hand-up, rather than a hand-out. There was consultation with Maori leadership, and the upshot was a policy strategy called Ka Awatea.

It's a Maori phrase meaning "new dawn", and Peters hoped to centralise delivery of services to Maori in one main agency, Te Puni Kokiri, that could more effectively administer and coordinate various initiatives.

Although he consulted widely within Maoridom, Winston hadn't sold it as well to his National Party colleagues and didn't get the support he was hoping for. The policy was announced in March 1991, and by October Winston Peters had been sacked as Minister.

Winston Peters dismissal was more to do with the ascendancy of the Ruth Richardson faction within National, and Peters' growing dissatisfaction at National's direction. Peters and Richardson had represented different wings of National since 1984 – the latter wanting to take the work of Roger Douglas even further. As Peters quickly lost influence in a New Right dominated cabinet, his position had become untenable. His battles were mostly being fought behind the scenes, around the cabinet table, inside the National caucus.

Team Richardson had won most of the fights, because the BNZ collapse had pushed National's manifesto out the window; "we're going to have some trouble with that," Prime Minister Bolger had told his caucus colleagues, looking at the manifesto document just after Treasury's horrific BNZ briefing.

National was going to need every ace up its sleeve. The BNZ required an immediate $380 million cash injection, and the Government was going to have to borrow a further $740 million.

Although his colleagues later accused him of not speaking up about the BNZ and Fay Richwhite at the time, Peters was able to prove they were wrong:

"I have a vivid recall of those events," he told parliament in a personal explanation. He said he'd expressed his "disquiet" at the very first cabinet meeting, because the decision to bail out the BNZ was "being imposed upon us when it had been around for 5 months since June 1990, and we were being asked to decide in five minutes, literally."[147]

Peters said he'd asked why Commerce Minister Philip Burdon was not being asked to advise on the banking crisis when he was "the one person qualified to have a grasp" of the problem.

"I raised the issue of why we were bailing out Fay Richwhite, when it was against all the party's philosophy in respect of the intervention of government in business."

That was a good question; as the evidence would later emerge that Fay Richwhite, a huge donor to the National Party, owed more than a billion dollars to the BNZ in secret borrowings at the time the bank went down.

Peters told his colleagues he had questioned why the BNZ's auditors weren't being "called to account" given the huge sums of money they'd charged in audit fees, and why the Reserve Bank wasn't being sent a "please explain" given its statutory role to oversee the banks.

"I asked why the Bank of New Zealand accounts were demonstrably and palpably inaccurate," said Peters, also wanting to know why the bank's highly paid directors were not being held to account either.

Of course, accountability was one thing. No one, not even Peters, denied that the life savings of ordinary New Zealanders could be placed at risk, and daily commerce would grind to a halt, if a government-owned bank like the BNZ was allowed to collapse.

While still Maori Affairs minister, shortly before his sacking, Winston

---

147 Hansard, Personal Explanation, 4 June 1992

Peters dared to write a letter to the Prime Minister and 19 other cabinet colleagues on 4 September 1991, requesting the Attorney-General and Justice Minister call "a proper inquiry" into the circumstances leading up to the BNZ collapse.

For his part, Bolger told parliament he could "not recall" Winston Peters raising any concerns about the BNZ in the initial cabinet meeting, and nor did he recall the 4 September letter. Bolger's memory was given a substantial jolt when Finance Minister Ruth Richardson's office admitted receiving the letter on 4 September.[148]

"You're going red, Jim," teased Labour's George Hawkins.

"There is no 'going red' about it," muttered Bolger. "I have acknowledged that such a letter was written by the member for Tauranga to the Minister of Finance."

Peters later revealed that as late as a Cabinet meeting they attended on 14 March 1991, Richardson said she had found "fertile ground" for investigation, but did nothing further about it.[149]

The Tauranga MP may have kept his BNZ disagreements to himself, but he was unable to hide his growing disdain for Ruth Richardson. Labour was quick to highlight the cracks, pointing out that Peters had described Richardson's figures on tax increases as "spurious" and "plain scaremongering".[150]

Bolger hit back at Labour saying Richardson's figures had been misquoted by a newspaper. "Everybody now knows," said Bolger, "that the newspaper report used as the basis for the remarks of the Minister of Maori Affairs was wrong and inaccurate."

All the same, the apparent criticism of one minister by another wasn't lost on observers, or the Prime Minister.

Historian Barry Gustafson, in the Muldoon biography *His Way*, writes:

"The 'intense jealousy' shown by many in the National cabinet and caucus towards Winston Peters worried Muldoon. He believed that for a long time some of National's more 'mediocre' MPs had been developing an antagonism towards Peters because of his superior political instincts and his ability to command media attention. That jealousy and hostility

---

148   Hansard, Questions for Oral Answer #2, 4 June 1992
149   Hansard, Fiscal Responsibility Bill, 7 June 1994
150   Hansard, Questions for Oral Answer #3, 12 June 1991

increased after the 1990 election and according to Muldoon even Bolger became involved and regarded Peters as a potential threat to his leadership.

"When Bolger 'excessively' criticised Peters' Maori policy Ka Awatea, however, Muldoon declared that it 'made sense' and associated himself with Peters by going to its launch.

"Although, perhaps with an element of wishful thinking, he speculated that Peters or Philip Burdon were 'two people who could be in line one day to become leaders of the National Party' and Peters 'could be our first Maori Prime Minister', on reflection he concluded that the jealousy of colleagues, the opposition from the New Right, and an element of racism within the National Party would prevent Peters from ever becoming National's leader."[151]

By July 1991, the relationship between Peters and Bolger was toxic, with the Prime Minister saying Peters was giving him "almost an open invitation" to sack him, after yet another lash at his colleagues.

"Winston has certainly got to recall the principles of Cabinet collective responsibility. There are times when it does appear that he's forgotten that," Bolger told Radio New Zealand, before aiming a shot directly at Peters:[152]

"If you find that too onerous then you have an honourable course open to you, and it's really pretty clear cut."

"What does a Minister have to do to be sacked from a National Government?" asked Labour's deputy leader Helen Clark.[153]

"It won't worry you, dear," cackled National's ghost-in-residence, Sir Robert Muldoon, from the dark corners of the back benches. Clark wasn't to be deterred.

"Given that the Minister of Maori Affairs has invited the Prime Minister to sack him, and that the Prime Minister has invited the Minister to take the honourable course open to him and resign, is there an invitation on which they can both agree?"

"When I want advice on such matters," snapped Bolger, "I shall consult the member for Auckland Central [Richard Prebble] who said that his Prime Minister was mentally unstable."

Challenged to follow the lead of former Ministers who had left cabi-

---

151 "His Way" by Barry Gustafson, Kindle location 13304
152 "Kiwi minister told to toe line", New Straits Times Malaysia, 2 July 1991, p11
153 Hansard, Questions for Oral Answer #3, 2 July 1991

net, Bolger called the departure of National's Derek Quigley as "a small start", before turning to the Lange years and reading a list that read like the Beehive had revolving doors:

"Between 1985 and 1990 the Minister of Foreign Affairs, the Minister of Labour, the Minister of Internal Affairs and the Minister of Agriculture were dumped; the Minister of Conservation retire late; the Minister of Defence was dumped and retired hurt; the Minister of State Owned Enterprises was fired; the Minister of Finance resigned; the Minister of Revenue walked out, a Prime Minister resigned –"

"Order!" yelled the Speaker as the Labour benches disintegrated into the kind of uproar you see in nature documentaries following a baboon pack. This wasn't the answer they had wanted.

"Another Prime Minister went," continued Bolger before being shouted down again.

"Order!!"

"And the latest Prime Minister was thrashed," grinned Bolger as he looked over at Labour leader Mike Moore who by now was on his feet with a hearty yet plaintive "Mr Speaker!?" of his own.

"Order!!!"

"Why don't you start acting like a Speaker and get him to sit down," demanded Moore.

Winston Peters, wearing the toothiest smile he could assemble at short notice, cheekily pointed out that Mike Moore had insulted the Speaker, "and I think that he should apologise".

"Order!" yelled the Speaker as Winston's tweak found its targets on the Labour benches and set the troop bellowing once more. "I have called Question No. 4".

At the end of September 1991, just days after Maori Affairs Minister Winston Peters began questioning the sale of Quality Inns to a Maori/Hawaiian consortium, Bolger redrafted his cabinet and Winston's chair was suddenly occupied by another's rump. His cabinet days were over.

Michael Laws reckons Winston's heart was never in it.

"Sure, he was interested in improving the general lot of the Maori people, but there was a hint of the ghetto about the appointment. His resentment was vividly expressed at the executive's swearing-in at Government House. The trademark grin was gone and he affected a manic, distracted air as if remembering that he had left the gas on back at the flat".[154]

Reflecting on the Ka Awatea process just days after his sacking, Peters called it a model for the way that a government should govern – by the consent of the people. He told parliament he'd asked his team not to impose top down orders, but to go to Maori and European alike and get their "advice, their consent, and their contribution" to the problems of Maori underachievement.[155]

"Some will recall that Ka Awatea was taken to Maori before it was taken to Cabinet. I make no apology for that, because, as Minister, unless the Maori gave it their blessings and consent I had no policy to present to Cabinet. Some people still refuse to understand the proper process of government. Government is about the consent of the people, for the people, and with the people."

Calling Ka Awatea "a beacon of light" Peters said his team had found 60% of funding for Maori wasted within bureaucracy, and that the new policy would end that waste:

"We will carve back 60 percent of bureaucracy; we will save 60 percent of the bureaucratic cost – and no ministry has contemplated that thus far. But it was accepted by Maoridom because the Government made a promise that the savings would go into real development – that is, education, training, health, and economic resource development. To take those savings and put them into the Consolidated Account when development is so important for Maoridom would be to commit a grievous sin."

It was a brave speech from the former Maori Affairs minister, given that Cabinet had actually scaled back a lot of his initiatives.

"I realise now why my good friend the former Minister of Maori Affairs became a little bitter and twisted in the past few months," remarked Labour's Peter Tapsell. "It is not quite what was promised in Ka Awatea, but that is neither here nor there."[156]

It is significant that busloads of Maori, including Dame Whina Cooper, came to Wellington to support Peters after he was cast adrift.

The National Government was in disarray, to some extent. Poll support after Richardson's mother of all budgets dropped as low as 16%, and

---

154 The Demon Profession, Laws, p210
155 Hansard, Ministry of Maori Development Bill, 17 October 1991
156 Ibid

caucus rebels like Hamish McIntyre and Gilbert Myles quit to become independents rather than continue to support Ruthanasia. There was a lot of speculation that Peters might lead a breakaway party – Michael Laws compared Peters' ambition to a helium balloon but complained a rope was keeping him tethered to the National Party. In truth, the time wasn't right. The history of breakaway parties under first past the post was poor. Additionally, Peters thought that if National's polls got low enough, caucus might beg him to take over as leader. As history and hindsight teach us, hell has not yet frozen over.

In fact, Bolger was doing all he could to encourage Peters to commit electoral suicide. At the Picton caucus retreat in the summer of early 1992, writes Laws, Bolger "was good enough to invite both of us to quit caucus now and swim home." The phrases "traitor", "treacherous dog" and "Muldoonist" turned up in polite conversation at the retreat. The impolite conversation didn't bear repeating.[157] Winston's reponse was to hire a launch with Michael Laws and buzz Bolger's lumbering caucus ferry boat.

In mid February 1992, Valentine's Day to be precise, the *National Business Review* published what would become one of its most highly-read articles, and Winston Peters found a new bone to chew on.

"Once upon a time, in a land far, far away," the tale began, "in Wogistan dwelt Ali Baba…"

Ali, so this allegorical tale went, was a tax lawyer who "devised schemes so cunning they did baffle the fiscal fiend, until one fateful day Ali and his band overstepped the bounds of what we self righteous Kiwis call moral rectitude and, in a rash moment, not only dodged the taxman but defrauded their clients as well."

Ali Baba's field of interest was bloodstock, "not ordinary bloodstock, mind, but racing camel bloodstock", and movies, particularly one starring "the Thin White Duke" – a nickname for the androgynous David Bowie. It just so happened the Duke had filmed a movie in Auckland in 1983, around the time he hooked up with kiwi *China Girl* model Geeling Ng. Readers began to wonder if Ali Baba's preferred office wasn't a tent, but a mirror-glass building in Auckland.

The thing that particularly tweaked Winston Peters as he read all this is that Ali Baba was said to be politically well-connected to, in particular

---

157 The Demon Profession, Laws, p212

a "leading legal Vasir ever so grateful to Ali for his help in filling pre-election coffers".

All over offices in Auckland and Wellington, mouthfuls of coffee were ending up all over computer screens as readers joined the dots and put the picture together. The Wogistan story was alluding to mega-lawfirm Russell McVeagh's film and bloodstock investment partnerships that had been pitched in the 1980s.

According to the Arabian Nights version, Ali and his band of financial pirates had suddenly been protected when the Vasir's tax department minions ceased investigating the frauds, allegedly on the nod of the Vasir as a thank you for all the election donations.

One of the country's dirtiest little secrets had hit the business media, and one of the country's most dogged political scandalmongers was reading it. Was there, he wondered, a connection between a Vasir whose electorate committee chairman had been a Russell McVeagh partner, and a director of the ill-fated BNZ bank?

As he later testified at the Winebox Inquiry:

"Now, the rumour within the National Party at the time was that the allegorical personalities included Russell McVeagh McKenzie Bartleet & Co, the Honourable Doug Graham and Robin Congreve. If the article was, in fact, meritorious, the matter deserved investigation and I decided to investigate."[158]

1992 was definitely going to be Winston Peters' year of living dangerously.

---

158 Evidence of Peters to Winebox Inquiry, reprinted in Lawyers, Guns & Money, p213

12

Enter The Gladiator

> *"My name is Maximus Decimus Meridius. Commander of the Armies of the North. General of the Felix Legions. Loyal servant to the true Emperor, Marcus Aurelius. Father to a murdered son, husband to a murdered wife – and I will have my vengeance, in this life or the next."*
>
> – ***Gladiator***

Winston's poll ratings after his sacking were back on the rise. As the black sheep in a hated government he gained points for every metre of space he put between himself and the Government. His suspicions of wrongdoing between big business and politicians also nagged at his traditional political instincts and he asked his Auckland barrister, Brian Henry, to do some digging.

Henry's feelers quickly put him in touch with lawyers Chris Dickie and Peter Edwards, from a mid-sized city lawfirm called McVeagh Fleming. At some point in the dark and distant past there'd been a family split within the McVeaghs, with one partner staying at Russell McVeagh and the other firing off to start his own practice. It's confusing, but not overly so. The Russell McVeagh lawfirm was being investigated by the McVeagh Fleming lawfirm. All the story needed was some Hatfields and McCoys and the picture would be complete.

Likewise in this story the name "Henry" pops up a lot. There's Winston's lawyer Brian Henry. There's the Commissioner of Inland Revenue David Henry, and the later Winebox scandal happened under the nose of Cook Islands Prime Minister Geoffrey Henry.

Michael Laws called 1992 the start of Winston's "conspiracy phase", a cheap throwaway line that gets an easy laugh, even now. The reality, as Wikileaks and Edward Snowden have shown, is that sometimes groups of people do get together to plot things to their own advantage; sometimes, conspiracies are real.

For Peters, the journey down the rabbit hole went like this.

In early April 1992, with Auckland still basking in the afterglow of an Indian summer, the MP was called to a meeting at the St Nesbit's Vineyard in South Auckland, owned by prominent independent tax barrister Dr Tony Molloy QC. Also in attendance were Dickie and Edwards from McVeagh Fleming, the MP's lawyer Brian Henry, Alan May – a senior investigator with the IRD, and two men from the Serious Fraud Office.

It was a briefing on adventures in Wogistan or, more precisely, the film and bloodstock frauds that had given rise to the rumours. For Peters it was a chance to hear first hand how one movie starring David Bowie may have duped the Revenue of $11 million. There were more than a dozen movie partnerships that McVeagh Fleming knew of; in fact, there were more than a hundred, the IRD later disclosed at the Winebox Inquiry. Potentially, huge sums of money were at stake.

So were reputations, and just a few weeks later Peters endured his first major misfire.

It was the start of June, 1992, and Peters had popped up on Australia's ABC TV network in a documentary called *Four Corners*, examining the alleged corruption of the political process across the Tasman in New Zealand. While various media reports paraphrased Peters' comments as alleging "bribery" and "corruption", he had not actually used those words directly.

Instead, in a lengthy personal explanation to Parliament, Peters – waving a copy of the programme transcript – explained what he had said, and why he said it:

"Part of this personal explanation is to defend what I said, not what others for their own purposes said I said. Words like 'bribery' and 'corruption' do not appear in the transcript, yet they have been glibly used by the leaders of the two main parties and sections of the news media.

"This is what I said on the ABC *Four Corners* programme: *'Well, for some time I had been asked to come and see a certain group in the Roundtable. In fact, it was put to me that it would be churlish not to do so; that it would be bad manners not to talk to them. So in the interests of public propriety I did. But I was pretty certain as to what the conversation would be about, and it was about that. It was about my swinging in behind a certain economic philosophy, and so it went. There was fine wine and the meal was lovely but there was going to be no business between us on the matter over and above what I perceived was the good of New Zealand.*

'And, further, I just as a matter of curiosity said: `Well, what do you mean by help? Do you mean money?'. And he said: `Yes'. And I said: `Well, how much?', and I nominated a few figures and each figure was agreed to. And I said: `Well, look, I'm not prepared to sell out the people I represent in either my constituency or nationwide.'

The question came: 'What sort of money was he talking about?'. The answer was: 'It seemed to me, there was no limit' – and here are the important words – `. . . to support my campaign, whatever they perceived my campaign to be.'. Question: 'What did he want in return?'. Answer: 'That wasn't made clear, but I had a suspicion that, once I was on a ticket, then I was clearly in my mind and publicly I would have been bought.'."

Listening to the personal explanation roll out, it became clear that two different events appeared to have been rolled into one, either by Winston Peters being loose with his phrasing while being interviewed, or editing by the TV crew to try and simplify the story line. Either way, here are the two ingredients. The first was a request for Peters to attend a meeting at the headquarters of merchant bank Fay Richwhite:

"On 26 October 1989 my diary discloses that I attended a 6.30 p.m. dinner at the office of Fay Richwhite in Auckland with the member for Fendalton, the Hon. Philip Burdon. At that meeting the following Roundtable members were present: Messrs Gibbs, Masfen, Richwhite, Myers, and Bidwell. All are, as you know, members of the Roundtable. The meeting was not at my request and, in fact, there is a senior journalist in the gallery who witnessed my reluctance to attend such a meeting.

Rt. Hon. J. B. Bolger: "Well, why did he go?"

"Simply because I was told that it would be damaging to the party's interests if I did not go. That is a fact, sir. As I told "Four Corners", I suspected what the meeting would be about, and I was right. What I did not tell "Four Corners" was that at the Auckland meeting I put to Mr Gibbs the question of why this group wanted to see me, given that they were already funding the member of Parliament for Selwyn, having shifted their allegiance from the then Government. Neither he nor anyone there demurred, or refuted my claim.[159]

"I put it to them that, that being the case, why would they want to talk to me? In reply, one member said that I should be using my skills and public support to swing in behind what the member for Selwyn was saying on economic matters, in which event it was clear in my mind that they would swing in behind me."[160]

Peters at this point tried to explain why the group were offering to fund him, but he was shouted down by his National colleagues and overruled by the Speaker.

"Let me go back to what was said on ABC *Four Corners*: 'To support my campaign, whatever they perceived my campaign to be'; and "what did he want in return?'; 'That wasn't made clear.'. And the remainder of my answer is my perception, having at that time been involved in party politics for 22 years. That is why I used the phrase 'in my mind'. That means that had I taken the money for my campaign I would have felt no longer free – that there would have been a new element in my mind when considering important economic matters. I would personally have felt bought."

That was the first incident – a 26 October 1989 meeting with David Richwhite, Doug Myers and others offering financial support if Winston would sing the same song as Ruth, thus at that time uniting National's rival wings. As I have indicated in the footnotes, this appeared to be a familiar pattern amongst the big electoral donors, so there is no real surprise in either their intent or Peters' reaction to it.

But Peters, whether flustered by the previous interruption or confused,

---

159 Peters in 1995 recounted the conversation in more detail: "I said to Alan Gibbs on my right that night, 'Why would I bother to prevail upon the public of this country to support Ruth Richardson when I know that you are supporting her right now…So come on Alan, you paid her $50,000, right?'. He got robbed. He did not get any return for that sort of money, but he did not deny it." – Hansard, Disclosure of Political Donations, 4 October 1995

160 That didn't mean the Roundtable would stop funding Richardson; what it meant was that the financiers were spreading their odds and possibly trying to forge a Peters/Richardson 'dream team', where a National Party led by Peters would endorse and continue the freemarket reforms. As I later discovered and published in the book Daylight Robbery, Richwhite and others were heavily involved in fundraising for Roger Douglas back in the eighties, but they had also ensured they donated to both sides of a debate, so as to hedge their bets. It's just that the preferred winner received larger donations.

then segues immediately into what appears to be a second, separate incident:

"Remember, sir, that the offer of financial assistance was direct: it was a departure from the conventional method of funding for political parties. The man belonged to a company associated with the Roundtable – in fact, a major shareholder, if not the major shareholder. And the man, even if his offer was genuine – and I leave that open, and believe it is possible – even if the offer was genuine, was a significant shareholder in a company associated with the Roundtable, and the political tactics of some members of that group had caused me grave disquiet. It was at the man's home that I recalled his business connection. I did not say at any time that this man may not have been genuine, because what was important to me then, as it is now, is how I would have felt about it.

"The three sums of money that go with the answers to the transcript are $20,000, $30,000, and $50,000 – not in addition, but alternatively. My diary for that day, rental car, and the man's business profile and business card are attached to this report. He is, sir, Mr Selwyn J. Cushing of Brierley Investments Ltd."

How did Selwyn Cushing end up in the thick of it? He wasn't one of those at the Fay Richwhite meeting. What appears to have happened was this. Cushing was not a Business Roundtable member. Despite being a senior Brierleys executive, he was more conservative than some of the other 'flash Harry' types, and disagreed with the social impact of raw free market policy. If anyone was going to be offering money to support Roundtable policies, it wasn't going to be Cushing.

That said, the man was a political donor. He'd given money to Michael Laws' campaign in the Hawkes Bay and had attended Laws' wedding. So had Winston, and that is in fact where Peters and Cushing had met and presumably exchanged business cards. It may have been that the two men discussed campaign donations, and one can understand the confusion later arising if the Fay Richwhite meeting in 1989 and the Cushing meeting in 1990 merged in the mind; you've seen one wealthy powerbroker offering money, you've seen them all, kind of thing.

Peters, I'm sure, came to believe – in a kind of Star Wars 'these are not the droids you are looking for' way – that it was Cushing offering him money for swinging in behind Ruth Richardson. The finer nuance – that Cushing may have been offering a generalised campaign contribution unrelated to that – could have been lost in translation. Indeed, at TV3 we quoted Michael Laws saying the naming of Cushing was "a tragic misunderstanding" on Winston's part.[161]

Adding to the fog around this donations for influence business is the overall position of Brierley Investments Ltd. Cushing had made contributions to Laws and others in his own name, not that of Brierleys, but there were nonetheless Brierleys donations floating around in the late 80s and possibly early 90s, creating a 'conspiracy of circumstance' where Winston felt he may be compromised.[162]

In *Daylight Robbery*, the story is recounted of a former top Brierleys executive making contact with *Investigate* magazine, a man who had "physically handled the donation cheques in the 1987 election". That person alleged:[163]

- That Brierleys knew the donations were not being routed via the Labour Party hierarchy, nor did it want the donations to be seen by ordinary officials
- That Brierley's put in $250,000 to the Roger Douglas fundraising effort for the Party
- That the company was expecting "no special treatment" other than a continuation of the favourable policies that Labour had introduced in 1984
- That the money was placed into a secret account

---

161 See The Paradise Conspiracy, 1ˢᵗ ed. p7
162 Michael Laws writes in his book that Cushing had asked Laws to arrange an informal meeting with Peters at Cushing's Hawkes Bay home, after the wedding. When Laws met up with Peters again after his honeymoon, he asked how it went with Selwyn: "Winston informed me that Cushing had been most generous with offers of personal financial support...We were later informed by the party's divisional staff that Cushing's principal donation had been relayed to National Party Headquarters in Wellington and that the sum had been in the region of six figures. The same indiscreet party official noted that Cushing had also been the party's largest individual donor in the previous election (1987) – brave stuff from a Brierley company director whose company profited so handsomely from Labour's economic and financial reforms...Certainly Winston mentioned that money had been discussed but in such general terms that I interpreted his remarks to mean Cushing had offered to finance Peters' election campaign in Tauranga...Equally, Selwyn Cushing's later public account of the circumstances leading to this fateful meeting did not square with either Anne's or my recollection of the facts. It was Cushing who eagerly pushed for a meeting with National's stellar attraction." Laws couldn't decide what to make of it, and put it down to miscommunication between both men. – The Demon Profession, p164-165
163 Daylight Robbery, 2ⁿᵈ ed. By Ian Wishart, HATM, 2012, p98

- That the secret account eventually totalled more than $2 million
- That businessmen David Richwhite, Alan Gibbs and Doug Myers were involved
- That Brierleys understood Roger Douglas, Richard Prebble, Mike Moore and David Lange were aware of the arrangements
- That details were kept away from so-called "straightlaced" MPs like Attorney-General Geoffrey Palmer
- That Labour Party secretary Tony Timms was not told all the details
- And that as a result of its efforts, Brierley Investments Ltd was expecting Ron Brierley to be given a knighthood the following year

Richwhite, Gibbs and Myers were of course all at the 26 October 1989 meeting with Peters and cabinet minister Philip Burdon.

Ironically, Winston Peters had himself come close to nailing Labour Finance minister Roger Douglas in the aftermath of the 1987 election, when he discovered Douglas had not only appointed some businessmen to well-paid directorships on Trustee Bank Holdings Ltd (the company referred to in the recent TSB Bank TV ads about the amalgamation of the local trust banks in the 80s ready for a sell off to the Australians), but that Douglas had then tried "seeking a financial contribution from Trust Bank for the Labour Party's political campaign."[164]

Thankfully, the appointed directors had the ethical sense to recognise a conflict of interest, and the board reminded Douglas that the bank's policy was not to involve itself in political campaigns.

Winston, in parliament, had asked Douglas:

"Before the last election, did he, as Minister of Finance, make any approaches to corporate bodies for party political funds when Government appointees were part of those bodies?"[165]

"No," answered Labour's Michael Cullen on Douglas' behalf.

You may be scratching your head at that given the evidence, and Peters waved the Trust Bank board resolution as proof. Michael Cullen had a lightbulb moment, essentially saying, 'Oh, you mean Mr Douglas the MP for Manurewa? Yes, he made some approaches, but not as Minister of Finance, just as a local MP'.

---

164   Board resolution of Trustee Bank Holdings Ltd, 24 July 1987
165   Hansard, Questions for Oral Answer #4, 30 September 1987

Even Bolger had piped up, wondering if Michael Cullen was seriously suggesting that government appointees on boards would have made a distinction between Roger Douglas, their boss, and Roger Douglas, local MP?

"The distinction is well known to every member of the House," affirmed Cullen.

Tricky things, politicians. Particularly when it is clear big business was setting out to buy influence in all the major elections. The central allegation that Peters made in 1992, that he felt the Roundtable was trying to compromise him with inducements to support Ruth Richardson, is probably an accurate reflection of how Peters felt, based on what we now know. The identity of the compromiser based on the evidence released to date does not appear to have been Selwyn Cushing, who promptly sued Peters for defamation.

Winston, however, wasn't backing down on the biggest campaign of his political career. As journalist David Robie put it, "Barely six months ago maverick Maori politician Winston Peters was by far the government's most popular cabinet minister. Today he is fighting for his political life."[166]

In parliament perhaps, but not out in suburbia. The willingness of Peters to speak out about secret donors tilting the level playing field of government struck a nerve not just in New Zealand but in Australia as well. Certainly the polls in New Zealand reflected it, with 81% of respondents in one survey stating they believed corruption was a factor in politics.

Inside the National Party caucus it was so cold towards Peters it made Antarctica seem like the tropics.

"You make me feel dirty, Mr Peters," snapped Police Minister John Banks, whose own political donations scandal awaited him two decades in the future. "When I walk down the streets of Whangarei, people don't know if I'm a politician or a crook."[167]

The funny thing about being perceived as a whistleblower is that you become a magnet. More people slip you notes and emails believing they've finally found someone brave enough to speak truth to power. In every sense of the phrase, Winston Peters was becoming a self-fulfilling prophecy, basking in his own afterglow.

He followed up his donations blast with new information being leaked to him about the Bank of New Zealand. A series of parliamentary ques-

---

166 "Rebel MP stirs NZ 'bribery' row," by David Robie, Green Left Weekly Australia, 1 July 1992
167 The Demon Profession, Laws, p218

tions during June were the preliminary jabs to what he hoped would be a knockout punch, which came on 30 June 1992.

The story, he said, was that Michael Fay, whilst a director of the Bank of New Zealand, summoned two BNZ loans managers to the Fay Richwhite building and asked them to rubber stamp a massive loan roll-over to his company of $42 million. This was March 1990, on the eve of the BNZ's collapse. The loan, said Peters, had questionable security and far exceeded the BNZ's loan-to-value ratio.

"Michael Fay was a director of the Bank of New Zealand with a serious conflict of interest; he was also a principal of the borrowing company that had made the application, yet he was present."[168]

"That's not correct," shouted John Banks.

"Step outside the House and say that!," echoed National MP and former policeman Ian Revell.

Once again, parliament erupted like a demented baboon troop, as the Speaker tried and failed to restore order.

"I understand members' rage when a speech of this nature is given," counselled Labour leader Mike Moore, "but I believe that we will preserve our privileges better if we hear this speech in silence."

The loan, continued Peters after a moment, "did not meet the underwriting criteria and it offended section 190 of the Companies Act, and Michael Fay was told that by the mortgage manager not once but three times." Michael Fay, he alleged, "breached his fiduciary duty" by attending the loan meetings and failing to recognise the conflict of interest. "This loan was blatantly preferential. Worse still, it is a case of a man using the Bank of New Zealand as his piggy-bank when others could not."

Attorney-General Paul East spoke next, expressing "sadness" at Peters' latest allegations.[169]

"An hour ago the Attorney-General was entertaining Sir Michael Fay," Winston accused from his backbench seat.

"That is absolutely untrue!" exclaimed East with all the outrage he could muster. "An hour ago I think that I was with the member for Mangere!"

Peters wasn't finished, accepting that maybe his timing was wrong but he knew who he'd seen:

---

168 Hansard, Perf. And Ops of SOEs, 30 June 1992
169 Ibid

"It is my vivid recollection...that he did receive Sir Michael Fay at the reception desk, maybe more than an hour ago, but this night, and the member over there is my witness."

East didn't cough to meeting Fay, but did admit he'd been working on Fay's case regarding documents Peters had tabled. "I was concerned that they might provide the basis of an allegation of wrongdoing on the part of a New Zealander was named in this parliament, so I took the time to check those documents, to discuss them...there was absolutely no substance to the claims that had been made."

The Attorney-General told parliament he could see no conflict of interest and no breach of s190 of the Companies Act, which allowed a company that someone was a director of to lend money to another company controlled by the same director, as long as the lending "is within the normal activities of that particular company."

Of course, it wasn't, on Peters' analysis, because the $42 million loan exceeded the loan-to-value ratio. And it wasn't within the normal activities of the BNZ by any other measure, either. Peters didn't know it yet, but he had just scraped the first frost off the tip of the iceberg. The BNZ's lending to companies associated with Michael Fay, its director, topped a billion dollars, and most of those loans had been hidden from auditors as "off balance sheet" transactions.

Instead, Peters was forced to endure the taunts. The BNZ, said National's Miramar MP Graeme Reeves, "has made provision for bad and doubtful debts of $2.8 billion – and the member for Tauranga focuses on a loan of some $42 million.[170]

"We heard tonight about meetings, and so on. We have no documents to substantiate those. Those documents should be tabled so that they can be challenged in the normal way that evidence would be challenged in the courts of this land. The member deals in hearsay and double hearsay. It is not good. It brings the House into disrepute. It is an abuse of the 350-year-old privilege that the member seeks to protect.

"If he has substantive evidence he should bring it before the Serious Fraud Office...anywhere but in here – and let his case be tested."

It was the same old story. Show us your evidence. Don't show us your evidence. You don't have any evidence. Show your evidence to the Serious Fraud Office.

---

170 Ibid

Fine, said Peters, we'll see about all that.

On August 4, Winston let rip on the Thin White Duke's movie, Merry Christmas Mr Lawrence, financed by unwitting investors lured into a tax scheme designed by Russell McVeagh and which was paying out – in tax breaks – an investment return of up to $2.44 for every dollar invested. Thus, a $10,000 investment returned not just the original capital but nearly $25,000 on top of that.

This was 'Wogistan' writ large on the silver screen, the unmasking of Ali Baba and his band of tax genies. Best of all, it had a link to the Bank of New Zealand:[171]

"The main perpetrators are: Robin Congreve, who invested $10,000, thereby defrauding New Zealand revenue personally of $34,400, and that is only part of the offence; Geoff Ricketts, who invested $35,000, thereby defrauding New Zealand revenue of $120,400--and, as we all know in this country, both Robin Congreve and Geoff Ricketts are directors of the Bank of New Zealand; they were running the bank in the time before the Government was required to bail it out--and the third person is Paul Carran, who invested $15,000, thereby defrauding New Zealand revenue of $51,600.

"The Inland Revenue Department determined those transactions to be a sham and that can be found in a letter, which I shall also table, dated 7 April 1988. The department wrote to the investors advising that this was its view. That information has been with the Inland Revenue Department for some time. Why has it not acted on what is clearly massive, criminal, fraudulent activity? What immunity from prosecution do those perpetrators of fraud have in this country? Is not the law in New Zealand to be applied in the same way for everybody?"

Peters was clearly gunning for the BNZ, gunning for Fay Richwhite, and gunning for senior National MPs like Remuera's Doug Graham, whose electorate chairman had been Geoff Ricketts. In short, Peters was in open war with the old boys network.

His revelations caused another firestorm of protested innocence and outrage. The allegations were "unsubstantiated". The IRD said it had investigated and "withdrawn" its fraud allegations.

Two weeks later, Winston was back with more:

"Is it true that New Zealand is Wogistan, and that what is set out by

---

171 Hansard, Appropriation Bill, 4 August 1992

allusion and implication is fact? What pressure was brought to bear on the Commissioner of Inland Revenue? Was he threatened by those two gentlemen from Russell McVeagh McKenzie Bartleet and Co.?[172]

"Oh, they're going to sue, Winnie!," exclaimed John Banks in some excitement.

"No, they are not!" barked Peters, pointing out that the moment Russell McVeagh sued they'd be liable to hand over all their secret documents under a principle known as 'discovery'.

"That is the kind of smart alec comment that the Minister of Police makes. Here is a law firm that says it has a QC and 52 partners. It told the news media 9 days ago that it was going to sue me. I rang the firm up the next morning and said: 'OK, boys, where's your writ? I want to come and pick it up.' Because when I pick it up I do not get that film; I have those documents--I get every other document of other films and other activities, just like this one. If the Minister thinks that I fear a defamation writ he is 100 percent wrong."

"They're big boys, Winnie," chuckled John Banks ominously.

"Yes, but they are not above the law. The Minister of Police says that they are big boys. There is not one law for those people and another one for the rest of the country. It is the same law."

To say there was fury towards Winston Peters in political and business circles would be understating it. Bare, naked, thermonuclear fusion would be a closer description. There were reports that National was considering harsh sanctions against the errant MP who kept on implying politics was corrupt. Peters, meanwhile, had a new person of interest to pursue.

In June 1992, young businessman Paul White had purchased a couple of boxes of old computer equipment at auction. Included in the haul were 90 floppy disks – the storage mechanism for data in the days before CD-ROM and USB sticks. When White began checking the status of the 90 disks, he found they still had information on – customer files and data that appeared to have originated from Citibank Auckland.

In July, White told Citibank he had the customer data and raised the issue of a "finder's fee", similar to the $62,000 an Australian court had ordered Brambles Australia to pay for the return of information accidentally sold.

---

172   Hansard, General Debate, 19 August 1992

White was immediately hit with a High Court injunction, but it didn't stop him meeting with and talking to National MP Winston Peters in the dark corners of nightclubs and taverns. White claimed to have evidence of a tax haven transaction involving the New Zealand Dairy Board, and other New Zealand corporates as well. There were deals involving the Cook Islands.

In the early hours of 5 September, 1992, Paul White's car slammed into an Auckland motorway bridge support, leaving him unconscious and fatally injured. Missing from the wreck was $15,000 in cash he'd been paid by Citibank in an out-of-court settlement the previous evening, and two disks it's believed he had retained in his possession. On one side of the wreck, otherwise undamaged by the crash, the rear wheel arch and panel showed horizontal scratches consistent with a nudge from another vehicle.

As news media began demanding answers from police, several new facts emerged: the involvement of Winston Peters, and the involvement of security and surveillance personnel, at one point formally identifying themselves as SIS.

When Winston Peters began asking questions in parliament, the police filed released under the Official Information Act disclosed that answers to all the important questions were secretly being provided by Citibank. Draft responses for Police Minister John Banks repeatedly showed in the space for the draft answers, "Further information will be obtained from Citibank".

Police, who supposedly had the Citibank disks in their possession after they raided White's storage unit, didn't even know the identity of the Citibank computer expert they had then permitted to examine and possibly manipulate the data on the disks.

By the time the disks got to the Serious Fraud Office, 35 of them were blank.

Police Minister John Banks told the media there was nothing on the disks of any substance, and Winston Peters said SFO official Phil Roigard had confirmed Banks – who was not minister of the SFO – "had been briefed".

That made the ears of Labour's Richard Prebble prick up. Not normally a Winston fan, he even passed up his almost weekly chance to drag up the Cook Strait ferry incident, and said Winston had some valid questions:[173]

"Does a person named Phil Roigard work for the Serious Fraud Office? Has he been contacted, and how much did that cost? Did he say to the

---

173 Hansard, Appropriation Bill, 17 September 1992

member for Tauranga that the Minister of Police had been briefed, and, if so, how does the Minister of Police square that off with answers that have been given in the House that clearly have led the House to believe that the Minister of Police had not been briefed by the Serious Fraud Office?"

"It's ships scraping the bottom," interjected Banks hopefully.

"Is it as bad as that?" replied Prebble hesitantly [Interruption.] "I refuse to get side-tracked by Cook Strait. What sort of briefing was given? The Minister of Police has publicly assured the nation that there was nothing on the tapes... However, it then turns out that the Minister of Police made that statement without having had a briefing. How can the Minister make such a statement if he did not get a briefing?

"It seems to me that the Minister of Police is hopelessly compromised. Either he has been assuring the public without having had a briefing--in which case, what faith can the House now have in that assurance--or, alternatively, he did get a briefing, in which case how could the House be told by both Ministers, or be led to believe, that the Minister of Police did not get a briefing? That seems to me to be a matter that ought to be cleared up, and that ought to be cleared up now," said Prebble.

Once again, Winston Peters had managed to get himself embroiled in a plot worthy of a major motion picture, and at the same time was successfully embarrassing his ministerial colleagues

The soil was barely dry on Paul White's grave before the National Party decided enough was enough. When Prime Minister Bolger asked, "who will rid us of this turbulent priest", fifty hands in the 62-member caucus shot up.

Winston Peters was expelled as a member of the National caucus on 1 October 1992. Now, it was open war.

13

Mutually Assured Destruction

"At my signal, unleash hell."

– Gladiator

There was absolutely no let up in the dirt that Peters was now prepared to dump on the government. "Put up or shut up," Bolger had told him. Well, on October 15, Peters didn't opt to 'shut up'. In his hand as he entered Parliament's debating chamber was an affidavit, sworn that day by Dr Larry Johnson, a California-educated lawyer, banker and commercial property valuer who'd worked at the BNZ on "helping clean up the mess".

At least, that was his old job. By the time he swore the affidavit, Johnson had been bankrupted by Marac Finance – at that stage a Fay Richwhite subsidiary – and had all his property mortgages held by his former employer, the Bank of New Zealand, foreclosed and ordered repaid immediately. His problems had started in June 1990, three months after he attended that meeting with Michael Fay about his building mortgage application.

"In the course of this discussion Sir Michael Fay became highly agitated and I was called a 'little effing God'. I personally advised Sir Michael Fay that he had a conflict of interest as he had his customer's hat on and asked what would he do when he put on his director's hat."[174]

"I told him that I was hired to clean up some of the mess at the Bank of New Zealand and now he was arranging his own loan which would be

---

174 Hansard, Appropriation Bill, 15 October 1992

far in excess of the loan to value ratios that had currently been fixed by the full board of the Bank of New Zealand, and that what he was doing involved a major conflict of interest. At this stage Sir Michael Fay became very irate and told me that it was quote 'my effing bank', and 'I will do anything I want to'."

The reason for Fay's displeasure is that he was seeking a $42 million dollar loan against a $55 million dollar security in a commercial building in a falling property market, when the BNZ rules were to go no higher than 50% loan-to-value on commercial property.

There was an aggravating factor, said Johnson – Fay Richwhite's total borrowing from the bank was far higher than Reserve Bank policy, and he was asking Fay questions "in respect of the $900 million current exposure that Fay Richwhite and associated interests had with the Bank of New Zealand."

There's a general rule of thumb in banking which, adapted to the problem at hand, goes like this: if you owe the Bank $900,000, the bank owns you. If you owe the Bank $900 million, you own the bank, because the pain for the bank if you failed to repay would be excruciating.

Johnson's affidavit was the first sworn evidence putting Michael Fay, as a director of the BNZ, in the room asking for special loan approval for his personal companies in a manner than bank staff allege was not acting in the best interests of the BNZ. Which of course, is where the conflict of interest arose, between his duty to steward the bank responsibly, and his personal desire to borrow more money.

"The following day I was summoned to a meeting at the Bank of New Zealand Tower. At the meeting were Sir Michael Fay's Financial Advisers, Mr Peter Thodey, a very senior officer of the bank; Jonathan Arthur, lawyers from Russell McVeagh, Roger Kennedy, and myself.

"Roger Kennedy and Peter Thodey asked me to step inside Mr Thodey's personal office. Once inside Thodey advised me he had received a phone call from Sir Michael Fay saying: I was 'being unco-operative given the time restrictions to make the deal work.' He stated: 'We can't let Michael Fay fall.' He told me that if I would sign off the loan as proposed, and anything happened to me, that the bank would be right behind me."

In the end the bank was so far behind Johnson it couldn't be seen when the shooting started and in fact there was good reason to believe some of the bullets hitting him in the back had come from the general direction of the bank. Johnson testified that he refused to sign off on the loan, but Fay got it anyway, and very soon after that Johnson's $200,000 a year job (in 1990 dollars) was terminated, leaving him unable to pay his bills. The BNZ cancelled his cheap staff low interest loan, jacked the mortgage up to market rates then demanded immediate payment of the full mortgage sum. And as stated, a Fay Richwhite owned finance company pushed Johnson all the way to bankruptcy.

Michael Fay hit back with a statement calling Winston Peters "a liar and a coward" and he gave indemnity to TV3 from any defamation suit if we ran the comment. Peters didn't react.[175]

The renegade MP opened fire from a second barrel, disclosing Cook Islands tax haven documents suggesting the BNZ had used a shell company in the Cooks pretending to be an insurance company, to hide its real financial losses from investors and taxpayers. This, of course, was fraud. The deal was called a "Captive insurance scheme", and it hid key financial information from auditors.

The documents themselves were damning:

"The insurance policy that is being taken out will ensure that the BNZ Group need not show the total extent of the write off of doubtful debts in their accounts in the present financial year and thus affect their financial position."[176]

Don't forget, shareholders had made purchasing and investment decisions on the basis of those official accounts. The National Government called it "more conspiracy theory" and invited Peters, "take it to the Serious Fraud Office". In taking that stand, the MPs sent a message to voters that Peters was right. Hundreds of thousands of small business owners knew that fudging your accounts could get you sent to jail, but here were the big boys getting away with it and calling it "profit smoothing". Any MP defending this kind of behaviour, they thought, probably was a 'crook', as John Banks had succinctly put it.

All the while, Winston Peters' public approval kept skyrocketing. He may have skewered his chances of being New Zealand's first Maori Prime Minister, but New Zealanders loved the fact he was prepared to put his

---

175 I wasn't surprised at Michael Fay's alleged ruthlessness. When I later wrote *The Paradise Conspiracy* I discovered Fay had hired former police inspector John Hughes to arrange for the manuscript to be stolen, and he then threatened publishing companies not to handle the book.
176 Hansard, General Debate, 7 October 1992

career and reputation on the line for what he believed.

One of the first to make contact with the exiled Peters after his 1 October expulsion was National Party Waikato-based electorate chairman Doug Woolerton. As soon as he heard Peters had been booted out, Woolerton wrote and offered his services:

"I said to him, 'look, you know, I'm leaving National as well, I'm pissed off with them too.' It was Jenny Shipley and Ruth Richard running amok and slashing benefits in a time of high unemployment if you recall. It was just total bloody madness and caused a bit of a recession as it was always going to.

"I said 'look, if I can help you either inside the National party or outside, give us a yell,' and heard nothing back – as is his way."

That silence at Peters' end was probably because he was still reviewing his options. Initially, he'd hoped to stay with National, seek the nomination for Tauranga and stand for National in the 1993 election. Around him, other 'rebel' MPs like Hamish McIntyre and Gilbert Myles, who'd formed the Liberal Party, urged Peters to make a clean break with National. There were discussions too with National's Brian Neeson and Peter McCardle, and of course Winston's brother Ian. Michael Laws was also part of that picture:[177]

"I approached him with the suggestion of leading a breakaway party into the next election," says Laws. "We were reasonably confident that Winston could garner seven or eight MPs for a 'New National' type party that might tap into disaffected National supporters but also cross over and gain support from potential Labour voters.

"A huge credibility gap had opened up in New Zealand politics, with both major parties not just disliked but distrusted and even despised. Winston could fill that void. This was the moment, all right. It just needed the right man."

Plan A for Winston was a legal challenge to the expulsion from caucus. Overall, it failed. But he didn't call Michael Laws, for which the latter was "bitterly" disappointed. He wrote of Peters lacking "the greatest attribute of leadership. Vision…the man did not just lack the will, he lacked the imagination."[178]

No, it wasn't Laws receiving the phone call, it was Doug Woolerton.

---

177 The Demon Profession, Laws, supra, p223
178 The Demon Profession, supra, p224

" He rang me and said 'look, I want to send a couple of guys over to see you'."

Winston explained that he was considering resigning from Parliament and standing as an independent. "He was cagey as buggery," Woolerton colourfully recalls. "He was really cagey. He's never any different, you know? There was never any name, 'New Zealand First' or anything like that, that came a lot later."

Part of Peters' caginess might have been his suspicions of being under surveillance over the Paul White/BNZ/Winebox/Film and Bloodstock fraud allegations. Woolerton agrees that's possible, but adds, "was he more cagey than usual? I dunno – he's always bloody cagey."

The lack of detail initially meant a lack of action:

"With a lot of things with Winston, it either continues or it doesn't, you know? And he doesn't actually tell you much on the way through."

Events had crystallised. The National Party in March 1993 vetoed Peters' selection as a National candidate. Peters decided to resign from parliament and seek a fresh mandate from the Tauranga voters. The writing was on the wall, and the abuse was in parliament:

"This by-election is a great waste of time," said Justice Minister Doug Graham. "It is a waste of time to this Chamber; it is a waste of time to the taxpayer; it serves no useful purpose whatever; and it is nothing more than an ego-trip by a former member of Parliament, who, on his own desserts, has found himself in a situation in which he has been disowned by his own people. What has happened – "

"He's been assassinated in a secret meeting," quipped long time Peters-baiter Richard Prebble.

"That is something, coming from the original jackal," retorted Graham. "I conclude by saying this: It's not very difficult to get your name in lights if that's what you want to do, and nothing else. All you have to do is to attack everybody around you and claim that you're speaking as the sole torch of humanity. That is what the former member for Tauranga did and he did it extraordinarily well, and he looks extraordinarily convincing. The trouble is that there is nothing below it, nothing there at all, and I rather suspect that the public will come to that conclusion before much longer."

"Government members have been happy to use this debate to slag off at the former member for Tauranga," jeered Labour's Michael Cullen across the chamber.¹⁷⁹ "Government members have been happy to attack him under the privilege of Parliament. It is worth reminding the people of Tauranga and the people of New Zealand that Government members were happy to license the former member for Tauranga as the mud-thrower extraordinaire when they were in Opposition. They were happy for him to take the bucket from the present member for Hawke's Bay and tip the contents all over whoever happened to be passing underneath. They were happy for him to lead the charge to wind up the redneck vote against Maori in this country and to be the leading anti-Maori Maori in New Zealand."

Helen Clark, then Deputy Opposition Leader under Mike Moore, was full of praise for Winston:

"The Minister of Justice said that the member for Tauranga had set out to denigrate his party and its policies. But members here remember how hard the member for Tauranga campaigned for that party and its policies. We remember. He was a real trooper. He went up and down the country. He fought for the elderly. He fought for the students not to have to pay those fees. He fought for the health policies. He put the effort in, and his putting that effort in and then reminding the Government of what it had promised and not delivered on was what did it for him."

National's John Luxton on the other hand was scathing, comparing Peters to Old Nick:

"He portrays himself as a paragon of virtue – the shining knight, the Prince of Darkness – and the only honest member in the House. That is the extent of the dishonesty in the public perception of the former member."¹⁸⁰

Luxton lashed out at Winston's previous 'conspiracy theories':

"The former member for Tauranga always had to focus on a villain. That villain was always unearthed in this House... We had the scraping of the bottom of the Cook Strait ferry, the incompetence of the Bank of New Zealand, the Maori loans, the Russian submarines, and the Mikhail Lermontov."

If Prime Minister Jim Bolger's ears suddenly stood upright at the mention of "Russian submarines", and a nervous look crossed his face, there was good reason. He'd recently had an offer from the Russians to supply him with a nuclear submarine if NZ agreed to wipe Russia's debts to the Dairy Board.

---

179 Hansard, By-election Tauranga, 18 March 1993
180 Hansard, Ibid

"Having spent my prime ministership explaining why I was keeping US nuclear-powered submarines out of New Zealand waters, how could I explain to the voters that I had bought a Russian one?," he later confessed in 1998.[181]

Right now, Bolger needed Winston Peters getting a whiff of the Nats being offered a Russian submarine like he needed a hole in the head. Memo to caucus, let's ease up on that whole 'Russian subs' gag…

National's Doug Graham had predicted Peters' star would fade fast. The voters of Tauranga had other things in mind.

Still in the mix, and they had been since Peters' sacking as a cabinet minister in late 1991, was Jim Anderton's Alliance. Already a hodge-podge of five small parties, Anderton had made overtures to Peters, probably figuring *a la* Lyndon B. Johnson that it was better to have Winston "inside the tent, pissing out, than outside the tent, pissing in."

Ruth Richardson's former disciple Martin Hames described it as an attempted arranged marriage which neither bride nor groom had any real intention of consummating. They "knew they needed to be seen to make an attempt to explore common ground," said Hames, but it was mostly about "form" rather than substance.[182] Winston, he wrote, had dragged his heels and wanted to know how the constituent parties could be legally bound so they couldn't waka-jump after the election. Peters had a vision of his name being used as a drawcard to get the "Alliance" elected into Parliament, only to have the parties breakaway after hitching a ride in on his coattails.

History shows Peters had good reason to be concerned about the stability of the Alliance, and he was the cause of part of that.

While Winston Peters concentrated on winning his seat back as an independent, Doug Woolerton offered to begin sounding out others who might be prepared to join a new party after the by-election, and Winston in turn sent a couple of his Tauranga officials over to go through the nuts and bolts. By the end of their brainstorming, Woolerton was hooked. "We just rolled on from there and I became the first president."

It was a massive leap into the unknown. Woolerton had been a true-blue Nat, joining the party at the age of 21 when MP Katherine O'Regan

---

181 "A View From The Top," by Jim Bolger, Viking, 1998
182 Winston First, by Martin Hames, Random House, 1995, p187

nudged him to become involved in politics. "O'Regan got me involved delivering pamphlets or something bloody dreadful and then I did all the usual things and was involved with Simon Upton and met Ruth Richardson through him."

He remembers Don Brash's ill-fated attempt to win the East Coast Bays seat for National, and also recalls going "to a couple of seminars where that mad bastard Alan Gibbs was promoting the new right, it was all in those days. They fingered a few of us to go along."

But Woolerton found the New Right economic agenda didn't sit well with him and he kept waiting for someone to notice his cynicism: "I was pretty sure they would have unfingered me quite quickly."

Instead, he had continued to rise through the ranks, becoming Simon Upton's electorate chairman. Woolerton was a spectator "when they sacked Muldoon and all of the mad stuff back then", although he says the minutiae of political history escapes him. "I'm hopeless with bloody dates. As soon as I've done something I close the book, chuck everything away, and move on, which is not a very good thing to do for history but it's a bloody great thing for your state of mind, I can tell you."

Like Peters, Woolerton had found National's lurch to the right with 'Ruthanasia' distasteful, and the Doug and Winnie show was a match made in political heaven.

"I knew it would be successful because, you know, you've got to have a charismatic leader to start a political party. You know that's the first thing. You can see this with Dotcom. With Dotcom and Hone and co, whether you like them, or whether you don't like them doesn't matter, but you've got to have the political X factor, you know? You've got it in publishing, you go where other people fear to tread, it's all those things.

"People like that are actually a bloody nightmare day to day, and you're no doubt a nightmare yourself, I don't know, but you've got to have somebody. If they're just run of the mill then they don't want to be a political leader, do they?

"So I know one when I see one and I know how political parties work and I've watched them."

For Woolerton, proof of Winston Peters' potential X-factor came in the initial polls following his expulsion by National.

"He was hinting at doing something, and I think those polls got up at like 20 something per cent."

In fact, it went much higher as polls taken after the decision to call a by-election showed:[183]

Winston Peters has the support of most of the public to stand as an independent candidate for Tauranga if the National Party hierarchy dumps him.

The latest National Business Review-Consultus poll, conducted last weekend gives the rebel MP 85% support to go it alone if the party's national executive rejects his nomination for the blue-ribbon seat. Only 7% say he should not stand as an independent and 8% are unsure.

The strong support for Mr Peters, unprecedented since the public adoration in the 1930s for Labour Prime Minister Michael Savage, is reflected in response to other his questions polled.

Nearly two in three New Zealanders – 64% – believe he should receive the National Party nomination for Tauranga compared with – 23% who feel the party should choose another candidate. His overall approval rating, too, far out-strips support for the leaders of the three main parties and has barely been affected by the latest controversy.

Some 61% say they approve of him, down only a point on a similar poll in December. His highest showing was 69% 11 months ago.

Twenty-two per cent of those polled say they disapprove of him, down four points on December, though the unsure vote has risen five points to 17% in the same period.

Mr Peters' approval is strongest among pensioners and those earning $25,000 or less a year. Clear majorities of supporters of all political parties give him their backing though the margin of support from National voters is less than for Labour and minor party supporters.

* The nationwide poll conducted by Insight Research, randomly surveyed 750 people aged 18 and over. It has a margin of error of 3.5%.

The precedent, for both Winston and Woolerton, had been provided by Bruce Beetham with Social Credit and Bob Jones with the New Zealand Party ten years earlier, in 1983/84. Both men had harnessed the protest vote to a massive degree. Could Winston do the same? He kept hinting at a new party, and the polls kept rising:

"I think it came close to 30 per cent which is just bloody off the wall," recalls Woolerton, who initially had wondered whether Peters could

---

[183] "Public backs independent Peters" by Graeme Hunt, The National Business Review, 5 Mar 1993, Page 7

achieve change by staying in the National Party. "I always knew it would be a success but I actually was in favour of rejigging the National party and getting rid of all the bloody right wing Nazis of those days. But he said, nah, nah, he didn't want to go there."

On Saturday 17 April, Peters romped home with 11,458 votes. Labour did not contest the by election because it wanted Peters to win and for National to stew in its own juices. Instead, the McGillicuddy Serious Party came second, which may sound impressive but quickly loses its sheen with the actual figure: 271 votes.

That was Winston Peters' majority in Tauranga, more than 11,000 votes. He had taken more than 90% of all votes cast. For a star quickly fading, it was shining brighter than expected – much to National's chagrin.

Election night was most widely remembered for National MP Michael Laws getting drunk and dissing his boss Jim Bolger, answering "who cares?" when a journalist asked whether he thought Bolger would mind him showing up to support Peters.

Nonetheless, even in a chardonnay-infused haze, Laws still managed to predict what others were loathe to but secretly feared:

"Hawkes Bay MP Michael Laws said this week he believed a Winston Peters-led party was inevitable, after the Tauranga MP's re-election as an independent this week.

"Mr Laws, whose public support for Mr Peters earned him a sharp rebuke from his caucus colleagues this week, predicted Mr Peters would emerge as a powerful force under mixed member proportional representation."[184]

Publicly, Peters was saying no such thing, and Laws was not part of the inner circle that knew. Indeed, Laws was chuffed when Peters later fulfilled his off-the-cuff predictions. The *NBR* newspaper noted Peters was staying mum on "overtures" from the Alliance's Jim Anderton and Gilbert Myles, but it quoted him appealing for donations, as long as he didn't know who they were from and therefore was not morally compromised:

"New Zealand got into its current political problems over non-accountability and non-delivery of straight-forward political commitments because of corporate supporters. It distorted the will of New Zealanders because of corporate funding.

"But if there's a corporate body that wishes anonymously to commit funds

---

184 "Peters won't say no to war funds," The National Business Review, 23 Apr 1993, Page 15

for this campaign it would be welcome. It has to be without my knowledge."

Instead of commenting further, Winston and Doug Woolerton pushed ahead with closely-guarded plans to launch a new political party, NZ First. And the polls kept climbing:

Tauranga's new independent MP Winston Peters is playing guessing games on whether he plans to form his own party, despite the support of nearly a third of respondents to the latest poll.[185]

A One Network News Heylen poll on Wednesday put public support for the hypothetical party at 31%, behind Labour on 34% but well ahead of National at 22% and the Alliance on 11%.

Mr Peters' only prediction was that "the National Party is finished".

The poll result comes as party members gather in Masterton and Hamilton tonight for the Waikato and Wellington divisional conferences.

Veteran journalist and political analyst Bob Edlin intimated the poll was earthshaking for National:[186]

"Peters would find himself at the head of a party strong enough to nudge the Nats into third place. According to the responses, almost half the Alliance's supporters would flock to his banner and collapse the Alliance's support to just 11%. Labour's support would dwindle by 11 percentage points and National by seven percentage points. In the resultant shake-out, the Peters Party would command 31% support.

"Thus the Peters Party would be running close behind Labour (on 34%), with National far back in third place (22%) and the Alliance a distant fourth."

Michael Laws might have accused Peters of missing "the moment", but Inside the Beehive, National Party strategists were desperate to find a way to neutralise the Peters factor, if they were to avoid a drubbing at the upcoming election.

Over in NZ First, they were just desperate.

Woolerton reckons Peters was ambivalent about party structure.

"I don't know whether he really wanted a party with the representatives and electorates and branches and all of those sort of things. He was more in a mind of a movement or something, but I knew if he had to do that – we never had any arguments about it – but I just said, 'look, if you're going to do this you've got to do it properly.' He agreed. I always

---
185 "Peters remains quiet on own party plans" The National Business Review, 7 May 1993, Page 2
186 "Pied Piper of Tauranga whistles up popularity", by Bob Edlin, The Independent, 7 May 1993, Page 11

felt that all of that humdrum stuff was a bit of a pain in the butt for him, which it probably was.

"So, he used to have these rallies which he used to get hundreds and hundreds of people along. I used to hate them because it required motivating heaps of people and making sure there were at least some people there in case crowds didn't turn up. What do they call it? Bussing people in they call it. In those days we didn't have the ability to bus people in, it was just about getting the word out."

It was a hand to mouth existence for the fledgling party organisation. Fliers had to be printed, and paid for.

"Various people would give him a bit of dough and he'd spend it on advertising and things like that, and that's how it started. But those things, they were pretty vibey, it was all bloody go."

Doug Woolerton much prefers a backroom role to stardom.

"I don't like big hoopla and fuss, I'm uncomfortable with it. My nature leads me more to organisation, back room sort of chitty chats and all that sort of thing, rather than the big public thing which he is so good at. Those were a phenomenon of the time, but they weren't my cup of tea. But, you know, you had to do your bit."

The next big target after winning the by-election was the launch of NZ First itself. The name had been stolen from a slogan used by the Liberal Party, but it encapsulated what the party stood for.

"What it stood for in those days," drawls Woolerton, "and I used to have this argument in caucus all of the time when I was there and still would today if I was there, which I'm not, but your mate Prosser is and he probably has the same argument, I don't know, but what it stood for is almost, we used to toss the campaign slogans around all of the time, but it was sort of a uniquely New Zealand thing. Quite nationalistic but none of the hand on heart like the Americans.

"It was the ability to, and this is never written of course, the ability for the average man, it might be old fashioned but it's a worthy aim even today, for the average man to be able to have a tinny and go down and catch a fish, to have any old sort of whare or bach or crib, whatever you want to call it, to be able to have access to all of those things and to get a feed and to look after the family without having a huge wage. So somebody, a labourer, can do all of those things."

In other words, it was about nurturing the New Zealand that people remembered; a bit working class, but an honest day's work for an honest day's pay. A place where you could aspire to and still reach your dreams.

Did that make New Zealand First racist? Many critics argued it did, but that raises a big philosophical argument: does a culture in its own homeland have the right to try and protect its culture and way of life? To argue 'no' is to accept the central doctrine of globalisation – that national borders should be abolished and New Zealand should open its doors to as many immigrants from as many diverse cultures as want to come here. After all, New Zealand is similar in size to Japan and Britain, with populations of 127 million and 65 million respectively. Clearly we are not doing our bit to house the third world's teeming millions with a population of only 4.5 million here.

Hand in hand with the free migration policy goes the democracy policy –one migrant one vote. New Zealand is one of the few countries in the world where non-citizens are given the right to vote, and influence elections and through them migration policy. It can become a self-sustaining cycle of change.

Official figures tell a story, and we may in fact have passed beyond the point of no return. Of the 3.4 million adults living in New Zealand in 2010, virtually half – 1.6 million – were either migrants or NZ-born children of a migrant.[187] That's a massive change from the demography of the 1970s, and it happened while we were sleeping.

It's not hard to see how it happened, though. Our natural population increase by birth has been artificially depressed because of abortions. One in every three pregnancies today ends in a termination, around 18,000 deaths a year. Regardless of one's views about the right to choose, the objective fact very simply is that abortion is the single largest killer of New Zealanders – bigger than cancer, bigger than heart disease, much bigger than the road toll and around one to two thousand times larger than the death rate from child abuse.

The reason there's a massive blip of ageing baby-boomers looking to collect pensions and burden our health system is because the free-love baby-boom generation didn't want kids cramping their lifestyles. The flipside of not having as many children is that you end up not having enough working-age taxpayers funding the welfare state that the baby-

---

187 http://nzdotstat.stats.govt.nz/wbos/index.aspx?datasetcode=TABLECODE7930#

boomers rely on. To make up for the lack of young workers, New Zealand and other Western countries have now become net importers of labour via migration.

None of these facts about migration or termination are included here as value judgements; they simply are the explanation for why things stand as they do today. Importing migrants is happening across the Western world for the same reasons.

In New Zealand's case, the media and politicians normally talk about "net migration" – that's the pool of migrants who remain in New Zealand over and above the portion of people who leave the country each year. Net migration, however, is a misleading term in itself because it tends to mask the size of the inflow. In the year to April 30, 2014, for example, net migration was 34,400, but in actual fact 98,800 immigrants arrived in New Zealand – that's a rate of around a million new faces a decade[188]. The difference of 64,000 people is made up of those New Zealanders leaving for medium to long term residency or study overseas. Like boomerangs, however, many of those end up coming back. To be fair, a chunk of the total immigrant pool are returning New Zealanders.

What cannot be avoided, however, is that New Zealand's population has skyrocketed from three million in the 1980s to more than 4.5 million today, and in a country with a birth rate barely replacing the death rate, that increase in population is almost entirely due to foreign migration.

This, then, is the context in which NZ First was set. This was a party, argued Winston Peters, trying to preserve a unique New Zealand culture, the ¼ acre section, the bach at Christmas, the 'kia ora/hail fellow, well met' attitude. If New Zealand truly was Middle Earth, NZ First would be the hobbit party.

Winston, of course, would be Gandalf.

His initial attempt at political wizardry fell a little flat however. With the polls showing support for a Winston-led party running at 31%, Peters booked the Alexandra Park Racecourse in Auckland for the mid-winter launch of NZ First on 18 July 1993. He had every reason to hope for a massive turnout. Between five and ten thousand people were expected.

It didn't work out as planned. Radio Pacific arranged to carry Winston's

---

188 "Kiwis moving to Australia at record low, pushing NZ's net migration near to all-time high", by Suze Metherell, NBR 21 May, 2014

speech live on air nationwide. Thousands of disgruntled elderly Winston supporters realised they could save themselves the busfare and the cold, and simply stay cosy at home with the radio turned up loud.

In the interim, the Alliance had finally pulled the plug on "negotiations" with Winston, just a week before Peters planned launch of NZ First.[189] There was no going back.

Around two thousand people turned up, big enough to fill the Auckland Town Hall, but nowhere near big enough to fill a grandstand, and the TV media that I worked for made much of the empty seats even though any other of New Zealand's political leaders would have struggled to fill a room with 200 people in those times.

Peters explained to his audience that NZ First would begin moves to abolish the superannuation surtax – a hated extra charge on pensioners who'd saved for their retirement, whereas those who'd blown their fortunes on wine women and song had been allowed to collect the full government pension. Peters didn't go the full monty on the policy, however, opting to make it conditional on investors investing in the NZ markets rather than offshore markets. It is significant that Peters did not vote against the surtax when it was introduced in 1991 – perhaps feeling bound by collective cabinet responsibility as a minister at the time.

He also promised a full inquiry via an anti-corruption commission into the billion dollar taxpayer bailout of the Bank of New Zealand. These of course, had been National Party policies at the 1990 election but National had refused to honour them.

Michael Laws would later accuse Peters of offering nothing new:[190]

"Instead of promoting innovative and exciting methods of democratic representation, Winston had instead resurrected the much-abused and now neglected National Party manifesto of the previous election as some kind of political nirvana. His answers lay in a mythical past."

Peters, of course, would argue differently. The manifesto of 1990 had not been put into place, its policies were still those of a yet-to-be-realised future. As for "exciting methods of democratic representation", Peters' views were well and truly on the record already.

---

189 "Double Decision: The 1993 Election And Referendum In New Zealand," by Jack Vowles and Peter Aimer, VUP, 1994, pp384-385
190 The Demon Profession, Laws, p 233

"When in power that party practised the tyranny of the few," Peters had lectured Labour during one heated parliamentary debate on electoral reform. "Nobody got a say. A small handful of men – about five – ran the country, ignored Cabinet, ignored caucus, ignored the party, and ignored the whole country. That is why it has 28 members tonight."[191]

"It has 29," interjected Labour's Larry Sutherland.

"Sorry," grinned Peters, not missing a beat, "it has 29 members who are despairing, lost, beaten."

The cure for such manipulation of power, he said, was to introduce proportional representation.

"By December 1992 we will fulfil our promise to the people. We will have true electoral reform. We will put to the masters of Parliament – the people of New Zealand – an opportunity to give their expression on electoral reform and proportional representation. The public will decide for the first time since 1893 the shape, form, and future of our democracy. That is a worthy promise."

As of party launch in mid 1993, the referendum for proportional representation was well and truly in place – the final version was to be held in concert with the 1993 general election that November

Indeed, commentator Patrick Smellie noted in a column for the Independent a fortnight after the launch that "Peters' big game is MMP reform" and "citizens' initiated referenda – a significant part of the Peters platform". Significantly, Smellie had filed these launch policies under a headline reading, "The Kook Problem", illustrating how anti-establishment some in the media viewed Peters. Today, MMP and referenda are part of life.[192]

"It is unclear how successfully Peters will make the transition from knocker to would-be statesman," said Smellie, "if he starts articulating fringe policies and attracting significant numbers of fringe group supporters."

Smellie – formerly one of Roger Douglas' press secretaries – began his piece asking the question "Does the Emperor have no clothes?". His reason for asking was a small snapshot poll by Heylen Research for TVNZ's Eyewitness that Smellie described as a "blow for Peters".

---

191 Hansard, Proportional Representation debate, 20 February 1991
192 "Peters the populist poll-axed but unbowed," by Patrick Smellie, The Independent, 23 July 1993, p12

The poll, he said, "sowed the seeds of doubt for many about Peters' ability to go on forever…could be the early harbinger of what his political opponents have hardly dared hope: that his bubble would eventually burst and that he will be a spent force by the election."

Smellie conceded that it was only a small poll, and a very early poll taken immediately after the NZ First launch, and that as Winston said larger polls taken two to four weeks later would be much more important than the "12% benchmark" Smellie quoted.

Even as the ink was drying on Smellie's article, Winston was already being proved right. Rival business paper the *NBR* published its own NBR/Consultus poll the same morning,[193] undertaken by Insight Research. It was a much larger poll with a sample of 750 people and a margin of error of +/- 3.5%.

Far from a poor showing, the bigger poll clocked NZ First at 24%, close behind Labour on 29% and National on 33%. Jim Anderton's Alliance was a distant fourth on 13%.

The Emperor adjusted his coiffed hair, brushed a speck of dust off the Italian suit, and took the stage with a grin to show he was indeed fully clothed. Not only that, but he led the preferred Prime Minister rankings on 28%, ahead of Labour's Mike Moore on 24% and Bolger on 15%. An hour can be a long time in political journalism, and it was one of the earliest examples in his NZ First incarnation of an attempt to write off Peters too soon.

Surprisingly, Peters wasn't cannibalising National's support, but Labour's, with NBR commenting "the poll shows a Peters party cutting savagely into the Alliance and Labour heartland support among the lower paid."

Just how savagely became clear from a closer examination of the figures. In a previous poll, 43% of households with a main breadwinner earning less than $15,000 supported Labour, and 39% supported the Alliance. Only 16% supported National.

Fast forward to this first poll of the NZ First era, and 45% of sub 15K homes had switched allegiance to NZ First, halving Labour's support to 20% and gutting the Alliance down to a wispy 14% support in its supposed voter heartland. Ironically, National had increased its share of low income voters to 20%.

---

193 "Peters front-runner in prime minister stakes", by Vernon Small, NBR, 23 July 1993, p4

As the most active political leader attacking big business and political corruption, Winston Peters had found an unexpected core of support from what Aussie commentators call "little battlers".

This was a torpedo heading directly for the Labour Party. Labour had earlier gloated that the launch of NZ First would offer "a home for National Party people who would never vote Labour but can't stand the present government. That helps Labour,"[194] said strategist Pete Hodgson. Hodgson was now forced to watch helplessly as Peters mowed down Labour's patch of grass and raced off with the clippings. This wasn't in the script!

Labour could only wait and see whether Hodgson's prediction would hold out long term; that the low-paid dalliance with NZ First was just a short term protest vote against Labour and a reflection that Peters was more likely to gain influence than Jim Anderton's Alliance. People like a success story, and at that point in time Winston Peters was a success story. If Hodgson was right, of course, then Peters' support was likely to taper off the closer they got to an election and people had to make a real choice.

Peters threw a news conference on 21 July, the Wednesday following his party's Sunday launch. Unfortunately he had little to say. He refused to name anyone who was a member of the new party and told journalists details would be revealed "in due course". There was to be a six member "interim committee" who he couldn't name either. One, I knew, was Brian Henry, but Peters wasn't talking. How had the "secret six" – as one journo dubbed them – been chosen? Equally cryptically Peters replied, the same way any "founding fathers" were.

It made it seem like Peters had something to hide:

"For an MP who has made so much mileage out of openness and democracy, the whole exercise looked curious," wrote Vernon Small.[195]

For most of his previous career, Winston Peters had been a darling of the news media. That was largely because of his charm and his willingness to feed journalists a good story every once in a while. He wasn't above sharing a drink with a few either. While Peters had been a core member of the National Party he'd been treated with media respect for the most part. As a rogue independent campaigning on big business and political corruption, the respect had wound down a notch. The spin coming from

---

194 "Labour the prime loser as NZ First party is born", by Vernon Small, NBR, 23 July 1993, p15
195 ibid

the major parties was that Peters had "gone feral", was "off the reservation", a "paranoid conspiracy theorist".

This new willingness of the media to begin pricking Peters' bubble had begun prior to the death of Paul White in the Citibank case, and escalated after it. Lacking the intellectual firepower or the resource to actually investigate complex tax haven financial dealings themselves, the media were reliant on spin doctors and Bolger's spinners were better than Winston. As commentator Colin James wrote, Peters could be hard to understand at the best of times:[196]

"For a quick lesson in the interview style that has infuriated the parliamentary press gallery, read a transcript of his press conference of July 21 or of his interview with Kim Hill on Radio New Zealand the next day. This device leads him into non sequiturs[197] and inconsistencies."

What commentators did not factor in, however, was the impact of surveillance on Winston Peters. It had become blindingly obvious to those of us working on the Winebox and Citibank investigations – Jenni McManus and Warren Berryman at the Independent, Fran O'Sullivan at the NBR and myself – that an incredibly high level of cloak and dagger spookery was going on. Peters' phone calls were being monitored; the offices of his lawyer had been broken into and searched. As the old joke goes, "It's not paranoia if they're really after you".[198]

For Winston Peters, that meant a philosophy straight out of the X-Files: "Trust no one". If you can imagine being interrogated by a Palestinian who thinks you are an Israeli spy, that pretty much describes Peters' attitude to the news media as relationships progressively worsened.

Winston Peters is a politician who doesn't suffer fools gladly. The media had just seen two thousand people turn up to the party launch at Alexandra Park, clearly the event had not been arranged and orchestrated by pixies, yet here they were, questioning him as if he had no support and no infrastructure, and wanting him to name names. The last thing Winston wanted was to disclose his inner circle to the people already watching everything he did.

---

196 "Will this party really put New Zealand first?", by Colin James, Management Magazine, September 1993, p90
197 A statement that doesn't make logical sense, it doesn't flow.
198 Enemy of the State movie, 1998

It all lent an air of utter surrealism to proceedings.

"More than any other politician," wrote Smellie, "he watches the media like a hawk and strikes back hard – sometimes justifiably, sometimes not… the cumulative effect has often been to make reportage critical of Peters less likely and more wary, while breeding resentment.

"When the tide turns against Peters in the media," said Smellie with what turned out to be a high degree of foresight, "and there were signs of that in this week's acrimonious press conference, he will face an additional, significant hurdle in the few short months to this election and beyond."

There were signs all right, and when it happened, it had all the sizzle of a sex scandal, minus the actual sex.

14

The Sarah Neems Mystery

> "Women hate revolutions and revolutionists. They like men who are docile, and well-regarded at the bank, and never late at meals"
> – H L Mencken, *Prejudices*

As August began in the race to the 6 November election, the polls were all over the place. The CM Research poll had what it called was "the first full week's polling" since the formation of NZ First back on 18 July. Journalists wrote of Peters "shaking up" support for the Alliance, which had its popularity "carved to just 6%" by Winston reaching 14%.[199]

This, of course, was a considerable difference from the 24% registered in the Insight poll, but CMR had a different sample and, interestingly, the trend in CMR was an increase for Peters from the previous poll and what was labelled a "rapid climb". In this poll, Peters was preferred Prime Minister by a country mile, at 26%, while Moore and Bolger slugged it out on 15% and 14% respectively.

A week is a lifetime in politics, and Peters was about to experience "utu" from within the news media.

"You are a passenger in a car travelling down Taranaki Street, Wellington, in the wee hours when you run into the cops and the driver gets out to take a breath test," wrote Tom Frewen in the NBR.[200]

---

199 Alliance falling fast: NZ First on rapid climb" by Bob Edlin, The Independent, 6 August 1993, p 14
200 "Breath test gossip hits the newsroom fast", by Tom Frewen, NBR, 20 August 1993, p47

"You are also the preferred choice in the polls as your country's prime minister and leader of a new political party in an election year. Do you sit in the car and shut up? Or do you get out and risk recognition?

"When Winston Peters relinquished the safe role of anonymous passenger for active protagonist and got out of the car to follow his driver and personal secretary Sarah Neems over to talk to the police, his recognition was inevitable.

"The seed sown, dissemination would have been rapid, spreading from cop to cop, then cop to reporter within hours..."

Sarah Neems was a young "ash blonde" Canadian who'd worked as Winston's executive secretary since the late 1980s. I'd met her several times and talked with her on the phone more often – usually in her role as gatekeeper of incoming calls.

"Sarah was smart, ambitious and politically aware," Michael Laws later wrote...the first of a new breed – a secretary who typed and also provided political advice."[201]

Laws described her as "Winston's closest confidante...closer than his university rugby mates; closer than his Salamanca Road political colleagues Philip Burdon, Paul East and Don McKinnon. Sure, the tongues wagged. This was closeness of the horizontal variety, whispered the gossips. Soon such gossip had been escalated into fact and then into living legend."

So much so, added Laws, that "Peters' alleged relationship with Neems was actively promoted within National circles as a knee-capping technique. Whether it was true or not was irrelevant. In fact, I observed not the slightest hint of proof."

Nor had I. Neems was very much a political activist who liked to be in the thick of it. She gave as good as she got:[202]

"Winston had no difficulty at all in chastising Sarah for the smallest of errors; it was as if Neems was the resident scapegoat. Yet Sarah refused to buckle or cower under his verbal attacks and would return any criticism with often conflagratory interest," wrote Laws, describing the turbulence as "a daily Punch and Judy show". Neither participant bore a grudge, but their tongues could have been used to strip paint from a wall at ten paces.

So, when Winston clambered out of a car at two thirty in the morn-

---

201 The Demon Profession, Laws, pp139-140
202 Ibid, p299

ing as Sarah Neems was breath-tested, it was like manna from heaven for the Press Gallery and Winston's political foes. Radio Pacific's (now Newstalk ZB's) Barry Soper hit the midday news with a leak from an unnamed police source, and Wellington's *Evening Post* newspaper wasn't far behind with the front page of its 12.30 edition. The Post wrongly claimed Neems had been charged – she had not. It was the number three story on One News that night – during my time in the TVNZ newsroom incidentally, although I was mostly working on the Winebox investigation by then.

What Frewen found fascinating was the wide range of media errors surrounding the reporting. National Radio was claiming Peters and Neems were on their way to a meeting (at 2.30am?), while NZPA more reasonably claimed the pair were on their way "from" a meeting. The police job sheet leaked to the media quoted Peters saying he'd asked Neems to drive after they'd worked late at parliament, and Barry Soper claimed Peters and Neems had come from a late dinner at Il Casino restaurant.

Another report said Peters was "asleep" in the car, which Peters denied. His wife, naturally, was mortified:

"I think they're both very foolish people," Louise Peters told the *Sunday News*.

"Her remark," noted Frewen, "was as close as anyone came to imputing a motive other than strictly business for the MP and his secretary to be out motoring at 2.30am on a Friday."

Unlikely as it seemed, it was entirely within the Winston Peters character I knew to be on his political beat at that hour.

One thing I'd learned of Peters was that the man was a night owl. There'd been late night meetings in the office of his lawyer Brian Henry during my investigations, and he'd also met the late Paul White at night – watched by a surveillance team according to the police file on White's death.[203]

Peters and White had exchanged phone calls more than once at four in the morning.

The *Independent's* Bill Ralston wrote a column bemoaning the media's stampede to report the Peters/Neems breath-test story. "No one, including me," said Ralston, "touched the Lange-Pope affair until Naomi rang the *Dominion* and spilled the beans…in fact, I have deliberately avoided

---

203 The Paradise Conspiracy, 1st ed. Wishart, p16

reporting every decent scandal to come out of Parliament in the last couple of decades. So did most of the capital's media."[204]

Ralston launched into a long litany of political indiscretions the media had ignored – Rob Muldoon, Doug Kidd, and David Lange's own traffic accident with multiple rumours of a female passenger that the media never bothered following up.

"The outrageous drinking habits of several other former politicians have never been reported. The personal tragedies within their families, the break-ups, the suicides, suicide attempts, drug addictions, the imprisonments have generally been ignored. And rightly so. Their families suffer enough for the politician's vanities.

"I chose, and so did most of the Press Gallery, never to report Deputy Prime Minister Don McKinnon's long-standing relationship with former RNZ reporter Clare de Lore, or Customs Minister Murray McCully's liaison with the *Dominion's* Jane Clifton. These became public eventually, when the people involved chose to make them so. The women involved were friends and colleagues, but I would like to think none of us reported the gossip because of wider principles of privacy.

"When you consider the legion of secrets buried deep within the private lives of journalists, who could have the double standards required to publish it?" he asked.

Over at the *NBR*, Tom Frewen argued Winston's late night car trip was relevant and that Ralston was wrong for wanting to suppress it. Frewen turned it into a matter of state importance and accused Ralston of paying too much credence to the MAD – Mutually-Assured Destruction – doctrine:

"Ralston's argument, and presumably the reasoning behind TV3's decision to ignore the story completely, was that politicians and journalists shared a moral glasshouse in which stone throwing would be not only dangerous but hypocritical.

"The story that Ralston would have suppressed is more than gossip, more than tittle-tattle to titillate the prurient public. Thanks to Soper and his colleagues it became a revealing test of a prospective leader under pressure and a legitimate challenge to the integrity of a man who would claim to be the last honest politician in New Zealand.

"More than the curious circumstances of the incident itself, Peters'

---

204 "Journos in glass houses shouldn't throw stones", by Bill Ralston, The Independent, 13 August 1993, p11

actions at the time and later reactions in the media provided voters with valuable information about how he handles minor crises."

Well, that's the theory. Again, what Frewen didn't know was that Peters was under surveillance and feeling justifiably jittery, or as Doug Woolerton would call it, "cagey". In my own dealings with Peters during this time over the Winebox, it almost reached the point where the sun would be streaming in through a window and you'd say, 'Beautiful day', whereupon Peters would look at you suspiciously and retort, 'Who says so?'.

Ralston's final line had asked "why the glee displayed in almost every avenue of the media?". The answer to the question came back to that aforementioned "utu":

"Win's mob believe the media has turned on their boy," argued Frewen. "They started turning more than a year ago but it did not become obvious until recently when his litany of leaks dried up and journalists felt deceived by his failure to deliver on promises – promises to provide information."

The attitude of New Zealand media towards Winston Peters surprised some of their counterparts both at home and overseas.

"Many media commentators have, almost gleefully, proclaimed that Winston Peters is on the road to political oblivion," Malaysia's *New Straits Times* had reported during the BNZ skirmishing a year earlier. The newspaper quoted respected left-wing writer Bruce Jesson, who was highly critical of kiwi journalists:[205]

"New Zealand has the tamest media in the world. Unwilling to challenge politicians or business interests, it will deal harshly with anyone who steps out of line."[206]

As the saying goes, the pen is mightier than the sword and Winston was suffering political death by a thousand ballpoints. Certainly, the political impact of the driving incident was serious.

"New Zealand First leader Winston Peters' approval rating has plunged in the wake of the incident in which his press secretary Sarah Neems was breath-tested," ran one front page story.[207]

---

205 New Straits Times, 8 July 1992, p6
206 As an example from Investigate magazine, we published a 17 page investigation with damning proof of police corruption, and the only thing the media were brave enough to run were two paragraphs in the story relating to a "chicken sex" video
207 "Peters dives in poll", by Vernon Small, NBR, 20 August 1993, p1

An Insight poll showed Peters' approval rating had dropped from 62% to 42%, and his disapproval rating had jumped from 30% to 44%. The Winston approval rating had never dipped below 61% in more than two years, so the plunge to 42% was breathtaking.

A TV3 Gallup poll a week later showed NZ First had dropped to 9% support, just ahead of the Alliance on 8%, squandering an eight point lead over Anderton's party in a previous poll. Winston's preferred Prime Minister ranking slipped to 20% from 26% the previous month, but he was still heading off Moore and Bolger by a comfortable margin.[208]

"He is still seen as having a positive influence on the country's future by more respondents (34%) than any other politician," the poll reported.

It seemed you could throw Gandalf off a cliff, but you couldn't make him disappear. Often down, but never out.

On 6 November 1993, New Zealand voters made history. Thanks to Winston Peters, who in turn had been prodded by Michael Laws back in 1988, National had carried out a referendum on electoral reform and the people had finally spoken, making the biggest change to our political system since women received the vote in 1893. Proportional representation, specifically MMP, was in.

MMP was the choice of voters. Peters had merely forced National to offer voters a choice of electoral alternatives. They chose MMP because it was the easiest to understand. It certainly wasn't the best system on offer, but it was a game changer.

November 6 was also a red-letter day for Peters. Not only had he won his Tauranga seat against all-comers, but little-known Tau Henare had broken a decades-long Labour stranglehold on the Maori seats, displacing Labour's Bruce Gregory in Northern Maori.

Peters had introduced me to Henare in the Auckland Airport Koru lounge earlier in 1993. "This is the future," Peters said, as Tau and I shook hands.

Although Winston and Brian Henry had tried hard to knock up a candidate list there'd been relatively few big names. Ian Shearer, a former Minister of Science under Muldoon, was the biggest but was unsuccessful in his bid for the Onehunga seat and took up an administrative role in the party with his wife Cheryl. Others to take up party roles included Democrats Terry Heffernan and Rex Widerstrom.

---

208 "MMP, NZ First and Winston losing ground", by Bob Edlin, The Independent, 27 August 1993, p14

So NZ First had two seats, the Alliance two seats, Labour had won 46 and National 49 – one short of the crucial majority it needed in the 99 seat parliament. It was New Zealand's first hung parliament since 1931. The Nats had lost 15 seats since their crushing defeat of Labour in 1990. Mike Moore was so certain he could stitch a coalition together he gave the best victory speech of his political career, and Jim Bolger's most memorable response was "bugger the pollsters". Most of the polls, including one on election eve, had put National eight to ten points ahead of Labour. In the end there was barely a percentage point between them.

There was business uncertainty surrounding the result, and long time Peters foe – Lion Nathan boss Doug Myers – said frankly that life and business was simpler under Muldoon:

"It was a known, controlled world. The unions beat you up, and the government was there to license and protect you, and to limit your capacity to be outstanding. If you were outstanding, you generally went overseas."[209]

"And the whole focus was on producers. The focus of everything we've done [post 1984] has been pro-taxpayer, pro-consumer."

Moore's election night ambitions proved premature. An official recount of the Waitaki seat saw it slip out of Labour's grasp, propelling the Nats to 50 seats and Labour to 45. Even with the Alliance and NZ First, there would be no coalition government.

Helen Clark was poised to swoop, knife in hand. Moore may have succeeded in bringing back a whole fresh intake of Labour MPs, but Helen Clark's supporters had made certain the bulk of the new candidates followed her worldview, not Moore's. He didn't stand a chance as the feminist and Rainbow wings of Labour clambered into power.

Two things resulted from this. Strategists like Michael Laws could see an opportunity for a new political party led by someone like Mike Moore, or even a joint Peters/Moore party. Secondly, Labour repositioned itself and began courting NZ First more seriously. The next election, Helen Clark knew, would be fought under the new MMP system and every single vote would count.

On Planet Peters, however, a new star was daring to hover above the horizon, and it concerned a box of tax haven documents. Those documents would change his life, and change history in New Zealand.

---

209 "Post election roundup," The Independent, 12 November 1993, p6

15

Conspiracy Fact

> "While dubious deals may be buried in the detail, it will be the headline that determines whether Winston Peters' papers will have the consequences of Daniel Ellsberg's Pentagon Papers. If it ever appears, that headline will contain the amount of tax that big businesses avoided, possibly legitimately but probably immorally. If it is tens of millions, it will be the story of the year. If it's hundreds of millions, it will be the story of the decade"
> – Tom Frewen, National Business Review, 1994

In mid 1993, I had quit my job as acting Chief of Staff for TV3 News, and joined a special investigative unit within TVNZ. The unit was assembled specifically to assist me with a story TV3 had found politically too hot to handle. Nobody knew, but I'd been given a copy of a mysterious set of documents known as "the Winebox". Mine came in a Xerox carton, but I was reliably assured the originals had been fermenting in a wine carton, hence the name.

If you wonder why Peters would be paranoid, the following story should suffice.

Cut back a few months earlier to October 1992, and I was in the middle of investigating the Citibank disks mystery. Chris Dickie, an Auckland lawyer investigating the film and bloodstock frauds involving Russell McVeagh tagged along with me this particular day, as I arranged to meet a businessman named Stephen Lunn. Lunn had been involved on the fringes of some Hong Kong and Cook Islands tax haven deals. The Asian ones interested Dickie, and the tropical ones captured my attention given Winston Peters' campaign about tax haven deals.

"Would you like a copy of the Winebox documents?" Lunn offered at one point in the conversation that afternoon. As if he needed to ask. Was the Pope a Catholic? Dickie and I drove away elated. He'd discovered vital new information and I had been promised a box load of vital new information. We didn't reckon on the intrusion of Big Brother into our little schemes.

As I wrote in *The Paradise Conspiracy*, it didn't take long for the first tremors to hit: they came the following evening. Stephen Lunn was relaxing at home on Waiheke Island in Auckland's Hauraki Gulf, pondering his next move in the European Pacific chess game, when his opponents forced his hand.

From out of the dusk came a helicopter, its blades thumping the still air ominously as the craft plummeted down onto the beach in front of Lunn's house. Too stunned to move, he could only watch open-mouthed as a man came running toward him and slapped a legal document into his hands. It was an injunction order restricting Lunn from any further dissemination of the European Pacific documents or discussion of them.

To his island neighbours it was like a scene from *Apocalypse Now*, or in Lunn's words "a James Bond movie", but to Lunn at the time it was the beginning of a nightmare. He rang European Pacific boss and old friend David Lloyd – what the hell's going on? Lunn later told *Metro* magazine Lloyd's response: "We have to injunct everyone". Shortly afterward came a phone call that resulted in armed men being called in to protect Lunn's home. It was a woman's voice on the end of the line, cultured and measured.

"Stephen?," she asked down the line.

"Yes."

"You must stop what you are doing. You must stop now. What you are doing is no good to any of us. If you don't stop now, we know where you are, at Onetangi. We will send some guys to break your f***ing kneecaps."

"We know where you are, where Anna is, where the boys are."

A shocked and frightened Stephen Lunn interrupted, "Who is this? What are you talking about?" The woman ignored him and continued.

"We will arrange for your boys to fall off the harbour bridge. Just stop it." Then she hung up.

Terrified for the safety of his family, Lunn sent them to spend the night at a friend's house. He then called police, and he called Chris Dickie. It was Dickie's house that was used by police as a control point while they decided whether to send reinforcements to Waiheke to protect Lunn's family.

The decision had already been made for them, however. By the time police had arranged a launch, Lunn phoned to say 20 or so of his neighbours had gathered with guns and dogs to protect the property and the family. The police, reluctantly, accepted the situation. Lunn's neighbourhood vigilante squad, armed to the teeth, would be allowed to stay in place.

Instead, police turned their attention to tracing the call. Naturally enough, the woman hadn't used her own phone – she'd called from a phone booth in Browns Bay. There the trail ended. Lunn and Dickie knew it was highly unlikely to be a crank call from the public given Lunn's non-existent public profile. As to the caller's motives and real intentions – given the highly charged atmosphere and the dramatic turn of events – they could only speculate.

It wouldn't be the first time that a mystery woman played a threatening criminal role behind the scenes as events gained momentum in later months. Someone, somewhere, appeared to have Lunn and others in his immediate circle of possible contacts under surveillance.

The previous week, on Tuesday October 20th, 1992, *National Business Review* journalist Fran O'Sullivan had taken possession of an envelope full of documents delivered to her hotel room. The following day she was attacked in a lift in Auckland's BNZ tower by a man who tried to snatch documents and computer disks she was carrying up to the newspaper's office. Some of the disks fell down the lift shaft and had to be retrieved later by maintenance staff. The offender escaped.

The documents she was carrying related to the so called "Magnum" transaction in the European Pacific winebox. At this point no one in the media realised the significance of that particular transaction. Magnum was the deal that would later be referred to in Court as a "criminal fraud" on the New Zealand Revenue to the tune of $2 million. Obviously someone had realised its devastating potential.

Whoever it was, they were undeterred at failing in the lift. O'Sullivan later went back to her hotel room, only to find evidence of a break-in, and her remaining documents had been ransacked.

Coincidentally, perhaps, Lunn was phoned up by a European Pacific executive around that time, and asked whether the Magnum deal was in the winebox. When Lunn replied in the affirmative, the tax haven banker couldn't hide his concern.

"I was afraid you'd say that!"

It was mid-evening on the 28th when I rang Dickie at home to chew over our discussions with Lunn the previous day. When he answered the phone Chris was panicky.

"I can't talk now, the shit's hit the fan, the cops are here, I've got guys with guns and dogs running around Waiheke -"

"Slow down Chris, I'm not with you. What's happened?"

"It's Lunn. They've served an injunction on him and he's had a death threat. I've rung a friend of mine who's a senior cop, we've got it under control."

I hung up the phone, stunned. Guns, dogs, death threats. To come so close to the full winebox and have the damned thing snatched out from under my nose. I was convinced then – somewhat egocentrically, I now hasten to add in hindsight – that the SIS must have bugged TV3's phones; they must have known I was meeting Lunn and decided to act. Expletive deleted!

Within hours journalists Warren Berryman and Jenni McManus of *The Independent* business newspaper were experiencing exactly the same thoughts. Lunn had phoned them to warn of the impending injunction. Naturally enough, they freaked. Fearing their own homes and phone lines were bugged, the two met on Jenni's front lawn to decide on their next move. Like squirrels on speed they did what came naturally, hiding their nuts – in this case their documents – in the ceiling of their office.

As dawn broke on the 29th, Dickie and Lunn were already plotting their next move. A court appearance at 10:00am left little room to manoeuvre, and the possibility of an immediate court order to return the winebox left even less room for choice. On Dickie's advice they dropped the winebox in the lap of the Serious Fraud Office, ensuring firstly that the authorities would now have to investigate them and, secondly, kicking the box out of reach of EP. But if they thought the SFO was glad to see the box they were very mistaken. Within the hour, a Serious Fraud Office investigator was on the phone to Chris Dickie.

"What are you trying to do?," he hissed, "set us up?"

Oh yes, humble reader. What possible reason could Winston Peters have had to be paranoid? Would the attempted abduction of his lawyer Brian Henry's son from the prestigious King's prep school in Remuera, four days before the July launch of NZ First, qualify?

"Listen, do you know Brian Henry's son? Somebody tried to kidnap him from school yesterday," barked jeweler Peter McCarty – one of Henry's clients – down the phone at me on 15 July 1993.

"Yesterday! No, what happened?"

"They managed to save the kid, and the woman fled."

"How did they try and do it?"

"I don't know. Talk to him. Because he was supposed to be in Wellington today, and he's had to call it off because of this attempt."

When I called Henry, he was shaken and wanted no publicity – for fear of prompting a nutcase copycat attempt. In addition, he'd been hounded by the media and refused to talk. A police file on the case had been opened, however. It appears a well-spoken woman had begun asking in the school corridors where she could find the boy, calling him by name. Another student guided her to Henry junior's classroom but, as the woman was about to go in, a teacher came around the corner and the mystery woman took flight.

We knew that it was a woman who'd rung Stephen Lunn just after the injunctions were served back in October 1992 and warned him his children would be thrown off the harbour bridge. The question was, was it just an attempt to scare Henry and others in the Peters/Lunn camp – to show that they could actually get to the kids – or would the mysterious woman have inflicted real physical harm to a child in a bid to get at the parent?

To me, as an observer chronicling these events as they unfolded, the cognitive dissonance between the media's reporting on the one hand of Peters as an empty windbag chasing a non-story[210], and the threats flying behind the scenes on the other hand, was unreal.

---

210 The media continues to get the facts wrong in forehead-smacking Homer Simpson style, even after all these years. In a 2011 obituary for one of the Winebox Inquiry lawyers, the Herald wrote: "The commission, which was headed by Sir Ronald Davison, heard evidence from several big New Zealand companies at the time – including the Bank of New Zealand and Brierley Investments. The inquiry concluded that there were no grounds to support the allegations." In fact, the Court of Appeal and High Court found there was prima facie criminal fraud, and overturned the Winebox Inquiry findings in 1999. Yet the mythology persists even now. Article source: "Formidable' QC involved in Winebox inquiry dies", NZ Herald, Apr 5, 2011

The even bigger irony was that leading up to the 1993 election, Winston Peters didn't actually realize how the Winebox transactions worked. Consequently, he had no idea of the dynamite he was sitting on.

This was no fault of Winston's. After all, at the eventual Winebox Inquiry, even the best tax experts at the IRD confessed that they didn't understand the Winebox deals either until I helpfully explained them in my June 1994 *Frontline* TV documentary. I kid you not.

The Cook Islands tax deals covered hundreds of transactions, but two in particular would later sit front and centre stage: the "Magnum" deal and the "JIF" deals. The way these particular deals worked can best be described as follows.

A company, let's call it Magnum Corporation, needed to reduce its tax bill in New Zealand by $2 million dollars.[211] It did so by investing in a Cook Islands money go round. Under the terms of the deal, Magnum would invest $34.4 million with a Cook Islands bank, earning roughly $5.8 million in interest.

European Pacific, the company that owned the Cook Islands bank and which was designing the deal, arranged for Magnum to pay $2,050,000 in tax to the Cook Islands IRD, ostensibly being the "withholding tax" on the $5.8 million interest earned.

As is normally the case for any taxpayer, if you pay tax overseas you can show a certificate to prove that to the New Zealand IRD and lower your NZ tax bill by that amount. That's an international rule of fairness, because let's say you own a business selling widgets in New Zealand and the USA, and the Americans sting you for tax on your American sales, but because you live in NZ our own IRD says your entire worldwide income is also taxable here.

You are not supposed to be taxed twice on the same amount of money, so governments have worked out "double tax treaties" where they recognize tax paid elsewhere and deduct it against your home tax liability. Say you earned $100,000 last year, incurring a $30,000 tax bill in NZ, but the Americans had already made you pay tax of $10,000. If you presented an

---

211 For ease of explaining, I have simplified the Magnum deal here. The principles are exactly what happened, but the detail is considerably more complex. If you want the full analysis with all companies and taxpayers along the way correctly identified, see The Paradise Conspiracy, Wishart, Howling At The Moon, 1995

American tax certificate to prove it, the NZ IRD would change your NZ liability to $20,000, and the US and NZ governments would work out their shares behind the scenes without bothering you.

Magnum Corporation, then, had a Cook Islands tax certificate proving they'd paid $2,050,000 in tax to the Cook Islands government. They presented the certificate to the NZ IRD, and their NZ tax bill was reduced by just over two million dollars.

So far, so good, although any smart person in the NZ IRD would surely have wondered why a big New Zealand brewery was paying millions in tax to a tax haven! Nobody in the IRD wondered that.

However, there was a secret twist to the Magnum deal that no one outside European Pacific Bank was supposed to know about: the Cook Islands government had not kept the $2,050,000 in tax, to help mend potholes in the roads and educate Rarotongan children. Instead, the same day they received the tax payment and wrote out the tax certificate, they actually gave the tax back.

Well, not quite all of it, they kept a $50,000 finder's fee for their part in the deal. So Magnum got its two million dollars in tax back, plus a tax certificate continuing to say they had "paid" the tax, and the Cook Islands government pocketed a $50K fee.

Everyone was happy, except perhaps New Zealand taxpayers who all had to pay an extra $1 each in tax that year just to compensate for Magnum breweries not paying $2 million in tax that it should have.

Now, European Pacific Bank had hidden this interesting little twist, but not disclosing the entire transaction in one document. Instead, as the Winebox documents in front of me showed, the tax "paying" part of the deal was contained in one transaction plan that made no mention of anything else, and the secret tax "refund" part was contained in another document that didn't even mention the name "Magnum".

Unless you knew what was going on, you wouldn't have a clue. You could hold the Winebox up and look underneath it; you could leaf through the documents till the cows came home; you could throw the 2,500 pages or so up into the air and clap happily as they fell to the ground making pretty little patterns; you could even dump them all on a big king size bed and wallow in them like Scrooge McDuck. None of that was going to make a blind bit of difference – if you didn't have the key to unlocking the Winebox transactions, you had nothing.

The only reason I knew what was going on is because a disgruntled former European Pacific employee told me. Which brings me back to the IRD's failure to launch on the Cook Islands deals. In talking about the key to the Winebox deals, I still firmly believe to this day that the IRD and the Serious Fraud Office should have detected the fraud at the heart of them.

Two reasons: first, these companies were paying tax in a tax haven. I mean, hello?? The average punter and certainly the average journalist might not understand the significance of that, but it should have set off alarm bells for complex fraud investigators. They might not realize at first how it was done, but by going over and over and over the transactions like I did, they would have worked it out. It's all about smelling the rat and then following the odour to its source. You don't just 'move on' simply because said rat hasn't surrendered and made itself visible by walking around with a sign saying 'Pick Me'. Second, it's the specific job description for the IRD and SFO to detect fraud. They don't get to weasel out of it that easily. If the IRD can't tell when its being rorted by a bunch of tax haven cowboys popping the magnums and laughing all the way to their own tax haven bank, then frankly, its investigators are incompetent in my view.

Now, the JIF deals were like the $34 million Magnum deal but much, much bigger. We're talking $2.4 *billion* dollars washing through the European Pacific Bank jointly owned by Fay Richwhite, Brierley Investments and the BNZ. That's not a typo. It really was $2.4 billion. The amount of tax money being laundered ran into the hundreds of millions, although the victim was the Japanese IRD, not New Zealand. Adding to the significance, the money go round began in the NZ government-owned Bank of New Zealand and washed through Citibank New York as well as the Cook Islands.

Again, just like Magnum, the JIF deals were done in two separate halves – one set of transaction documents to "pay" the tax, and an entirely separate set to "refund" the tax which never mentioned the name of the clients.

There were a whole bunch of JIF transactions, in fact only a few of them were actually in the Winebox, a lot more were disclosed at the eventual inquiry. If you looked at a "JIF" deal, it appeared to be just a US$200 million loan from the Bank of New Zealand to a tax haven bank. Odd, risky perhaps, but not criminal.

Knowing that like Magnum there had to be a second half to this deal I was quickly able to find it by cross-referencing transaction dates and amounts.

In essence, the JIFS were a series of massive criminal frauds against the Government of Japan perpetrated by a tax haven bank part owned by the New Zealand government, and using the NZ government owned trading bank the BNZ to handle the transactions. You couldn't ask for something more politically embarrassing – a crime against one of our biggest trading partners.

No wonder somebody wanted to shut Winston Peters down. Except Winston Peters didn't actually know how the JIFs worked. I discovered that by chance, and my discovery changed the course of the 1993 general election, although only three people in New Zealand knew that.

As I explained in *The Paradise Conspiracy*, an accidental meeting with Winston's lawyer Brian Henry resulted in the discovery that he and Peters were working on a transaction called JIF.

"How the hell did you find out about JIF?," I inquired in utter disbelief.

"It's one of the transactions in the wine box we've been trying to figure out," he grinned. "But don't worry, it'll all be public in a couple of weeks. The winebox is about to be tabled in three foreign parliaments."

The sense of panic rising up within was hard to quell. Here I was frantically looking for documentation on JIF, only to find it was in the winebox after all, and then discovering the whole lot would be laid bare in a multinational free-for-all within a fortnight.

Even if we'd had the go ahead that day to produce a programme, TVNZ could not have had one ready within two weeks. I needed to stall for time.

"What do you know about JIF?," I probed, trying to gauge what kind of spin was likely to be put on JIF if it did see the light of day. That was my second problem. Peters had been criticised previously for not hitting the correct points in some of his earlier Parliamentary outbursts. If he muffed this one, no one would be able to understand it even if TVNZ broadcast the correct version, people would only get even more confused.

"JIF appears to be a US$200 million dollar loan from the BNZ to European Pacific," Brian replied, his face now starting to betray some confusion at my line of questioning. "Why?"

"You're looking at JIF the wrong way around," I told him bluntly. "It's much bigger than that." It took a lot of persuasion to get Henry to try and talk Peters out of Plan A. The wheels had already been set in motion, he said, and two wineboxes were already in place overseas awaiting their fate.

"Peters has to hold off," I pleaded. "JIF could be the granddaddy of the winebox tax evasion schemes. If he goes off half-cocked we'll never be able to get the full story out, and TVNZ is already committed to a one hour documentary on this. What's the best Winnie can do? 10 minutes? He can't do it justice and no one will ever understand it."

The November 1993 General Election was only six weeks away. Peters had been planning a campaign for the new New Zealand First Party based on revelations from the winebox. Politicians in a number of other countries, including Australia and the Cook Islands, had been planning to cook up storms of their own based on the documents.

I was asking a lot. I was asking, said Henry, Winston Peters to sacrifice his chances in the upcoming election in return for a promise that the state television network might vindicate him down the track. A state network, Henry reminded me, that had "repeatedly bagged" Peters during the setting up of his new political party earlier in the year. It was a point I had to concede.

After the MP had stepped up his campaign for an inquiry into the Bank of New Zealand in 1992, powerful interests had been moving to nobble him. He became increasingly ostracised by his own party, culminating in his expulsion from caucus at the end of 1992. Peters' problems had escalated with a letter on March 4, 1993, from the National Party. It contained his marching orders.

"I write to advise you the National Executive has decided not to approve you as a candidate for the National Party," wrote executive director Marg Skews.

The effective expulsion forced a by-election the following month in the Tauranga seat, and during the campaign Peters' lashed out at what he called a "hysterical analysis of me" on TVNZ's *Holmes* programme, the previous week. At an 800-strong rally he called it a smear campaign directed against him, and that was the nicest thing he said!

"Ladies and gentlemen, in 25 years of politics and political involvement that is the most biased, disgraceful and unprofessional TV report I have ever seen. But I've got news for TVNZ, and it's this: if you think you are going to get away with that, those that made that decision, I've got news for you and it's all bad."

When the TVNZ camera crew covering the meeting turned their camera off during the monologue, Peters demanded that they turn the camera back on and keep recording.

"Shove it on and give us a fair go here. You're meant to be the watchdog for democracy, not a poodle or chihuahua."

The crowd loved it, joining in with cries of "shame" and "go home", directed at the TVNZ contingent.

Throughout the year, a state of undeclared war had remained between TVNZ and the politician. Here I was walking into the middle of it, trying to wave a white flag while both sides were still firing at each other.

"Look Brian," I said wearily, leaning back in the chair, "You're going to have to trust me on this. I can't force Winston to do anything, and I don't actually want to interfere in whatever shenanigans he's got planned, but hear me out: If he messes this one up, it's going to wreck our chances of getting a well researched, reasoned documentary investigation to air. It's his choice."

Driving away from that meeting was a white-knuckle experience. I knew Brian Henry would take on board what I'd said, but Winston Peters was a different matter. Only weeks away from an election campaign, and here I was trying to snaffle his election thunder.

All this time, Winston's poll ratings had been falling. He'd had journalists publicly mock him, like NBR's Tom Frewen, saying "where's your evidence?" I had the evidence. I could have given it to Winston and boosted his election chances. But I was an independent journalist, I had a documentary to make, and Winston reluctantly agreed to keep taking the insults and jeers, on the offchance that I would set the record straight eventually.

By putting the greater good ahead of his own instant gratification, Winston Peters earned my trust that day.

The IRD and SFO had each had a copy of the Winebox documents since my lawyer friend Chris Dickie had dumped it on them in late 1992. Both agencies claimed to have subjected the transactions to "expert scrutiny" and found nothing untoward.

They were either stupid, or they were lying, in my view. Winston Peters said as much in May 1994, two days after the Frontline documentary had finally gone to air and the whole country had seen how the deals worked. The documentary had only been cleared because the Court of Appeal had ruled there was prima facie evidence of criminal wrongdoing in the documents – documents that had just been cleared by the two law enforcement agencies:

"Eminent lawyers and tax specialists call it criminal. Should not New

Zealand's law enforcement authorities, at the very least, lay charges and let the court decide? But they will not. The collusion between this Government and its business network has taken care of that," railed Peters.

"Charles Sturt of the Serious Fraud Office is supposed to be the Government's hired gun to combat fraud. He could not hit a barn at 10 paces. Today I am calling for the immediate suspension of the Director of the Serious Fraud Office and the Commissioner of Inland Revenue. These men are, at best, incompetent. In nearly 2 years of having access to the documents, Sturt and Henry could not find any evidence to lay one criminal or tax evasion charge.

"In contrast, in just 2 days, the Court of Appeal found there was enough in the "Magnum" and "Jif" documents to indicate that serious fraud had taken place. Henry and his Minister told this Parliament they had examined the schemes and they were legal. The Court of Appeal did not fall for that. Instead, the court found "a seriously arguable case" that fraudulent tax evasion had indeed taken place. Are the Inland Revenue Department and the Serious Fraud Office so inept that television is now doing a more professional job of detecting criminal fraud?

"I believe that sufficient evidence is now available to suspend David Henry and Charles Sturt. I have had contacts from senior investigators from both the Inland Revenue Department and the Serious Fraud Office who say their bosses are plainly wrong. Some say they are lying when they claim these schemes are within the law.

"David Henry told Parliament that he got independent legal advice on "Magnum" from a barrister with extensive commercial and criminal expertise but he will not name that person. I know for a fact that the Inland Revenue Department did not consult its usual legal adviser on this matter – an independent QC with enormous taxation experience – and I know from calls to my office that other legal advisers within the Inland Revenue Department consider the "Magnum" transaction to be criminal fraud on the New Zealand revenue to the tune of $2 million.

"I call for a royal commission of inquiry into such dealings. I can say that there are those within the Inland Revenue Department and the Serious Fraud Office who can testify to the ineptitude of their bosses, and will do so if they are given the immunity and protection of a proper inquiry.

"Concealment is at the heart of this issue. If you or I failed to declare income to the Commissioner of Inland Revenue, we would be prosecuted for criminal tax evasion. Yet on the Fraser programme Mr Henry claimed that tax havens not making proper disclosure are within the law. The last paragraph of a letter from Treasury to the Minister of Finance of 19 December 1986 states that that is plain drivel. That paragraph 10(b) on page 3 states: "Note that the Commissioner has authority under existing legislation to require taxpayers to furnish the necessary disclosures of tax haven transactions."

It was the speech of Winston Peters' career. His abuse of the two civil servants heading the IRD and the Serious Fraud Office was a step too far in the Government's eyes – Jim Bolger ordered a Commission of Inquiry so the two men and their agencies could clear their names.

But clear their names of what, precisely? Critics of Winston Peters, and there are many, loosely paraphrased Peters in a way that implied the two civil servants were part of the alleged criminal conspiracy. Then, when Peters provided no evidence to the inquiry showing they were criminally involved with the perpetrators, mountains of abuse was heaped down on Peters, as we'll see later in the book.

Read back over the speech just given, and you'll see Peters was making these allegations:

- Incompetence. That the two men and their staff had failed to properly analyse the transactions yet had persisted in clearing European Pacific of any wrongdoing
- Incompetence or lying when they claimed the deals were lawful. In the IRD's case Peters drew specific attention to David Henry telling TVNZ that the IRD could not force companies to disclose their tax haven transactions, when a 1986 Treasury briefing and in fact the law itself clearly showed IRD had powers to penetrate tax haven secrecy. Was David Henry stupid, asked Peters, or lying?

Nowhere in that particular speech that resulted in the setting up of the inquiry, does Peters go further than the above.

Let's examine some earlier speeches he made. On 16 March 1993 Peters, for the first time, explained to parliament how the Magnum deal worked. His knowledge of this by that stage was no mystery. My TVNZ team had been injuncted (technically 'enjoined') by European Pacific to stop our documentary from going to air. At the Court hearing in February to argue for lifting the ban, we had to disclose in open court how the transactions worked. Media and one of Winston's lawyers, were among those watching and listening to the legal argument.

Peters' advisors had simply gone through the Winebox as a result of what TVNZ revealed in Court, and found the key to unlock the transactions. So on 16 March, he described the Magnum deal and, thanks to a National Government error in strategy, he was allowed to table the Winebox documents in parliament after being denied permission 16 previous times.

On Friday 18 March, two days after Peters had laid out the criminal fraud on the Magnum deal chapter and verse, SFO Director Charles Sturt issued a press statement saying not only was there no evidence of criminal fraud in the Winebox, but his office was not permitted to investigate tax fraud either.

Now, you could take such a press statement with a grain of salt earlier in the scandal, when no one actually knew how the transactions worked. But to issue such a press release two days *after* the fraud had just been described in all its gory detail, who would stick their neck out like that wondered Peters, and continue to argue black was white in defiance of the evidence now staring them in the face?

On 22 March 1994, Winston Peters gave his response to parliament:

"Today I am calling for the resignation of Mr Charles Sturt for the most serious reasons.

"Mr Sturt lied to the news media and he lied to the people of New Zealand. Section 37 of the Serious Fraud Act 1990 states: "Any member of the Serious Fraud Office may disclose any revenue information to any other member of the Serious Fraud Office for the purpose of investigating or prosecuting any inland revenue offence;". There is his power, yet he put out a press release saying that he was without power. That was a demonstrable, palpable lie, or he is totally incompetent. Under his own Act – the only Act that he need know – Mr Sturt's claim that he cannot investigate tax fraud, if made in a court of law, would warrant a charge of perjury.

"Mr Charles Sturt is prepared to turn a blind eye to corporate criminals when they are the same men who donate money to political parties. Was Mr Sturt's pursuit of the Equiticorp boss, Allan Hawkins, really motivated by a desire for justice, or had Mr Hawkins simply failed to pay his political dues on time?

"If the director of the Serious Fraud Office is so incompetent that he does not realise his powers to investigate tax fraud he should resign immediately or be dismissed forthwith. I take issue also with Mr Sturt's contention that he could find no breaches of the Crimes Act in the documents of European Pacific that were tabled in this House. I ask honourable members to familiarise themselves again with the documents of the Magnum Corporation transaction marked July 1988, already tabled. I am itemising and particularising these documents to overcome the ruling of the Speaker and the Clerk with respect to their publication and distribution to the remainder of New Zealand.

"The Magnum Corporation transaction marked July 1988 is all documented, complete with the signatures of all the criminals involved, and the politicians and inland revenue officials from the Cook Islands who conspired to give away their people's tax money. Every document necessary to prove criminal fraud is contained in that transaction, even down to the false tax certificates used to help steal $2,050,000 from the New Zealand Inland Revenue. That is one transaction alone that I have tabled. Not only do the documents show that a criminal fraud took place, they clearly show a conspiracy to defraud, which is covered by the Crimes Act and punishable by five years in jail, as well."

Inland Revenue boss David Henry had also chosen Friday 18 March to issue a press release giving the Winebox documents a clearance in regard to fraud. Peters, again, couldn't believe his ears, not after having explained how the deals worked. Surely these men and their departments could not be that incompetent?

"Apart from the tax evasion charges that arise from the Magnum Corporation transaction there is also clear prima facie evidence of conspiracy to defraud and of using a document to gain pecuniary advantage, knowing the document to be false. These are criminal charges punishable by long jail terms," Peters told parliament. Remember, the Court of Appeal later came out and made similar comments.

"To those ... who suggest that I have misinterpreted the facts, I quote from a tabled memorandum of 25 November 1987 – tabled here – which is headed: "Cook Islands Withholding Tax". Paragraph 8.5 of that memorandum states: "The Cook Islands Government would refund the amount of the tax, less its cut." What is to misunderstand? What is to misinterpret? The intent was to manufacture fake tax certificates and then to use them to defraud unsuspecting foreign governments.

"If the Serious Fraud Office cannot find enough evidence in the Magnum

Corporation transaction alone to put a number of these men behind bars, then the Serious Fraud Office should be immediately suspended from operating, pending an inquiry into possible corruption of that office."

If the Winebox had been the only isolated incident not properly investigated by the Serious Fraud Office, Winston Peters' allegation of possible corruption of the Serious Fraud Office would have been unfair. But this was the SFO which had done strange things in the Citibank inquiry, and which had refused to properly investigate the film and bloodstock frauds referred to earlier, and which had failed to investigate irregularities inside the BNZ and its dealings with Fay Richwhite. One cock-up is unfortunate, two is a tragedy, three just doesn't bear thinking about, and four leads to the kind of allegations Peters was making.

"If the Inland Revenue Commissioner, David Henry, can find no evidence of tax fraud in the Magnum Corporation transaction alone, he should resign or be sacked. If the Commissioner of Inland Revenue stands by his press statement of last Friday and today, and continues to claim that all of this – including the use of fake tax certificates – is legal, he should be fired immediately and charged with conspiracy to pervert the course of justice in New Zealand.

"There is a clear prima facie case and evidence of criminal dealings. Those responsible should be charged and the evidence presented in an open court, so that a judge and jury can independently decide whether crimes have been committed, and, more important, where New Zealanders can see justice really being done.

"Decisions by the Serious Fraud Office and the Inland Revenue Department not to prosecute have been made behind closed doors, and I ask, what right have they to be judge and jury away from the scrutiny of justifiably suspicious New Zealand people? Who knows what favours are being called in or bribes are being paid, even as we speak, to save the reputations of some of New Zealand's so-called leading business figures and top political campaign donors. It is time for charges to be laid and the evidence to speak for itself – thousands of pages of tabled evidence and criminal deal after criminal deal."

Again, looking back at this speech, let's carefully isolate the key allegations:

- SFO Director Charles Sturt was incompetent or lying when he said his office was not permitted to investigate tax fraud

- That Sturt's and/or Henry's inaction may have resulted from political instructions as a result of donations paid to the National Party
- That Sturt and Henry were incompetent for failing to discover fraud in the Magnum deal
- That the continued insistence of both men that they would not prosecute, even after the details of the fraud had been carefully pointed out to them, amounted to a possible conspiracy to pervert the course of justice

These were the main speeches that cumulatively caused the Government to launch a Commission of Inquiry. In those speeches, Peters essentially narrowed it down to just two possibilities: incompetence or corruption. Not corruption in the sense of taking part in the original crime, but corruption in the sense of not doing your job.

Exiled Burmese leader Aung San Suu Kyi wrote a precise definition of corruption in 1991:

"It is not power that corrupts, but fear. Fear of losing power corrupts those who wield it, and fear of the scourge of power corrupts those who are subject to it. Most Burmese are familiar with the four *a-gati*, the four kinds of corruption.

"*Chanda-gati*, corruption induced by desire is deviation from the right path in pursuit of bribes, or for the sake of those one loves.

"*Dosa-gati* is taking the wrong path to spite those against whom one bears ill-will, and *Moha-gati* is aberration due to ignorance.

"But perhaps the worst of the four is *Bhaya-gati*, for not only does *Bhaya*, fear, stifle and slowly destroy all sense of right and wrong, it so often lies at the root of the other three kinds of corruption.

"Just as *Chanda-gati*, when not the result of sheer avarice, can be caused by fear of want or fear of losing the goodwill of those one loves, so fear of being surpassed, humiliated or injured in some way can provide the impetus for ill-will."

On those definitions, there were at least a couple that appeared to fit the Winebox scandal and the law enforcement agencies inaction; had they refused to investigate because of ill-will towards Winston Peters, or was their aberration due to ignorance? Were the IRD and SFO fearful of political repercussions if they gave Winston Peters' allegations any oxygen?

The bigger question remained unanswered: was there any evidence supporting a conclusion that the IRD and SFO were either incompetent or corrupt? Could Winston Peters back up his biggest allegations?

On 25 August, 1994, Prime Minister Jim Bolger finally gave in to the inevitable and established a Royal Commission of Inquiry. Its terms of reference were limited to the Winebox transactions, but specifically the Commission was not to make findings about the transactions themselves, only about whether the IRD and SFO had investigated lawfully, properly and competently.

There would be a time of reckoning, but first there was a political party to build.

16

It's 2am, It Must Be Winston

> *"To stand upon the ramparts and die for our principles is heroic, but to sally forth to battle and win for our principles is something more than heroic"*
>
> – **Franklin D Roosevelt, 1928**

Tuariki Delamere remembers well the first time Winston Peters made contact with him. For Delamere, it was a wake-up call.

"Winston called me about 2am sometime in 1993 wanting to know if I would run for New Zealand First in the Wairarapa seat, because I was living in the Wairarapa."[212]

Two o'clock in the morning?

"About that, yeah. Winston calling at two in the morning is not unusual. Gets an idea and oh, whatced the hell, every other bastard in the country's asleep but never mind. About two in the morning when he called me and I distinctly remember, I think he was in Hastings at the time."

Delamere had the pedigree Peters was looking for. One of New Zealand's top Maori students in 1969, Delamere was awarded a scholarship to Washington State University in the USA. One thing led to another, and Delamare ended up serving for a time in the US Army, even joining the acclaimed West Point military academy as a member of staff. An athlete, a scholar and a soldier, he had unsuccessfully sought the National Party

---

212 Interview with author

nomination for the West Auckland seat in the 1990 election. He didn't get it, but he had caught the attention of Winston Peters.

It helped that Winston's brother, Ian Peters, himself a National MP, had been Delamere's high school basketball coach. "He was an ornery bastard," he chuckles.

Delamere says the idea of running in the 1993 election for a new party didn't appeal at two in the morning, "I just wasn't ready to do anything like that and to be honest I didn't really want to run for the Wairarapa anyway."

The seat he had his eye on was Eastern Maori, held by Labour incumbent Sir Peter Tapsell, but Winston had already chosen someone for that seat, accountant Doc Wirepa.

"Now, you may not recall this," says Delamere with a wry smile, "but Doc Wirepa got too clever. He got the media in there to record him putting in his nomination five minutes before it closed off, in Gisborne I think it was. He went in with a flourish, 'Here I am, you've read all about me, I'm Doc Wirepa, here's my nomination, here's my application, and here's my personal cheque for my fee'."

The returning officer stared at Wirepa, blinking nervously in the gaze of the news media: "I'm sorry Mr Wirepa but the law says we can only take cash. Or a bank cheque."

"But it's five minutes to 12!"

"No Mr Wirepa, it's now three minutes to 12. You have three minutes."

No one had any money, laughs Delamere. "Doc rushed down to the bank, came back, 'here's the money!'

" 'I'm sorry Mr Wirepa, it's now two minutes past 12, your nomination cannot be accepted'."

Winston, says Delamere, "never forgets a mistake". The mistake in this instance meant New Zealand First had no candidate to stand for Eastern Maori in the 1993 election, having spectacularly failed to file its nomination in time. Delamere's mind returned to that 2am call from Peters weeks earlier.

"Winston had no one to run. When that happened, I decided 'I'm going for that seat'. Others told me 'oh, no, Winston will put up Doc Wirepa next time.'

" 'No he won't, Winston never forgives anyone who screws up in that way'."

Knowing he had at least two years to plan his run, Delamere shifted from the Wairarapa back to his homeland in the Bay of Plenty.

"Because of my family connections, it was the only seat I could run for, but you needed to be back there."

When a position as regional director for Te Puni Kokiri, the rebranded Maori Affairs Department, came up in Whakatane, Delamere snatched the opportunity with both hands. "So I went back home and I had this brilliant job in 93, which basically allowed me to run around all of Maoridom in my electorate, slowly building up the support for three years later."

Another who was to be shoulder-tapped was former SAS soldier Ron Mark, recently returned from serving as a Major in the Sultan of Oman's special forces. Mark's mother-in-law Marie Berry was a Labour electorate chair in the South Island seat of Selwyn, then held by Ruth Richardson. Recognising political talent, Berry signed Ron Mark up as a card-carrying Labour Party member while he was off chasing Islamic radicals in the Middle East, and when he returned to New Zealand he suddenly discovered she had already put his name forward to run for parliament in the 1990 election.

"I pulled out in 1990 but ran in 1993 because she forced me to," Mark – now the mayor of Carterton – exclaims, "and there were a bunch of people in that campaign supporting the NZ First candidate, and they always came up to me saying 'you're in the wrong party, you need to join NZ First', which I laughed at."

But the 1993 election result ushered in the Helen Clark coup, "and by then I'd become close friends with Mike Moore." Mark was offended by the viciousness of the coup, and despite "nearly tipping Ruth out of Selwyn on her ass" (he reduced her majority to just 888 votes), when Richardson resigned from parliament in 1994 forcing a by-election Mark told Labour he wouldn't stand, not for them.

"I couldn't honestly stand up and say I supported the leader," Mark says. From being a close second in the seat, Labour's next choice when Mark blew them off, schoolteacher Marion Hobbs, came a distant third in the by-election, won by National's David Carter with the Alliance second.

Ron Mark, as a loyal Moore supporter, initially threw his energies into the possibility of creating a new Mike Moore party. It dragged on for over a year.

"I'd been working with Michael Laws, Geoff Braybrooke, Peter McCardle, Jack Elder – there were a bunch of people who wanted to be involved with Mike in that party – like Margaret Austin and a lot of others.

"We'd done so much work, and Mike had garnered up some good financial backing from Gil Simpson [now Sir Gil, of Aoraki Corporation] and some other people he mixed and mingled with, but then it got messy."

When Mark heard that Michael Laws had jumped to NZ First, then Peter McCardle and Jack Elder, he realised that Moore's party was never going to happen: "All of these were the people who'd been working with Mike to set up Mike's new party that he was going to lead."

There was a meeting at Tusker's Bar, on Church Corner in Christchurch. Mike Moore was there, Clayton Cosgrove too, Tony Day – the chair of Labour's regional committee, and Ron Mark.

"We just tried to drill down into Mike and find out once and for all what he was doing. He never said, but it became patently obvious that he wasn't going to leave Labour. After 18 months work, he just didn't have it in him to leave.

"There was a lot of talk from Mike about 'those bastards' – being Helen's crew, but we just couldn't get a commitment out of him."

When Moore popped away for a few minutes, Cosgrove, Day and Mark just looked at each other. It was Cosgrove who voiced the unspoken thought in Ron Mark's mind. "I think you should probably join NZ First," he said.

Another factor that will have given Moore the speed wobbles was the creation of United New Zealand in 1995 when a group of National and Labour MPs – many of whom had toyed with the Moore party concept – quit the big parties to establish what we now know as United Future. The only name readers might recognise today was Peter Dunne, formerly Labour, but there were six other defectors, Labour MPs Margaret Austin and Clive Matthewson, and Bruce Cliffe, Pauline Gardiner, Peter Hilt and John Robertson, all ex-National.

With the first MMP election looming, the centrist seven hoped to occupy the middle ground and head off NZ First. The problem with United, however, was its inherent blandness. It failed to resonate with voters. Nonetheless, Austin and Matthewson were two Moore had hoped for, and they'd now given up waiting for him.

In a harbinger of the fate that befalls most third parties, commentators noted soon after its formation that "United, which has a coalition agreement with the Government, is copping a lot of flak because it is being seen as the Government's lackey."[213]

---

213 "Defections to NZ First leave National and Labour tied," Mike Booker, The Independent, 4 April 1996 p3

Sensing that Ron Mark had electoral mana, two senior regional figures in NZ First had made numerous approaches ever since the 93 election. They were later joined in their overtures by former National Cabinet Minister Bert Walker, who'd established the "Sunday Club" in the eighties as a pressure group to influence National. Bert told Mark he should be in NZ First. Mark initially maintained them at a polite arms length. The collapse of the Moore party initiative in early 1996 changed all that.

"When Labour had asked me to stand in 1993, leader Mike Moore came to my home and actually asked me," says Mark. "My conversation with the NZ First guys went along similar lines, I said 'if NZ First wants me to stand, then Winston will come and ask me himself. If he can't do that, then I guess I won't.'

"Bugger me dead, a couple of weeks after that conversation I get a phone call from Winston Peters saying he'd like to come and see me. I immediately rang my mother-in-law because she had been instrumental in getting me involved in politics and had given me a lot of good advice along the way."

When Winston turned up at Ron Mark's home in Christchurch with Doug Woolerton, the party president, Marie Berry was already there in the lounge, waiting to grill Peters. Mark says it was NZ First's unique blend of "social conservatism" that appealed, "the hand up not hand out sort of mentality", with a focus on the needy.

"Of course one of his core constituencies was the elderly, and I guess as a former soldier you are inculcated with that deep respect for elderly people, because they are the people who fought through the war years, whether they did it at home or did it offshore.

"I also like the nationalistic flavour. I'd come back from five years in Oman, working for a Sultan who had laws I thought were eminently smart, that protected his people from being taken over by foreign investors – in fact, he still got all the investment that we were told we wouldn't get, and he still kept control of his country, his economy and his people's future.

Ron Mark says conversations with Winston about "controlling immigration so it benefits the country rather than swamps it, those are issues I had empathy for…Of course I was chuffed to bits to find out that Jack Hinton, the Victoria Cross winner, was a member and that Charlie Upham (another VC winner) was sympathetic to the party."

It was his mother-in-law, Marie, who gave the nod of approval.

"Yep, do it, join NZ First."

Mark later received something deeply personal from Mike Moore.

"Mike gave a friend an envelope to give to me, and inside it I found a letter from Mike confirming that I was his first choice to replace him.

"When I went to NZ First I think Mike was fairly gutted. He'd wanted me to stay out there in the ether until he finally left parliament, and then take over his seat, but of course with me going – ironically partly on the recommendation of Clayton Cosgrove – he then handed it on it Clayton."

Although Ron Mark would later play a key role in New Zealand First, his first steps were political baby steps and he describes himself as "a newbie" who was initially outside Winston Peters' circle of power.

"I certainly wasn't moving at the levels Michael Laws and Peter McCardle were, and definitely not Doug Woolerton. That was to come later," says Mark.

Laws was "energetic, on fire, ideas pinging, I thought he was bright, positive and very astute politically. He could smell a populist issue, fifty fathoms down in a sealed concrete basket. A very, very sharp political nose and great at writing policy, it just oozed out of him, and he clearly had far more energy than anybody could ever contain, that was my first impression. I remember thinking, 'Mmm, if you were one of mine I'd bloody put my foot on your throat and hold you down, just to slow you down a bit!'"

Michael Laws was coordinating most of the political preparation for the 96 election, although even Laws wasn't privy to everything, as Laws himself writes:[214]

"My first meeting with the inner circle of the New Zealand First organisation took place at the Northern Club in Auckland and proved welcoming, if slightly fraught, for reasons that soon became apparent. Apart from Winston and Deputy Leader Tau Henare, I was introduced again to Winston's personal assistant, Sarah Neems, new party president Doug Woolerton, treasurer Kay Urlich, legal representative and close Peters confidant Brian Henry, and parliamentary staffers Terry Heffernan and Rex Widerstrom.

"There was also a mystery participant whose identity was considered so hush-hush that I wondered if the Second Coming was really at hand. Instead, former TVNZ journalist and *The Paradise Conspiracy* author Ian

---

[214] The Demon Profession, Laws, p297

Wishart appeared – a sufficient reminder that the Winebox hearing was considered a critical factor in New Zealand First's strategic deliberations."

For the record, I don't recall ever meeting Michael Laws, not even when we later worked for the same radio network, albeit from different cities. My appearance was so 'hush-hush' on the occasion referred to that I actually wasn't there.

It is true there was an inner circle operating above Laws, and some of those mentioned above were on it. I'd been asked by Brian Henry to brief Grey Advertising, which was handling the NZ First campaign strategy, on aspects of the Winebox case. I only attended one meeting – at Grey's corporate offices, not the Northern Club – and Laws didn't make it.

Laws has been highly critical of NZ First's level of organisational preparedness for the 96 campaign, and left wing political scientist Bryce Edwards has talked of the "shambolic"[215] party organisation. Ron Mark says he saw no evidence of that in Christchurch:

"I only knew it as what it was, and down in the Christchurch area it was huge, Christchurch was massive. The party went over 30% in the polls at one time, and down in Christchurch it was vibrant. Every electorate had a committee that was running hot. They were always running functions of one sort or another, raising funds, it was doing really, really well."

Mark acknowledges the breakdown in personal relationships between Winston and some of the party's original 1993 team, like Brooke McKenzie or Rex Widerstrom and Wellington Central candidate David Stevenson, slowed progress down from time to time but with no lasting damage.

"The ship might have shuddered occasionally, but it didn't stop. It didn't bother me; I'd just come from the Labour party where I saw people getting their throats slashed from behind, left, right and centre. It didn't seem as bad as that, not by a long shot."

Of course, in most other parties such attacks usually focused on an identifiable 'other'. NZ First, on the other hand, was the home of the political suicide bomber, people who managed to do often spectacular damage to themselves, not so much the enemy. Take Laws as an example.

Michael Laws' NZ First career was meteoric in the traditional sense of the word; it flared, burned brightly, then crashed to earth in a trail of smoke and debris. At the end of February 1996, NZ First had just two

---

215 "NZ First Party History: The Shambolic Party Organisation," by Bryce Edwards, 27 November 2008

MPs – Winston and Tau. By the first week of April, they had five, and the increase was almost entirely down to Michael Laws.

The Hawkes Bay MP had quit National and joined NZ First on 6 March 1996, when the Moore party fell through. He immediately turned his attention to persuading National's Peter McCardle and Labour's Jack Elder to join him with Winston. Both men had low rankings within their own parties, both had been prepared to join Moore. On April 4, they also took the leap.

National's 50 seats from the 1993 election had now been whittled down to 41, thanks to defections. MMP waka-jumping had become a national sport, even before the first vote was cast.

Laws was particularly chuffed to have scored McCardle: "Employment is his forte. He really gives us a lot of grunt in that area."[216]

The defection of one Labour and two National MPs in the space of a month was a massive PR coup for NZ First, giving the impression of a party seriously on the move. That image had been enhanced when Winston Peters began attacking immigration policy in late February.

Coming out of the summer break, with the Winebox Inquiry in recess, the party polled 6% support in February 1996. Within a week of the February immigration speech it had risen to eight percent in the polls, and within two weeks to 12%. Clearly Peters had hit a nerve.

For decades, New Zealand had followed a mostly white immigration policy – with a surge of Pacific Islands migrants to staff factories in the early to mid-seventies as well. The last big wave of migrants from the UK had arrived in 1974, but Britain's announcement in 1984 that it had signed an agreement to hand Hong Kong back to China by 1997 opened up new opportunities. The Lange Labour government believed it could entice expat Brits and leading Hong Kong Chinese who didn't want to remain there, and New Zealand loosened its immigration policy to achieve this.

There were stumbles along the way, like the 1988 decision by Labour to appoint a Hong Kong criminal to run the new Serious Fraud Office in Auckland; the mistake was only caught in the nick of time. In an interview with radio station 89FM (now merged with Newstalk ZB), Justice Minister Geoffrey Palmer defended in 1988 the migrant policy in regards to security, telling listeners that background checks were provided "by the Hong Kong police".

---

216 "Two more MPs cross the floor to NZ First", Evening Post, 3 April 1996, p1

Of course, it may no longer come as a surprise to learn that Triad gangs controlled the Hong Kong police, which is why people with shady backgrounds have turned up so often in New Zealand, including the nominated first pick to run the SFO.

"I was a victim of my own success," one of Hong Kong's top former security officials said in the 1990s. He has to remain nameless for blindingly obvious reasons.[217] "I kept digging into the bad guys, and I found that the money laundering, gun running and drug trafficking was intertwined with some of the major corporates here, Government officials and even the British security services.

"When I wouldn't stop investigating, they let me keep my title, but gave me a desk without an in-tray. I was given nothing more to investigate. The Hong Kong police force is run by the Triads.

"That's one of the reasons that you now have Asian organised crime in New Zealand," he added. "When the Labour Government opened up immigration in the late 1980's, it naively thought it could screen the immigrants and weed out the undesirables. Even more naively, your Government was allowing Hong Kong Government agencies to do the vetting, and Hong Kong's got the best agencies money can buy."

And in case you don't believe it, try an entirely separate conversation, where Hong Kong lawyer Colin Leaver was trying to explain to a kiwi counterpart that he could not just "take" his information to the Hong Kong Serious Fraud Office:

"Then why don't I take this to the Hong Kong Serious Fraud Office, or whatever it is that you have here," said Dickie. "They can investigate, they've got the power to deal with these people."

Leaver felt like smacking his forehead with the palm of his hand in a gesture of exasperation.

"I obviously haven't explained this properly. This is Hong Kong. Organised crime runs this city, and they run the law enforcement agencies too. You cannot trust any of them. If you go to a law enforcement agency with this information, you will be dead before you reach the airport to leave."[218]

In 1987 there were 7,036 migrants to New Zealand from non-English

---

217 Interview with author, published in Lawyers, Guns & Money, by Ian Wishart, HATM, 1997, p248
218 Lawyers, Guns & Money, by Ian Wishart, HATM, 1997 p247

speaking backgrounds. By 1995 more than 30,000 migrants to NZ had difficulties speaking English.

Speaking to a receptive audience in Auckland's Howick, Peters talked of "rows of ostentatious homes in this very suburb, occupied in some cases by children whose parents have no ties in this country other than the price they paid for the house, and who prefer to remain outside its shores."[219]

There had been screeds of articles on TV and in the newspapers about Asian migrants who had effectively purchased residency in New Zealand as a bolt-hole to escape Chinese rule in Hong Kong, who had dumped their teenage children here to take advantage of New Zealand's free education and health systems, but who nonetheless remained in Hong Kong or Taiwan where their businesses were.

When journalists accused Peters of being racist about Asians, his response was blunt: "Can I suggest you go back to your own archives and look at the sheer volume of stories you have written about Asian home-alone teenagers, left to roam a strange city out of control for months at a time."

The problem, incidentally, hasn't gone away. As a major feature in *Investigate* magazine noted this year,[220] big accountancy firm Andersen, in a 2013 briefing to clients, noted "that the ease with which non-residents can buy property in New Zealand contributes to unnecessarily high house price inflation, causing harm to New Zealanders who cannot, as a result, afford to get on the housing ladder.

"There is a related issue that also often features in the media. This is the case of so-called 'astronaut' families, where the wife and children live in New Zealand, enjoying the benefits of New Zealand's education and health care system, while the husband works overseas. The breadwinner usually visits New Zealand for short periods of time. Anecdotally, the evidence is that most breadwinners in this situation do not pay tax in New Zealand. We believe that in many cases New Zealand income tax is actually payable."

Again, not only are New Zealand citizens subsidising the government's migration policy through interest rate rises and hefty house price inflation, but the migrants are often not paying tax here either, according to Andersen's.

---

219 "Politicians gambling with the race card," by Brent Edwards, 24 February 1996, p14
220 "The $elling Of New Zealand", by Ian Wishart, Investigate June/July 2014

Knowing what we now know, nearly 20 years after Winston Peters began warning about it, are his original criticisms "racist and xenophobic"? Or was he simply stating the obvious whilst his opponents tried to shame him into silence using the language of political correctness?

The issue is painted by the media as one of race, but it's more one of nationalism – the right to maintain economic and political sovereignty over one's country. It doesn't really matter whether 20 million Australians or 20 million Chinese eventually apply for residency in New Zealand or a mortgage loan on an investment property – the end result is an economic, political and cultural impact on those already here, of all backgrounds.

The recent revelations that many migrants are not even paying tax in NZ, whilst enjoying taxpayer-funded services, adds fuel to the fire now that wasn't there back in 1996.

Prime Minister Jim Bolger, at the time, said he was outraged by Peters questioning migration:

"Politicians through time, when seeking a new populist plank to attract the disgruntled, have sought to channel that anger against a separate and distinct minority. The trick is old but the obscenity of the tactic does not diminish. I hope we will hear no more of the New Zealand First leader's slander against Asian or other migrants."[221]

Bolger, retorted Winston Peters, was a hypocrite:

"Who called it a 'surge of people' when somewhere between 12,000 and 25,000 additional immigrants were allowed into the country? Who referred in the debate to not wanting a 'deluge' of people entering the country? That was Jim Bolger," Peters told parliament, happily quoting a 1987 speech from Hansard where Bolger was opposing Lange's decision to open the migration floodgates.

Peters went on to question the Prime Minister's assurance that immigration numbers were now trending down as a result of 1995 category changes. How could that be, he wondered, when the figures to February 1996 showed a net migration gain of more than 30,000, compared with 21,000 in the 1995 period. "Somebody has not been telling the truth," he accused.[222]

Bolger was furious.

---

221 "Politicians gambling with the race card," Evening Post, supra
222 Hansard, Appropriation Bill, 21 March 1996

"Truth is an interesting objective statement from that right honourable member, who is often a stranger to it –"[223]

"I will show the liar that he is," yelled Peters, "up in the Winebox inquiry –"

It took the intervention of the Speaker to disentangle the verbally-brawling protagonists, but not before Bolger had some sport of his own with an old Winston speech:

"The member should recall his speech he gave before the 1990 election. He said as follows, and I invite him to listen: 'New Zealand needs a third wave of migration if it is to become an effective trading nation in the 21st century'."

It was a speech given to an Australian trade delegation in Wanganui.[224]

" 'Migration would help develop the necessary skills, attitudes, and access to capital and trade markets. This does not mean we neglect to train and educate our own people. However, anyone who does not subscribe to the necessity of immigration ignores the devastation of our economy at least partially caused by minimal regeneration of New Zealand society in past decades."

What Winston Peters had identified was New Zealand's low birthrate; because of the high number of abortions our population growth was essentially stagnating, just treading water between an almost balanced births and deaths. If you are going to exterminate the next generation, the only way to get growth and more workers was immigration.

Ironically, Jim Bolger himself had identified this as a problem the previous decade, when questioning a new forecast that New Zealand's population could hit four million within ten years – by 1997:[225]

"At present the population is 3,300,000. The population projection of the Department of Statistics for 1997 – based on medium fertility and low migration – is 3,400,000 people. Therefore…NZ is 600,000 people short of Mr Fay's projection.

"This means, of course, that we require an extra 60,000 births a year, or an extra 1154 births a week."

That was over and above the existing birth rate of 53,000 a year.

---

223   Ibid
224   Wanganui Chronicle, 18 October 1990
225   Hansard, Address in Reply, 23 September 1987

"As all members know," joked Bolger, a father of nine, "my wife and I have done our bit to assist the birth rate, but I have to say, when looking at Mr Fay's forecast of four million people in ten years' time, that other members will have to do much better – and faster!"

Bolger worked out that even with more realistic policies to encourage more baby-making, NZ would still "have to have a policy of bringing in 500,000 extra immigrants during the next ten years." That wasn't going to happen, he laughed, "I suggest that we should not give too much weight to that forecast."

Except it did happen. Labour threw open NZ's doors making us one of the highest migrant nations per capita in the world. The Statistics Department projection of 3.4 million was hit, not within ten years but just three, in 1990.[226] Massive migration, mostly from Asia, had boosted New Zealand's population to 3.74 million people in 1996, when Bolger and Peters found themselves slugging it out over migration in Parliament.

Back in 1990, argued Bolger, Winston Peters had called for a smart migration policy "aimed at attracting the best people to New Zealand. More than any other issue it must be faced positively if we are to create a sustainable economy and society in the future."

"That was the member for Tauranga!" trumpeted Bolger, waving a copy of the *Wanganui Chronicle* article around. "This is the same hypocrisy we have to put up with."

Michael Laws tried to raise a point of order. Bolger just sneered: "Oh, the rabbit is hopping up and down."

Peters' argument, naturally, was that it hinged on the definition of smart migration. Was it smart to bring in tens of thousands of migrants a year who couldn't speak English and couldn't find work? The main centres, particularly Auckland, were overrun with foreign doctors driving taxicabs because their foreign qualifications were not to a New Zealand standard. What sort of social pressures were being created as a result?

Even critics like journalist Brent Edwards – whilst still accusing Peters of "playing the race card" – had to acknowledge Peters had made at least an arguable point:[227]

"Virtually no resources have been put aside to help integrate those new

---

226 http://www.indexmundi.com/new_zealand/population.html
227 "Politicians gambling with the race card," Evening Post, supra

New Zealanders into Kiwi society. Non-English speaking adults find it almost impossible to learn language skills. The West Auckland Polytechnic was 1000 people on its waiting list this year and just 60 places available for adults wanting to learn English...in response the Government has imposed an English proficiency test on migrants but it requires just a rudimentary command of the language."

Bolger then attempted to embarrass Peters over an advertisement placed in a South African newspaper which read:[228]

"New Zealand Immigration. New Zealand is actively seeking professional, technical and business migrants." Prospective South African migrants were urged to contact "A Fenwick at Lyon Lucas, Barristers and Solicitors. W Peters, member of Parliament, on legal staff."

It was a cheap shot. Peters' old lawfirm still had his name on the letterhead as a "consulting partner". Even Parliament's acting speaker Peter Hilt, no Winston fan, had to intervene:

"I am sorry to interrupt the right honourable Prime Minister, but I do have specific recollection of the member for Tauranga making a personal explanation to Parliament in which he denied receiving any remuneration."

The same caveat applied to a Lyon Lucas immigration ad that ran in Bangladesh.

Labour's Annette King backed Winston Peters up, talking about migrants "coming into New Zealand and sitting on the dole, unable to get jobs, unable to contribute." And as for smart migration, she wondered, "Why is the Prime Minister not aware of the impact that people from Soweto, Bangladesh and Pakistan will have on New Zealand? Why has he not undertaken any research into what impact immigration has on New Zealand, and why does he continue to blame migrants for the mistake that the Government made?"[229]

Bolger looked across at King.

"I would commend to the Labour member Annette King and her leader Helen Clark, the speech just given by the new Governor-General of New Zealand when he talked about those who came to New Zealand to make their lives here, and are equal citizens in this country. It was a superb speech."

---

228 The Sowetan, 19 June 1992
229 Hansard, Questions For Oral Answer #4, 21 March 1996

The bigger implication of the immigration debate was a fundamental one going to the heart of democracy: as one of the only countries in the world giving migrants the vote when they were not actually citizens, what about the rights of people who were in fact citizens? They suddenly found their votes were only worth as much as someone from Pretoria, Islamabad or Beijing who wasn't even a New Zealander, who hadn't made a commitment to the country other than buying or renting a house, and who as big accounting firms are now warning often don't pay taxes here either.

Yet these people were getting the vote, making donations to political parties, having an influence on future immigration and business policy.

"What price should we place on owning New Zealand – either its land or its citizenship," asked Peters. "Such questions go to the heart of determining our future. It is not racist or xenophobic to ask them... This year, choose to have a say in the future of the nation we share. To have that choice you must first join us in putting New Zealand and New Zealanders first."[230]

Journalists covering Peters' speeches in the mid-90s were often surprised to find Asians and other migrants cheering in the audience as well, yet ethnic community leaders who didn't attend were invariably scathing of Peters as a 'racist'. Former party president Doug Woolerton has a theory on that:[231]

"You see, they hear, Winston's got lots of sayings, one is 'put the caveat up the front'. And he puts the caveat up the front although New Zealanders never hear it. What do they call it, dog whistling nowadays. Which is far too sophisticated in my view.

"Immigrants always hear the caveat, the caveat is, and you will hear this in his speeches, 'if you are here, you intend to stay here and you have been here six months' or whatever the hell else he says, 'you are a New Zealander. So I'm including,' and he doesn't say this bit, 'I'm including you as a New Zealander in this speech when I speak to these other pricks who are here illegally.' And they hear that. New Zealanders never hear that. That's the caveat in his speeches when he talks immigration."

The media never reported the caveat[232], "and I don't know whether they

---

230 "Politicians gamble with the race card," Evening Post, supra
231 Interview with author
232 As a TVNZ journalist covering some of the speeches, I heard it. I may not have mentioned it.

pick it up," says Woolerton, who nonetheless feels guilt at how easy it was to generate poll ratings. "This is the bad part now, we used to be able to get two per cent from one day to the next raising immigration. Two per cent right there, any day you like. You just write a speech, bang, there it is."

As evidence of migrant support for Peters, take the case of a 2013 debate on migration on Newstalk ZB's Danny Watson show one afternoon. Watson was staggered to get calls from Chinese and Indian New Zealanders lamenting the lax laws surrounding migration and foreign ownership. "You can't just go to India and buy land," said one, "why on earth are you letting foreigners come here and do it?"

There may be a United Nations reason for that.

Breaking down national borders and allowing unrestricted migration into what the OECD calls the "settlement countries" of Australia, Canada, New Zealand, the UK and USA[233], is part of a long held United Nations blueprint for globalisation that went hand in hand with promoting lower birthrates in settlement countries so they would eventually have room for migrants.

The plan worked. OECD documents show that in 2005 in New Zealand, the number of 15-19 year olds entering the workforce as a 'cohort' was 169%, or 1.7 times, the size of the number of 60-64 year olds about to retire. That meant that in 2005 we were still putting more workers and taxpayers into the workforce than the number of pensioners who were leaving it – a key measure of taxpayers/welfare recipients.

By 2020, reports the OECD, the cohort of young people entering the workforce will be smaller (at 96%) than the number of people joining the pension. The burden of paying for the upkeep and health care of the baby-boomers will fall on half the number of new workers than it did in 2005. The ratio will become far worse by 2030.

There are only two ways out of that nightmare. One is for every New Zealand woman to have a minimum of four children, preferably by the age of 25, and for their daughters to do the same. The other, as the OECD points out, is mass migration. The migration rates we are seeing today will have to increase even further.

The United Nations has cunningly made it almost impossible for nations like New Zealand to pursue a repopulation strategy based on more births. The UN's Agenda 21 document that emerged from the 1992 Earth Summit

---

233 http://www.oecd.org/els/mig/46656535.pdf page 10

at Rio has become part of "soft law" that New Zealand, in particular its local councils, adheres to.

Agenda 21 stipulates that humans should be strongly encouraged to abandon the countryside and live in concentrated city enclaves in order to make the environment "sustainable". Agenda 21 forms the basis of our Resource Management Act, and the basis for town planning in most cities. Auckland's Unitary Plan seeks to turn suburban homes – where one house sits on a 600 m2 section – into three unit apartment complexes on the same land footprint: much less grass for kids to play on, but supporting three families instead of one per section. Auckland's population could conceivably triple, but the roading infrastructure would remain the same. Who in their right mind would have four kids living in a crammed city apartment? The Unitary Plan is based on Agenda 21. A million migrant workers, however, might find Auckland apartment living attractive.

Given that almost all of New Zealand's population increase from 3.3 to 4.5 million has come from migration, so will the next million people that Auckland is planning for. Migration remains a huge bone of contention.

It is not just permanent migrants who factor in the policies. New Zealand has the highest ratio of international students in the world – 67,000 a year in 2006 as the OECD's comparison year, compared to double that number in Australia with five times our population. Even the top international student destination, the USA was accepting only quarter of a million overseas students a year, despite having a hundred times the population of New Zealand.[234]

New Zealand also takes in more than a hundred and thirty thousand migrants on temporary work visas each year.

New Zealanders, Winston Peters told rallies up and down the country in 1996, have never been asked their views on migration policy by the Government:

"This is an issue about ownership of one's country and its future, and ownership of individual futures as well...neither does this Government have any idea what a sound population policy for New Zealand would comprise. Worst of all, the Government has no desire to include the New Zealand people in a debate on this issue."[235]

---

234 Ibid, page 24
235 Hansard, Appropriation Bill, 21 March 1996

To Bolger's jibes about hypocrisy, Peters challenged the media: "Put a microphone under his nose and ask him whether he ever stands by anything he says – back in 1987 [he] was bitterly vituperating about the Labour Party's policy. He called it the worst mess in immigration history. He said he did not want a flood or a deluge, and then he went on to talk about not selling his turangawaewae for thirty pieces of silver... ask him, 'Prime Minister, do you ever, ever stand by anything you say?'"

The immigration debate made headlines, understandably, in Asia. One newspaper questioned why 51% of voters "believe New Zealand has too many Asians, even though they make up less than 0.5% of its 3.5 million people?"[236]

Fast forward to the 2013 Census, just 17 years later, and 18.9% of Aucklanders are now of Asian descent. Overall, 11.8% of New Zealand's population. By contrast, 11.1% of Aucklanders, the biggest Polynesian city in the world, are Maori.

The firestorm surrounding immigration policy continued to burn for NZ First. It rose to 14% in the polls in March, then 22% in the UMR Insight/NBR poll at the start of April; "the second month in a row support for the anti-foreigner party has surged," warned the NBR, "one of the most spectacular turnarounds for a minor political party."[237]

Translated into seats under MMP, National would have 46 seats, Labour 28 and NZ First hot on Labour's heels at 26 seats. The Alliance would have 12. "Labour and New Zealand First are feasible partners," said NBR, stirring up expectations that Winston would join with Labour in any coalition.

Two things were about to happen to NZ First however, and they threatened its election chances to the point of snatching defeat from the jaws of victory.

---

236 "Newcomers unite New Zealand foes", Star-News Manila, 24 March 1996, p6
237 "Peters emerges as MMP kingmaker" by Graeme Hunt, NBR, 4 April 1996 p1

17

A Funny Thing Happened On The Way To The Poll

"Everything is funny as long as it is happening to someone else"
— Will Rogers, 1930

It was an unfortunate own goal by Michael Laws that provided Winston Peters with his first major crisis of the 1996 election campaign. Not only was Laws an MP, he'd also decided to stand for his local council in October 1995.

Elected with the largest popular vote of all candidates, Laws decided he could cut through council red-tape by getting a company part-owned[238] by his wife to do some polling research for the council at a lower cost than other polling firms were going to charge.

The Audit Office eventually investigated and found a "technical" breach of the rules which it was prepared to write off as an "honest mistake". That "technical" breach was that Laws had failed to declare his wife's financial interest in the company and therefore the contract. Laws subsequently paid the $2000 bill that his wife's company was charging from his own pocket, so that no one could accuse him of having his family benefit from a private council contract. Laws says his wife's company was only used so the contractors could be paid and IRD PAYE paid on their behalf — the job was otherwise being done at cost.

---

238 Out of interest, Companies Office records show Karen Laws was left as the sole director and only controlling mind of the company when her fellow directors resigned on 26 September 1995 – before the polling work was commissioned

However, like many things in politics, the devil was in the detail. Some of the polling work had been carried out by Louise Sampson, the parliamentary assistant to Laws – he was still a National MP at the relevant time.

Apparently in an effort to avoid muddying the waters around the use of a taxpayer-funded worker to do private contractual work, Sampson signed off her polling report using a fictitious name, "Antoinette Beck".

When Laws' opponents on the Napier City Council, including councillor John Harrison, got wind of the fact that a company linked to the Laws family had secured a private council contract, they started poring over the documentation looking for something they could hang him with. Who was this "Antoinette Beck", they wondered.

Initially Paul Sherriff, another Laws associate who'd worked on the poll, claimed the signature was his and he'd done it as "a gay prank". Sherriff had sometime previously switched from being what Laws described as "outrageously heterosexual"[239] to someone who preferred men, leading to rumours, Laws writes, that he himself was "a pooftah"[240] having an affair with Sherriff, hence the 'prank'.

For several weeks the scandal over the fake signature and the family contract bubbled away in the Hawkes Bay newspapers and stayed out of national politics, although both National and Act were being secretly briefed:

"Mr Harrison's was no lone ranger battle," wrote NBR's Fran O'Sullivan later.[241] "As Mr Harrison's campaign widened he had major behind-the-scenes support from both National Party and Act New Zealand strategists, National cabinet ministers and local businessmen who were fed up with Mr Laws' antics…

"The *National Business Review's* inquiries disclose that Mr Harrison was feeding both National and Act strategists with details of his campaign right from the start."

When a local newspaper compared the 'Antoinette Beck' signature to Paul Sherriff's handwriting, it was chalk and cheese. When they compared it to parliamentary secretary Louise Sampson's handwriting it drew comment in parliament, even though Sampson wasn't named in the report:[242]

---

239   The Demon Profession, p75
240   Ibid, p308
241   "Laws' fall comes giftwrapped" by Fran O'Sullivan, NBR 26 April 1996, p 11
242   Hansard, Questions for Oral Answer #10, 18 April 1996

"Does that news report contain further information regarding the signature of one Antoinette Beck that was used by the polling company," asked National's Roger Sowry in the House, "and does that information indicate that the person Antoinette Beck, who to date has been suggested as the author, may in fact not be a person at all?"

"That is for experts to determine," replied Attorney-General Paul East, but one does not have to be an expert to see from the newspaper photograph a remarkable similarity between two signatures, and one of them is not the handwriting of the person who to date has been suggested as the author of the signature."

Winston Peters then entered the fray, and made a fatal, if unwitting, mistake.

"Could the Minister confirm to the public of this country…in respect of this signature, that it is not the signature of anyone in the office of New Zealand First, full stop?"

Sampson, although she had worked for National at the relevant time, was now in the NZ First office. Michael Laws claims he'd earlier tried to tell Winston the full story:[243]

"On more than one occasion I attempted to tell Winston the entire truth but Peters would hold up hand and stop me in mid-sentence: 'Michael, don't tell me anything. When I look down the barrel of the camera I want to honestly say that I have absolutely no evidence to doubt your public word. Ride it out, it'll go away'.

"Peters' later explanation in the House, that no one within the NZ First parliamentary offices was responsible for the poll signature, was not based on any assurances provided by me. As was his tendency, Winston had carried the rhetoric one step too far. I listened to the speech in horror —my failures had become the tar-baby with which to entrap Peters as well. I had been careful throughout the whole issue not to mislead the House; inadvertently Winston had done just that."

Laws blames Peters, but in my view Laws could only have been "careful throughout…not to mislead the House" if in fact he had known it was Louise Sampson's signature from much earlier. That meant Laws was a co-conspirator in the 'gay prank' lie. No great surprise as Laws knew very well he had never employed an 'Antoinette Beck' to work on the poll, and he had only hired one typist.

---

243 The Demon Profession, Laws, p310

Laws had told parliament back at the end of March[244] that "my contact throughout this whole matter has been Mr Paul Sherriff, Director of Harlequin Research Associates," but he wrote in his book that he himself had co-ordinated the whole thing:[245]

"My electorate office was to be used as the polling base...I asked my parliamentary secretary, Louise, if she would mind doing some extra typing; and I sought out my former research colleague Paul Sherriff to complete a cursory analysis of the initial raw results."

Laws also states in his account of the scandal that he has "never been a director of PNZ [the company controlled by his wife] or its public relations predecessor Harlequin."[246]

Unfortunately, Companies Office records show Laws was indeed a director between October 1991 and October 1992. Sherriff was never a "director".

It wasn't the use of his wife's company to provide the interface at cost that did Laws in, it was lying about the whole shebang. I recall Brian Henry phoning me up:

"What should Winston do about this?"

The answer to me seemed obvious, and Brian already knew it himself. I think he was just seeking reassurance.

"Laws has lied about the signature and helped cover it up. In doing so, he appears to have allowed Winston to mislead parliament. If Winston lets Laws stay on he can kiss the integrity issue that he likes to raise goodbye. If he acts decisively now, he'll be seen to have imposed accountability and held his friends to high standards."

It was no skin off my nose. I had a winebox inquiry to cover and *The Paradise Conspiracy* was the #1 bestseller in the country. I certainly had a soft spot for NZ First's political ambitions, but I was also being feted by officials from both Labour and the Alliance wondering if I would be interested in standing for parliament in the 1996 election. The answer to all requests from all parties was a polite 'no'. I'd worked in the Beehive, I'd seen the machine first hand. I was having far too much fun as an author and publisher.

Within 24 hours of passing my own ten cents' worth to Henry, Laws was gone, just after lunchtime, and it was clear Winston had been sitting

---

244   Hansard, Questions for Oral Answer, 28 March 1996
245   The Demon Profession, p305
246   Ibid, p307

on Laws' letter of resignation for two days, presumably seeking counsel as Henry had done with me:[247]

"On 21 April, I received a letter from Michael Laws, which read, 'Dear Winston, this letter is to formally offer my resignation to you, both as a member of the NZ First caucus and a member of parliament. I have failed my own standards with regard to this matter, let alone anyone else's'...

"Since then," added Peters, "I have had a chance to talk with Mr Laws. This is a grave, responsible offer and decision by Mr Laws. It is also an extremely sad one, potentially curtailing a brilliant political career. But New Zealand First means what it says on the issue of political accountability, and I have therefore accepted his offer."

In most political parties, MPs circle the wagons around embattled colleagues and attempt to tough it out – the excuses trotted out when Labour's Minister of Social Development David Benson-Pope was found to have slapped the thighs of teenage girls and made them stand in the freezing cold in their nighties are an example. At the time Laws fell on his sword back in 96, no minister had taken responsibility for the Cave Creek tragedy which had killed 14 students and teachers when a DOC viewing platform collapsed on the West Coast. To have a politician, any politician, admit they'd done wrong and quit was a breath of fresh air for the public. Even NZ First's enemies were astounded, their guns unexpectedly spiked:[248]

"I think it's a triumph," Act party strategist Simon Carr told the NBR. "It's the first time that a parliamentarian has resigned on something like this and actually I give him a lot of credit for it."

"He resigned," wrote journalist Russell Brown.[249] "And Winston Peters was quite right to point out that that simple fact set him apart from anyone else in the current government. Lockwood Smith did not resign over student fees, despite his signed promise to do so; Simon Upton did not resign over the bad blood scandal which saw haemophiliacs infected with HepC; Denis Marshall did not resign over Cave Creek. Peters needed Laws to fall on his sword to maintain New Zealand First's credibility and Laws, the good soldier, did so with a flourish – quitting the council, parliament and his newfound party in one fell swoop."

---

247 Hansard, Personal Explanation, 23 April 1996
248 "Laws' fall comes giftwrapped," NBR, supra
249 "Hard News", 26 April 1996, http://nznews.net.nz/hardnews/1996/19960426.html

It was also a sign that Winston Peters was prepared to seek wider counsel when confronted with issues where he felt conflicted. Peters and Laws went back a long way together, and as Laws acknowledges in his book Winston felt a sense of loyalty to Laws and tried to persuade him to stay. Regardless of his personal feelings, however, Peters had sent out feelers and acted on the advice. Maybe the party was not a one man band after all.

The man responsible for bringing Laws down, Napier councillor John Harrison, sent a message to Prime Minister Jim Bolger's office:

"I've told them in the PM's office, I want a knighthood and a job in Washington!"[250]

When Bolger saw the next round of poll results, however, a knighthood slipped off the agenda rapidly. NZ First was surging on the back of the Laws scandal, hoovering up Labour's support and moving within striking distance of National:

"Labour has become the latest victim of NZ First's rise in opinion polls, with a third of its support dropping away, largely to the Winston Peters-led party," reported the *Dominion*.[251]

"Last night's TV3-CM Research poll showed Labour's share of the party vote has fallen 10 points to 16 per cent since March, while support for NZ First has risen seven points to 25 per cent. The remainder of Labour's support seems to have jumped to the Alliance, which gained four points to 12 per cent. The Alliance appears to have stopped losing support to NZ First. National was up one to 40 per cent. Richard Prebble's ACT reached 4 per cent, just under the critical 5 per cent threshold for party votes.

"Translated into seats in Parliament, the poll would give NZ First and Labour 53, meaning they would have the numbers to form a government. However, NZ First would have the upper hand in any coalition, holding 32 seats to Labour's 21. National would have 52 seats and the Alliance 15.

"Mr Peters continued to dominate the preferred leader stakes, with 27 per cent support. Prime Minister Jim Bolger was steady on 19 per cent, while the Alliance's Jim Anderton and Labour's Helen Clark were on 7 per cent and 4 per cent respectively.

"A slight majority agreed with Mr Peters that immigration was excessive, while more than a third disagreed. A majority also agreed that disgraced

---

250 Ibid
251 "NZ First continues poll surge," The Dominion, 15 May 1996, P1

NZ First MP Michael Laws was right to resign after becoming embroiled in a fake signature cover-up. However, 49 per cent thought he should stand again, compared with 37 per cent who said no."

Just as a point of interest, note how yet again the media were laying out expectations that Labour and NZ First would "have the numbers to form a government". It wasn't an unreasonable assumption to make, given Bolger's toxic relationship with Peters and his description of NZ First as a party engulfed in "a sordid story of deceit".[252] The previous week Bolger had even likened Peters to Adolf Hitler.[253] Nonetheless, the Labour/NZ First ticket was a theme constantly repeated in the media, and the public were soaking in it, as the old Palmolive commercial might say. The theme that Labour and NZ First would naturally team up did get in.

Labour, however, realising it was in for a caning, tried to neuter the NZ First message and was prepared to mislead the public to do it.[254]

When Peters was attacking National's foreign investment policy in Parliament, Labour's David Caygill opened up a broadside on Peters' exposed flank, claiming to quote from a Winston speech that said New Zealand had to have investment and "if we cannot fund it ourselves, we must have it funded off-shore".

It was a deliberate misquote, and what Winston really said was "if we cannot fund it ourselves, because of the absence of a national savings strategy, we must have it funded off-shore".

When Peters tried to object he ended up being thrown out of the House by the Speaker.

"Labour MPs were cock-a-hoop and gave Mr Caygill the thumbs-up for prompting the New Zealand First leader's ejection," reported one newspaper.[255] It would take more than a stunt like that to derail the NZ First election express, however, and luckily for his rivals a much bigger threat was looming. Winston Peters had a one way ticket to his destiny, but the light up ahead wasn't a tunnel exit; it was a potential train wreck at Winebox Junction. Peters was about to use up five of his nine lives in one short burst.

---

252 "PM blasts NZ First for 'story of deceit'," by Brent Edwards, Evening Post, 27 April 1996 p1
253 Hard News, by Russell Brown, 26 April 1996
254 "Clark labours the point as Peters continues to rise", by Brent Edwards, Evening Post, 11 May 1996, p2
255 Ibid

18

The Battle Of Black Stump

> "The tree of liberty must be refreshed from time to time with the
> blood of patriots and tyrants. It is its natural manure"
> – **Thomas Jefferson, 1787**

When the Winebox inquiry kicked off for real in 1995, Bolger and the National government were hoping it would be the noose around Winston Peters' neck; not because he was wrong about the Cook Island tax deals – even blind Freddy could see they were dodgy – but because the terms of reference were so narrow.

As we've seen, for three years now Peters had been making massive fraud allegations against some of the most powerful and politically-connected individuals and companies in New Zealand. They were not just Winebox deals, which had only turned up relatively late in the piece, but also related to the billion dollar collapse of the BNZ bank and multi-million dollar frauds against hundreds of investors in film and bloodstock financing partnerships designed by mega lawfirm Russell McVeagh.

That lawfirm, known colloquially as "the Black Stump" after the building it was housed in, had hired Winston Peters when he graduated from law school back in 1974. Now, two decades later, they faced off like two giant Transformers ready for battle.

Among the Russell McVeagh staff in Peters' sights were tax designer Robin Congreve, and partners Geoff Ricketts and Paul Carran. Ricketts had been National's electorate chairman for Justice Minister Doug

Graham's Remuera seat. We covered the main allegations in an earlier chapter but now the day of reckoning was approaching: Winston Peters was due to testify at the Winebox Inquiry.

Initially, there had been grave fears the Inquiry would be a rubber stamp for the government view because of its limited terms of reference; it wasn't to make findings about the Winebox transactions, only about whether the IRD and SFO had competently investigated those transactions.

Commissioner Sir Ronald Davison, a retired Chief Justice, decided to take a 'robust' view of the terms of reference, ruling that he couldn't very well determine whether the IRD and SFO had done their jobs competently unless he first determined the nature of the actual transactions, and whether there was evidence of fraud or not.

That decision sent shockwaves through the tax-planning and business communities, and also through the National cabinet. The man widely regarded as a tame shoe-in had suddenly gone free-range feral and was widening the inquiry up.

Remember, Peters had accused the IRD and SFO of either incompetence or corruption as an explanation for the way they had reached decisions not to fully investigate or prosecute over the film and bloodstock deals, the BNZ collapse and latterly the Winebox deals. The Inquiry only had powers to examine the Winebox documents.

This meant that although Peters felt he had good evidence on the BNZ and the movie and horse deals to back up his incompetence or corruption allegation, he was not allowed to rely on that evidence. He could present it – to a limited extent – but when making his ruling about incompetence or corruption the Commissioner was required to ignore it.

To see whether Winston Peters genuinely had enough facts upon which to voice his suspicions, let's examine the different scandals from the evidence that emerged from the Inquiry.

THE WINEBOX DEALS: SFO ANALYSIS

Did the SFO and IRD investigate these transactions properly? The evidence that emerged at the Inquiry clearly shows they did not. Serious Fraud Office director Charles Sturt testified that if something "doesn't pass the smell test, then I order an investigation".[256] Sturt must have had a

---

256 The Paradise Conspiracy, 1st ed, Wishart, p298

head cold when the Winebox documents arrived in his office in late 1992.

On the Magnum transaction, the SFO admitted it had seen TVNZ's legal advice that the deals were fraud, but its chief forensic accountant told the inquiry the decision to prosecute did not depend on whether the deal was fraud, but whether those involved "knew" it was dodgy. As a consequence, the SFO's initial investigation did not analyse the transactions to look for fraud itself, only to look for clues as to whether the participants admitted anything in writing that proved they "knew" it was fraud.

You may be laughing, thinking how many fraudsters admit they are being criminals, in writing, in advance: "quick, hand me a pen and paper so I can give you my signed confession along with the transaction documents". Laugh away, that is precisely the level of investigative grunt that the SFO brought to the table.

"What I was looking for was evidence of conscious dishonesty," said Sturt.[257]

Sturt was the one who handled the winebox initially, bending over it, sniffing the pages, smelling nothing suspicious. This was strange, because he admitted to the inquiry that there was reference to the "criminality" of one Winebox deal for Aussie billionaire Alan Bond, but Australia was outside his jurisdiction. Perhaps, but the "criminality" reference, on the SFO's own box-ticking list, should have sounded alarm bells that these were tax planners who perhaps were prepared to walk on the dark side.

Instead, Sturt put the Winebox on a shelf, cold-case style, after just "40 hours" of work on the 2,500 pages. He didn't let any of his other staff examine the winebox, and he was unable to present any timesheets or notes to the Commission of Inquiry that proved he had even worked for the 40 hours he claimed.[258] There was not a shred of evidence that Sturt had done anything more strenuous than simply stare at the box in the corner of his office every lunch hour for forty days, while chewing on a doughnut.

Sturt had issued a news release to parliament at one point stating that a team of SFO 'investigators' had examined the transactions and found nothing:

"Who were the investigators to whom you were referring?" asked Colin Carruthers QC, the legal counsel assisting the Commission, when Sturt took the witness stand.

---

257   Ibid p291
258   Sturt's testimony here is covered at pages 50 and 51 of The Paradise Conspiracy 2, by Ian Wishart, HATM, 1999

"I was wearing an investigator's hat for that particular purpose," replied the Director.

"There is only one of you Mr Sturt. Who were the 'investigators' to whom you were referring?"

"In the plural sense," admitted the SFO boss, "that would not be correct".

Carruthers called it "an abuse of language" to describe Sturt as an investigator.

Even when Sturt had dusted off the Winebox again after TVNZ's discoveries became public, he assigned the file to a forensic account to review.

"So we get to the position that one accountant looks at the papers for, at the outside, 31 hours, over a period at the outside of three weeks?" pushed Carruthers.

"Yes".

How then, the QC asked, did Sturt reconcile that with the press statement to parliament which claimed that "hundreds of documents" were "examined by accountants and investigators in this office over a period of several months"?

The press statement concluded by stating "the investigation satisfied me that there was no evidence of criminal fraudulent offending."

Carruthers paused, looking at the press statement for a moment longer, then fixed Charles Sturt in his gaze. "There never was an investigation by the SFO involving accountants and investigators over a period of several months, was there?"

"There was never an investigation carried out, no," Sturt admitted.

Let's stop it there for a moment, and look back at the events that had led to the inquiry. Sturt had issued the offending news release immediately after Peters had laid out the criminality of the Magnum deal in Parliament. Sturt had leapt to European Pacific's defence, telling politicians, the media and the public that the documents had been fully investigated and the fraud claims were groundless.

Peters had been outraged. He told Parliament the SFO director was "either lying or incompetent" and that he should be suspended pending an inquiry into "possible corruption" of that office. The Government called Peters' attacks on a senior public servant "outrageous" and eventually called the inquiry.

It turns out Peters was right. Sturt had lied to parliament. He had cleared the Winebox despite doing no investigation.

Under Aung San Suu Kyi's eloquent definitions of corruption, Sturt's behaviour was clearly corrupt in my view. But there was more evidence of strange behaviour as well. Sturt was accused of trying to discredit the man who'd given him the Winebox, Stephen Lunn, claiming Lunn had tried to sell the Winebox for a hundred thousand dollars. In a press statement to Parliament, Sturt went so far as to say, "the Director was not prepared to make any offer of payment of public funds to Mr Lunn."

Challenged by Carruthers, Sturt was again forced to admit the claim was a lie, Lunn had never once asked him for money. Why would a supposedly independent law enforcement agency repeatedly lie and run interference on behalf of big businesses connected to the Government who were accused of fraud?

Sturt, it turned out, had lied repeatedly. It also transpired that the SFO *had* seen documents in the Winebox hinting at the possible illegality of the deals, but it chose to ignore them.

"The reference to 'detection' attracts the eye," testified the SFO's Gib Beattie about one document. "So too does the reference in para 5 to payments from an entity that 'purported' to be a Pacific Rim Development Bank. Also of interest is the apparent ability of European Pacific to rewrite the laws of the Cook Islands."[259]

"I would also comment on the sentence which states 'no legal difficulties that there is any intent to defraud persons revenue of monies owing'."

Another document overlooked by the SFO read, bluntly, "Therefore, the Cook Islands withholding tax is not a 'tax', promotion of the note constitutes a criminal offence by company officers and those knowingly involved in a conspiracy to defraud the Australian Revenue."[260]

There was also a reference in the Magnum deal which read, "This money 'run around'…is likely to be a breach of s62 of the Companies Act 1955".[261]

In fact, Gib Beattie had not been asked to look at the Magnum transaction that generated two million dollars' worth of fake tax certificates, until after the SFO had watched TVNZ's June 1994 *Frontline* "bouncing money bags" doco that showed how the whole rort worked. His more detailed investigation came three months after Sturt's claim that a team

---

259 The Paradise Conspiracy, 1st ed. Wishart, p292
260 Legal opinion by Brian Oslington QC for European Pacific, quoted in The Paradise Conspiracy, p294
261 The Paradise Conspiracy, 1st ed. Wishart, p297

of investigators had spent months examining the files and cleared them. They had not even looked at the main transaction, it turned out. Incompetent or corrupt? That is the question we will return to.

WINEBOX DEALS, IRD ANALYSIS
Winston Peters had called IRD boss David Henry a liar or incompetent under privilege as well.

"If the Inland Revenue Commissioner, David Henry, can find no evidence of tax fraud in the Magnum Corporation transaction alone, he should resign or be sacked. If the Commissioner of Inland Revenue stands by his press statement of last Friday and today, and continues to claim that all of this – including the use of fake tax certificates – is legal, he should be fired immediately and charged with conspiracy to pervert the course of justice in New Zealand."

The first piece of evidence is David Henry's 18 March 1994 news release, which claimed to have subjected the winebox documents to expert scrutiny and found no illegality. What emerged at the inquiry was that Commissioner Henry had exonerated the Magnum deal *before* he had received legal advice about it.

What kind of credible investigating agency clears a crime before it actually investigates it? Having issued his Friday 18 March release, on Monday 21 March David Henry decided to ask barrister Grant Pearson for a legal opinion on Magnum. He gave the lawyer 48 hours to complete it and report back. Normally the IRD consulted two senior QCs, Tony Molloy or Peter Jenkins. Neither man was asked to work on the Magnum transaction.

The IRD and SFO press statements of 18 March 1994 appeared to be jackups. They were used by lawyers for European Pacific to try and get the winebox investigation by TVNZ permanently suppressed, on the grounds that David Henry and Charles Sturt had both cleared the winebox transactions of any wrongdoing.

Was there some kind of political/corporate/civil service conspiracy to shut the whole thing down and deprive Winston Peters of oxygen?

The IRD "all clear" of 18 March looks even more suspicious when its testimony to the inquiry confirmed proper investigations of the winebox documents actually began on 29 April 1994, six weeks *after* the supposed clearance.

Those suspicions of a corrupt motive grow larger in my view when the testimony of BNZ taxation manager Spyros Papageorgiou is taken into account. His file notes of discussions with the IRD about the winebox reveal that the IRD felt "pressured" by Winston Peters, and senior IRD investigator John Nash was quoted as saying the IRD investigation was just for show: "the process we were going through was basically an attempt to placate the Commissioner in respect to Winston Peters' allegations."[262]

Nash allegedly told the BNZ that he was doing all this just "in case a subsequent internal quality review (IRD) was undertaken by the Audit Office or some other organisation", that the winebox was "a pain in the neck", and that if anyone asked the IRD had to be able to say it had "reviewed the papers".

Does any of that sound like an honest investigation by the IRD? If it doesn't, does it mean that the IRD acted corruptly in the way it approached the Winebox, just as Peters had alleged?

Remember, the IRD issued a news release on 18 March clearing the transactions of fraud. They'd received a copy of the Winebox in March 1993 from the Serious Fraud Office, and had some staff in the Tax Intelligence Unit trying to analyse the deals. The head of the unit was Tony Loo, and he told the inquiry he didn't even understand the Magnum deal until he saw it explained on TV, four months after he'd finished his team's analysis.[263]

"At the time I did my analysis in March 1993, I didn't understand how it operated."

When Counsel Assisting the Commission, Colin Carruthers QC, showed Loo the main planning document for the Magnum deal, his response was essentially, "what's this?"

"I don't particularly understand it because I have never read the document before."

Carruthers couldn't believe it, nor could anyone else. How could the IRD's Tax Intelligence Unit have analysed the Winebox deals and "cleared" them if it did not actually understand them and the key documents had not been read?

So far, you've seen, I suggest, clear evidence of incompetence and, if the documents accurately record the position, corruption involving the IRD trying to whitewash the Winebox for political reasons so as not to give Peters any momentum.

---

262   The Paradise Conspiracy 2, Wishart, 1999, p30
263   Ibid, p32

But it wasn't just the winebox deals. The inquiry heard evidence outside its terms of reference in relation to the film and bloodstock partnerships.

THE RUSSELL MCVEAGH DEALS

First of all, do you remember what Winston Peters had alleged about the bloodstock and film deals leading up to his expulsion from the National Party in 1992? Let's revisit the parliamentary speeches to refresh the memory.

On August 4, 1992, Winston Peters laid bare the details of a movie called *Merry Christmas Mr Lawrence*, alleging it "defrauded the revenue of the sum of $11,472,400. This is a substantial conspiracy to defraud for which the perpetrators, once found guilty, should go to prison."[264]

Those of you who've read John Grisham's bestseller *The Firm*, or seen the movie starring Tom Cruise, will appreciate the next bit. Peters accused one of New Zealand's mega lawfirms, Russell McVeagh, of engineering this massive $11 million rort on taxpayers, using complicated company trails winding through exotic overseas tax havens.

"Some partners of Russell McVeagh McKenzie Bartleet were clearly a party to the conspiracy," Peters said. "The main perpetrators are: Robin Congreve, who invested $10,000, thereby defrauding New Zealand revenue personally of $34,400, and that is only part of the offence; Geoff Ricketts, who invested $35,000, thereby defrauding New Zealand revenue of $120,400--and, as we all know in this country, both Robin Congreve and Geoff Ricketts are directors of the Bank of New Zealand; they were running the bank in the time before the Government was required to bail it out--and the third person is Paul Carran, who invested $15,000, thereby defrauding New Zealand revenue of $51,600."

Peters told Parliament the IRD had determined the movie's tax haven transactions to be "a sham", a legal term for fake, and he tabled an IRD letter to investors advising them of this dated 7 April 1988.

"That information has been with the Inland Revenue Department for some time. Why has it not acted on what is clearly massive, criminal, fraudulent activity? What immunity from prosecution do those perpetrators of fraud have in this country? Is not the law in New Zealand to be applied in the same way for everybody?"

Given the lack of action by the IRD, Peters laid a complaint with the

---

264 Hansard, Appropriation Bill, 4 August 1992

Serious Fraud Office. After all, his arch-rival Ruth Richardson, Minister of Finance, had often challenged him to:[265]

"I am aware that the member has made a number of unsubstantiated claims of white collar theft, serious breach, fraud, massive criminal fraudulent activity, lies and deceits. No evidence of that has been tendered to any of the appropriate authorities…as I have repeated on many occasions…if anybody has evidence he or she is honour-bound by the law of the land to front up to the appropriate authority with that evidence."

Back in the 80s, massive tax breaks were available to investors in New Zealand made movies and horse-breeding syndicates. For every dollar you put in, you could generate tax write-offs of up to $2.50. It was money for jam for investors, or at least that's the way promoters of the schemes sold them.

Two hundred people, putting in $10,000 each, could finance the making of a movie, or buy a share in one of the world's best thoroughbred mares.

Problem is, some of the horses investors had paid for did not actually exist. They were fictitious horses managing to chew their way through very real grass, oats and even stud-servicing fees all billed to the investors by the management company for the syndicates. Some of these fictitious horses even had fictitious foals, for which further very real expenses were charged back to the investors.

Turns out most of the horses had actually been bought from the original stud farms indirectly, although again the investors didn't know this. The paperwork they saw said Horse X had been purchased from a top Irish stud for $2 million, when in fact it had been purchased for maybe a quarter of that price by a tax haven company controlled by a Russell McVeagh lawyer, who then onsold the old nag to the investors for the $2 million price – the said lawyer and his tax haven company pocketing the $1.5 million mark-up for each animal.[266]

The horse-droppings had hit the fan behind the scenes. The IRD had

---

265 Hansard, Questions on Notice #6, 15 October 1992
266 This is a generalised description of the "hydraulicking" of prices that went on. For more detailed, 'price-accurate' and specific information, see Lawyers, Guns & Money by Ian Wishart, HATM 1997. The real irony was that even the secret middleman got ripped off, paying about twice as much for the horses as they were worth. "There's been armed robbery here," explained the British Bloodstock Association when it saw the prices paid for the horses. See p293 of LGM

tumbled to the expense frauds and was disallowing around 60% or in some cases 100% of the claimed tax expenses. During the course of its investigation, IRD investigators led by John Nash had raided the offices of Endeavour Productions in Wellington, a company controlled by film and TV producer John Barnett who later went on to produce *Shortland Street*. The IRD raid was illegal, the tax department had exceeded its powers.

While Russell McVeagh geared up its legal teams to fight over the IRD raid, the tax department finished investigating another company that produced a Tatum O'Neal movie, *Prisoners*, which was so bad apparently that it was never released. Hundreds of investors in that movie had been hit with massive tax bills after the IRD disallowed 60% of the movie's expense claims as bogus.

Russell McVeagh, however, saw a chance for some "negotiating leverage". The lawfirm arranged a "special deal" – not for all the investors, but just for the investors who also happened to be Russell McVeagh lawyers or their very special friends. That special deal was that if the IRD agreed to let the Russell McVeagh partners keep most of their expense deductions, and if the IRD promised never to prosecute the Russell McVeagh investors for tax fraud, Russell McVeagh would find a way to solve the problem over the Endeavour Films raid that had left the IRD exposed.

Hundreds of other investors in *Prisoners* would remain in the gun, but the Russell McVeagh investors would have much lower tax bills and the IRD would not charge them with fraud. It was, just as Winston Peters had alleged in parliament years earlier, a secret "non prosecution" agreement, a copy drafted by senior Russell McVeagh tax lawyer Geoff Clews was tabled at the Winebox Inquiry. See for yourself:[267]

"The agreement for settlement with partners in *Prisoners* is limited. The offer is to be extended by the Commissioner only to those persons whose names are set out on the list attached as schedule 2.

"The terms of the offer are to be relayed in a way which makes it clear that the offer should remain confidential from other partners in *Prisoners*."

And why should it remain confidential from other partners in the same movie? Because the Russell McVeagh lawyers were getting a financial advantage from the IRD not offered to other investors in the same movie.

---

[267] Quotes taken from Winebox Inquiry evidence, reprinted on pages 204 and 205 of Lawyers, Guns & Money

This deal was being offered by the IRD to the Russell McVeagh partners "in consideration of those persons [the Russell McVeagh lawyers] not financially supporting or supporting further (as the case may be) the litigation" in the Endeavour proceedings.

According to one IRD document tabled at the inquiry, Clews was acting for nine colleagues from within his lawfirm and promoter John Gow.

Senior IRD Auckland tax investigator Denese Latimer testified to the Winebox Inquiry that Russell McVeagh had blackmailed the IRD into not prosecuting them:

"I had been told by Clews," testified Latimer, "that Russell McVeagh was funding it [the litigation against the IRD over *Endeavour*] – that they pulled the strings. Clews was blackmailing us, by saying if you want out of [*Endeavour*] you will give in on [*Prisoners*]."

Clause 4.11 of the deal between the IRD and Geoff Clews is arguably illegal and unenforceable, but nevertheless, it was part of the deal they struck.

"No partner accepting the Commissioner [of Revenue's] offer to settle that partner's tax liability arising from participation in one or more of the partnerships shall be subject to any impost of penal tax or to prosecution.

"This agreement shall apply notwithstanding any request by the Commissioner of that partner for a personal explanation of any alleged discrepancy or any advice to that partner that his case is to be considered under the penal provisions of the Income Tax Act 1976 or otherwise."

Such a deal had never been seen in the Auckland IRD office with its 1200 staff. It was unprecedented, a special financial benefit for a small group of lawyers, an amnesty from penal tax or prosecution, and a promise by the IRD never to re-open the investigations.

When Denese Latimer refused to sign off on the non-prosecution deal, Geoff Clews threatened to go to people in high places:

"If we were not prepared to continue the discussions," she testified, "he would have to go to a higher power…the Commissioner, the Minister of Revenue and the Minister of Finance."

Remember, this was a secret, quite possibly illegal non-prosecution deal, and Russell McVeagh felt so well connected it was allegedly mentioning the Commissioner and the Minister in the same breath.

Clews denied making such a blatant threat although he did admit mentioning the Minister of Revenue. In a form of damage control, Fay

Richwhite's lawyers tried to get Latimer to agree that it wasn't blackmail, merely "negotiating leverage".

Michael Scott, another senior IRD investigator, told the Winebox Inquiry, "The settlement appeared far too low, and purported to benefit unnamed persons. Mrs Latimer had been requested three times to sign the settlement letter by Messrs [John] Nash, Bouzaid and [IRD lawyer Angela] Satterthwaite and refused to do so.

"Eventually, as I understand it, Mr Bouzaid signed the settlement letter agreement on behalf of the Inland Revenue Department."

When Latimer refused to sign the final version of the agreement on December 4, 1991, she had been rung by Satterthwaite, who told her to get on with it. Later the same day John Nash – the man who'd blown the *Endeavour* investigation in the first place – phoned and told Latimer that she wasn't aware of the background circumstances, and that she should "put the past in the past".

Let's pause a moment and look back at what Martin Hames called those wild and unsubstantiated allegations of Winston Peters, besmirching innocent people and linking them to some non-existent conspiracy; what was it Peters had said again?

"Decisions by the Serious Fraud Office and the Inland Revenue Department not to prosecute have been made behind closed doors, and I ask, what right have they to be judge and jury away from the scrutiny of justifiably suspicious New Zealand people? Who knows what favours are being called in or bribes are being paid, even as we speak, to save the reputations of some of New Zealand's so-called leading business figures and top political campaign donors. It is time for charges to be laid and the evidence to speak for itself – thousands of pages of tabled evidence and criminal deal after criminal deal."

Another intriguing movie was *Merry Christmas Mr Lawrence*, still available on DVD and movie download services. Starring rock legend David Bowie and filmed at both Auckland Grammar and the Cook Islands, this prisoner-of-war movie managed to come second behind *ET* in Japan in terms of box office earnings, and third behind the James Bond movie *Octopussy* in Britain.

The IRD went after *Mr Lawrence* investors like rats up a drainpipe:

"The initial contributors to this Partnership were Messrs R L [Robin] Congreve and P C [Paul] Carran of the legal firm of Russell, McVeagh,

McKenzie, Bartleet & Co. of Auckland," noted an IRD status report tabled at the Winebox Inquiry.[268]

Documents obtained by the IRD indicated the company Mr Lawrence Productions Ltd had declared a fake loan of NZ$4.6 million as a business expense when the loan didn't really exist, and that the film company had failed to declare $3.8 million of film income, disguising it as a loan instead.

The IRD investigation status report makes it clear the tax department considered fraud was involved:

"The following investors, based on the weight of evidence obtained, appear to be parties to the deception. These are: Mr C G P [and] Mr C J K, ex Broadbank Investments Ltd, [and] Mr P C C [and]Dr R L C, [of] Russell McVeagh."

Despite stumbling on hard documentary evidence that US$2.9 million of movie profits had been transferred to a Channel Islands tax haven company and hidden from both ordinary investors and the IRD, the IRD's Auckland office suddenly found themselves under pressure to stop investigating the many movie deals. Chris Dickie, the lawyer suing on behalf of disgruntled investors, found out why in a meeting with Russell McVeagh tax partner Geoff Clews.

"Mr Clews informed us that he would not deal with the investigating officers at Otahuhu, including Mrs Latimer, but would only deal with the head office of the Inland Revenue Department at Wellington.[269]

"He further informed us that he was endeavouring to obtain a settlement in not only Merry Christmas but also in a number of other film partnerships. I do not know the names of the other partnerships, but it was plain from that meeting that the settlement proposals which Mr Clews was undertaking certainly included more than just Merry Christmas."

In fact, just like the *Prisoners* deal, Clews was 'negotiating' with the IRD head office to back off on 16 movie partnerships.

IRD Auckland had discovered what it was convinced was clear tax fraud in Mr Lawrence – the missing US$2.9 million that had ended up in a tax haven bank account. Geoff Clews tried to neutralise that in 1991, suddenly producing a letter dated 1983 supposedly explaining that the movie investors had agreed to relinquish their rights to US$2.9 million. If the

---

268 See Lawyers, Guns & Money, p141
269 Chris Dickie in testimony to the Winebox Inquiry, 1996, see LGM p160

money no longer belonged to the investors, argued Clews, it couldn't be their taxable income now, could it.

The IRD's Denese Latimer, smelling another giant McRat, went and had the get-out-of-jail-free document tested by forensic examiner John West, a police documents expert. West compared the letter to other Russell McVeagh documentation from 1983 and concluded it was probably a forgery, according to a report tabled at the Winebox Inquiry:

"An interim reply from Mr West," she wrote, "indicates that his best guess is that the document [dated 1983] could not have been prepared prior to 1985 based on the print type.

"By way of a note, *Mr Clews confirmed* [author's emphasis] at the meeting on the 8/11/91 *that the document was prepared by his firm in 1983*, but this appears unlikely as the type setting bears no resemblance to similar dated documents prepared in their office."[270]

The IRD in Auckland now had the top forensic document examiner in NZ as a potential witness alleging a major lawfirm was presenting forged documents in a tax fraud inquiry. IRD Head Office in Wellington, however, was hell bent on shutting down the inquiry into Merry Christmas Mr Lawrence.

The IRD, through Tony Bouzaid in Head Office, negotiated a deal where any further inquiries by the IRD into tax fraud in Merry Christmas were to be stopped immediately. Russell McVeagh's Robin Congreve and Geoff Ricketts – directors of the BNZ and Fay Richwhite Ltd respectively – were off the hook.

When Winston Peters began raising these matters in parliament, IRD Deputy Commissioner Robin Adair ordered his 1200 Auckland staff not to talk to Chris Dickie or Tony Molloy about anything, and announced that the bloodstock investigations were to be stopped forthwith as well. When the IRD's second in command in Auckland, Norman Latimer (Denese's husband) discovered the Wellington head office was still in contact with Russell McVeagh, he wrote an explosive letter to Adair:

"I note with concern in this regard," he wrote, "that subsequent to Mr Peters' disclosures in Parliament, the department has been in communication with Messrs Russell McVeagh in respect of the matter.[271]

---

270 Lawyers Guns and Money, p196
271 Evidence tabled at Winebox Inquiry, see LGM p257

"I am extremely concerned that the department's actions in communicating with Russell McVeagh, while at the same time limiting communication with Messrs Molloy and Dickie and suggesting that the bloodstock investigations have been 'stopped', might wrongly be construed by an independent third party, acting upon inquiry, as being evidential of not only a cover-up, but also of a conspiracy between the department and certain taxpayers or their representatives."

Does all this sound like an "honest" IRD? A "competent" IRD?

When Peters dropped his *Mr Lawrence* bombshell in parliament, IRD Commissioner David Henry was warned by his senior staff that Tony Bouzaid had signed a non-prosecution agreement and closed down all further investigations, on the basis of a document likely to have been forged. Testimony at the inquiry suggests Henry didn't care when he rang up Denese Latimer after Winston Peters started raising the issue.

"Tony made that decision, and that's enough for me."

Henry, who just the previous evening had told journalists and politicians there was no truth to the Peters allegations, and no suggestion of "fraud", decided to finally ask the senior investigator on the case the big question:

"Was there a fraud against the investors?"

"Yes," answered Latimer.

"What about us?" asked Henry.

Remember, this was a man who had already publicly stated the previous day that there was no fraud. It was very late in the day to be asking these questions.

"By accepting Mr Clews document without properly finalising our inquiries," Denese Latimer told her boss, "we were virtually saying no."

"Well," said Henry remembering his comments to the media a few hours earlier, "we withdrew the sham and fraud claims."

"Actually, we didn't," said Latimer. "The settlement chose not to deal with these aspects, but the end result, in effect, was yes."

"The department isn't concerned with who got the money," continued Henry.

"Under the settlement, we agreed not to look at anyone associated with the film and therefore that wasn't looked at," explained Latimer.

"If the Serious Fraud Office contact you," he concluded, "you are not to give them any records, and you are to contact me."

"I'll do that," promised Latimer.

Which brings us to an interesting point. Remember Ruth Richardson's repeated 'put up or shut up' demand to Winston Peters – "If that member has evidence, he knows where to take it". Well, Winston Peters did take it, to the Serious Fraud Office, but although they said to the media and parliament that they investigated, it turns out they didn't.

Here's what Peters wrote:

"It is clear from the documents that a significant conspiracy to defraud exists. Mr King, a senior partner in the law firm Russell McVeagh McKenzie Bartleet & Co has publicly stated that the Inland Revenue complaint of 7 April 1987 has been withdrawn.

"Mr Henry, Commissioner of the Inland Revenue Department, has publicly stated that this matter was fully investigated and completed in December 1991.

"I understand that the great majority of investors in the film *Merry Christmas Mr Lawrence* are being required to repay the money deducted in reliance on the investment. This can only be the case if the Department of Inland Revenue's view, as expressed in the 7 April 1987 note to investors, remains unchanged and an improper deduction has been made.

"I believe the perpetrators named in my speech in the House have reached an agreement with the Commissioner of Inland Revenue, which is recorded in writing and includes an agreement not to prosecute. I believe such an agreement is unlawful and that a serious criminal conspiracy has been wrongfully covered up in circumstances where the Commissioner of Inland Revenue had, and still has, a duty to initiate a prosecution."

That was the complaint to the SFO. Peters didn't have a copy of the secret non-prosecution agreement, but he was as sure as hell that it existed and that the SFO should find it.

"I asked them to investigate an agreement between a civil servant and a so-called taxpayer that was unlawful," Peters later told the Winebox Inquiry, "and, more importantly, to find the document which I believed was in existence."

So what did the SFO actually do?

Literally two weeks later, SFO director Charles Sturt issued a press statement clearing the IRD of any wrongdoing:[272]

"There is no information before me that would lead me to conclude that Mr Henry has been involved in any way in a cover-up of a criminal conspiracy."

---

272 SFO news release, 21 August 1992

It was a very odd statement to make because just the previous evening IRD boss David Henry had told journalists, "when the Serious Fraud Office agrees to discuss it with me, I will be happy to do so."

"I drew the inference," Peters told the Winebox Inquiry in 1996, "that the Director of the Serious Fraud Office had made little or no inquiry, and certainly not of the Commissioner."

What had the Serious Fraud Office done? Nothing. Sturt however, was prepared to lie to Peters – long before Peters had ever attacked him for being either incompetent or corrupt. In a letter to the MP, Sturt talked of his "investigation" into the Bowie film:

"You may not have been aware that the *investigation* [author's emphasis] into the allegations surrounding the film partnership *Merry Christmas Mr Lawrence* and other film and bloodstock partnerships were commenced by this office in 1991," wrote Sturt.

And then came a bare-faced lie from the director of the Serious Fraud Office.

"Furthermore, the *investigation* of the allegations relating to Mr Henry, Commissioner of the Inland Revenue Department, were likewise commenced and completed many months ago. The findings of our *investigation* satisfied me completely that the allegation of any criminal wrong-doing by Mr Henry was groundless. As would be expected, this was treated in the strictest of confidence.

"The matters to which you referred recently in Parliament and the material you forwarded to this office were already well known and did not alter in any way the conclusion I had already arrived at some time ago."

We all now know, of course, that when Charles Sturt tells the media or politicians he has done an "investigation", he might not have.

SFO senior counsel, Willie Young QC, outlined to Peters the extent of the SFO's inquiries.

"Following the publication of the Wogistan article (February 1992), the existence of possible corruption in relation to the IRD was discussed within the Serious Fraud Office.

"The investigators dealing with the films investigations were asked to keep an eye out for any evidence that supported that allegation. Now, the SFO will say that the allegations of corruption against Mr Henry were seen in the light of the inability of anyone ever to produce anything concrete."

"Mr Young," snapped Peters in response. "Did your client ever *ask* the

Inland Revenue Department for that agreement? Did they ever ask Inland Revenue for this agreement which sets out clearly an agreement not to prosecute and other favourable privileged matters?

"One simple question by Mr Sturt to Inland Revenue would have found all the evidence that you, or anybody else, required!"

"Mr Peters," snarled Willie Young back, "you are not here to ask me questions!"

"Mr Young...a Member of Parliament is making serious allegations about a non-prosecution agreement. 'Mr Henry, does such an agreement exist?' Simple question. The most rudimentary of questions and procedures to follow, and it appears to me your client didn't bother to take that very minor step."

Peters was right. The SFO had done nothing. Nothing, that is, except exonerate the IRD over what the SFO later admitted to the inquiry was an illegal non prosecution agreement without ever bothering to check out the evidence.

What was it Finance Minister Ruth Richardson had taunted Winston Peters with?

"I am not prepared to do other than have confidence in the appropriate regulatory institutions. If anybody has evidence...front up to the appropriate authority with that evidence."[273]

Little wonder senior ministers could be so "confident" – the regulatory institutions could apparently be relied on to sweep alleged corruption under the carpet, no questions asked.

There was a highly entertaining interlude at the Winebox hearings involving what Ruth Richardson knew and what she did, which I recounted in *The Paradise Conspiracy 2*[274].

In 1992, at least one senior Minister knew the truth about the deals.

Russell McVeagh tax lawyer Dr Geoff Harley confirmed he'd been attacked at a Fay Richwhite function by the then Finance Minister, Ruth Richardson, who berated him over $400 million worth of winebox deals involving Fay Richwhite and the BNZ.

The Minister angrily called the deals "tax avoidance".

Dr Harley, a man with a wicked sense of humour and a great sense of

---

273   Hansard, Questions on Notice #6, 15 October 1992
274   P41

theatre, enthralled the inquiry as he described the Minister's demeanour.

"This wasn't a conversation that permitted any explanation [of Fay's side of the story]," he told Winston Peters' lawyer Brian Henry.

"The only reason she could be angry," said Henry, "is if she thought something wrong was being done, surely?"

"There's no doubt that's what she thought – and communicated in clear terms!" replied Geoff Harley as a smile began to play at the corner of his mouth.

"Do you recall the exact words she used?" continued Brian Henry eagerly.

"No," said Dr Harley, seizing the moment, "I was more surprised at having her finger stuck in my ribs, several times, with emphasis."

On the media bench, hoots of laughter could now be heard openly as Geoff Harley fought to keep a straight face and an even tone in his voice. Elsewhere, lawyers were sheltering behind computer screens to stop Sir Ronald from seeing their smiles.

"She was basically going ballistic about it, is that it?" asked Henry, his own voice breaking.

Geoff Harley, with masterful understatement, kept his answer short and to the point.

"I understood that she was *displeased* with me."

It was too much. The hoots had become long, gut-wrenching, eye-watering howls that rolled uncontrollably throughout the hearing room, the mental image of the short, feisty Minister with the *Split Enz* hair-do scolding the naughty tax lawyer had become too much to bear. Even Sir Ronald's mouth was twitching.

None of which explains how Richardson knew about the deals, or why the Government kept taunting Peters and telling him "where's the evidence?" when the Minister of Finance already knew.

There were further bombshells on the agenda when one of the most senior staff at the SFO, former police inspector Geoff Downey, testified that SFO Director Charles Sturt had shut down a BNZ investigation for political reasons.

THE BNZ INQUIRIES

Unbeknownst to Winston Peters, a former senior BNZ manager, Brian Perry, had tipped off the Serious Fraud Office in early 1992 about what he believed were massive amounts of illegal lending from the BNZ to Fay Richwhite & Co, a merchant bank associated with one of the BNZ's major shareholders. The BNZ had lent a billion dollars to Fay Richwhite despite having capital reserves of only $389 million. In other words, the BNZ's loans to one customer were almost triple the BNZ's reserves. The lending had endangered the very existence of the BNZ, two of whose directors, Robin Congreve and Geoff Ricketts, were associated with Russell McVeagh and Fay Richwhite. Ricketts had been a National Party chairman in Justice Minister Doug Graham's Remuera seat.

Winston Peters knew there was something highly suspicious about the BNZ collapse in 1990, but he didn't know about Fay Richwhite treating the taxpayer-owned BNZ as its private piggy bank. Geoff Downey, the SFO's Chief Investigator, was asked by Sturt to investigate and ended up going around the world talking to former BNZ senior executives, who all told a similar story.

"At that time I was involved in compiling and checking the bank's reported large exposures to major customers," Brian Perry had written to the SFO, "I noted that the transactions for Fay Richwhite/Capital Markets did not appear to be included on the reporting lists for large exposures.

"If included, the exposure of BNZ to that group would have been in excess of $1 billion. I was told at the time by the head office executives that these transactions had been structured specifically so they did not need to be reported.

"My concerns about this matter related principally to what appeared to be a carefully constructed concealment of the true exposure of BNZ to that customer. This concealment appeared to be at the highest levels in the bank, and I was concerned to note that [BNZ CEO Lindsay] Pyne appeared to be aware of it, if not actually concurring with the concealment.

"I also believe it may be worthwhile exploring these transactions in respect of section 62 of the NZ Companies Act. This is the section that prohibits a company from providing funds or assistance for the purpose of purchasing its own shares.

"I am unable to offer any opinion on whether section 62 was breached, but merely make the observation that this should be investigated."

Returning to New Zealand, after verifying these allegations overseas, Chief Investigator Downey briefed Charles Sturt in April 1993 and was shocked to discover a change of heart by Sturt.

"He indicated to me that he did not want the matter to go any further, whatsoever. He told me that our friends in Wellington would not appreciate the office inquiring into the Bank of New Zealand and, in particular, he did not want to give Winston Peters any further ammunition or cause in regards to his call for an inquiry into the bank."[275]

Asked by Commission of Inquiry lawyer Colin Carruthers QC what he thought was meant by "our friends in Wellington", Downey answered "I clearly took that, and had no doubt, that he was referring to members of the National Party who were then in Government.

"It was a definite decision not to take it any further."

Downey says he specifically asked Sturt if he could interview two other BNZ executives that his contacts had recommended talking to, and claims he was told "No."

Downey says he was then ordered to hand over to Sturt all his files, documents and interview tapes on the now-quashed BNZ investigation.

"It is my understanding that the director placed it in the safe in his office."

For the record, Charles Sturt vehemently denied Downey's version of events, calling it preposterous". He would not call Downey a liar, but claimed his Chief Investigator must have misheard or misunderstood. Sturt's position was that no hard evidence of fraud had been forthcoming, and it was time to cut the losses and get on with other investigations.

Except here's what emerged at the Winebox inquiry:

Imagine, if you will, that you have been alerted to billion-dollar dealings that are allegedly placing the very survival of the taxpayer-owned state bank in jeopardy. Imagine next that you are suddenly given a huge carton of documents, most of them involving either said bank or the party allegedly behind the massive borrowing.

Would you, as a seasoned and sophisticated investigator, go through the windfall documents meticulously to see if there was any evidence to back up the earlier allegations?

One would think so, but not if you were Charles Sturt.

Hard physical evidence of the deals Perry had alerted the SFO to turned up in the winebox when Dickie and Lunn dumped it on the SFO's doorstep in October 1992. Page, after page, after page of hard evidence.

Appallingly, Charles Sturt admitted to the Winebox Inquiry that he'd failed to link the substantial evidence in the winebox with Perry's complaint, and so it went uninvestigated.

---

275   Downey evidence to Winebox Inquiry, reprinted in Lawyers, Guns & Money, p309

Massive borrowing, allegedly concealed from those with a right to know, involving the BNZ and its shareholder Capital Markets/Fay Richwhite, went uninvestigated. In fact, at the stage in April 1993 when Sturt shut down Downey's BNZ investigation, Sturt himself was sitting on the winebox documents that contained the evidence of the excessive lending to Fay Richwhite, so when he told the inquiry there was no evidence, he again was either lying or incompetent.

Shocked at these revelations at the inquiry and the inaction of his boss, the Deputy Director of the SFO, Terence Healey, independently reviewed the evidence on the BNZ and launched a formal "Part II" investigation while Sturt was on sick leave in 1997. The Part II categorisation meant the SFO had "strong suspicions" of fraud. When the SFO director found out on his return, he again quashed the investigation and in this instance forced Healey to resign from the SFO.

"The man is dangerous. He's got to be stopped," Healey said of his boss.[276] Sturt blamed all these revelations alleging corruption on "malcontents" within the SFO, but the alleged 'malcontents' did not exactly rush forward to give evidence voluntarily, however. Against their wishes they were summonsed by order of the Commission to appear and tell all. Hardly, as Colin Carruthers QC pointed out to Sturt, "exploiting" a situation for their own ends.

Sturt had also rejected as "preposterous" any suggestion that "our friends in Wellington" meant political pressure had been applied to the Serious Fraud Office. Yet in Sturt's own autobiography, published a few years later, he alleged that Attorney-General had pressured him by questioning why Sturt was prosecuting Equiticorp chairman Alan Hawkins.

"My thinking was that I did not need his advice as to which cases I would take on."

Sturt then alleged further political pressure over his decision to investigate Sports Foundation boss Keith Hancox over a $70,000 fraud. Paul East, said Sturt, rang him and "questioned whether a fraud of that value warranted an SFO investigation."

East, for his part, made a ministerial statement to parliament denying it and saying Sturt had got his facts wrong.

The point is, Sturt told the Winebox Inquiry he had *not* been subjected

---
276 Interview with author, 1997

to political pressure, then once out of public office wrote a book and claimed he *had* been subjected to political pressure.

What we do know from the inquiry is that under Sturt's management documents within the SFO were falsified in regards to its work on the Winebox, that various major investigations had been quashed, that Sturt had a "pathological hatred" of Winston Peters that pre-dated any of the MP's allegations about Sturt, that the Director had arranged for one of his staff to mislead the inquiry through "the creation and documentation of a fictitious conversation".

There was one final postscript to all of this.

Three former or current SFO staff gave damning evidence against Sturt. For my research I had tracked down two more senior SFO staff, one of them second only to Sturt in the office. All of them had equally damning evidence to give, particularly in regard to how controversial investigations had been shut down by Charles Sturt.

One of the sources explained how the Serious Fraud Office had been looking into the film and bloodstock frauds carried out by lawfirm Russell McVeagh. All was going swimmingly, said the source, until Sturt received a visit from Lyn Stevens, a lawyer associated with Russell McVeagh and the son of Sir Laurence Stevens – the Chairman of Fay Richwhite. Almost overnight, said the source, the atmosphere inside the SFO changed and the bloodstock investigation was effectively shelved. Lyn Stevens then became a contracted prosecution barrister for the SFO. In the view of my source this sequence of events reeked of conflict of interest.

In his book, Sturt attempts to explain away the SFO's lack of action on the deals by claiming that Chris Dickie and Dr Tony Molloy QC, lawyers acting for disgruntled investors in the schemes, had not found any evidence of fraud. Interestingly, their evidence was sufficient to get Russell McVeagh to cough up in full to the tune of almost $20 million dollars in a civil case, and when Molloy's book *Thirty Pieces of Silver* was published he was inundated with comments from leading QC's and even judges who believed the evidence was more than proven to a criminal standard.

Unfortunately, most of what you have read in this chapter was given in evidence after Winston Peters had already appeared on the witness stand. In other words, when he was facing cross examination, he didn't have the benefit of knowing what you now know.

There's one other thing Winston Peters didn't know: that Michael Fay had met the SFO Director after stealing *The Paradise Conspiracy* manuscript, and assured Sturt he'd seen to it that the 'explosive' book would never be published.

Was that evidence of a "conspiracy" between Sturt and Fay? I was there in the inquiry room when Winston Peters took the stand to be cross-examined at the Winebox hearing, and I diarised it at the time. Here's how it unfolded.

19

Winston On The Witness Stand

"I have a problem. No matter how I look at it, I think I'm going to have to classify several sets of Winebox transactions as fraud! I can't see any way around it"
— Sir Ronald Davison, Commissioner, July 1997

The sweet little old lady gazed around the packed Winebox Inquiry hearing room as they adjourned for the day, and shared a sweet little old lady thought with a passing journalist.

"The sods," she exclaimed, "they're just trying to trick him, but Winnie's too clever for them!"

If she'd had an umbrella, she probably would have poked it at someone. Under normal circumstances, the hapless victim would probably have been a journalist. But these were not normal circumstances, and today anyone dressed like a lawyer was fair game.

She and 50 others had bussed up from Tauranga to see New Zealand First leader Winston Peters in action at the inquiry, all of them wearing NZ First campaign buttons and not afraid to show a little verbal solidarity for the man whose parliamentary speeches caused this inquiry.

Added to a 150 strong crowd of other interested observers, the tour bus contingent completed a sizeable welcoming force for the MP – spontaneous applause marking his entrance, and fellow NZ First MP's Tau Henare and Jack Elder providing the honour guard.

Winston Peters was entering the ring with one hand tied behind his back. Whilst Fay Richwhite, European Pacific, Brierleys, the IRD and SFO had all been allowed to call their own expert witnesses to testify about the legality or otherwise of the winebox transactions, Sir Ronald Davison had forbidden Peters from calling any expert witnesses of his own. Winston was not only the star performer; he was the only performer on that front. Still, Winston did what he does best: smiled.

An American General once recalled how, as a young platoon commander in World War 2, he'd managed to get himself and his troops trapped on the business end of a vicious German assault. Faced with insurmountable odds, the platoon commander and his boys kept pumping lead into anything that moved on the perimeter, at the same time dodging the massive volleys of return fire.

"What the hell's going on?" crackled headquarters over the radio.

"It's alright sir," replied the future General optimistically, "they've surrounded us again, the poor bastards!"

At one time, 25 media personnel, including three television crews and a battalion of newspaper photographers, were darting all over the hearing room looking for vantage points and photo-opportunities.

Wednesday was definitely Winston's day. From the moment the bell rang and Winston came out of his corner, the MP took time between punches to play his audience like a piano, talking easy to understand concepts like "one tax law for everybody".

Every time he scored a point against his foes, it was as if a Mexican wave was surging through the public gallery.

"Good on yer, Winston!" rang one voice in the midst of one particularly telling exchange.

At times, also, it took on the flavour of a tennis final at Wimbeldon, as the politician and the SFO lawyer served and rallied to the ooh's, ahh's and tut-tut's from the back of the room.

Not that SFO QC Willie Young was working from Dale Carnegie's book on winning friends and influencing people.

"I meet people every day around this country," Peters had said, "possibly I have spoken to 180,000 of them in the last year at public meetings. I have not had one get up and say: 'Mr Peters, you should not be saying those awful things about the Serious Fraud Office.'"

"Perhaps you mix in the wrong company," said Willie Young, forgetting for a moment that some 200 ordinary New Zealanders were sitting behind him.

They hissed, booed, and sucked in their breath as one, leaving Winston Peters to capitalise on the moment.

"Well, if you regard the New Zealand people as being the wrong company, I can understand that given the circles you mix with," the MP snapped back.

Surprisingly, there were no more NZ First busloads for the rest of the week, but nevertheless a large cross-spectrum of ordinary people managed to fill the public benches, and still managed to tut-tut in the appropriate places.

As I wrote for the Christchurch Press at the end of the first week, they wanted bread and circuses, they got Christians and a lion at the Winebox Inquiry when it took a decidedly political and primal turn with the appearance of New Zealand First leader Winston Peters. Rather than a biblical Daniel entering the lions' den, it was more akin to Rome's Christians inviting 300kg's of furry, slavering trouble into their midst.

Trouble wasted no time making his presence felt.

His counsel, Brian Henry, started proceedings by declaring open season on Serious Fraud Office boss Charles Sturt and former Inland Revenue commissioner David Henry. The reason? Both men had made public statements pouring cold water on Peters' winebox allegations.

"It is the decision not to investigate, not to inquire and ultimately not to prosecute for which there is no check or balance in New Zealand society, save the integrity of the civil servants and their staff," explained Peters' lawyer.

Like a big cat feeling confined by the inquiry's narrow terms of reference, Peters first tested those limits and then sprang right over the top of them.

He talked of the BNZ bailout and the flow-on financial trouble it caused – Sir Ronald Davison stepped in and told Brian Henry to put Peters back on his leash.

"Mr Henry," warned Sir Ronald, "I notice there are references being made to the Bank of New Zealand which I have ruled is not the subject of the inquiry."

The leash didn't hold for long. Winston Peters said there was a much bigger background picture to his corruption and incompetence allegations than the one he was being allowed to paint.

He questioned "the role of the Director of the Serious Fraud Office in respect of the Paul White affair", before quickly adding "however, I'm advised by my counsel that this simply can't be brought within the terms of reference."

Even so, like flies to fly paper or lions to a carcass, the MP and SFO lawyer, Dr Willie Young QC, couldn't leave the mysterious death of Paul White alone.

"With respect to the Citibank tapes," said Dr Young, "Phillip Roigard [of the SFO] made contact with you on the 11th of September 1992...and he would, if necessary, say that he asked you four times whether you had evidence [of fraud], was unable to get a straight answer and concluded that you didn't!"

"With respect," retorted Peters, "here is a Serious Fraud Office that uplifts a series of tapes which an expert in that technology told me would take about two weeks to clear. They cleared it in 48 hours."

The lion-tamer running the show cracked his whip again.

"Mr Peters," intervened Sir Ronald Davison, "this is not relevant."

"But he asked me, Your Honour," said Winston plaintively.

"Whether he asked you or not, I am telling you it is not relevant," said Sir Ronald in a tone of voice that indicated Winston Peters would be sent back to his cage if he didn't behave.

The MP also alluded to the "orchestration of an attempted cover-up inside and outside of Parliament in respect of the winebox," and "the sad public televised spectacle" of the Government preventing the documents from being tabled.

But Winston Peters roared longest and loudest about the document that he says proves his claim of corruption – the infamous, previously secret, agreement by the Inland Revenue Department not to prosecute partners in the law firm Russell McVeagh for their role in the Merry Christmas Mr Lawrence film partnership.

This was a document that one senior IRD officer refused to sign – she told the inquiry last year she felt the IRD was being "blackmailed". When she refused to agree to the terms of the deal, including a promise not to prosecute, it was signed on her behalf by her boss, Tony Bouzaid, in Wellington.

"I believe such an agreement is unlawful," growled the NZ First leader at the SFO QC, Dr Willie Young.

"In this country we have tax laws and they are for everybody, not one law for one group of people and a different set of tax laws for others.

"A serious criminal conspiracy has been wrongfully covered up in circumstances where the Commissioner of Inland Revenue knew he had, and still has a duty, to initiate a prosecution. I am talking here about the law being applied equally, identically, to everyone."

Winston Peters laid a formal complaint with SFO director Charles Sturt about the alleged cover-up by the IRD, but says the SFO never even picked up the phone to ask the IRD for a copy of the settlement document before clearing it.

Dr Young later acknowledged that there was a "real issue" as to whether a non-prosecution agreement was legally enforceable, but he said that was a different matter entirely from suggesting that parties to such an agreement were criminals.

I suspect, however, that both sides in this primal struggle will be claiming victory. Winston Peters keeps on punching in words of one syllable that most people can understand. The SFO and IRD lawyers, on the other hand, have also scored points, showing an MP with a sometimes inaccurate memory when it came to chronology.

Peters told the inquiry that he hadn't had time to familiarise himself with previous evidence or transactions, and it showed. When it came to detail on some issues, he was out of his depth, a casualty – he said – of having to run a political party and having to fight off up to 14 current lawsuits.

"Mr Peters," asked Willie Young at the close of his questioning, "isn't the position here that in this respect and in other respects, you have made allegations of dishonesty and corruption where you simply haven't understood what was done and why, and can't even explain it now?"

Winston Peters, for his part, says he was never a financial "whizz-boy" and took expert advice on transactions, basing his views on that advice.

Nevertheless, the politician showed consistency. He began this quest by asking hard questions. He came to the inquiry still asking those questions, not offering answers. That, he maintains, is the job of the inquiry.

Peters had started the week well, but around 3pm on the Friday his blood sugar levels must have dropped, and he allowed Fay Richwhite's dangerous QC Rhys Harrison to back him into a corner.

Steering clear of the wider allegations of illegality in the winebox deals themselves – Harrison repeatedly asked Peters to produce any evidence specifically showing his clients had been responsible for the alleged corruption of the IRD and SFO.

"Mr Peters, you have made the most serious allegations of criminality over many years against those two civil servants and my clients. You don't have the courage now to acknowledge that those allegations have no factual basis whatsoever, do you?"

"Yes I do Mr Harrison, with respect. We have sat here for month after month, over two years, looking into the most serious transactions which were given preferential treatment by the Serious Fraud Office and the IRD, and no amount of shouting at me is going to change that!"

Harrison's biggest coup came by accident however, when he badgered an angry Peters into repeating some hearsay evidence which he said showed SFO boss Charles Sturt knew Sir Michael Fay. Little did Peters know it, but he'd inadvertently grabbed one of Chas Sturt's "boomerang chickens".[277]

Peters promised to find the source of the claim and bring her to the Inquiry the following week, so in the interim Fay Richwhite's cross examination on other matters continued.

Peters had, of course, failed to have the BNZ issue placed on the Inquiry's agenda, after strenuous opposition by all parties except the IRD.

Trying to rectify some of the collateral damage suffered by David Richwhite and Sir Michael Fay during Peters' brief unauthorised sojourns into the BNZ affair, Rhys Harrison wanted to take Peters to task on some of those matters, but only succeeded in creating more collateral damage, mostly at the expense of the SFO.

On the subject, for example, of the 1989 BNZ sale to Capital Markets and the 1990 bailout, Peters said the SFO should have investigated given the huge public controversy and concern.

"My evidence, Mr Harrison, is that on [the SFO's] formation, presumably for very similar issues like this, it did nothing. That's evidence of neglect, slothfulness, idleness!"

"Mr Peters," snapped back the QC with a hard edge to his voice, "if this was a matter of such moment to you, why did you not write a letter of complaint?"

"Because, Mr Harrison, when I became a member of Cabinet, I had

---

277 Charles Sturt had a propensity, when irritated or excited, to mix his metaphors. He once gathered all his staff together at the SFO to complain about "that swine" Peters and, whilst exhorting his troops to scale new heights against Winston, gave them some 'sage' advice: "If the oven's too hot, stay out of the chicken". Sturt became the laughing 'stock' of the intelligentsia as a result of the Independent running the story and causing a right 'flap'.

become a member of a Cabinet that had promised a full scale inquiry into this very matter, and when the National Government got into power it did exactly nothing on this matter...I would have thought in that situation, the Serious Fraud Office would have done that investigation."

It was all too much for SFO counsel Nick Davidson, who interjected to ask for the issues to be brought back within the terms of reference. Sir Ronald's response was swift.

"Mr Harrison, I am going to put a closure on this line of inquiry as far as the Bank of New Zealand is concerned. I have allowed it to go on, but I have had enough."

The ruling is understood to have provoked furious discussions within the Fay Richwhite team as to how to deal with the Peters problem.

David Richwhite was seen arguing loudly with Harrison as they walked up Auckland's steep Shortland Street a few minutes later.

"Shut it down! We've wasted enough money on this already. If we can't ask the questions just shut it down."

Across the city, Sir Michael Fay was enjoying lunch in a chic restaurant when his mobile rang. His conversation indicated he agreed with Richwhite.

The result of those discussions was revealed on the following Tuesday afternoon.

"Commissioner," began Rhys Harrison, "I am instructed to terminate my cross-examination of Mr Peters at this point...in view of your direction that I am unable to cross-examine Mr Peters on any issues relating to the Bank of New Zealand which are not winebox-related."

Harrison set out a number of areas in the transcript where Fay Richwhite or its directors had taken hits outside the terms of reference.

"In view of Your Honour's ruling, I am prevented from testing the credibility of those allegations. I simply wish to record that those allegations are emphatically rejected by the parties whom I represent."

The irony of Fay Richwhite finding itself restricted by the narrow terms of reference hadn't been lost on Winston Peters either.

"If you think that this matter requires further investigation," he'd growled during one of their earlier arguments, "why didn't you join me and my counsel in opening this matter up, but you did your best to shut it down and, more importantly, you asked for a secret inquiry Mr Harrison. Now you are on your back saying something else!"

Of all those to take a tilt at the MP however, it was arguably Brierleys' QC Jim Farmer who scored the most points on behalf of his client, and he did so without beating Winston Peters around the ears.

In a largely relaxed, sometimes humorous and mostly gentlemanly exchange, Winston Peters and Jim Farmer appeared to strike a rapport with results that satisfied both sides.

Peters said he accepted the word of BIL chief executive Paul Collins that the company hadn't been involved in the captive insurance transactions, although he expressed a strong opinion that Collins, as a director of European Pacific, should have known about the $200 million dollar insurance deal that EP carried out for the BNZ, and said he couldn't believe that Collins didn't know.

Nevertheless, he agreed with Dr Farmer that he had no evidence with which to challenge Collins.

Peters also provided an assurance that his allegations about fraud in the winebox related to the tax credit deals, not Brierleys transactions.

Alone among the cross-examining QC's, Dr Farmer was the only one to go to the heart of Peters' concerns about alleged fraud in the tax credit deals, effectively saying that even if the deals were illegal, Collins and the other non-executive directors had acted on good faith on legal opinions from respected QC's, just as Peters had relied on expert legal opinion in coming to the view that they were criminal deals.

While the QC and the witness remained at odds on the issue of how much criminal intent flows from acting on a legal opinion there was, even on this crucial issue, no shouting.

European Pacific QC Richard Craddock, widely expected to take a swing at Winston Peters, followed the Fay Richwhite lead and decided not to cross-examine, partly because the MP's parliamentary speeches were out of bounds but also because some of their questions had already been answered.

But the boomerang chicken was hovering above, and Peters was about to get clucked.

Victory for Fay Richwhite came the following Thursday afternoon, when the woman who'd passed the hearsay about Fay and Sturt and the babysitter to Peters was called as a witness.

Peters ended up retracting an allegation that Sir Michael Fay and Serious Fraud Office director Charles Sturt had met each other at Sir Michael Fay's house, chaperoned by a babysitter.

The NZ First leader had relied on information that he said came in a phone call from the former head of the Phobic Trust, Marcia Read. "I mentioned to Mr Peters," Read told the inquiry yesterday, "that I believed that Mr Sturt's second wife had previously been a nanny to Sir Michael Fay's children and had met Mr Sturt via that position.

"She had later run a child daycare centre where Sir Michael Fay's wife occasionally took her children. I had been told this in a social context previously and had no direct personal knowledge of it.

"I acknowledge that it is possible that Mr Peters may have taken my remarks as having been from personal knowledge."

Winston Peters, recalled to the witness stand afterwards, later acknowledged that in fact the information was wrong, and it related instead to David Richwhite, not Sir Michael, and he retracted his allegation about Sir Michael Fay and Sturt meeting.

Richwhite's two children went to a private creche run by Sturt's wife, Leonie, although Peters now accepted that the two men had not spoken to each other.

David Richwhite told reporters afterward that there was "no evidence whatsoever" to support claims that he or Sir Michael Fay had corrupted the SFO or Inland Revenue Department.

"There is no conspiracy, there is no fraud, there is no bribery and there is no corruption," he said, before launching a stinging attack on Peters, accusing him of "fabricating evidence to suit his political agenda," and "lying to Parliament and this Commission."

Those of you who paid attention earlier will of course know that Sir Michael Fay and Charles Sturt did in fact meet, after private investigators working for Fay Richwhite managed to misappropriate a copy of the unpublished manuscript of a book called *The Paradise Conspiracy*. At a meeting between the two men in 1995, a year prior to Peters' appearance at the Inquiry, Fay revealed to Sturt that he had taken care of it, and the SFO director wasn't to worry, because "steps have been taken to stop it from being published."

I alerted the Winebox Inquiry to the existence of this meeting, but it was never raised in evidence, and Winston did not know. The fallout from Winston Peters being suckered into a sideshow about babysitters was pretty much immediate.

QUESTION: What's the difference between the US WWII officer who once told his commanding officer "they've surrounded us again, the poor bastards!", and Winston Peters?

ANSWER: The US officer proceeded to pull the pin and hurl a grenade at the advancing Hun hordes, Winston Peters grabbed a grenade and threw the pin at advancing winebox lawyers.

As the soot clears, Winnie-the-singed-battered-but-not-broken-Pooh will undoubtedly pause to reflect on the vagaries of war – after numerous bombshells under numerous winebox witnesses to date, it was Winston's turn to take some of the punishment that he's revelled in seeing others suffer up until now.

It began Friday a week ago when, finding himself in stormy seas courtesy of Fay Richwhite QC Rhys Harrison, Peters reached out for a cement lifebuoy.

Harrison had been badgering the MP over whether he believed the SFO and IRD had been corrupted by Fay Richwhite. Repeatedly, Peters had answered no, qualifying it by saying that he believed the two Government departments had effectively been intimidated at the thought of investigating Fay Richwhite, and he described that as a form of corruption.

In one of the more esoteric twists of the inquiry to date, Peters found support for his definition of corruption from the currently besieged Burmese Opposition leader, Aung San Suu Kyi, in her essay *Freedom From Fear*.

"It is not power that corrupts but fear," she wrote in 1991. *"Fear of losing power corrupts those who wield it and fear of the scourge of power corrupts those who are subject to it.*

"It would be difficult to dispel ignorance unless there is freedom to pursue the truth unfettered by fear. With so close a relationship between fear and corruption it is little wonder that in any society where fear is rife corruption in all forms becomes deeply entrenched."

Moral of the story? If things get chucked in the "too hard" basket for the wrong reasons, that's corruption.

Needless to say, the wisdom of the east failed to save Peters from himself. Cleverly baited beyond his endurance, the MP finally lashed out at Rhys Harrison, saying he knew a woman who'd seen Sir Michael Fay and SFO director Charles Sturt together at the Fay home in the company of a babysitter.

Given, he said, that Sturt had previously testified to never having met

Sir Michael, he suggested Sturt may have lied to the Commission.

Had the MP not taken the bait, he would have sailed through his six day stint in the witness box largely unscathed. Instead, Peters found himself forced to call an unscheduled witness, the head of the Auckland Phobic Trust, Marcia Read.

Read confirmed she'd passed the information to Peters, but said there appeared to have been a communication breakdown.

"I mentioned to Mr Peters that I believed that Mr Sturt's second wife had previously been a nanny to Sir Michael Fay's children and had met Mr Sturt via that position. She had later run a child day care centre where Sir Michael Fay's wife occasionally took her children.

"I had been told this in a social context previously and had no direct personal knowledge of it. I acknowledge that it is possible that Mr Peters may have taken my remarks as having been from personal knowledge."

So where the MP had thought he had an eyewitness, he simply had a woman passing on information which she said was hearsay, and needed further investigation.

Worse still, the evidence would show that in fact Leonie Sturt ran an exclusive creche attended by David Richwhite's children, not Sir Michael's. Right hearsay, wrong man. Even so, there was no evidence that Charles Sturt and David Richwhite had actually met, let alone spoken.

Like Wylie Coyote's eternal quest for culinary supremacy over the Roadrunner, Winston Peters gulped, looked down at the fizzing explosive he found himself holding, looked up to see a grinning Rhys Harrison go "beep-beep", smiled weakly and went bang.

Peters said he accepted Read's testimony, and accordingly retracted his allegations about Sir Michael and Charles Sturt. He also accepted that Sturt had not met Richwhite through the creche.

It would be churlish to suggest that Peters failed to bring evidence to the inquiry. After all, he was responsible for the winebox papers tabled in parliament and delivered to the inquiry. Commission investigators are asking pretty specific questions about those deals, including whether the Crimes Act has been broken in three places.

Nevertheless, asked whether he had specific evidence on the more nebulous issue of whether Fay Richwhite had actually corrupted two Government departments, Peters chose to turn his "no" answers into a "yes", and suffered accordingly.

It is certainly not the end of civilisation or the western world as we know it, and when the sun rises on Tuesday, the Winebox Inquiry will still be there, still churning through the detail as it endeavours to find out who did what with the winebox and why.

⁂

Despite the fact that Winston Peters had come through his interrogation almost unhurt but for the babysitter debacle, his confidence, and his credibility, took a massive hit. It was a demonstration of the triumph of flash over substance. The sheer theatre of a senior QC in full flight ripping pieces out of the country's toughest MP was compelling grab-some-popcorn television, each frame of video footage worth a thousand words.

It looked like the MP had no evidence to support his allegations, yet as you have now read there were plenty of facts in my view that could support an opinion of corruption. The fact that virtually everyone studiously avoided asking Peters about the criminal transactions in the Winebox and instead played with the fluff around the edges speaks volumes.

Nonetheless, as a journalist covering the inquiry, I gave credit where it was due, writing a story for the *National Business Review* acknowledging Fay's "win" over Win. David Richwhite told reporters afterwards that there was "no evidence whatsoever" to support claims that he or Sir Michael Fay had corrupted the SFO or Inland Revenue Department.

"There is no conspiracy, there is no fraud, there is no bribery and there is no corruption," he said before launching a stinging attack on Peters accusing him of "fabricating evidence to suit his political agenda," and "lying to Parliament and this commission."

Richwhite also thanked me for the "fairness" of my coverage the following week. He wasn't quite so happy a few weeks later.

Although Peters had taken a dent in the polls, relatively speaking it was more of a 'ding' than a 'prang':

"NZ First's meteoric rise has stalled, bringing support back to the National Party, according to the latest public opinion polls...NZ First's startling four month rise halted for the first time, falling four points to 25% of the party vote."[278]

---

278 "NZ First star no longer rising", by Ruth Laugesen, The Dominion, 20 June 1996, p1

Yep, those were the days. When a rough poll for Winston Peters had him sitting at 25%. To put that in contrast, here's what the Dominion's Ruth Laugesen had to say about Helen Clark:

"Labour strategists will be breathing a sigh of relief after the party's vote shows no ill-effects from the attempt on Helen Clark's leadership during the past two weeks."

Given David Cunliffe's nightmare year in the polls you may be wondering where superstar Helen Clark had Labour just a few months out from the election. After all, the media have told us for years how Winston Peters was supposed to go into coalition with the Labour powerhouse. So how popular was Labour in late June 1996?

"Labour's support stands at 16%, up one," wrote Laugesen. You read it right: 16%. And Labour was 'relieved' to be there.

"Helen Clark's personal support has almost doubled to 7%, but rival Mike Moore's support has risen even more, up six points to 8%."

Staggering stuff – Mike Moore wasn't even running as an alternative leader any more, and he was still managing to trounce the hapless Clark whose Labour Party was sitting on a healthy 16% in the polls. It makes Cunliffe in 2014 look positively presidential, really.

Of the other parties, the Alliance had announced it was bringing Pam Corkery on as a candidate, and dropped two points in the poll to nine percent, while National was up six to 41% support.

National could not have governed alone on those figures, and clearly from NZ First's four point drop and National's six point rise there was some overlap in terms of both parties' core constituency. Labour could not have governed either, even with NZ First as a majority partner; it's baseline support was just too low. Bringing in the Alliance might have taken them to 50% overall, but not necessarily a clear majority or mandate for a three-headed political hydra. Winston, said Laugesen, would be "kingmaker".

Nothing to smile about there for David Richwhite. His company had spent a fortune preparing to dump all over Winston, and he was still being hailed as 'kingmaker'.

Peters wasn't out of the woods yet, however. He'd leapt straight from his Winebox appearance to being sued in the Wellington District Court the following week for the comments he'd made alleging Selwyn Cushing was the man who had offered him money before the 1990 election.

Cushing had deliberately sued for only $50,000, a threshold that forced the case to remain in the District Court before a judge alone. Had the lawsuit been for more, Peters could have elected trial by jury in the High Court, and Cushing didn't want the popular MP anywhere near a jury full of little old ladies.

It was a fascinating case from a legal perspective. Cushing had originally sued on the basis of what Winston Peters had said on the Aussie *Four Corners* documentary – where Cushing was not named –and on what Peters had later said in parliament because, said Cushing, that's where Peters finally identified him and closed the circle for defamation purposes.

Speeches in parliament, however, are absolutely protected by parliamentary privilege. It is the one place in the country where you can say anything you like, and that's because in ancient times if the King didn't like what you said about him or his mates in parliament you'd lose your head. When parliament overturned absolute rule by kings in the 1600s, it wrote laws allowing MPs to truly speak their minds to the nation without fear of the consequences.

In New Zealand law, no court has the power to call into question anything said in parliament. No court, that is, except the Wellington District Court in June 1996.

Peters refused to mount a defence to the defamation suit, because doing so, his lawyers argued, would be submitting to the Court's jurisdiction. Peters argued the Court had no jurisdiction over a parliamentary speech, and therefore he could not turn up to Court.

Peters' counsel, Sandra Moran, told Judge Dalmer, "If this court proceeds to give judgment for the plaintiff it will have...overturned 300 years of settled constitutional law. It cannot be said too often or too plainly that such a decision is totally without precedent, is totally contrary to principle, and will defeat the whole purpose of the privilege of the House."[279]

Making it murkier, Cushing had added a further allegation of defamation to his lawsuit a year after the original, claiming that an interview Peters gave on TVNZ's *Holmes* show defamed him even though it didn't name him either. So Peters faced two alternative defamation claims from Cushing in the Court.

Peters of course presented no evidence, did not appear in court, and

---

279 "Winston Peters ducks for cover", by Steve Evans, The Independent, 21 June 1996, p12

his lawyers refused to cross examine Cushing on the witness stand. It was like an America's Cup race featuring only one yacht, with the rival crew remaining stubbornly on the start line waving a protest flag and refusing to sail. Judge John Dalmer dutifully heard all of Cushing's evidence, waited for him to cross the finish line, then awarded judgment.

Cushing when he finished had tried to get his damages claim boosted from $50,000 to $200,000, but the judge rejected this on the basis that Peters had no prior notice and might have run his defence "differently" if he'd known $200K was on the line. Peters, he added, would also have been entitled to a High Court jury trial for that amount.

On 3 July, Judge Dalmer let rip. Peters, he said, didn't get one thing right about the Cushing case except his name. He said despite the constitutional objections from Peters' lawyers that he had accepted the parliamentary Hansard transcripts into the court because they were simply "extrinsic facts" that established Cushing as the target of the earlier, unnamed, defamation on TV.

Peters, railed Dalmer, had made no effort to explain himself in court or defend his actions. The words amounted to an allegation of "bribery", the MP had "titillated" the public to build up interest in a "non-existent incident", and he had "cynically manipulated" the media and the public.[280]

Even if he was wrong to enter judgment on the parliamentary speech, Dalmer said, the second allegation that Peters had defamed Cushing a year later in a TV broadcast by implying Cushing was a liar was capable of being proven regardless of what was said in parliament.

Peters, accused Dalmer, had acted "with malice" and that his claims were "false". He awarded Cushing the full $50,000 plus costs.

Constitutional law experts quickly swung in behind Winston Peters[281] – not because they liked the guy but because the lower court judge had seriously overreached his powers in ruling that he could seize hold of a parliamentary debate.

Auckland University law professor Dr Bill Hodge, Victoria law professor Andrew Ladley and a senior QC were among those who accurately predicted Judge Dalmer's ruling on the Hansard transcripts and his com-

---

280 "Clear cut case of malice – judge," Evening Post, 4 July 1996, p2
281 "Peters to appeal defamation case", The Independent, 5 July 1996, p3

ments surrounding them would be struck down on appeal.[282] They were right, but that was a long time in the future and Peters had to live with this judgment in the here and now.

A TV3/CM research poll taken a week after Cushing's "damning" defamation win registered a slide of four points by NZ First, from 28% a month earlier to 24% now.[283] Although journalists linked the slide to the court case, the figures were actually very similar to the rival poll in late June and may simply have picked up the same trends. Labour, for example, was on 16% and National on 41%.

Pundits who thought Winston Peters' bubble might be bursting were in for a shock, however, and Michael Fay and David Richwhite were left ruing the day they'd not heeded Charles Sturt's sage advice: "if the oven's too hot, stay out of the chicken". One of those chickens was coming home to roost...

---

282 As a postscript, in 1999 those predictions were proven correct, when the Court of Appeal ruled parliamentary privilege and the need for MPs to answer questions without fear of civil consequences outweighed the power of the courts. They allowed the later TV defamation claim against Peters to stand, but threw out the claim based on the Four Corners documentary and naming in parliament, and the criticisms of Peters resulting from that.
283 "NZ First hit in poll," Christchurch Press, 11 July 1996, p1

20

Winston's Secret Deal With Ratana Church

"There is no salvation outside the Church"
— St Augustine, 400 AD

Sharp-eyed readers might have picked up in the last chapter a reference to Winston Peters taking the witness stand at the Inquiry in front of a phalanx of media, including three television crews. In a country with only two news channels at the time, the identity of the third crew was a mystery.

There was no identifying logo on their equipment, they were not known to any of us working for TV One or TV3, and they were spending money like it was going out of fashion. They had three people on their crew, a luxury long since lost at the big networks, and they were rolling tape on hour after hour after hour of Winston Peters' testimony, missing nothing. They told the rest of the media they were from the "National Archives", but that seemed like a huge waste of taxpayer money. A two person crew cost $1000 a day, and a three person crew even more, let alone the cost of the tape. They'd been there for nearly two weeks.

I had suggested to Commission of Inquiry staff that they might like to check out the bona fides of the mystery crew, because something wasn't quite right. TVNZ producer and North & South writer David McLoughlin did even more digging, and tipped off the Commission to an explosive scandal – the mystery crew were filming undercover.

McLoughlin suspected Fay Richwhite. He asked Michelle Boag, handling PR for Fay Richwhite and also an election campaign strategist for

National leader Jim Bolger, whether she knew who the mystery crew was. "I don't know," Boag had replied.

The chicken had landed.

On 18 June, behind the scenes, the Commission called on the mystery crew to identify itself. The name they'd given to the Inquiry when seeking permission to film – Hauraki Films – did not exist on the companies register. On June 27, the film crew's contact wrote back to the Inquiry saying their client preferred to remain anonymous, but that they were no longer planning to make a TV programme.

This was news to the Commission, because they'd originally been told, like the media, that this was filming archival footage for the National Archives.

On 11 July, Commission executive Susan Evans turned up the heat, stating it was now obvious the Commission "has been under a misapprehension" about Zee Films' role. "From the information given previously, the Commission had understood that your company had an official role in obtaining material for film archives. If the Commission had understood the position as it now appears, you would not have been allowed to film.

"The present situation is unsatisfactory," she warned. "The Commission is not prepared to allow use of the material without its permission. You are required to answer [the earlier questions] within 7 days of receipt of this letter. Failing this, the Commission will require you to deliver up for destruction all copies of the film in your possession and to provide an affidavit to the Commission confirming you have done so."

Finally, Russell McVeagh coughed up. The film crew, confessed the lawfirm, had been filming Winston Peters on behalf of Fay Richwhite so as to use the footage against him, but they requested that this information "be kept confidential" so as "to ensure that the issue of the filming of Peters' evidence does not develop unnecessary political overtones."

With Boag acting as an election strategist for National, a party accused of being in the pocket of big business, and acting as PR for a company caught filming their main accuser, the leader of the second most popular political party, of *course* it would be kept confidential to prevent the public developing the wrong idea about "political overtones".

Not.

In the last week of July, Michelle Boag, Russell McVeagh's Mark Gavin, and a series of hapless creatures from the film company were all subpoenaed to appear for questioning in public at the Winebox Inquiry.

Like the cast in a movie of the Nuremberg War Trials, the film producers admitted they'd lied about who they were and what they were doing, they were really named Zee Films and the plan had been to discredit Peters in election advertising, and documents established that Fay and Richwhite had given the go-ahead for the ill-fated project.

The whole shebang was best summed up in a Tom Scott cartoon featuring a Bolgerish character standing hands on hips being interviewed by a crew from Zee Films: "Congratulations guys, in the absence of any other evidence you have single-handedly proved to the talkback nation that Winston is the victim of a vast conspiracy…"

Although Peters had continued to slide in the polls after the Cushing ruling, the undercover film crew did indeed change that trend. Two new polls taken after the plot was uncovered saw NZ First gaining one point to 21%. TV3's poll saw Labour remaining on 19% where it had crept in the interim, but the One News/Colmar Brunton poll had Labour slipping from that recent gain, down four points to 15% with the Alliance now at 13%.[284]

Winston Peters, in the TV3/Gallup survey, remained the most preferred Prime Minister at 24%, ahead of Bolger on 21 and Helen Clark on 7%. Mike Moore, now that he was staying with Labour, was ahead of Clark on 9%.

Peters, however, didn't have time to bask in the public approval ratings. This was his first MMP election, and there were things to be done.

Rather than sit on his hands and weight for candidates to apply to stand for the party, Peters and the NZ First board had been proactive, drawing up lists of people they wanted. On that list was Tuariki John Delamere, the athlete turned West Point officer turned public servant who Peters unsuccessfully approached in 1993.

In August 1995, he was shoulder-tapped again for Te Tai Rawhiti, the new name for what had been the old Eastern Maori seat, still held by Labour veteran Peter Tapsell. "I let Winston know it was my intention to win that nomination. And then all of a sudden around about August 1995 I was told to go to Ratana Pa."

Delamere says Winston had gathered together the five men he wanted to stand in the Maori seats, and was presenting them to Ratana secretly, for the Church's blessing. While commentators over the years have assumed NZ

---

[284] "Labour still trailing NZ First in polls," by Anna Kominik, The Dominion, 6 August 1996, p2

First broke Labour's stranglehold on the Maori seats despite the longstanding Labour/Ratana alliance, and saw the result as a diminishing of Ratana's influence, Delamere says Ratana gave its approval to NZ First in 1995. NZ First couldn't have done it if Ratana had backed Labour for that election.

"That's where I met Tau [Henare], Rana [Waitai], Tu Wyllie and [Tuku] Morgan. But Winston said, 'you are my candidates' if we kept the blessing of Raniera Ratana, he was the head of the church at the time."[285]

Delamere says the five candidates and Winston spent a long day at Ratana with the leadership.

"It was all secret, and we got his blessing and then Winston basically says, 'right, you are the candidates as long as you do the ground work to make sure you get it all in place'. That was the challenge to us that we, as far as he's concerned would be the candidates. But it was for us to set up."

That task involved going through the motions of a selection process. Delamere's was at the Waahi marae at Whakarewarewa, his grandmother's home turf.

"I had one challenger but one of the elders threw him out, so it was all done. I presume Rana, Tuku, you know, had similar situations where we went around, garnered support. So it happened. We were the Anointed ones, but no one knew about it."

Indeed, each of the candidates presented to Ratana back in 1995 sailed through their selection panels, with obstructions smoothed out of the way.

Winston Peters sold Delamere a vision of the future, that NZ First was to be "a vehicle where he would bring Maori and Pakeha together. And so it happened. In fact it was elderly Pakeha mostly, and Maori. Maori came in behind Winston, like it didn't matter who ran in the Maori seats. It wouldn't have mattered if he put in a monkey, the monkey would have won, because they were bloody pro Winston. They didn't vote for me or Tau, or whatever, even though Tau was going back a second time. Maori were voting for Winston and the Pakehas were voting for Winston."

Each candidate worked his patch, building the grassroots contacts and support needed to ensure victory. After a while, the news media began sniffing the wind and sensing a change within Maoridom. In an article predicting NZ First was about to 'unlock' the Maori vote, the Dominion noted the "raw and new" party that had attracted "ambitious" candidates

---

285 Interview with author, June 2014

like the Maori five, men who were "contemptuous of the 'Browntable' as well as the Pakeha establishment...young to middle-aged, independent, self-made. They make up a ticket well-tailored to appeal to the growing ranks of middle-income, moderately conservative Maori voters."[286]

Despite all this, the newspaper said "NZ First is not about to destroy Labour's Maori support. Other than Mr Henare, Mr Morgan is the only NZ First Maori seat candidate with a good shot at victory.

"Winston played that card pretty well," says Tuariki Delamere, "Maori and Pakeha together. But when we got to parliament it was then, 'oh you Maori keep your heads down, shut up cause you're pissing all the Pakehas off.' That started the rumbles that finally blew up a couple of years later."

In August 1996, with the polls running above 20% and the media predicting a strong Maori vote, Winston Peters called Delamere to a meeting at NZ First supporter Tommy Gear's home in Tauranga. Top of the agenda, he claims, was a preference to go with National after the election.

"There was me, there was Winston. Tommy was in the background, but he wasn't a member. There was Doug Woolerton and Richard Charters. The whole meeting, there were two topics, the main one being to make sure that we got in there – as Winston says, 'we're going to win the Maori seats, we're going to win a whole bunch of seats through MMP', is to make sure that ultimately we go with National. Winston did not want to go with Labour and it was just discussing how to make sure we got in with National, because Winston was also sure that a large number of incoming MPs would likely be pro-Labour."

If that was the case, Peters may have been influenced by a recent media poll. A One News/Colmar Brunton survey of 1000 voters back in June had found – surprisingly – that voters actually preferred a National/NZ First pairing, seeing Winston as someone who could force National to be honest.

"Prime Minister Jim Bolger and NZ First leader Winston Peters may detest each other," reported the *Dominion*, "but voters would like them to work together."[287]

The combination was seen as "the leading choice" with 21% approval,

---

286 "Ambitious NZ First set to unlock Labour's grip on Maori vote," by Graeme Speden, Dominion, 5 August 1996, p2
287 "Poll shows support for Bolger-Peters coalition", Dominion, 21 June 1996, p2

while an "NZ First/Labour pairing...was preferred by only 11% of voters."

Incredibly, voters would have rather seen Labour go into a so-called "grand coalition" with National (16% support for that idea) than seen Labour team up with Winston.

Twelve percent of respondents backed a "Labour, Alliance and NZ First government, though the Alliance has ruled out coalition with any other party." Remember that last point, because it turned out to be directly relevant to NZ First's eventual decision to go with National.

Delamere was sympathetic to National as well, having previously sought a National Party candidacy in the 1990 election. Deputy leader Tau Henare, however, was problematic. He told journalists he would never serve in a coalition where Bolger was Prime Minister, Bill Birch had control of finance and Jenny Shipley had a social welfare portfolio. Clearly if Tau Henare had his way, Labour was the only option. Ironic, given that Henare would later end up as a National MP in his own right.

Delamere says Winston wanted to depose Henare:

"He wanted to replace Tau as his deputy leader. Eventually he decided he didn't want to do that, but at the time that was part of the meeting. But the main agenda item was how to go with the Nats."

A scan of the newspapers during this period gives no real reason for voters to believe that NZ First would automatically go into coalition with Labour. Arguably it was the media itself planting that expectation in the minds of voters.

On one occasion, for example, when Labour's Helen Clark decided to back National's decision to sell off another state asset, ForestCorp, for $1.6 billion, Winston Peters lashed out with full force at Labour for betraying the public, describing the party as "rotten at the core" and "without a soul".[288]

"The Labour Party," raged Peters at a public meeting, "are the ultimate political quislings. Whilst pretending to defend New Zealand assets, they sanction the sale of Foresty Corp."

Reporting the event, a *Christchurch Press* journalist was shocked at the attack on Labour because NZ First, he said, would be "needing to form a coalition with Labour to have any hope of forming a new government after the election."

---

288 "Gloves off for 'war of words' between NZ First, Labour," by Jeremy Kirk, The Press, 27 August 1996, p7

It's little wonder the public came to believe Winston had 'promised' to go with Labour, when journalists just kept repeating the mantra even in the face of contradictory evidence. Of course NZ First had another option, the media just chose to ignore the possibility when it suited them.

In fact, Peters' consistent refusal to rule out a coalition with anybody, even National, was one of the main factors impacting his vote. From the heady heights of 29% during the peak of the Winebox Inquiry, latest polls in mid September had NZ First sliding three points to 15% support. Labour on the other hand had moved from its low of 15% back in the day to 19%, showing Labour voters were factoring in the possibility that Peters might choose National.

Labour campaign strategist Pete Hodgson went so far as to publicly talk of internal NZ First tensions resulting from "Michael Laws' studious efforts to transform NZ First into a coalition partner for National."[289]

It's not as if Labour-leaning NZ First voters were not being warned, as many now claim. But there were some mixed messages emanating from NZ First. In terms of creating expectations, Michael Laws has put his hand up as the man responsible for the speeches where Peters was bagging National. "National, ACT and the Christian Coalition were politics' 'toxic trio'," wrote Laws, "illiberal, insensitive and infelicitous – and I worked the insult into all of Winston's campaign speeches."[290]

Laws says he was infuriated at Winston refusing to declare a coalition preference – he says Winston was wanting to play the game straight and not give a preference – and says he "faxed Winston a four page memo establishing my concerns over the party's coalition stance and proposing that New Zealand First declare the Labour Party its preferred early option."

It was only at the end of a conference call that Laws realised what Tuariki Delamere claimed to have known since August: "Winston had already chosen his post-election partner. And the audacity of that choice stunned me."[291]

There were some things within NZ First, it seemed, that even its chief campaign strategist wasn't privy to.

Adding to the confusion were the increasingly anti-National state-

---

289 "Odds favour centre-right coalition", by Jeremy Kirk, The Press, 17 September 1996, p3
290 The Demon Profession, Laws, p357
291 The Demon Profession, Laws, p364

ments of deputy leader Tau Henare, and even public speculation that Labour-leaning Tau Henare would be "dumped as deputy leader after the election".[292]

Tau Henare's problems, however, were of his own making. He'd given an interview in 1995 suggesting Maori treaty claims could be settled if the Government gave back all Crown land to Maori. Three weeks out from the election, the Government dug out a copy of the interview and spun it for radio talkback land: vote Winston and you are voting for a Maori radical Trojan horse.

That, too, was creating bite-back amongst the support base and also amongst the traditional Left, like commentator Chris Trotter, who noted Henare's left-wing union background was already a source of tension. "Even less palatable is Henare's obvious sympathy with much of the Maori nationalist movement.[293]

"Whether the rumours of a coup against Henare in the immediate aftermath of the election are true or not, their very existence points to the degree of factional conflict now gripping the party."

Trotter, ironically, blamed Michael Laws for transforming NZ First "into a moderate party of the centre-right", and he noted that the party list rankings "indicated a substantial shift towards the right of the political spectrum."

The Left knew NZ First might go with National. It might have been a surprise to Michael Laws and some journalists, but not for those who could read the signs. The irony that Laws was getting the blame for the lurch rightwards may have been lost on him at the time.

New Zealand First's final two weeks before election night 1996 were shaping up as akin to a space capsule re-entering Earth's atmosphere at speed: it was too late to change course, this was going to be either fiery and spectacular or fatal, strap on your seat belts and pray.

Just 12 days out from the election, and "New Zealand First leader Winston Peters is steadfastly refusing to rule out a post-election deal with National," reported a major story in the *Dominion*. Alliance leader Jim Anderton very prominently warned voters that only the Alliance and Labour could guarantee a centre-left government.[294]

---

292 "Odds favour centre-right coalition," supra
293 "Faction-ridden NZ First courts Right and Left," by Chris Trotter, The Independent, 20 September 1996
294 "Peters shuns pressure to shut door on National," by Graeme Speden, The Dominion, 1 October 1996, p2

For his part, Peters refused to rule out either National or Labour, saying that regardless of his personal preferences it was up to the voters to dish out the cards. "This campaign has become a binge of speculation on answers only the whole country can give," he told a packed hall in Wellington. "I don't know what it's like to play cards without seeing them, but apparently we're meant to."[295]

The cards were more like those trick-cards of the seventies with the mousetrap spring on the back designed to whack your finger when you pulled the card out. And Jim Anderton was the joker in the pack. At a campaign rally in the Wairarapa, Alliance supporters whooped, whistled and stamped their feet in satisfaction when Anderton floated the possibility of a pre-election deal with Labour. Labour quickly ruled the idea out, much to the anger of the Alliance.

The reason for that, said Chris Trotter, was simple. Labour was factionalised down the middle between a right wing led by Mike Moore and a left wing led by Helen Clark. He called the balance of power within Labour "fragile" and "precarious". For Helen Clark to have begun talking to Anderton would have sent a clear message to Labour's right wing that their views didn't count.[296]

"Unable to respond positively" to the Alliance overture, Trotter wrote, "Clark and Labour were forced to weather the growing volume of negative public feedback."

Sensing the pressure, Winston Peters rode to the rescue with a Michael Laws idea. Why confine cabinet postings to the winning parties after an election? Winston broke the deadlock by announcing he would welcome Opposition MPs like Mike Moore into a "Cabinet of all the talents" in an NZ First government, the idea being that Cabinet chose the best person for the job, even if they came from a rival party.

"Peters emerged looking statesmanlike. Mike Moore was dealt back into the political card game, and Clark's heartfelt sigh of relief was audible throughout the country," wrote Trotter. Winston's offer stole attention away from the Alliance and made it look like Labour and NZ First could work together. According to Trotter, internal Labour polling was showing it bleeding support heavily during its refusal to deal with the Alliance and

---

295 Ibid
296 "Why Labour rejected Anderton's advances," by Chris Trotter, Independent, 27 September 1996, p11

in danger of "a fall into fourth place" if no circuitbreaker emerged. Peters stemmed the bloodloss, he said.

They may not have formally dealt the cards, but voters continued to send a message through the opinion polls. Yet again, just a week out from the election, a UMR-Insight poll found a National/NZ First coalition the most preferred outcome, with one and a half times the support of the next best option, a Labour/Alliance/NZ First coalition.[297]

"It was significant," reported the NBR, "that the biggest groups of National voters (22%) and NZ First voters (26%) in the survey believed a coalition government involving their two parties was the most likely outcome, despite the friction between their leaderships."

Jim Anderton had gone on the record months earlier to say he wouldn't coalesce with any party, not even Labour, unless a pre-election deal was done. Even now, just one week out from the election, he was sticking with that demand: negotiate with me now, or don't negotiate with me ever. It was not a recipe for stable government because it ran the risk of skewing the election and inviting a public backlash.

It made a coalition with NZ First impossible, as Peters had given his word there would be no pre-election deals, and Anderton had given his word he would only respect pre-election deals. For Anderton and Peters to both end up in a governing coalition after the election, one man would have to become a liar.

Even worse, Anderton had published a list of what he called the Alliance's "12 Non-negotiable Principles". That left utterly no room for meaningful coalition discussions – Anderton had not one bottom line but a dozen, and he was telling all his supporters they were "non-negotiable".[298]

As NBR reported just one week out, "Jim Anderton's condition of a pre-election deal had yet to be met."

One senior NZ First figure at the time believes Michael Laws was to blame for the media's continued speculation that Peters would go with Labour which, unless voters removed the Alliance, was going to be an impossible dream. Laws was setting the public up for disappointment.

"So we had this big disconnect with the public at that time that we

---

297 "National and NZ First lead voters' coalition preferences," by Stephen Ward, NBR, 4 October 1996, p14
298 "Why Labour rejected Anderton's advances," by Chris Trotter, Independent, 27 September 1996, p11

were a bunch of traitors and all the rest, but I maintain to this day, and Winston has come to believe me, but I told him back then, 'Laws is telling the news media that we're going with Labour.' And that's what he was doing. So we were the big bastards when we went with National."[299]

Some circumstantial corroboration of Laws-spin can be found in the *Independent* the day before the election, when it reported Peters was trying to hose down speculation that he would coalesce with Labour, by attacking Labour in his final speeches.

"Peters' U-turn was against the advice of party strategists concerned his refusal to shut the door to National is losing NZ First support...NZ First strategists say Peters returned to a neutral stance as a matter of principle."[300]

Given that Laws was virtually the only NZ First 'strategist', and that the comments above match those in his book, his identity wasn't hard to guess. The newspaper noted however that the more likely it looked that Peters would go with Labour, the less Helen Clark would have to offer at the negotiating table because Peters was cornering himself. The more he dropped his drawers for Labour, the less they would have to pay to see. That was the problem Laws appeared to have overlooked – by declaring one's hand, there was nothing left to negotiate. Peters didn't want power for power's sake, he wanted policy concessions. And he wasn't going to get those by tipping people off about his preferences.

The final TV3/Gallup poll of the campaign delivered some bad news. Published on the Thursday ahead of Saturday's vote, it showed NZ First had slipped to 13% in the polls, and the Alliance had shot up to 17%. Anderton flexed his muscles even more.

"The Alliance's insistence that coalition deals be done pre-election almost certainly rules it out of being in the next government," said the *Independent* on election-eve. "However, the party insists it would expect concessions in return for shoring up a minority Labour-led government."[301]

That's called wanting to have your cake and eat it too.

The final poll indicated the Christian coalition had dropped below five percent support, but that ACT looked like it would break through the threshold. As Winston Peters cast his vote on Saturday 12 October in New

---

299 Interview with author
300 "Win Peters rediscovers his infinite adaptability", by Frances Martin, Independent, 11 October 1996
301 Ibid

Zealand's first MMP election, the outcome was anyone's guess except for one thing: barring a catastrophe, NZ First was about to be in government.

21

Great Expectations

"Politics is the art of the possible"
— Otto Von Bismarck, 1867

After hitting highs of 29% in the polls before he took the stand at the Winebox Inquiry back in mid June, and for a while being the second most popular political party in New Zealand, by election night New Zealand First recorded its biggest intake of MPs – 17 in all – on the strength of a 13.3% share of the vote. Among those was a clean sweep of the five Maori seats – the secret Ratana deal had paid off.

"Yeah, I was pretty confident we'd win all the seats," says Tuariki Delamere reflectively. "You always harbour doubts because you should harbour doubts. If I look at it now and try and be dispassionate, it was game, set, match. I mean, Maori were ready for a change, Labour hadn't done a hell of a lot for them, but more than that it was, 'wow, here's a Maori leader who can mix it with the very best that any party, culture or whatever can put forward'.

"Winston was the key man and Maori wanted to support that. We just rode in on his coattails. I was lucky enough to be the Johnny on the spot."

To put the election, and therefore the coalition negotiations that followed, in context, it's worth spending a second examining the actual hand of "cards" that got dealt.

In the 1993 election, National under Bolger and Labour under Moore had been virtually neck and neck, with 35% and 34.7% of the vote respectively. The Alliance in 1993 gained 18.2% of the vote and NZ First tail-ended with 8.4% support in 1993.

Pundits in the media portrayed election 1996 as a Labour "win", which we'll analyse in a moment. First, the figures.

National's share in 1996 was 33.9%, a swing against them of 1.18%. Labour under Clark had done much worse than Mike Moore, the man she ousted. In 1996, Labour's share of the vote suffered a 6.5% swing against them, dropping to 28.2% of the popular vote. If this was the voters delivering a "victory" to Labour, they had a funny way of showing it.

The Alliance, the other Left wing potential coalition partner, suffered even more. An 8.1% swing against the Alliance saw its election night vote slip to just 10.1%. So much for the TV3 Gallup poll on election eve with its predictions of 17%. In other words, the so-called Centre-Left parties had suffered a massive swing against them.

What about NZ First? In 1993 it captured 8.4% of the vote. In 1996 it experienced a positive swing of five percent to reach 13.3% of the vote. Act had gained a positive swing of 6.1% from a standing start of zero, not having been around in 1993.

Translated into seats, National had 44, needing 61 to form a government, Labour had 37, NZ First had 17, the Alliance had 13, Act had 8 and Peter Dunne as United New Zealand had one – managing to lose all the six MPs who'd waka-jumped with him to form the party.

On the one hand, National and Act could get to 52 seats, while Labour and the Alliance could reach 50. With 61 needed, the only option for either side was Winston Peters. National and NZ First could reach 61, and they knew they could count on the Act party's support for confidence and supply. The Labour equation was more problematic. The Alliance had to be part of the mix, yet the Alliance had been difficult to deal with all the way through with its "12 Non-negotiable Principles" and couldn't be relied on to play ball.

The news media were not seeing it that way, however. Whether it was a rush of narcissistic blood to the head, or a deliberate strategy to ratchet up voter expectations and pressure on NZ First, Labour's Helen Clark allowed herself to be introduced to rapturous applause at her Mt Albert headquarters as "New Zealand's next Prime Minister", and proceeded to give a speech suggesting she truly believed it.

Reuters even flashed a photo around the world with the caption, "Helen

Clark holds aloft a child early yesterday in celebration of her election victory."[302]

It took someone with big nuts to say it, but Clark was that person. Staring down an election night drubbing where Labour had managed to lose more than a fifth of its support base since 1993, and from a woman who'd been polling last as preferred Prime Minister only weeks earlier with her party as low as 15% in the polls, "next Prime Minister" wasn't exactly the phrase that sprang to mind.

Bolger, on the other hand, was much more subdued. It wasn't quite "bugger the pollsters" this time around, instead he congratulated Peters and told supporters "We will manage things calmly and rationally in the days ahead."

New Zealand First, he added, had "by far the most rational economic policies of the parties on the left."[303]

For his part, Peters too was conciliatory, "This is not the time for settling old scores."

To call it a victory for the centre-left, which Helen Clark did, when the Alliance had lost nearly half of its support, was stretching the word 'victory' one election cycle too far, torturing the concept until it screamed. Mike Moore back in 93 had made the mistake of declaring victory, and he had a lot more justification to do so than Clark.

The centre left had won just 38% of the vote this time around, well down on the 53% they'd earned in 1993. But again, that's not how the news media reported it.

Agence France Presse reported confidently, "observers believe NZF will back Clark's bid to become the country's first female prime minister."[304]

Donna Chisholm, an intelligent and otherwise astute senior journalist at the *Sunday Star-Times*, woke the country up to the news: "Helen Clark seems set to become New Zealand's first woman Prime Minister of a new centre left Government after last night's historic first MMP election."[305]

Nearly two thirds of NZ had actually voted against the centre-left, but that got lost in the euphoria.

---

302 New Straits Times, 14 October 1996, p13
303 New Straits Times, Ibid
304 Ibid
305 "Winston the kingmaker", by Donna Chisholm, Sunday Star-Times, 13 October 1996, p1

"National's only chance of continuing in power is if New Zealand First leader Winston Peters agrees to prop it up," Chisholm continued.

Labour was spinning Election 96 for all it was worth. Former prime minister David Lange assured journalists with a straight face that Helen Clark would be leading a government as a result of the election. Party president Michael Hirschfeld agreed.[306] Either Labour's senior team had collectively developed Alzheimer's, or this was deliberate: to snatch victory from the jaws of defeat they had to make the public believe that NZ First was honour-bound to support Labour.

As history now shows, it was one of the great propaganda stunts of all time, pretty much akin to the General in WWII saying, "they've surrounded us again, the poor bastards!". It was great propaganda, because it worked. People began to believe that Winston had promised to support Labour.

Things weren't that rosy inside Labour however. New NZ First MP John Delamere flew to Wellington on the Monday morning to meet Winston and the team. "I had just finished lunch with Winston. We were at level three, Winston and I waiting for the elevator there, and who walks up but Mike Moore! Mike didn't know who I was, but he was just ropable and he was going on about 'that effing b.i.t.c.h,' you name it. Mike's rather flowery language. He was talking about someone, a female named Helen, it turned out. He was just spewing."

Delamere never found out what it was, but it's highly likely Moore had just been told he would not be getting a Cabinet post after all. This was a huge slap in the face because he'd issued a news release prior to the election saying he felt duty-bound to serve the people from Labour's front bench. With Moore out-polling her, Clark didn't want him anywhere near an oxygen supply.

"I didn't really understand what that was about," says Delamere. "Winston seemed to know. That whole feeling between the Moore camp and the Clark camp came through in the negotiations. What I noticed in the negotiation with Labour was there were two sides who hated each other's guts. They weren't unified in the sense that this was a team. You just felt that, there was Mike Moore's side and there was Helen's side and they couldn't stand each other."

Delamere says the Clark team were incredibly arrogant.

---

306 Ibid

"I think it had quite a huge impact because, I believe Labour was under the impression that New Zealand First had no choice. New Zealand First had to go with Labour, that's how Labour played it. 'You guys have no choice because Maori are expecting you to go with Labour'."

National's Deputy Prime Minister Don McKinnon tried to counter Labour's spin, telling journalists the country had clearly swung to the centre-right, away from the centre-left. After noting the same statistics you read at the start of this chapter, McKinnon pointed out that in the electorate seats, National had lost just one sitting MP while Labour lost six.[307]

He also had some fascinating breakdowns on the way people had split their electorate and party votes. In the Alliance stronghold of Wigram, held by leader Jim Anderton, for example, National gained 7,000 party votes there against only 4,000 for the Alliance – even though the Alliance won the actual seat. In Helen Clark's seat Labour and National had split the party vote between them despite Clark's big electorate majority, and National had even scored more party votes than NZ First in Winston Peters' Tauranga seat.

The message from all this, he said, was that voters had abandoned the Left; Labour had no moral right to govern.

In a snap TV3/Waikato University poll released five days after the election, a National/NZ First coalition was still the most preferred option, at 48.4%, against 46.2% support for a Labour/NZ First coalition. The question was badly phrased, however. There could not be a "Labour/NZ First coalition" without the Alliance. It couldn't happen. Even asking the question without mentioning the Alliance was misleading by not giving those polled the real creature they were being asked to support.[308]

This, again, was another way the media skewed public expectations.

The Alliance, meanwhile, was being as difficult as it could be, with MP Pam Corkery labelling Winston Peters "a political prostitute" just hours after the election, and Agence France Presse noting a coalition deal involving the Alliance was almost impossible:[309]

"Alliance leader Jim Anderton flatly refuses to join a coalition with Clark, but after what Clark called an 'amiable' telephone chat they agreed to hold hands on the big public issues."

---

307 "McKinnon says poll backs right-wing coalition," by Brent Edwards, Evening Post, 17 October 1996, p11
308 "Peters receives only 11pc backing," The Press, 17 October 1996, p6
309 "NZ Politicians go courting for power," New Straits Times, 15 October 1996

Clark's attempts to phone Winston Peters didn't go so smoothly. She left a message on his cellphone voicemail but the callback number couldn't be clearly heard. Instead, when Winston Peters dialled it from a boat in Tauranga harbour, it rang somewhere in the wop-wops:

"The phone rang," a surprised dairy farmer named Peter Paterson later told journalists, "and I was bloody sure it was Winston Peters, and he said 'can I speak to Helen Clark?'"[310]

Former Prime Minister David Lange described the first MMP election as "a bad joke played by the electorate on itself."

Negotiations to form a government were never going to be easy. NZ First had no infrastructure capable of resourcing such negotiations. Winston had 15 new MPs, many of whom needed political babysitting, and the demands of the media, the public and the competing leaders to juggle. He also had no stomach for trying to keep a coalition government with a minority Labour government running while Jim Anderton decided he was there for some purposes and not for others.

Peters was leaning toward National, so too were ex National MP Peter McCardle and former Labour MP Jack Elder. Michael Laws could see which way the wind was blowing and resigned just four days after the election. If journalists had properly understood Laws and his machinations, they would have known then it was a sign National was shaping up as the likely partner.

NZ First's negotiating team – led by Peters – included deputy Tau Henare, McCardle, Doug Woolerton and Winston's brother, lawyer Wayne Peters who, according to the Evening Post, was paid to provide consulting advice to NZ First. The other parties, of course, already had their advisors on public salaries. It was the job of the negotiators to report progress to the wider caucus. Woolerton later dropped out of the team, and Labour reckoned he'd been leaning their way:

"I think he was genuinely keen to see an accommodation with us and he had been playing a lead role every day – then suddenly he was gone," complained Labour's Michael Cullen to journalists.[311] Woolerton, however, says he was recommending that Peters not rule out the Nats.[312]

---

310 Ibid
311 "Cullen: we were set up for failure," by Anna Kominik, Dominion, 12 December 1996, p2
312 Interview with author

"Winston never liked Bolger particularly, because he sacked him a couple of times. I used to say to Winston, 'look, he's the bloody sheep and beef farmer, he counts pretty bloody good.' Bolger understood that he had to make coalitions. All the Tony Ryalls and all the new right acolytes, they would sooner have been pure and out of government. But Bolger understood the bloody deal straight away, and he just got to it with a will. So did Clark, she understood straight away too. But the rest of them didn't. There were people who were lining up behind them."

Jim Bolger later admitted he'd been negotiating behind Winston's back, directly with Helen Clark, trying to convince Labour to join a grand National-Labour coalition and lock Peters out. Clark and Moore were present at the meeting with Bolger in November 1996:

"They both said Labour couldn't discuss a coalition with National as it would destroy the Labour Party. I told them I disagreed," Bolger wrote in his autobiography, *A View From The Top*.[313]

The fact that Bolger was prepared to cut Peters off at the knees, and display that willingness to Labour, may have given Helen Clark extra confidence that Peters would join her in a marriage of convenience.

Over at NZ First, they continued to brainstorm.

"We had bloody big graphs on the board and numbers on the board, and lists of things that we wanted and lists of things that were important to us," explains Woolerton.

"The big lie, of course, which everybody knows and which I learnt subsequent to that, the big lie is that you have to have ministers who protect your policies. Remember that? What'd we have? We had about five. It was huge."

In fact, National was offering nine: five ministers inside cabinet, four associates or under-secretaries outside cabinet, with the prospect of boosting to 11 in total, including eight in cabinet, if the deal lasted two years.

The big lie is that having ministerial responsibility made you part of the problem, not the solution. You go into coalition, "and you are dead, because everything you do up to that point, and there's a huge element of the knight on a white horse about Winston, as soon as you join with the enemy, be it National or Labour, there's no difference. It's poison."

As a centrist party, New Zealand First's supporters had come in roughly

---

313 "Nats sought union with Clark – book," The Press, 5 October 1998

equal measure from both sides of the political spectrum, which meant whatever decision the negotiators made, you were going to "piss off a chunk of your support base, and there was only one silly bastard that had to face that and that was me," mutters Woolerton.

"I'd go around to all these meetings all over the damn place, people ripped my bloody ears off. So that was the big lie, you needed ministers to protect your policies. Untrue. The fact of the matter in every negotiation I've seen, and I've seen a few, are that the more ministers you have the less policy you get.

"Because those two big parties, they just sit there and say well okay, what do you guys want? You want free doctor's visits? You want the old age pension card (although that came later). You list the stuff you want and then they say righto, fair enough, there's some of those we can do, some of them we just can't. So what about position? Do you want a chairman of a select committee, do you want this or that or the other bloody thing, and then bang, there's ministers on the table as well."

What the big parties did, says Woolerton, was sell ministerial positions, salaries and trappings, and deduct policies in return.

" 'What do you want there?' 'We want minister of this, I want to be deputy prime minister, I want to be minister of finance, I want to be this, that, and the other bloody thing'. 'Ooh', they'd start to say, because these guys are from business in the case of National and Labour, they'd say, 'oh no, you ain't getting all that mate.' They'd just start to deduct policies. If you say, 'no, I don't want any ministers,' they 'say great, fantastic.' Because they've got their tensions in their own parties of course."

Although not part of the "A-team", Tuariki Delamere had been given glimpses of the inner sanctum, and was accordingly courted by Bolger.

"Bolger played his part, I think, unbelievably well. Very smart, that Uncle Jimmy. The National MPs hated the whole process. They resented being held, what they believed, to ransom, and they should be allowed to do the governing by themselves. They had trouble accepting the new system so to speak. But Bolger, on day one, and Birch and those older guys there, they knew damn well that there was only one game in town and that's being the government. There ain't nothing good about being in opposition.

"Bolger played the social card very well. He was brilliant at it. Called a bunch of us after about four or five weeks. We got a call around 11 o'clock, it was Bolger, because we're upstairs, like the 15th floor of Bowen tower, whatever it was. Bolger says, 'oh, I can see your guys' lights on up there, what are you doing? Who's up there?'

"There were four of us. Me, Deborah Morris, McCardle, and I think Wayne Peters. Anyway, we're on the way down to the whip's office, John Carter's office for drinks about two in the morning. By the time we got to the decision, everyone liked Bolger."

Ron Mark, NZ First's parliamentary whip, agrees the social connection built a rapport.

"That was the amazing thing. I only knew about Bolger's relationship with Peters from what I'd seen on the campaign trail and in the media, which was pretty septic. Clearly it had been difficult, but I didn't know either of them that well."[314]

"The big breakthrough came when they got together that evening, when Bolger and Dick Griffin and Max Bradford came across to Winston's office and sat down to talk. They had a very long conversation until the very wee hours of the morning. Doug was there too. That was very useful for creating a platform that showed maybe these too could work together. At the end of the day though the decision had to be made by the caucus and then by the council, which it was."

Tuariki Delamere says that within the NZ First caucus, Labour was the first choice.

"Right up to the last minute Labour was still leading, because fundamentally most of our caucus were Labour leaning."

What tipped the deal National's way was Labour's refusal to offer NZ First anything meaningful.

"All the major jobs were promised already. Other than really Winston and maybe one other, they weren't interested in giving any ministerships out."

Not only ministerial roles, they were offering few policy concessions either.

"Not really, they weren't really offering anything. Which is what surprised me," says Delamere. "The person who hugely impressed me was Heather Simpson. I called her the red hedgehog because of her red haircut. But very, very smart lady. Very smart. But it still came down to, at least as what was reported back to us by Wayne Peters, Labour were offering us nothing. I'd be interested to see what Labour says they offered us, because

---

314 Interview with author

we had no confirmation other than what Wayne told us. But when the Nats came back, what was it, nine ministers? I mean, we had 17 MPs, of which 13 were new, so that meant five, brand new, off-the-street bloody MPs, wet behind the ears, five of us were going to be ministers. That's a pretty persuasive offer when Labour wasn't offering us much of anything."

Delamere believes his fellow 'tight five' MPs – Tau Henare, Tuku Morgan, Rana Waitai and Tu Wyllie – would probably have pushed for Labour regardless, if they'd sat down and thought through the implications for the Maori seats.

"They were angry that we weren't offered anything," he says of the Maori caucus, "but if they'd thought about self-preservation then they would have gone with Labour.

"I was pretty confident that if we went with National – I was always supportive of going with National, because they've got the bulk of the numbers, they've got the bulk of the decision and I preferred their economic policies anyway – but I also knew that I was possibly consigning myself to being a one-term MP. The other four were seeing this as a lifetime job. Because for Maori MPs, once you got in there you tend to stay in there for a long time and if they'd thought about it then they would have forced us into Labour.

"I was totally supportive of going with National. I thought that was the better decision for the country. Winston at that time was very pro-National. He didn't want a bar of Helen at the time, although obviously that changed years later. He was still fundamentally – he probably still is fundamentally – right of centre. National was a better fit for him. If National didn't come to the party then he would have gone to Labour, I'm sure."

In fact, according to the public record, Labour was offering more. Deputy leader Michael Cullen told journalists Labour had offered six cabinet positions in a 15-person cabinet to NZ First, and the Deputy Prime Minister's job. If it was baubles Peters was after they were there in spades. It was policy that Labour wasn't willing to compromise on.

Senior negotiator Mike Moore said Labour wasn't prepared to budge on its policy of repealing the Employment Contracts Act, or setting up income-related state house rentals. Labour also insisted on keeping asset testing, which NZ First's core base hated. But the biggest sticking point was whether NZ First could have the Finance portfolio.

"Our bottom line," said Michael Cullen, "was only finance and prime ministership,".³¹⁵ NZ First could have anything it wanted in terms of ministerial titles, but it would never be given the purse strings. Nor would Cullen share it, as NZ First suggested, in a split portfolio.

The elephant in the room, however, almost never spoken about by the news media, was the Alliance. It had made a point of refusing to go into coalition. Nor would it give confidence and supply, ensuring that a Labour/NZ First minority government wouldn't fall at the first hurdle. Instead, in a written letter, it reserved the right to bring the government down on any issue the Alliance deemed "detrimental to the interests of the country".³¹⁶

The Alliance would literally be sitting there with its fingers on the nuclear option, waiting for a moment they could strike and look like heroes in the detonation process.

One of the few journalists to realise that Jim Anderton was deliberately driving Winston Peters into National's arms was left wing columnist Chris Trotter, writing in the *Independent* only two weeks into the coalition discussions. Remember when you read what follows, he had not yet seen the Alliance ultimatum to NZ First and Labour above:

"The Alliance…has become the critical factor in the coalition equation. If Jim Anderton gives Helen Clark and Winston Peters his commitment to support a Labour/NZ First coalition on all matters of confidence and supply, then New Zealand is likely to have a centre-left government. If he refuses, he will give Winston Peters and the NZ First caucus all the excuse they need for throwing their support behind National."³¹⁷

Trotter wrote that if Anderton was his arrogant self and true to form, he would not give confidence and supply. "If he refuses to believe the Alliance was severely punished by the electorate [losing nearly 50% of the party's support base] and that he is largely responsible for the poor showing, then Clark's chances of becoming prime minister are slim…the sad probability is that the Alliance leader will learn very little from his party's defeat."

The *Independent* columnist went on to argue, persuasively, that it was

---

315 "Cullen: We were set up for failure," by Anna Kominik, Dominion, 12 December 1996, p2
316 "Labour, Alliance dug their own grave," by Michael Laws, Evening Post, 11 December 1996, p3
317 "Will the Alliance founder on Anderton's intransigence?" by Chris Trotter, Independent, 25 October 1996, p13

actually in Anderton's Machiavellian best interests to keep Labour out of government for now, until the Alliance could regroup. If Helen Clark successfully gained power she could make the Alliance look irrelevant, because she was taking Labour leftward anyway. Indeed, as history later showed, Clark did make the Alliance irrelevant and it disintegrated.

"The long term interests of Anderton and the Alliance are, therefore, better served by insisting on the preconditions it knows NZ First cannot accept (repealing the Employment Contracts Act, for example."

In other words, the Alliance never had any intention of allowing an NZ First/Labour coalition to survive, and would have gained kudos from the hard left for blowing Clark and Peters out of the water at the first sign of compromise with NZ First.

"In short, for the Alliance to survive, Labour must once again be cast in the role of traitor," wrote Trotter. "The Alliance campaigned on the slogan, 'We won't sell out'. But if, in attempting to remain true to the flawed and destructive strategy of political purity which cost it so dearly at the polls, the Alliance makes it impossible for a centre-left government to be formed, it will be guilty of doing exactly that.

"And, in 1999, the vengeance of the voters will be biblical in its severity."

That's the only thing Trotter got wrong. Yes, Anderton did not learn his lesson from the election. Yes, the Alliance deliberately sabotaged the coalition of NZ First and Labour so Helen Clark could not become prime minister. Thus, the fault was not Winston's but Jim Anderton's. However, no, the public never really knew. Not until now. For fifteen years the public – with "biblical" severity – and the media have blamed NZ First for betraying voters, but as former Labour candidate Ron Mark explains, it was entirely Anderton and Clark's doing. Regardless of whether Winston preferred the Nats, Anderton had no intention of any other outcome being possible. From the moment the negotiations began, the only outcome ever possible was National.

Ron Mark says he saw no evidence of Peters signalling a preference for National to the caucus:

"Not from what I saw. What I saw was a person who was very astute, very deliberate, who was determined to negotiate the best damn deal he could get. And at the end of the day he handed the negotiations over in so many portfolio areas to people like Peter Brown, Peter McCardle, Brian Donnelly – and if anyone wants to tell me that Donnelly had made up his mind before that caucus, I would say one, they don't know what the hell they're talking about, two, they don't know Brian Donnelly at all, and three, they're talking through a hole in their backside.

"Brian Donnelly was one of the most incredible men I'd ever met in parliament and had an ability to work with anyone. If anything, his leaning was Labour. Now where had I come from? Labour. As much as I had a lot of friends in Labour, and I would have loved to be working with Mike Moore in coalition – back with my mate – I would have loved it. But you can't do it if the Alliance haven't given you supply and confidence."

Mark remembers the whiteboard comparisons between offers.

"There wasn't a huge amount of difference. There were pluses on one side and minuses on the other and vice versa the other way. We could have run with either of those coalition deals and been very happy about what we achieved. Let's be clear about that.

"Without remembering the detail, and I do have a copy of the original coalition document in my drawer at home, if you looked at those policies I think you'd find Labour gave more on social stuff and our economics policies were more meshed, but National got very, very tight in some areas but were keen to progress some in law and order and traffic etc.

"If you looked at the two deals either of them would have been good to sign and we would have been proud of both of them."

One thing Mark is angry about is the 'armchair historians' and media commentators who talk about the time it took to get a coalition deal. None of them had negotiated a coalition agreement before, it had never been done and no one knew how to do it. "We had no resources, I didn't even have a desk, let alone a computer. We didn't have any staff. No party funding allocation. We were trying to negotiate with the government on one hand, and the leader of the opposition on the other, who had money to burn.

"People complain about the nine and a half weeks it took – longer than it took to make the movie – well excuse me, we got to parliament and we had no bloody staff. We had to go out and recruit people, then we had to go out and get some specialist advisors. Before we could do that we had to get money. People initially weren't too keen to give us money. They were happy to negotiate with us using whatever resources we had, like trying to negotiate a treaty settlement with a piggy bank – bloody hopeless!

"No journalist wrote that, because they wanted to demonise Winston for going with National. Let's be very clear about that.

So NZ First spent the first few weeks getting money, getting resources, moving into offices, getting desks, getting computers, "and then teaching all these newbie recruits how to be a parliamentary executive secretary. How to set up our research unit so we could start doing some damn research work. We were simply a brand spanking new party with absolutely nothing, expected to leap headlong into negotiations with the two major parties who'd been around a hundred years.

"Did anyone write that? Like hell they did. They weren't interested in writing that," Ron Mark mutters bitterly.

Watching the caucus react to the negotiations was like watching the women's final at Wimbledon.

"Quite honestly, I was in the caucus and I spent a lot of time, as the whip, talking to caucus members, and on one day they'd say 'We're more inclined to go with Labour, we know them better, we trust them, we came from there', and on another day they'd say, 'For heaven's sake, can you imagine working with that lot?'"

When the caucus reached the final stage and had two coalition agreements it could look at, Mark says "there were a couple of things that leapt out. I sat through that whole presentation and let people go through it, and I held my peace until the end. I only had two questions.

"The first question was this: for any coalition agreement to be workable, to be of any value whatsoever, we need to know that the money is committed to make it happen. The last thing we need is the Minister of Finance saying 'uh oh, we've had a bit of a turn of events and the money's not there, so we are cutting this, this and this'. I said, 'with that in mind, I've got a question: Do you have the Minister of Finance portfolio, Winston? Have either of these parties offered you Finance? Do we have control of the purse strings?'

"His answer was 'With Labour, no, they will not concede the Finance portfolio'. Someone asked, 'And National?' Winston looked at us and said, 'National have agreed to the establishment of a Treasurer, they will hold the Minister of Finance appointment. I will have the Treasurer's appointment and we will also have an associate Treasurer.'

"So now we had some certainty around the money.

"The second question was the Alliance. We didn't have the full numbers on our own to form a government with Labour. Everyone said afterward, 'you were meant to go with Labour'. What a dumb bunch of thick-asses.

Labour and NZ First could not form a government, we needed the Alliance. 'Do we have Alliance support on supply and confidence?' and the answer was, 'No.'

"We had a flaky, dodgy letter which I hope to God that Winston has kept for his own sake, Anderton saying the Alliance would support them on policies they agreed with.

"You can't form a government on that sort of a letter. You've either got supply and confidence or you haven't.

"With that, all Maori MPs got a bit agitated. Winston called a break, a pause, before we made our decision, to give people a chance to have a think about it. Tau got up and walked out, and all the Maori MPs fell in behind and followed him. Me, being a whip, wondered where they were going so I got up and tagged along.

"They went into Tuku's office and shut the door, I walked in behind them, they looked at me and shut the door behind. Tau sat on the desk, pulled the phone around, punched the buttons on the speakerphone and dialled Helen Clark. Dialled Helen Clark. Having been in our caucus, which told me he'd been talking to her all along.

"He said 'Helen, we've just been told that Labour won't agree to NZ First having the Minister of Finance portfolio. How firm are you on that?' She said, 'Tau, that is correct, and I'd be surprised if you got a better offer.'

"Tau said, 'Right, thanks', and hung up. And he looked around and you could see the shoulders dropping. All the shoulders dropped. Tu Wyllie walked over to the window, Rana moved to the window. People had their hands in their jacket pockets, looking out the window. I'm not sure whether it was Rana or Tu, but one said, 'Well, that's that, then. How are we going to tell our people?' And they all just nodded, and it was silent. They were in total disbelief. I seriously believe that Tau thought Helen would agree to the Minister of Finance portfolio. And they knew it was game over at that point.

"Because we needed a finance portfolio to ensure our policies were funded, and we needed confidence and supply from the Alliance. And without those two, there could have been no other decision. Caucus moved that way and it went to the national executive, who ratified it, and the deal was done. Then we got slagged and bagged for the next three years. Still are being slagged and bagged.

"Nobody held the country to ransom. In fact, quite the contrary. We continually got drip fed, and I believe there was actually a conscious strategy by the Government to have the business community apply pressure through the media by talking about the instability and the cost economically for the nation as we wavered around without a government. And what was Winston doing? He'd gone fishing.

"He went fishing because he was sick of negotiating, looking over his coffee cup and seeing a damned camera lens staring him in the face. He couldn't have a conversation anywhere without media following him," says Ron Mark.

Winston Peters may well have wanted National, but the choice was always one for caucus alone. After considering their options, and the prospect of a surprise attack by the Alliance, there was, and could only have been, one answer.

22

Crash And Burn: 1997–1999

> *"Your actions and statements...are unacceptable"*
> – Prime Minister Jenny Shipley to Deputy Prime Minister Winston Peters, 14 August 1998

The verdict unfolded in a live TV broadcast, just before 8pm on Tuesday 11 December 1996. It had been almost two months to the day since the October election. This was no once-over lightly deliberation; the caucus and then the party's executive council debated the competing offers for nine hours on the 13th floor of Wellington's Bowen House.

Tau Henare's infamous phone call, full details of which emerged for the first time in the last chapter, was made to Helen Clark at 5.30pm. At 6pm Wayne Peters and National's Doug Graham were still thrashing out the wording of National's final pitch.[318]

When Winston told the TV cameras he was going with National, Helen Clark burst into tears. Jim Bolger couldn't hear himself think for the tremendous cheer that went up from his assembled caucus. Neither the Nats nor Labour knew which party NZ First was going to choose. Even Winston didn't know, it had all come down to the vote.

The screaming of the news media was so loud it rang in the ears of the public for weeks. All those journalists who genuinely couldn't see the cognitive dissonance of their confident predictions, turned their anger

---
318 "Bidding war went to the wire" by Sarah Boyd, Evening Post, 12 December 1996, p2

rapidly on Winston Peters. For some strange reason, even though the left wing vote collapsed in a heap, with the Alliance support slashed nearly in half and Labour down more than a fifth from where Mike Moore had it in 1993 – to in fact its worst performance in six decades – journalists had convinced themselves that Helen Clark had a right to be Prime Minister regardless.

No one was gloating more over the media's discomfort than Michael Laws, who used his new position as a newspaper columnist to go 'yah sucks boo hiss'. It was a little personal for Laws. The Dominion's Graeme Speden who covered a lot of the NZ First beat had confessed he regarded them all as "bullshitters", and he was typical of many in the media who disliked NZ First.[319]

So you can hear the relish dripping from Laws' pen when the coalition was announced:

"There will be Press Gallery hacks with sufficient egg on their faces today to feed the starving hordes of Africa and still allow for seconds... Anderton wanted the talks to fail. He has his wish."[320]

One of the only other media voices to pick the outcome was Christchurch talkback host and columnist for the working-class *Sunday News*, George Balani. "I'm surprised so many people are shocked at the outcome...logic would suggest it was a foregone conclusion."[321]

The slide in the share of the Left's vote was a big decider, he argued. "Winston Peters made it quite clear before the election he wanted to hear what the people wanted before getting involved in coalition talks. The people spoke 34% for National and 28% for Labour on election night. The people also rejected the Alliance, and any coalition with Labour needed the Alliance to work."

While the media spent weeks debating the offers of the two main parties, it was almost irrelevant. The two bottom lines – a finance portfolio and confidence and supply from the Alliance – had been rejected by Labour and the Alliance. In some areas, Ron Mark had noted, Labour was better, in others, National.

Labour had offered a better deal on state asset sales, promising a blanket

---

319 The Demon Profession, Laws, p 366
320 "Labour, Alliance dug their own grave," by Michael Laws, Evening Post, 11 December 1996, p3
321 "Coalition easy to pick from outset," by George Balani, Sunday News, 15 December 1996, p20

moratorium. National promised not to sell strategic assets like Electricorp, Contact, Transpower, NZ Post, TV1, Radio New Zealand, but other assets like TV2, Coalcorp, Timberlands, the Met Service and Airways Corporation were not listed as protected.

NZ First had to give away – in return for Treasury – its immigration policies. Again, Labour had agreed to implement migration restrictions. NZ First however scored an extra $824 million in education spending over the next three years.

In the key health area, gains included boosting health funding by $1.7 billion over three years in a range of areas. Easy to remember highlights included:

- Establish guaranteed maximum waiting times for surgical and specialist treatment.
- Remove hospital user part-charges.
- Providing free doctors visits and prescription medicines for children 5 years and under
- Remove income and asset testing for long stay geriatric public hospital care services and asset testing for long stay geriatric private hospital care

On Maori policy, the hand-up not hand-out doctrine of Ka Awatea came back, along with a plan to drop the $1 billion cap on Treaty settlements on the grounds that:

- there is respect for the settlements already effected, which would not be reopened
- the Parties confirm that the Crown will endeavour to settle claims on their merits using the settlements already effected as benchmarks
- be fiscally responsible

The coalition's general mission statement on Maori development read:

"The Treaty of Waitangi is fundamental to the relationship between Crown and Maori. Within that broad framework, government is committed to working with Maori to achieve full and active participation in NZ society. Maori have dynamism and vitality to determine own social and economic development. Justice and equity are over-riding principles in improving education, health, housing and economic outcomes, and in settling Treaty claims."

Another biggie was the removal of the hated superannuation surcharge, from 1 April 1998.

For women, NZ First pushed for and gained greater access to mammograms: "Parties are committed to the National Cervical Screening Programme. Parties are committed to the introduction of the National Breast Screening Programme over the next three years to cover all women from 50 to 65."

These were all big ticket items. The total value of extra government spending as a result of NZ First's negotiations was in excess of $5 billion over the next three years. NZ First was instrumental in the coalition agreement for shifting the Reserve Bank's inflation target from the 0-2% it had been since the days of Rogernomics, out to 3%, where it remains in 2014. Peters had argued a wider target allowed for better economic growth and more stability.

All of the major policy agreements can be found in the Coalition Agreement itself, still available online.[322] An extra addendum of the last minute initiatives National agreed to was published a few days later. Again, from a historical perspective, it's interesting to see what was set in motion back then.

The parties agreed to

- Investigate the bad blood hepatitis C scandal with a view to boosting compensation to victims
- Boost funding for the Children's Commissioner
- Assist with legal expenses for kiwi victims of British nuclear testing on Christmas Island
- Encourage a big increase in New Zealand content on TV and radio
- Analyse the preparedness of the Earthquake Commission to ensure its reserves are "adequate to meet substantial disasters
- Examine setting up an Independent Commission Against Corruption

Key policies like free health care for children and the cultural benefits of encouraging more New Zealand music and TV shows have stood the test of time, argues Ron Mark. In comparison, he says, more recent coalition 'baubles' pale into insignificance:

---

322 http://www.hinz.org.nz/journal/1996/12/1996-Coalition-Agreement-Between-New-Zealand-First-and-The-National-Party-of-New-Zealand/77

"I don't think there's been a coalition agreement as comprehensive, as detailed, as formidable as the one that we negotiated, ever since. Everyone's now so scared of the media chastising them for taking too long that they roll over like a puppy dog getting their tummy tickled and take gratification in whatever baubles they get handed out. Then run around trumpeting for the next three years, 'oh, we got $50 million for healthy homes' or a cycleway.

"Great. Really helpful. How does that match up with free healthcare for children under six?"

It took nine and a half weeks, he admits, but it wrung more than $5.4 billion of extra spending on issues that most people could agree with.

Getting there was only half the job, however. When the doctrine of Cabinet collective responsibility kicked in, Doug Woolerton realised his NZ First team were going to be dining on rodents for a while. With nine of the caucus either sitting at the cabinet table or with associate portfolios, Woolerton says the ministers became the enemy in some ways:

"You'll often find, as we've found, the ministers are on the opposite side to you. You've put this bastard or bastardess there, and then he or she comes back to the caucus and then says, 'well I've got 45 dead rats here and you're going to have to swallow about 18 of them.'

" 'Oh, great,' you know, 'I'm going to unfriend you aren't I?' You get these huge bloody tensions, most of which I had to contain, but it wasn't part of my role. You just have to go around and talk to people and say 'we'll be okay', all the b/s," recalls Woolerton.

The party, slowly, grindingly but increasingly competently got to grips with its new workload and new mission. Surprisingly, after declaring he would never work in a Bolger cabinet, Tau Henare became Maori Affairs minister.

For Tuariki Delamere, with Michael Laws gone, he quickly realised where the real power in NZ First lay – Sarah Neems.

"There were all these rumours. As far as the personal relationship I don't have any personal insight, never went out with them socially. She was a very, very highly strung lady in my view. Smart. If there was a sounding board that Winston had, it was Sarah. They were always together, they often left together. What happened after that, I had no idea. You heard all sorts of stories, rumours, but I really don't know. But she was very, very influential in New Zealand First.

"Officially she was Winston's PA. Everything was routed, through

Sarah, who had her hands, ears, eyes, fingers, everything on the pulse for New Zealand First. Nothing happened without Sarah knowing about it, nothing really happened without Sarah giving it her blessing almost. If you wanted something done, you had to get it through Sarah. She had total control of access to Winston.

"It was very volatile between the two of them. At times it would be embarrassing. They'd get in caucus, they'd have screaming matches, the two of them, occasionally, over . . . a very highly personal relationship. But again, what level at I don't know. But certainly they were very close personally. It was like, they would have quarrels, and it was like no one else was in the room, just those two going at each other. And then next minute it's all over. It's like nothing happened."

Despite the predictions of the media commentators that the marriage between Bolger and Peters wouldn't last, Ron Mark says it ran smoothly.

"Things worked really well. Bolger, once he'd given his word, had given his word! And he did everything he bloody could to make it work, even when some of our MPs were being a total pain in the ass, and even when some of his MPs were being a total pain in the ass. The spats between Neil Kirton and Bill English, and Michael Laws back in there with Neil Kirton, ramping up the tension, it didn't make things easy. But the two of them did their very best to keep the coalition on an even tack.

"I was on the coalition communications committee with Wyatt Creech and Max Bradford, I was also on the coalition disputes committee, and the coalition strategy committee, and we did a lot of work. The working relationships that developed between the ministers was superb, it really was.

"We had National ministers saying 'I'm so pleased you negotiated that in, I've been trying to get the party to agree to that for years, and now we are and it's the right thing to be doing'. We started to get more of those comments coming across the table and we had a damn good working relationship. It was working fine, and it would have gone the full term under Bolger."

It wasn't to be, however. Not long after getting their feet back under the desks after the summer break, NZ First was hit with the Tuku Morgan underpants scandal.

Tukoroirangi Morgan was Tainui, and also Tau Henare's brother-in-law. He'd been a TV journalist for both TV1 and TV3, before setting up a company to help run Aotearoa Television on a public contract. Over

Christmas, it emerged that Tuku had spent $4,000 of a company clothing allowance allegedly after leaving the company, including the purchase of an $89 pair of boxer shorts from a menswear store in swanky Newmarket.

There were other suggestions of serious financial irregularities, but the Serious Fraud Office found no criminality in its investigation, but there was an overwhelming stench of what the Act party gleefully described as "troughing" on public monies. Instead of making fine programmes, money was being spent on fine feathers for directors.

When the story first broke, Tuariki Delamere was in the middle of a ministerial meeting with Bill Birch.

"Ted, my press secretary, came in and told me what was going down, so I told Birch and we kicked out the Treasury official and called Bolger and Peters."

The Prime Minister and Deputy arrived minutes later in Delamere's office, and the awesome foursome hatched a damage control plan. "Ted briefed them, then Winston and Jim decided the first thing that all parties had to do was go to ground – that's Tuku, Tau, and Broadcasting Minister Maurice Williamson.

"We got hold of Williamson first and Maurice was at home in Pakuranga, and Maurice, being Maurice, laughed, 'ah don't worry Prime Minister, I'm hiding under the f**king bed already'. That's Maurice. And he did, he went to ground and you didn't even get a word out of him for about two or three weeks.

"It took us until the middle of the afternoon to track Tau and Tuku down, and Winston made it very clear they were to go to ground. If you check your records you'll find they turned up on the *Holmes* show, because Tuku's position was 'I'm from the media, I know how the media works, I can handle this'. Of course, one side of the camera and the other side of the camera are two different beasts. Between them Tuku and Tau kept digging the bloody hole deeper and deeper.

Delamere listened to the allegations of fraud and wastage of money, but considers the scandal a storm in a teacup:

"My perspective? It was a bloody set up for months on end. First, it was always Tuku's money. He had a contract, he fulfilled the contract or the company fulfilled the contract, he owned the company, so once you fulfilled the contract, the money's yours, nothing to do with the bloody government. We could never get the story out there because Tau and Tuku wouldn't shut their bloody mouths. They wouldn't go to ground. It would have been easier to handle and work our way through it."

Delamere still blames Labour for what was maybe a little utu on Tau Henare for failing to bring home the coalition deal.

"It had been planned and executed, we couldn't get a bloody grip on it because Tau and Tuku wouldn't shut up. Even then, when Tuku comes in he's boasting, 'I've got a deal with bloody Campbell', and Campbell of course, had conned him and cut his knees off during that interview with TV3. I told Tuku, 'This is what you do Tuku, go to the house, get a big old bloody cushion, put a pair of bloody grundies on it, and seek a point of order, and say Mr Speaker the country is fascinated by these, I'd like to donate them to the nation.' Bring the bloody thing into you, make a joke of it, which is what it was."

It was a tough time for the NZ First caucus and the fledgling coalition government, and it dragged on for months. By the end of it, Tuku was still standing but Peters was tarnished from having to defend his MP – the leader who had campaigned on integrity was being hammered over the morality of the underpants scandal. The public were quick to seize on the contrast between the Winston Peters who had stalked the Maori Loans Affair demanding accountability, and the new one whose nickname seemed to be "Wince-ton" every time a new allegation arose to make the party squirm.

Peters, however, continued to take the bullets for Tuku Morgan and Tau Henare.

NZ First's poll ratings plummeted to as low as 2%. The party that had begun with a hiss and a roar was now a laughing stock. Delamere is adamant the fatal mistake was not 'owning' the errors in judgement.

"When those things happen, my belief is you don't push it away you 'pull it right in', like Judith Collins should've over Oravida. 'You're right, I had a cup of milk, you're right I went to dinner, and why wouldn't I? They're exporting millions and millions of dollars of New Zealand products and therefore employing hundreds of New Zealanders.' But no, she chose to fudge it. Of course, once you've done that you're in the crap. Same with Tuku, just tried to push it away. But yeah, that was certainly a diversion for about four months from memory."

Delamere began keeping receipts for his own smalls, just in case.

I even got myself a certificate from Farmers' general manager, attesting to the fact I paid $3.45 for my underpants, which I tabled in cabinet."

Bolger, if he was worried about the implications of the scandal, didn't show it, says Delamere.

"I don't think he worried about it. He came up to give counsel. I love Bolger. I think the guy was an awesome manager of the cabinet, as opposed to prime minister. As a manager – as a prime minister I thought he was great too – but at managing the cabinet the guy was great. He didn't let things like that rock him, and he'd been around for 20-30 years. These things come, these things go, whereas some of my colleagues are all pulling their hair out. And he's always like 'look, yeah it's on the front page today but by next week it's across the road wrapping up fish and chips. Don't go stupid, it'll play itself out'."

It didn't really get a chance to play itself out. Instead, it festered like an untreatable wound and cast a pall over the coalition that just didn't lift.

The tension manifested in a clash that made world headlines, "Maori leader in fracas row: Peters apologises for assault".[323]

"New Zealand Deputy Prime Minister Winston Peters apologised yesterday for a late-night fracas with a fellow politician who alleged the flamboyant Maori leader had been drinking."

The alleged victim was John Banks. The pair had not seen eye to eye since Banks accused Winston of making him feel like a dirty crook back in 1992. Banks alleged the Deputy PM had abused and physically assaulted him in a parliamentary corridor late at night.

"I was assaulted. I was grabbed by the shoulder and close to the scruff of the neck and given one hell of a good shake and push," Banks claimed.

"I didn't touch the man," Peters responded. "We were walking down the corridor side by side having a strong conversation. That's not an assault, that's not an abuse, and you'd have to get a forensic scientist to try and find anything that would back that up."

In parliament, however, Peters later said he had "clearly upset" Banks, and "I wish to tender my apology to him unreservedly ". He admitted having a drink, but denied being under the influence. The incident was witnessed by Alliance leader Jim Anderton who told reporters it was clear Peters had been drinking, and that he "manhandled" Banks. Peters rejected it as political opportunism.

---

323 "Maori leader in fracas row," The Nation, Bangkok, 7 March 1997, p8

"Anderton is sitting there like some prissy, who is the morals and behaviour cop now in parliament, when he knows full well that there have been events far worse in his own caucus."

In July 1997, Peters became collateral damage from a leaked briefing paper compiled for Australia's Foreign Minister Alexander Downer. The Aussie diplomats were hurling abuse at virtually ever Pacific and Asian government, calling Malaysia and Papua New Guinea "corrupt". The Australians told their boss New Zealand's National Government was out to "spoil" Australian foreign policy in the Pacific, and in a section on the new coalition structure called Winston Peters "a loose cannon" and an "opportunist".[324]

Below Bolger, some of the other National MPs were worried. The next election was two years away, the government was looking damaged, and if the coalition continued NZ First would become eligible for three more seats around the cabinet table towards the end of 1998. Those were jobs that ambitious National MPs believed should be theirs, not wasted on a party whose popularity was lower than the margin of error.

There'd been skirmishing too, involving NZ First's Associate Health Minister Neil Kirton, who clashed with National to the point where he was fired from cabinet in late 1997, becoming a renegade NZ First dissident at first, and later an independent MP. Kirton had a pro-Labour perspective and accused National of breaking the coalition agreement on health, "deceitfully".

Ron Mark says to an extent the new MPs had let power go to their heads.

"The one thing that I've come to appreciate which I found very frustrating at the time was that I often felt I needed to know more information. No different to being in the army, really, you can never have enough information and you always feel you need to know more.

"A couple of things I did know very clearly: Winston never demanded loyalty, but he did expect it. And if he gave loyalty – I just think it really hurt and it really hit home when those people who he trusted and took in and gave such opportunity to, did the dirty on him and walked away. I saw that.

"He would never, he might have his moments in close and private company where he'd say what he really felt, but most of the time he would keep it to himself.

---

324 "Diplomatic flap over secret papers" New Straits Times, Malaysia, 22 July 1997, p10

"Some people got upset because they believed things had been done without their knowledge, well, welcome to the real world. I guess, looking back on it, I could have been one of those people. But it was a different position for me because I was a whip. One, I did know more because I was a whip and I had to. Two, even if I didn't know I still understood and recognised the value of collective responsibility and loyalty and trust. To me it's really simple. If you don't trust the captain, then leave the ship. Get off, you've got a choice.

"People who felt they were kept in the dark, might have been right, might have been wrong. Truth is, you are on the ship because he's built it and he's picked you and he's given you the opportunity. Shut up and get on with your work. If you need to know, you'll know."

The party, which had suffered the leak of a confidential memo to candidates during the election campaign, was accused of being secretive, but Mark says Winston was learning through bitter experience that faith in others was sometimes misplaced.

"I've seen myself, not just in politics but in a range of areas, where you give people information in confidence, only to be disappointed that they then go and inappropriately share that information. He's the sort of guy who's learnt the hard way, and learnt from experience, to play things close to his chest and only trust a very tight, small group of people who have proven that they are worthy of that trust. I can't fault that."

National MPs, meanwhile, had some secrets of their own that they were keeping – a plot to break the coalition. Ron Mark says he heard the jungle drums:

"Jenny and her team, ably assisted by Jim Bolger's whip David Carter, which is the most – for a whip to actually be involved in a coup against his boss is absolute unspeakable in my view, it's just not how the whip's code works at all. They had orchestrated one, to depose Bolger, and two to orchestrate the coalition split, and they had the numbers the night they forced it.

"I think Winston knew, because I knew that the chitter chatter was underway. I knew that certain MPs had already been approached, and I knew the numbers – if it went to a vote – what way it was going."

The coup came early November. Shipley and her plotters delivered Bolger an ultimatum. Ron Mark knew, because Shipley's team had put out feelers to some of the more 'dissident' NZ First members to see whether their action would force a break in the coalition. National needed at least some NZ First MPs in order to maintain a majority in the House, Shipley wasn't planning on fighting an early election. She had a bigger card yet to play.

It took NZ First a week of internal discussions and communication with Shipley before Peters agreed to continue supporting the coalition. But to Ron Mark's consternation, as the clock ticked over to 1998, the jungle drums began beating again, this time about a possible break in the coalition. NZ First MPs were being secretly approached to gauge their interest in supporting National.

"It was after the Bolger coup, so we knew it was only a matter of time. The Nats needed that lead time to socialise more with the caucus members they were targeting. As Doug Woolerton, political supremo, used to say, 'to tuck you up'. They needed to get enough NZ First people – because they didn't have the numbers to govern otherwise – 'tucked up' so that if they forced the issue and broke the coalition, or if Winston pulled the plug, they would have the numbers to continue to govern.

"I mean, Jenny Shipley had dropped the hint on to me, sitting on an aeroplane, in a private chat. I respected Jenny and I liked her, but she was an ambitious woman planning to be the prime minister of New Zealand, and the first woman prime minister come hell or high water, and she was one of that caucus that was not happy that National had had to do a deal with NZ First nor that they had given so much.

"It was a question that had a subtle hint in it. She'd already tested it on her people and most of them told her, 'No, you won't get Ron, he's loyal'."

They did get others though, and Mark could do nothing but watch:

"We heard whispers about who was going to jump, oh hell yeah. The one thing Tau's not good at is keeping confidence and doing things smart – he may as well have painted his intentions in red fluoro paint on the side of the Beehive, as far as I was concerned as a whip.

"One of the whip's main roles, as well as managing the House and administering the caucus, is risk management. I had some brilliant teachers, I had Bill Birch, Don McKinnon, Roger Sowry and John Carter. Once I realised that you were an adjutant, you were a brigade-major, a sergeant major, roll those things all into one and add to the list the function of protecting your boss and the party, you've pretty much got it all summed up.

"I had my own sources of information and I had my own observations, and I knew precisely what Tuariki, and Tau, and Rana and Tuku were all doing. I knew precisely who, at the end of the day, had been hoovered up. The only one I got wrong at the end of the day was Ann Batten, whose husband assured me and my deputy whip Robyn McDonald, that Ann would stay with Winston if push came to shove. But she didn't, because Tau promised her she could be deputy leader of his party.

"This all built up over a period of time. When I broke news to Winston of what was happening he took it quietly, with a nod. Winston's not one to go throwing his toys around the room waving his arms. It was just a quiet nod, because deep down he already knew. He wasn't a bloody idiot, and they weren't rocket scientists."

Sensing that Tau Henare was doing the numbers for a tilt at the NZ First leadership, MPs loyal to Winston made a pre-emptive strike mid-July, stripping Henare of the Deputy Leadership he'd enjoyed since 1993. Journalist Joanne Black noted the "tall good looking" MP with the Dirty Dog sunglasses and his controversial brother-in-law Tuku "has never appeared bothered that his personal style has alienated many people against both NZ First and the Maori cause generally. But that alienation has been of huge concern to Mr Henare's leader, Winston Peters, who has watched support for the party he personally built up all but disappear."[325]

In late July 1998, renegade MP Neil Kirton finally quit NZ First entirely, reducing the coalition's paper majority to zero, although National could always rely on Act for confidence and supply. The resignation made the newspapers in the USA – admittedly on page 91.[326] Within a fortnight, it was 'game on'.

The end, when it came, was swift, at a late cabinet meeting. National revealed it wished to sell the Government's 66% stake in Wellington Airport, the country's busiest terminal. Winston Peters couldn't believe it. He hadn't campaigned against state asset sales and protected the ones he knew about, only to be blindsided with the sale of a controlling stake in a strategic asset like the airport. The media quickly heard reports that Peters had "stormed out of cabinet".

The remaining NZ First cabinet ministers – Delamere, Tau Henare, Peter McCardle and Jack Elder looked at each other in disbelief.

---

325 "Henare pays price for perceived arrogance," by Joanne Black, Dominion, 15 July 1998, p2
326 "New Zealand coalition loses one-seat majority", Milwaukee Journal-Sentinel, 29 July 1998, p91

" 'What the hell?'" said Delamere after a moment.

"After Winston stormed out we just sat there wondering what to do, and no one knew what to do. It never happened before and the cabinet secretary, Marie Shroff, the Prime Minister wanted to know from her 'what does the cabinet manual say on this?', and she didn't know.

The cabinet meeting ended abruptly.

Ron Mark, hearing the news spreading like wildfire on parched summer grass, raced up to the Deputy Prime Minister's floor.

"I went up and saw Winston in his office. He was sitting there having a smoke. It was very dimly lit, most of the lights were off. I'd already heard and wanted to see what was going on. He didn't say a lot. I was doing the numbers. And I knew we had a problem. 'How many do you think will leave if the coalition breaks?' he asked. I gave him some names, and I think the other side were still one short at that stage. But as it turned out they got Ann Batten.

"He was reflective and pondering, but thoroughly alert, dragging on a cigarette. It was quiet. He told me, 'They knew not to go there, we had an agreement'. I think he'd had an agreement with Bolger or Shipley earlier on, but the option they put up at the cabinet table was not an option, and that they had deliberately pushed it.

"He was in one of those moments – I'd call it 'battle mode' from my experience – where you're taking stock and you are thinking it through. I still think he was waiting for a phone call bringing him back to the cabinet room saying 'Let's start this again', but it didn't come."

Instead, Winston headed downstairs for an emergency caucus meeting. He told his 15 other remaining MPs that Shipley had been acting "treacherously" and that she had lied to him. He didn't tell his caucus that he knew some of them had been secretly approached by National in advance of the policy ambush.

Delamere maintains that as far as he was concerned Peters was lying to caucus:

"I was just stunned. I just remember thinking, 'Winston, you're bullshitting.' I should have probably said something. I guess I was a chicken shit by not doing so.

"For me, it was when that whole thing over the Wellington airport happened. I was quite shocked when we walked out. I said 'Winston's bloody lying, this is not what happened at all'. But I was the only member of caucus who knew, because I was involved in the whole thing as the associate finance minister."

Delamere did break his silence, telling journalists that Shipley was right, that Wellington Airport was not a strategic asset under the terms of the Coalition Agreement. It's true the airport was not listed as a 'protected' asset, but as one source close to NZ First said, "you'd have to be an idiot to think that wasn't going to push Winston's buttons, and whatever you think of Shipley she's not an idiot."

The first and most obvious crack in NZ First came with Tuariki Delamere, who leapt to Shipley's defence "Some of the things Winston has said were shocking," he told the media. "I have nothing but the highest respect for Mrs Shipley's integrity."[327]

Except Winston and Ron Mark knew better. They knew MPs had sold out to National. They knew Shipley had been making sure she had the numbers to keep her government alive.

For her part, rather than attempting dispute resolution as the Coalition Agreement required, Shipley simply tore up the Coalition deed and fired Peters, telling him, "You have publicly criticised government policy regarding the sale of the Crown's share-holding in Wellington Airport, and your actions and statements…are unacceptable."[328]

The mystery deepened, however, when the Alliance got its hands on a "leaked report" written by Delamere with the New Zealand Maori Council.[329] The report floated plans to set up a new "Maori led" political party and named all five of NZ First's Maori MPs as "automatic starters". Delamere's report complained of tensions between the Maori and Pakeha wings of NZ First, and accused Winston Peters of being "a Pakeha MP".

In true smoking-gun fashion, the report pre-dated the Wellington Airport stoush that had blown the coalition apart. Delamere's difference of opinion with Peters over Wellington Airport was genuine, but it was still just an opinion about an indisputable fact – the airport was being sold. The report, however, showed Delamere was plotting to break NZ First apart and had been doing so before the airport crisis.

Peters hit back:

---

327 "Bitter Delamere defends PM's integrity," Evening Post, 14 August 1996, p1
328 "NZ coalition rift deepens as deputy PM is fired", The Nation, 15 August 1996, p5
329 "Delamere admits role in Maori party," by Pete Barnao, Dominion, 14 August 1996, p1

"What Mr Delamere has done is to have sought to undermine the interests of this party from a very early time. I have never seen, in my time in politics, such a betrayal from one who has been rewarded probably better than anyone else."[330]

Delamere says one Pakeha MP had made life unpleasant for the tight five, referring to them as "black monkeys".[331] His report for the Maori Council alleged "Peters, Brown and many of the other Pakeha MPs of NZ First" had made it clear that "the interests of Maori constituents should somehow be suppressed."

At the time the issue was red-hot, so was Tuariki Delamere. Sixteen years after the event, Delamere has mellowed, he and Winston now talk from time to time, and he concedes "Tau had been plotting."

A lot of the caucus, he says, were unhappy at where the party was going. "I'd been approached by a couple, I won't say who they were, who wanted me to stand as leader. It's all very, you know, it's great for the ego, but when you step back, I actually did step back and think about it. It's just crazy. The only reason we existed is because of Winston."

Delamere took heed of Ron Mark's unspoken advice. "If you don't like the captain, get off the ship". On 18 August, 1998, Delamere quit NZ First. He did not form the new Maori Party he'd floated. Instead, he remained a cabinet minister in Shipley's government.

NZ First party president Doug Woolerton says he tried to explain to the tight five long before this that they were part of a bigger political movement.

"I said, 'Now look you bastards. You're all here because of New Zealand First, so bloody toe the line!'

"Winston didn't do anything and it just got worse and worse and then something had to be done. People started walking out of caucus and doing dumb things. They had meetings in people's offices. I knew because I went around the party the whole time and I said, 'Winston, you've got a Maori breakaway thing happening here'.

"The people who weren't part of it were mystified and didn't know what the hell was going on, as you saw when Tau formed his party. Various people joined it, didn't know what side to be on, didn't understand. It was just a 'bugger's muddle' as my grandma would have said."

---

330 "Bitter Delamere defends PM's integrity," supra
331 Ibid

Woolerton says the coalition quickly disintegrated following Winston's sacking as Deputy Prime Minister on 14 August and NZ First MPs were asked to choose which side they were on.

"He and I got in a bloody room and they wheeled through. Like who was with us and who wasn't. Most of them weren't. And that was that."

How did that affect Winston?

"Well he's the toughest bastard that God ever breathed life into. You can see Judith Collins has had a bit of pressure and then she starts, the voice changes and she starts to do some crazy stuff. Winston does crazy stuff sometimes too but he just staunches it through, man. Like the crap he's been through – privileges committees, being sacked from the National – God knows, just staunches it through.

"I had tears in my eyes and he said, 'Doug, if there's only me and you left we'll just carry on.' And that was it. How many were left? Bugger all."

When the dust settled, Ann Batten and Jack Elder had joined Tau Henare, Tuku Morgan and Rana Waitai in the shortlived party Mauri Pacific. Delamere had struck out on his own, as did Deborah Morris and Peter McCardle. Neil Kirton had already gone.

Remaining in NZ First were Peters, Woolerton, Peter Brown, Ron Mark, Jenny Bloxham, Robyn McDonald, Tu Wyllie – the only member of the tight five to stay loyal – and Brian Donnelly.

"There were some good times with the boys, the brothers, before the bust-up," Ron Mark reminisces. "Hugely important to me in terms of connecting me back to my people, because I wasn't raised a Maori, I was just Ron Mark, raised in foster homes, and knew nothing of my background. To this day I am grateful to Rana, Tuku, and Tutekawa Wyllie for that. Always grateful that Tutekawa Wyllie stayed true, he didn't jump. To him it was really simple, he asked what would his people expect of him? And he knew. He asked me, and I said, 'your people expect you to be loyal to Winston' and he said, 'Yeah, they do'.

"Rana summed it up by saying 'vengeance is best served cold'. There'd been a blow-up between Tau and Winston, Tau had aspirations of being leader and that was never going to happen, and Tutekawa Wyllie had already had a crack at taking the deputy leadership off Tau. Looking back on it though, I'm still pleased I met all those guys and I see them today as friends. That was then."

Mark says there were elements of to-hell-with-the-world comedy, when he looks back on it.

"The funniest thing for me was when the Coalition had just broken; everyone was down and a bit sad, and knew there were huge implications – not the least being that staff were going to get laid off, people were losing their jobs. There was that song, 'I get knocked down, and I get up again, you're never going to keep me down', it was on the charts.

"I had a CD player/radio in my office and my staff were looking down, everyone was upset. I grabbed the CD and slapped it on, punched the button, turned the volume up loud. All the media were sitting outside with their cameras, poking through the glass, and we all walked out of there with this music blaring! We knew Winston would get up again, and we were determined to be part of that."

It had been a rough 12 months. The ship had more than "shuddered"; it had gone the full Rena, splitting in half on the reefs of political intrigue. To make matters worse, in late 1997 the Winebox Inquiry had issued its final report exonerating the Cook Islands tax deals and making the outrageous finding that there was "no evidence of incompetence" within the Serious Fraud Office and Inland Revenue Departments – these were the agencies, sharp-eyed readers will remember, who publicly cleared the Winebox deals of any wrongdoing months before actually doing an investigation, and who didn't even fully understand the deals until they saw them explained on TV.

Additionally, despite evidence that the SFO boss had shut down investigations into the BNZ, the film and bloodstock frauds and the Winebox frauds, and that the IRD had signed a secret non-prosecution deal to protect the culprits, Winebox commissioner Sir Ronald Davison ruled there was "no evidence of corruption" either.

Davison's ruling was a jack-up. He'd been talking fraud only weeks before issuing his report, but had suddenly gone weak at the knees. In the view of many winebox watchers, the old judge had been got at. There was no other rational explanation for a verdict that bore absolutely no resemblance to the actual evidence.

The IRD and SFO, he said, cannot be judged incompetent for failing to find fraud where no fraud exists.

I knew that the two lawyers who'd been given the task of investigating the Winebox by Davison were equally stunned. As I later wrote in *Paradise Conspiracy 2*:

"I can't believe it," the lawyer had sobbed to me as she read the report. "This country is so bloody corrupt!"

I watched as fury welled up in her eyes, teardrops falling like molten lava. Sympathy? I had it by the bucketload. Fury? That too. For three years we had both endured the Winebox Inquiry, and 'endured' is definitely the right word.

Three years of blatant lying, obfuscation and the kind of collective corporate amnesia that suggested to me that most of the executives and company directors involved in these so-called leading companies were unfit for their jobs and cheating their shareholders by the mere act of drawing a salary.

Suzanne Clark's fists were clenching and unclenching – she knew something that the rest of us could only guess at. As 2nd Counsel Assisting the Commission, she had helped uncover the stunning evidence at the centre of New Zealand's longest running Commission of Inquiry.

It was obvious that she now believed corruption had permeated the very Commission of Inquiry set up to investigate allegations of corruption. What wasn't clear was why she believed this. The mere existence of such a belief, coming from one of the Commission's own lawyers, rocked me to my very core.

Clark and her colleague, senior Counsel Assisting, Colin Carruthers QC, had seen the Devil. One of perhaps only five people in the world who knew what lay at the centre of a giant web. She looked up at me and I could see it in her eyes: knowledge. Knowledge of the kind that haunts you forever. And right at that moment, I would have killed to know what she knew…

Winston sighed when he saw it. It was as if the Universe was conspiring to destroy NZ First.

In the face of news media and political scorn, Peters set out to appeal the clearly dodgy Winebox findings. In late 1998, he was rewarded with a victory. The Court of Appeal slapped down Davison's verdict with the full force of the law. Davison, a five-judge panel, said, didn't know what he was talking about.

"The Commissioner *initially* indicated a proper understanding of the function of a Commission of Inquiry," Justice Ted Thomas' ruling began, ominously.

The Government, he said, must have expected Sir Ronald Davison's Inquiry to proceed on the basis of correctly applying the law.

"Otherwise, why have an inquiry? What would be the value of the resulting report?"

Thomas said that if Davison had misunderstood the law around what constituted fraud, then the inquiry report was about as useful as a 1975 telephone directory. The Court of Appeal and the Privy Council had both previously examined the Winebox deals and found evidence of prima facie fraud. They were not about to let Davison get away with this. To be polite, they called Davison's work a "misperception" of the reality of the tax frauds:

"This perception led the Commission to disregard that part of the prearranged scheme relating to the repayment of the tax in the Cook Islands when determining the effect of the Magnum transaction, and it contributed to the restricted view which he took of European Pacific's disclosure obligations under s301 [income tax] and ss229A and 257 [of the Crimes Act].

"Whatever one's view of the doctrine of form over substance, it does not apply to instances where the transaction is a sham, that is, where the form merely conceals the fraudulent reality. There must be a strong argument that this was the case with the Magnum transaction."

By the time the Court of Appeal sent the case back to the High Court for a final verdict in 1999, the election was nearing. The findings of the Winebox Inquiry, achieved at a cost in excess of $13 million, were null and void.

They'd been knocked down, but they were up again. The irony was that the positive publicity arising from the final Winebox verdicts may have been the thing that saved both Winston Peters and NZ First politically, but it was the narrowest of squeaks as you are about to see.

23

And They Got Up Again

> "When I became Deputy Prime Minister of New Zealand, I got rid of the surtax, I preserved the right of the elderly to get a decent retirement, we gave free medicine to under-six year olds – all things that people now believe are good – pay parity to primary school teachers who for decades had been paid on a different scale to secondary teachers with the same qualifications – there's a hundred things we've done and it's not 'exacting a price', it's doing what's right for the country. We took the minimum wage from nine dollars to twelve dollars in three years flat, and no other political party in history has done that."
>
> – Winston Peters, 2014

If Jenny Shipley thought booting NZ First out of the Beehive was going to give her government an electoral transfusion, she got it very wrong. National's support by February 1999 had slumped to the low 30s, and the previously unelectable Helen Clark was looking for all the world like a Prime Minister in waiting.

Peters had long since gone back to more familiar territory, acting as a vociferous member of Her Majesty's loyal opposition. Keeping the government honest was a role that, in truth, Peters enjoyed. Additionally, it gave him the chance to get back on the right side of voters who'd felt betrayed by the 1996 result.

In parliament, it was a time of goodbyes. As the session closed, it closed also on some of New Zealand's best known MPs. David Lange, who'd taken New Zealand anti-nuclear and once boasted his back had so much scar tissue you couldn't stick a knife in it, remembered the funny moments in his valedictory:

"In 1984 I opened at the town hall too, and that was the one where Geoffrey Palmer was the warm-up man. Can members believe that? He was down there like an embalmer's cosmetician, trying to warm the show. His other job – because we had 30 minutes – was to wait; we had to cut off after 27 minutes so we could show a 3-minute commercial. There we were, and his job was to hand me the stop-watch. So I came along, and I came out of the back and was swept up in this tide of applause. I marched up and Geoffrey shook my hand as though I had just won the 100 metres. He was smiling and his teeth were showing – it made Lockwood Smith look as though he had dropped his dentures. He was absolutely all over the place. He said through clenched teeth: 'The stop-watch has broken!' Somehow or other we got through the next 27 minutes to a T and we signed off at the end. There were other moments like that, but those were days of real exhilaration and real enjoyment.

"I thought of that when Joe [Walding] was with me one glorious night in Oxford, where in those timbered stone rooms, with a worldwide audience, we talked to the world about New Zealand's antinuclear position. And there was Joe. He was in that amazing dinner suit; he had that vast expanse of white dress shirt with the diamond studs absolutely blatantly sticking out the front. He sat there with great pride like a pregnant morepork. He sat at the end of this great hall, and we were able to talk, and I was uplifted by the fact that a person like that who was part of my very political being was there.

"I think Winston Peters is a person who brings his own particular style to this House. He would have been with us today, would he not, Tau, if he had not been detained by a full-length mirror! I heard Winston say something absolutely remarkable earlier this week. He had just said something, and I said to him: 'But that's the opposite of what you said last week.' He replied: 'I know. I've changed my mind. At least I'm consistent.' That is the sort of vigour and energy that one needs in politics, if one does not expect to be running the show immediately.

"But there are people here who are like that. I often think of Bill Birch, who, when I was ill last year, wrote the most moving personal letter I received in hospital. Yet I have spent a political life portraying him as a heartless, venal, mechanical, robotic, uncaring fiend – and it did not quite work! Then, of course, we blamed him for everything he did, and he took credit for everything we did. He got his own back in that spectacular fashion."[332]

Mike Moore, also, was going, and wanted to remember ordinary kiwis. In doing so, you get an idea of just how close he and Winston Peters were on some issues:[333]

"I wish I could have done more for them. They are the real battlers, who want to own their own homes, who, in the main, look after their kids, run the netball teams, and wash other people's children's football jerseys. They are the cream. They do not want a Government to tell them what to eat, who to meet, and how to greet. They simply seek the gift of opportunity, and that their children have a better life than themselves. As Norman Kirk, who represented Kaiapoi as mayor, said: 'They don't ask much: someone to love, somewhere to live, somewhere to work, and something to hope for.' To serve them has been the highlight of my life. To be asked to hold hands at a hospice, to join in a family christening, and to share their hopes and represent them – that is the privilege.

"My biggest disappointment is the fact that we still do not have a compulsory savings scheme, as envisaged by Norman Kirk, Roger Douglas, and, later, Winston Peters. When Bismarck put up the first pension, less than 3 percent of the population was covered. Within 20 years it will be 25 percent. No nation or family can long prosper and survive, or even be independent, if it is not living on its own savings, and is sucking money in from other countries and living off other people's savings. That is something we will have to address, and something I was unable to do much about.

I think the defining issue of our age – against which we will measure our progress as a civilised society – is race relations and treaty issues. Of course, I do not expect all members to agree with me, but race relations have been the stone in New Zealand's shoe. We could get everything right here – I doubt it, but we could – inflation, employment, health policies, and debt. But if we fail on this issue we fail at everything. We keep talking

---

332 Hansard, Valedictory, 22 August 1996
333 Hansard, Valedictory, 24 August 1999

about the Crown and Maori at Waitangi. I do wish we would substitute the words 'New Zealand Government', 'New Zealand people', and 'New Zealand taxpayer' for 'Crown', and I would like us to stop using the word 'beneficiary' when we speak of Maori claims, and instead talk of 'owner' and 'stakeholder'.

"Let us think of that fateful morning at Waitangi. There on the lawn were assembled Maori and representatives of the British Government. Was that the deal? Not entirely. There was a third partner – the church, God, the missionaries. It was the missionaries whose mana and prestige gave confidence to the partners. Remember, this was 1840 not 1640. It was not America or Africa, where the church was the villain. Europe had gone through the age of reason and enlightenment. The church had a moral mandate based on the principle that we are all created in God's likeness, therefore we are all the children of God, and therefore we must be equal. That is the moral basis of democracy. That is the force of the democratic impulse. Those are the core values that have driven civilised society. That is why I get uneasy when people say that partnership could mean Maori having 50 percent of the seats in Parliament, or could mean having a State within a State.

"Sometimes I do fear for our country. We are in danger of dividing ourselves. Any nation that bases its law and destiny on the colour of skin will perish, and so it should. When faced with a hostile Congress because of the slavery issue, President Lincoln said these words. He had a civil war on his hands, and he knew that the Union could be over, that it was in peril. He said: 'We are not enemies but friends. We must not be enemies. Though passion may have strained, it must not break our bonds of affection. The mystic chords of memory, stretching from every battle-field, and patriot grave, to every living heart and hearthstone, all over this broad land, will yet swell the chorus of the Union, when again touched, as surely they will be, by the better angels of our nature.' The better angels of our nature can win through.

"We need to think of what we are doing. This Parliament has passed legislation – and I have been guilty of this – without really knowing what it means. I am not quite sure what 'taking into regard the spirit of the Treaty of Waitangi' means, but let us do it, anyway. We are painting by numbers. We have no clear picture and vision of where we are going. Therefore we are surrendering the rights and prerogatives of Parliament.

Because we do not know what it means, we expect a court or some commission to determine what it means.

"Perhaps we should be inspired by the preamble of the new South African constitution. I will read it to members, because every sentence and every word resonates and has meaning. Who would have thought we would learn from the South African constitution? 'We, the people of South Africa, recognise the injustices of our past; Honour those who suffered for justice and freedom in our land; respect those who have worked to build and develop our country; and believe that South Africa belongs to all who live in it, united in our diversity.' As Nelson Mandela said, there are no white South Africans and there are no black South Africans; there can only be South Africans."

And with that, parliament ended. Could Winston Peters survive long enough to help create the kind of New Zealand that both he and Mike Moore believed was possible? Only if he could reconnect with the voters who'd been burned off by the events of the Coalition.

Most sensitive of all, perhaps, were the humble citizens of Tauranga. In 1993 they'd given Peters a massive majority and a massive vote of confidence, by electing him at the head of a new party. Back in those days he could do no wrong.

Now, in the weeks leading up to the 27 November date with electoral destiny, it was easy to find the disgruntled and disillusioned.

"He has let himself down," local businessman John Baty told the *Herald*. "The reason for his demise is his choice of other party representatives, the likes of Tau Henare and Underpants Morgan. They ruined his credibility, not him. They ruined it for him. It shows poor judgement on his part."[334]

Another voter vox-popped by the newspaper told them she didn't like his defensiveness:

"What he usually does is argue against everything," said restaurant supervisor Lydia Skinner. "I find him quite arrogant. It would be all right if he was down to earth. He has promised people a lot of things he hasn't delivered on, like keeping the Government honest."

Clearly Peters still had some work to do, although at least one voter grudgingly supported him:

"This country needs the likes of Winston Peters to stay in," said Roger Magee, a PR consultant. "He's a mischief man. We need one of those.

---

334 "National weighs Tauranga challenge," by Audrey Young, 9 December 1999

We've got enough mavericks. He did his apprenticeship as a maverick. We need a little bit of educated mischief."

In mid-November, polls placed NZ First on 4.8%, tantalisingly close to the 5% threshold needed to enter parliament without a seat. But of course, the party had two of those – Tauranga held by Peters and Te Tai Tonga held by Tu Wyllie. In better times, NZ First wouldn't have blinked. But these were no longer better times.

A TVNZ Marae Digipoll placed Peters support in Tauranga at 31%, and for the first time in a decade he was behind a rival challenger, National's Katherine O'Regan on 32%. Again, the difference fell within the margin of error, but combine that kind of tightness with the 4.8% and there's not enough piggy in the bank to guarantee a return to power.

"We're going to shock you all on election night," Peters challenged the always doubtful *Herald*.[335]

He was right, but possibly he was as shocked as everyone else. NZ First's share of the party vote dropped to 4.3%. It was pretty clear only an electorate seat could save them. Tu Wyllie's was the first to fall, returning to Labour. Peters was now his party's only hope, but National's Katherine O'Regan was holding a provisional lead.

It was close to midnight at Peters' campaign headquarters, still no final count. On stage with him, unusually, his children – 19 year old Joel and 17 year old Brittany – all three getting the shock of their lives when the TV progress reports rolling in the background finally placed Winston Peters back in the lead in Tauranga.

"It was too much for the fragile emotions of a caring daughter – Brittany broke down," reported the *Herald*. "Mr Peters forgot his politics for a moment or two and turned away to console her and her brother in a family embrace. No one else mattered as he kissed away her tears in a private moment shared live with the country."[336]

Turning back to the TV cameras, as his daughter wiped a tear away and composed herself, Peters made a rare introduction:

"My boy Joel and my girl Brittany, who you've not seen much of over the years because its important in politics that you keep your family protected from the agony of politics."

---

335 "Make or break week for Peters," by Audrey Young, NZ Herald, 22 November 1999
336 "Winston has his finest hour…" NZ Herald, 29 November 1999

As election night close, Peters had a provisional majority of just 323 votes. By the time the votes had been officially recounted, his majority was slashed to just 62.

Sixty-two Tauranga voters had made the difference between political life or death for the NZ First party. It was enough to keep the seat, and bring back four other MPs. Wyllie was gone. So too were the two loyal female MPs Jenny Bloxham and Robyn McDonald. They'd dropped below 20 on the party list. The new core of NZ First, apart from Peters, was Peter Brown, Brian Donnelly, Ron Mark and Doug Woolerton. From 17 down to five, NZ First had suffered a nine percent swing against them.

Winston told interviewer Mark Sainsbury that at times like that it is about family, and tuning out for a little while:

"When things are seriously difficult, you need to go home, play some music, and realise that there's far more important things in life. One of the things I've learned is that if you haven't done enough that day to fix it, don't worry about it until the next day."[337]

It was time to rebuild the party. That meant some fundamental lessons being learned. Perhaps the biggest was the ability of the major parties to destroy the brands of smaller parties they coalesced with. NZ First had become largely invisible beside National, and the Labour Party began to do the same to the Alliance in its first term from 2000 to 2002. The Greens had already splintered from Jim Anderton's monster, and had polled a healthy 5.2% of the vote for their initial appearance, winning an electorate seat in Coromandel and bringing in six more list MPs.

By remaining outside government – admittedly not completely of their own choice – the Green brand survived. Keep that in mind, because it will become relevant in a page or two.

Former NZ First party president Doug Woolerton gets a conspiratorial tone in his voice as he relives the memories of the 1998 break-up and its fallout. Unlike Ron Mark, Woolerton hints that Winston might have been playing chess with Shipley the night he stormed out of the cabinet meeting.

It wasn't as Delamere claimed at the time, "Winston telling lies", he says. Nothing so gauche. Rather, it was Winston looking for a way to save what was left of the party, to get it out from under the crushing goliath that was Jenny Shipley.

---

337 Peters interview with Mark Sainsbury, Radio Live, 29 June 2014

The trigger had been former prime minister Jim Bolger's resignation from parliament, forcing a by-election in his King Country seat in May 1998. Winston Peters had not wanted to stand a candidate in the poll, figuring it was a waste of the party's time and money. Woolerton, on the other hand, was absolutely insistent that they should.

"He never wanted to fight that by election, and I and a few others absolutely insisted on it, just rarked it up. The purpose of that was to show Winston that we were dead in the polls, and he wasn't wanting to accept it, which is why he didn't want to fight the by election.

"When he fought the by election, he realised that we were dead which I knew he would, when he got out on the road. There's a huge disconnect when you become a minister, it really removes you from the humdrum everyday stuff."

NZ First scored only 2.77% of the vote. Its candidate polled sixth behind the Christian Heritage Party. The Alliance meanwhile, in Jim Bolger's home turf, scored more than 15% of the vote. It was a sign to Winston that his brand was in trouble.

"Like a lot of things that Winston does," says Woolerton, "he didn't tell lies; it was the Wellington airport, but if he hadn't been involved in the by election, between you me and the gate post, he might have let it go. No lies were told but when you're going down the dunny you've got to toughen up a bit." He chose to make an issue of the airport because he could.

"It's the same today with the Maori party. They haven't toughened up, so they've supported John Key and the National government. What the hell have they done for the Maori party? Killed them? Stone cold dead. Te Ururoa Flavell is going to have to rebuild the whole bloody thing from scratch now.

"The same thing was happening to us, and Winston knew that which was why I wanted him to stand. He will never forgive me for that, but it was for survival, I believe."

Not that Winston ever admitted this to Woolerton. "He just said 'well there you are Doug, I told you we shouldn't have run in that. That was a complete waste of time,' which it wasn't of course. So he blamed me and anybody who supported me running the election. Of course, the folk in New Zealand First said 'what a drongo we've got for a president.' In my humble opinion I'd just saved the bloody day for God's sake."

Woolerton says the shock of the low poll motivated Peters, gave him a sense of purpose. "He just gets motivated with elections, fullstop. I used to tell funny stories about that which I won't repeat to you. Between elections Winston does this, that and the other, just carries on. Election time comes, oh man, he's up and into it."

The "funny" story Woolerton refuses to repeat actually popped up in parliament one afternoon in a valedictory speech from a Green MP, recounting a conversation he'd once had with Woolerton:

"I asked him what it was like working with Winston Peters. Perhaps I should not tell this one. Doug said: 'Look, he's like a racehorse. For 10 minutes every day, his eyes are bright, his ears are pricked, and his nostrils are flaring. He races around the track and just hates to be beaten. But after the roar of the crowd dies down, for the rest of the day he's just like the other horses. He's back in the stalls, snoring and farting and rolling in the hay.' Sorry, Doug!"[338]

"Yeah, okay," concedes Woolerton with a chuckle, "well you know the quote. I told him. It was a great joke at the time. Well, not so bloody funny, I had to go, when he did that I wasn't in parliament that afternoon hearing it. And when I heard that I thought, 'oh shit.' So I had to go and apologise to Winston. He just stared at me. I just did my thing and took off."

"Did he see any humour in it at all?"

"Well not that I could see, no."

As Woolerton sees it, the success that NZ First achieved in the Helen Clark years was because Winston opted to stay on the cross benches as Jiminy Cricket, getting his MPs to act as parliament's conscience. That, says Woolerton, is why parties like NZ First are needed and where they can do their best for the country. He points to the Greens' good run on the Left.

"The luck that they have had is they've never been accepted into a coalition. When they do, if they do, their polls will go through the bloody floor. Absolutely. The tide will go out, instantly.

"Because the people, and this is the same phenomenon with New

---

338 Hansard, Valedictory Ian Ewen Street, 2 August 2005
http://www.parliament.nz/en-nz/pb/debates/debates/47HansD_20050802_00000965/valedictory-statements

Zealand First, all of the people who are pissed off with both National and Labour, and especially today, when both leaders come from the right wing Chicago School of Economics, and David Cunliffe can talk about that and do what he likes, all the rest of it, but he and Key, basically, have the same background financially and the belief system. So it's hard for Cunliffe to differentiate the difference.

"Easy for Winston. It's just like a bloody turkey shoot. You could write the speech: 'Here I am sticking up for the average Joe who's fixing the bloody tractors and digging the wells down in bloody Canterbury and fixing up the bloody hedges that have all been blown over, you know? 'I'm looking after you bastards, and all these other ponces come from the Chicago School of Economics or whatever.'

"And then, at the end of that, he goes and joins one of them. They just say 'eff you,' and the tide just goes out. I couldn't keep up with the letters of resignation. I answered every one I could. The tide just goes out and it will with the Greens, because you cannot go into a coalition and maintain your purity, totally the wrong word, but maintain your brand. Everybody's proved it, we've proved it a couple of times."

Woolerton says there are lines small parties need to learn they should never cross:

"After the first coalition with National, I just opposed any offer of ministers, anywhere, anytime. And the next time I resigned as president when Winston went with Labour – not that I'm against Labour, no problem with Labour, no problem with National either, I get on with lots of people. And the public understand coalition. They understand coalition absolutely. They do not accept a minister because they know, and the newspapers never write this, they never write this stuff, but the public inherently has the wisdom to perceive you cannot be a minister in a National or Labour government and be your own person."

But of course, Winston did accept a ministerial position from Helen Clark, and that had consequences…

24

The Price Of Politics

> *"Democracy has a romance and glamour about it that is worth striving for. It keeps me interested. I do not think it's about personal power or egregious self interest. I could have been a lot of things a lot quicker and faster, but I never did and I don't intend to."*
> – **Winston Peters, 2011**

The funny thing, when you listen to or read media coverage of NZ First, is how the criticisms keep getting recycled like it's a 1993 or 1996 Groundhog Day. This, despite the fact that many of the journalists now writing the stories were at primary school back then; some were not even born. Yet the institutional memory, the knee-jerk dismissal of people with a different perspective, has been passed on.

The real issue with NZ First is that the party's worldview is totally out of step with the globalisation now automatically programmed into our education system and thus journalism graduates. Concerns about the level of immigration to NZ – one of the highest per capita rates in the Western world – are automatically dismissed, without any debate, as "racism" by young journalists who go out to find critics who will sing that song for them.

In *Investigate* magazine's January 2003 issue, we ran a test across both main TV news channels for a week to detect worldview bias in their coverage of major public issues. One of the issues that surfaced during the test week was immigration. Here's how the magazine article played out:

Take the immigration debate. In the last week of November and first week of December, we ran the video recorders over One News and 3 News. One of the biggest news stories in this time concerned Winston Peters' comments on immigration.

On One's Late Edition, anchor Peter Williams opened with this:

"Winston Peters is unrepentant in the wake of a new poll which suggests many New Zealanders think he's increasing division in the community."

Let's pause there for a moment and search for liberal-loaded newspeak. We're told Peters is "unrepentant". Unrepentant for what? Who elected One News to be judge and jury on what politicians should be repentant for? If One News wants to editorialise, it should broadcast editorials and state clearly that's what they are.

But it gets better. Late Edition then tells us there's a new poll suggesting many New Zealanders think he's increasing division in the community.

"The One News Colmar-Brunton poll," continues Williams, "shows the majority believe his comments on Asian immigration raise tensions."

"Auckland," begins the reporter, "is home to one in three people born in another country. It's often portrayed as the start of what will be an increasingly changing face of New Zealand. Changes Winston Peters warns will lead to a divided and mutually exclusive society.

"But in a One News Colmar-Brunton poll, it's Winston Peters who's being called divisive. Seventy-one percent of those polled say his views increase tension between Asian immigrants and the rest of New Zealand. Only 23% disagree."

The facts were presented as if Moses had just held up stone tablets and read from them, and on the face of it they appeared damning of Peters.

But, again, was it really that simple? Once again, no.

You see, opinion polling is an art form. I know. I worked in the industry for a year. The answer you get in a poll is almost 100% dependent on what question you ask and how you tilt it. In a truly objective poll, questions are phrased as neutrally as possible so as not to skew the results. But in polls designed by news organisations, the questions are often far more obtuse.

The value of this One News poll on immigration was about to be defined by whether or not its questions were horribly biased. Let's take a look:

QUESTION 1: "Winston Peters' views and statements increase tension and division between Asian immigrants and the rest of New Zealand... Agree...Disagree...Don't Know."

As you can see, it's not a question. It's a political statement and it could have been drafted by the Prime Minister's office for all the objectivity it displayed.

One News is telling survey respondents that Peters is being divisive. In polling terms, One News has loaded the dice for what some may believe are political reasons. By making a firm statement portraying a negative image, One News is inviting respondents to see it that way before they've even opened their mouths to respond.

QUESTION 2: "Asian immigration is a good thing. It makes the country more multicultural and the economy stronger...Agree...Disagree...Don't know."

Again, a political statement rather than a polling question. One News is telling those surveyed that they should believe immigration is a good thing. The final 'question' in the poll asked whether the Government should stop any further Asian immigration (given that we've now established Peters is being unkind to Asians and that Asian immigration is good for our economy and good for multiculturalism), to which 71% disagreed and said the Government should not stop Asian immigration.

Having set up their straw-man, One News then tries to set him alight.

"The Government," continues the report, "says the poll is proof Winston Peters has read it wrong."

"I think this is a very telling poll indeed," Labour's Immigration Minister Lianne Dalziel is quoted as saying.

The liberal prejudice running through the report – that Peters is being divisive and causing tension by daring to comment on the issue, that he should shut up because immigration is a good thing and multiculturalism is a good thing – these are the prejudices of staff in the news organisation, not scientifically-tested facts.

Ironically, the reporter and producers who worked on the story, and the person who dreamt up the poll 'questions', may not even realise they have the biases – the attitudes are so ingrained they are accepted as "the way it is".

But One News hadn't finished the hatchet-job. Anchor Peter Williams came back after the break to interview sociologist Paul Spoonley from Massey University.

"Is Winston Peters' reading of the issue all wrong? Is he the one actually out of touch with what New Zealand is thinking? Are you surprised Paul that New Zealanders, at least according to this poll, appear to have a pretty liberal attitude towards Asian immigration?"

"No, not really," replied Spoonley. "I think what they're beginning to realise is that our economic future is very much with Asia, and we're beginning to accept that Asians coming here is part of that future."

What One News never declared in their coverage was that Paul Spoonley has been highly critical of NZ First leader Winston Peters on his immigration stand in the past, and that Spoonley is funded by the United Nations to help the UN plan for immigration.

"Embracing cultural diversity and demonstrating a tolerance of others is surely one of the most significant challenges of this period of our history," Spoonley told an audience in 1996, before getting stuck into people whipping up hysteria about migrants.

"Some national politicians, notably Winston Peters of the New Zealand First party, have articulated these concerns. These politics reflect the beliefs held by significant numbers that 'at the economic level, the nation-state is threatened by globalisation; at the cultural level (so it is thought), it is threatened by immigration'. Racist politics are one result.

"Peters has always denied any racist intent...but, inevitably, his rhetoric is seen as an endorsement of certain racist views in the wider community. It is reinforced by an increased and declared interest by the New Zealand police in the involvement of Asians in various criminal activities, and especially the possibility that Triad gangs are operating in New Zealand.

"This is an irony because one of the post-war myths was that Chinese migrants were law-abiding and had a strong work ethic. In fact, the statistics for those charged with drug offences in 1965 show that 103 of the 113 involved were Chinese. Few knew about the statistics and the popular mythology that prevailed in a post-war era meant that Chinese were viewed benignly. But with the racialisation of Asian migrants in the 1990s, the mythology has been discarded and one of the stereotypes which sustains this racialisation of Asian involvement is organised crime. It contributes to the generally negative perceptions held towards Asians by New Zealanders.

"These negative and hostile reactions have been articulated in a variety of ways. In its most extreme form, they result in racist and neo-fascist politics as expressed by skinhead and motorbike gangs...The most significant expression of the anti-Asian sentiments are provided by New Zealand First, and specifically its leader Winston Peters, whose statements encapsulate the guarded racism of middle (and typically elderly) New Zealand."

In other words, Paul Spoonley is hardly an "independent" academic in the immigration debate. Politically, from his speeches at least, he appears to be a globalist and is certainly happy to take funding from UNESCO whilst pushing multiculturalism as a cure-all for the world. In addition, he's not a Peters fan.

Meanwhile, across on 3 News they were running this:

"Proof today that Winston Peters has been mining a very popular prejudice. A TV3/NFO poll has surveyed feelings about levels of immigration, and Asian migrants stand out.

"Asians were the only ethnic grouping to attract a majority disapproval rating among those surveyed.

"53% said they felt too many Asians were coming here."

Different TV channels, different polling companies, and diametrically-opposed poll results. TV1 saying 71% favour Asian immigration. TV3 saying 53% disapprove of Asian immigration. Both polls had a margin of error of plus or minus 3.4%.

Even so, TV3 still labelled Peters' comments as prejudiced. Who says so? How can one possibly "pre-judge" the immigration issue? Surely it's a simple question of whether New Zealanders want new immigrants or not, end of story. How can there be a moral side to this that one could pass pre-judgement on?

Yet both news organisations pitched the story as if to say that people who questioned immigration levels were "prejudiced".

For the record, as those who've listened to me on Radio Pacific will know, I'm in favour of even higher immigration levels than we currently have – maybe 100 to 150,000 a year. But that doesn't mean that I would label opponents of immigration as "prejudiced" or "racist".

∽

As you can see, journalists were caught red-handed spinning the issue for all it's worth.

With such a public profile on 'foreigners' It thus came as a surprise to many when Winston Peters accepted the role of Foreign Minister in 2005 from Helen Clark, in return for NZ First providing confidence and supply. How could New Zealand have a 'racist' Foreign Minister, the pundits chirped.

Others wondered, how could Winston Peters be going with Helen Clark? "There was a meeting in Rotorua," leading up to the election, says former party president Doug Woolerton, "and getting advice I was bloody just beside myself and I said to Winston, 'look, you have got to stay on the cross benches. No bloody nothing. Otherwise we're buggered.' So he did that and I was friendly with Brian Donnelly bless his soul, but he saw Winston's speech the night before he gave it, and he changed a couple of words and I was waiting for that, and I just went bloody apeshit, but to no effect. Those words stay and I can't for the life of me remember them now but it's this business of saying one thing and meaning another.

"He delivered the speech, all of the people in the room jumped up and gave him a standing ovation because they thought the speech was what I'd wanted it to be. There'd be no talks, no bloody nothing. Anywhere, anytime, nothing. They got up and applauded. I watched the polls. The polls jumped straight away."

When Winston broke that assurance, Woolerton knew the party was 'toast'.

Ironically, the one thing the NZ First story shows is that on occasions when the party has power-shared, it has recognised that it won't get all its views across the line. Peters was forced to compromise on immigration in the 1996 coalition, and that was simply a political reality. As it transpired between 2005 and 2008, Peters was widely regarded as one of the best foreign ministers in recent history.

"And he was, and I never doubted that he would be," agrees Woolerton. But it hurt his brand:

"Wrecked it. He eventually lost the 2008 election. I resigned when he accepted that posting. I can say I was the only one who opposed him doing that and I said 'you'll have my resignation by 2 o'clock this afternoon as the president, not as an MP, but as president because I can't go around the party supporting this', and lots of people never got the difference. As an MP you can plod along quite happily, in fact the best years of my bloody MP's life was then. But as the president I couldn't go around supporting something I knew would kill the party. I bloody wasn't going to do it. I did it once under National and I knew what drama that caused. I wasn't going to do it again, so I resigned."

I asked Peters about that in a major 2005 interview. Why had he offered confidence and supply when the party had assured voters it would stay on the crossbenches? Peters told me it came back to pragmatism – doing what was best for the country, even if it meant pain to NZ First again.

"Look, the moment it became 57/57, the position we'd taken at Rotorua became untenable. Neither side could command a majority, and neither side could guarantee that their social or economic policy initiatives could be passed through Parliament. We could not, in good conscience, continue with our policy of sitting on the crossbenches. My team understand that now.[339]

INVESTIGATE: Here you are, part of the Government but not in Cabinet, ostensibly free to criticize. Really?

"I'm free to agree to disagree outside of my portfolio areas, and that's a reality."

INVESTIGATE: How public can you be in your disagreement?

"Entirely public. What's unprecedented, when you talk about the baubles of office, is a person who was in cabinet twice and never took a car or a house or anything. So when I say I'm not concerned about the baubles of office, I've got a record to back it up and a long career. And I've taken on big issues at enormous financial cost and time and effort, so when I look at the pygmies who criticize me and who've never invested five cents on anything in their whole lives, I just find it an issue of absolute mirth and comedy. When have they ever stood up for anything? These are the same people who for seven years berated me for going for the Winebox. Up hill and down dale, wrote 57 editorials in one case and 68 in another case, two major newspapers in this country and never said sorry when they were wrong. Or the Maori Loans affair or anything else for that matter. They're just a bunch of cynics whose record in terms of being a public watchdog is a disgrace."

The problem for Peters was that his offer of stability meant joining Labour past its use-by date, with all the odium that was bound to follow from being seen, yet again, to support an unpopular government. Even Peters admitted National should have won in 2005:

"They lost the unloseable election with more money than you could throw a bank at. Some people who were doing the analysis should be coming forward and explaining to the country today why they're still employed.

INVESTIGATE: Yeah, I want to expand on that. If you were in Brash's

---

339 "Having Affairs" by Ian Wishart, Investigate, December 2005

shoes or Steven Joyce's shoes in the National Party, what were their failures – what broke the camel's back for National?

"Their Orewa speech was a straight steal, a purloining of another party's policy without understanding. I've said it's one thing to walk out of a saloon and steal someone's horse, it's quite something else to stay on its back trying to ride out of town!"

INVESTIGATE: So in other words they got the rhetoric, but they didn't understand what you were actually getting at?

'No, no. And my justification for saying that is that the election was hardly over and they were going back on it."

Peters pointed at National's attempt to stitch together a coalition with the Maori Party and even include NZ First in some way. To coalesce with the Maori Party however meant abandoning the Orewa speech. Peters says he explained to the Maori Party why he could never work with them, and he criticised National for being prepared to sacrifice virtually all of its principles just to get back into power:

"Don't forget, they were talking to the Maori Party about reversing everything that they said at Orewa One and Two. Now, you can go from that 'apex of deceit' all the way down. But there's nothing more significant than that preparedness to change their policy. Problem was we weren't prepared to change ours. Our view of long term race relations has never changed, their view is a transient purloining of some other party's policy."

INVESTIGATE: Could you have worked with the Maori Party in any way?

"No we couldn't have, because we are too diametrically opposed on what, long term, is good for NZ."

INVESTIGATE: Could one have put those issues, on both sides, to the side to work on other core areas?

"No you couldn't, because that party was formed specifically to do just that, which the Maori Party was. Privately, I spoke to the Maori Party about the impossibility of this, and they privately recognized it."

INVESTIGATE: So they came to the same conclusion you did?

"On the last day, they came to the same conclusion I did. It was a respectful conversation."

Peters was optimistic, that late Spring day in 2005. And he had reason to be. He went on to forge a strong personal relationship with US Secretary of State Condoleeza Rice, and suddenly the nuclear ships issue was ancient history.

Winston, says Woolerton, was even Condoleeza's man on the ground in North Korea at the height of the nuclear stand off in 2007:

"The minister thing is huge with Winston. It's not the money and the international thing, it's the red carpet when you get off the aeroplane. It is like, if you go to China they close bloody roads, they do! You've got this fleet of cars whizzing through. Everybody's blocked up on the side roads giving you the fingers. God knows what it's like in America, I've never been there and don't want to go. It's all of these sort of things. It's the red carpet.

"They sent bloody Winston to Korea, the yanks did. Nobody knows about that. He was just in Korea, was the report back here. Well the yanks sent him there because he's a bloody wonderful negotiator. This was the training the dogs business, you know? The father trained the horses. Immense patience. You go off for an hour, 'now we'll just come back to that point'. 'I thought we'd covered that point?' 'Well, you know, I just had another thought about it.' And they said totally 'no, piss off,' and he's coming back for it. There's not many men can do that, I tell you. People said 'no, no, we're not going to revisit that, bugger off!' Whereas he'll say 'no, no,' and he'll wheedle away and get it back on the agenda! You think, 'shit, how did that happen?' He's amazing like that, the skills are bloody unbelievable.

"In political terms he will overreach himself. But in a negotiating room it's a more sophisticated bunch of people. I don't like that word. There's a more understanding bunch of people who know people will come back to things. In politics, 'you said that, now you've broken it, you're buggered, see you.'

"In a negotiating room you know that until the thing is signed, even then it's not very good these days, people will revisit things. He's just amazing at that. He likes all of that stuff."

Money, says Woolerton, was never a motivation for Peters, although the party never had enough of it. At one stage Peters was fighting nearly half a dozen lawsuits and defamation writs totalling more than $4.5 million in claims. The only award he had to pay was the Selwyn Cushing judgement of $50,000 plus $75,000 in costs.

He has had to fundraise to pay the legal costs of fighting the various court actions, however, even though close friend and lawyer Brian Henry has done much of the work free, where he can. Henry's like that; as the Sunday Star-Times reported, he also represented RSA shooting survivor

Susan Couch through a landmark battle all the way to the Supreme Court to win her compensation, and didn't charge her a cent.

"I think he's a lovely man who just stands up for what he believes in," Couch said of Henry to the newspaper.

It was Henry who helped, with the other lawyers surrounding Peters since the Winebox days, set up the trusts to gather public donations for the legal fighting funds. These were already set up in 1993, because I was in Henry's office at the time when he explained it. Winston was publically calling for donations to a fighting fund over the Cushing case and the other lawsuits he'd been hit with. Along with money from ordinary members of the public, business leaders sometimes made contributions but they made sure neither Peters nor anyone else found out who they were lest they experience a business backlash from the clique suing Peters.

One of the few rich enough and powerful enough to rise above such fears was Sir Robert Jones, who reportedly gave $50,000 to the party in 1994 and $100,000 to Peters' legal funds.

The amounts obtained by NZ First have paled into insignificance alongside the multi-million dollar donation totals collected by National, Labour and Act, always hidden behind the same kind of "trusts" arrangement s NZ First uses and for the same reasons – donors don't want a backlash.

Peters, of course, found himself in a serious spot of bother leading up to the 2008 election when it was revealed controversial businessman Owen Glenn had given the party or Winston $100,000. The perceptions around that issue helped contribute to the disappearance of Peters from the political stage in 2008.

A politically motivated Privileges Committee investigation found Peters guilty, but stripped of the theatrics Ron Mark maintains the issue was "a beat up". Glenn, he says, made a donation, apparently hoping to get a favour returned down the track with an appointment as honorary consul to Monaco. Peters, when he realised what was up, did not let the donation corrupt his duty and said no. Owen Glenn then threw his toys out of the cot. It is the way donations to political parties should work, but usually don't – as the latest donations scandals involving National and Labour and the sale of citizenship to wealthy foreigners show.

"Why is Act now in disarray?" adds Mark rhetorically, given Act's leading role in prosecuting Peters over Owen Glenn. "It's over donations. Talk about pots and kettles and black."

Is Winston Peters a man of principle?

"Principle?" gasps Mark. "That's his problem. An absolute adherence to the letter of what is right and correct, and not giving in when he's being slandered and bagged up and down the country because he truly believes he's right, no matter what it's doing to the polls, no matter that it's kicking you out the door and in 2008 you're looking like you'll be thrown out of parliament. Yeah, he's a man of principle alright, a stubborn bastard at that."

Ron Mark was no longer in the upper echelon of NZ First when the Glenn scandal hit, no longer a whip, he wasn't deputy leader and he wasn't on the board of directors, which means he has no direct knowledge of where or when donations were banked. But he was there for the fallout.

"For me, the guts of that, Owen Glenn wanted a political appointment, he didn't get it, he'd given a donation, clearly, he'd given it and it had been treated in exactly the same way that the National Party does, ie they had the Waitemata Trust, you donate it there and the Waitemata Trust donates it to the National Party.

"I was not involved, I was just a footsoldier fronting my portfolios and that's what I concentrated on. But all I could see from all of the discussions we had, all the explanations, no matter how critical I might have wanted to be of Winston, at the end of the day the actual story was a beat-up, and National used it with the privileges committee to achieve their aim, and Murray McCully's stated aim was to get Winston out of parliament.

"There were a whole bunch of things that I could see pointing to Rome. "Rome" was governing alone, without NZ First, and for Murray McCully it was as simple as 'I want to be the next Minister of Foreign Affairs and that bastard Peters has got my job and he's not going to have it.'

"For Murray McCully, Simon Power and Pita Sharples, their whole motivation was to make sure Peters was damaged as much as possible and that hopefully he wouldn't be back in parliament again. With Winston's help, they succeeded.

"You can look back at how he handled it, and he admits – he will quietly admit to you today – that looking back he could have handled it differently. But you back him into a corner on a matter of principle where he knows he didn't do something wrong, and he will fight you until he bleeds to death. He will die fighting a point of principle if he believes absolutely and emphatically that he is right. Whereas others would say, 'let's find a way through this'.

"I put it down to some bad advice that he received as to how it should have been managed, but sometimes you will not manage Winston, no matter how good you think you are as a press secretary, no matter how good you think you are as a deputy leader and no matter how good you think you are as a whip – at the end of the day he'll make is call, and if you are in the waka then row, shut up and row.

"I actually like that, because right or wrong, I like to know that everybody behind me with a loaded rifle is on my team."

Peters later apologised to his MPs and party members for his failings in the 2008 campaign where the party was conclusively booted out of office. With repentance and time off came a fresh perspective, and NZ First made it back again, in defiance of the doomsayers, in 2011.

Losing, says Woolerton, would have hurt, personally, but the biggest pain was inflicted when the Maori people turned their backs on NZ First after the coalition split.

"There was a defining moment, we never won the Maori seats again. That hurt him."

It hurt, he says, because behind the scenes Winston Peters had put so much work into helping various iwi get reparations. Woolerton cites the Taranaki Maori land being leased to dairy farmers at a pittance, "all of the Taranaki farms, those guys made a bloody fortune. They were paying peppercorn rentals to Maori. When I say peppercorn rentals, a few grand a year. Just a bloody outrageous situation. Winston sorted all that out. The whole thing was Winston.

"The thing with Maori, not winning the Maori seats, that would have hurt."

It may have taken two coalition deals and nearly destroyed him on both occasions, but it looks like Winston Peters won't get a rush of blood to the head three times. He's now saying his party will stay on the cross benches, regardless.

Peters says he has never stated his preferences before an election because parties can suddenly find themselves in an unhappy marriage.

"I don't know what policies they [other parties] are going to announce in the next few months of this campaign. One needs to know that. And the other thing that one needs to know is, who will you end up having to deal with?"[340]

---

340 Peters interview with Mark Sainsbury, Radio Live, 29 June 2014

"All I say to people is, we don't know what policies they're going to announce, the second thing is I'm bound to consult with my caucus and the wider party when the election is over. We are not going to go into any government where it is based on race, where certain races have special privileges.

"Unlike all the others who are all tied one side or the other, left or right, we are not. We are the only middle party in this country, the only centrist party. We speak common sense and we are prepared to sit on the cross benches, which is what I announced in 2011 in the campaign, that we would not go with any of the parties because their policies were too divergent from ours.

"We are prepared to make that sacrifice. We're in for the long haul on matters of policy and principle. I've taken a heavy hit in politics for this, going from being the Deputy Prime Minister because I would not compromise on things that were important."

Is his heart in the right place?

"Yeah, absolutely," says Woolerton. "He wants a New Zealand that stands up for itself internationally. He thinks we have a role to play internationally, which is why he loves those things. His heart's definitely in the right place."

Ron Mark, despite turning his back on NZ First after the 2008 election, feels the same.

"He's been in the game longer. Regardless of the love/hate relationship that may exist between Winston and the media, he's still the most experienced politician out there. And he's still, nine times out of ten in the long, long, long run, been proven to be right. And in the long, long, long run, people will see that."

25

Keeping The Bastards Honest: Snapshots

> *"I give people a lot of liberty and a lot of freedom because in the end they will never be able to mature as politicians without that. Contrary to what everyone says, you ask anyone in NZ First about decisions we've made; I ensure that the full crew of caucus has to take responsibility for it, because if they do get consulted and they do make the decision, they can't later on back away from it."*
> — Winston Peters, 2014

THE PRIME MINISTER'S RUGBY DASH[341]
Rt Hon Winston Peters: How could she not know about the speed of the car she was travelling in on the day in question, when the windscreen of her car had to be repaired and replaced, and a front paint job done because of the gravel and stones coming off the car in front of her car, the one she was riding in, and would not that be something she would notice in her busy schedule of reading her documents, at 140 kilometres an hour?

Rt Hon Helen Clark: As I have said, I will not be making any comment on a matter before the courts.

Dail Jones, NZ First: I am sure that if the Rt Hon Winston Peters was travelling in a car at 180 kilometres an hour, and the windscreen broke and the car was damaged, he would be fully aware of what was going on. The leader of Labour – the Prime Minister – tells us that she can travel in a car

---

341 "Hansard, Questions for Oral Answer", 2 August 2005

in those circumstances and not know what is happening. What a disgrace! She is letting down our fine New Zealand police force by indicating she had no idea what was going on. Of course, as usual with Labour, she lets the police force carry the can. Someone else, as far as Helen Clark is concerned, can always carry the can. How many Labour Ministers have been sacked? It is always someone else's fault; she will never accept responsibility herself.[342]

GREEN CALLS POT BLACK?[343]

Keith Locke: I raise a point of order, Madam Speaker. When I was speaking there was a reference to Pol Pot. I seek leave to table Hansard of December 1979 at page 4844, when Mr Peters was in the National Government, and where the Acting Minister of Foreign Affairs, David Thompson, explained that Government's support – that is, the Government Winston Peters was a member of – for what he called the Pol Pot regime, in answer to a question from Stan Rodger.

Madam Speaker: Leave is sought to table that document. Is there any objection? There is objection.

Rt Hon Winston Peters: I do not oppose the tabling of that document, but I seek leave to table two documents that show effusive support of both Pol Pot and the Soviet Union's invasion of Afghanistan by this reformed man, Keith Locke, who wishes to excuse his past stupidity and idiocy.

IMMIGRATION DOUBLE-STANDARDS[344]

Dail Jones: Why is it that immigrants such as Mr Dean Kenny and his wife have to produce passport documents twice, documents to prove that their children are actually theirs, photos of them holding hands, and numerous other documents to prove that they have been living together in a genuine and stable relationship, and have to wait for 12 months before they get a decision; and does an 8-year Western marriage with two kids not speak for itself?

Hon Paul Swain: As I say, I do not know the details of that case. What I can say is that if the system was lax, the New Zealand First members would be the first to scream, whinge, and whine about it.

---

342 Hansard, Appropriation Bill, 3 August 2005
343 "Hansard, Questions for Oral Answer", 2 August 2005
344 Hansard, Questions of the Day, 23 June 2005

Dail Jones: Why does it appear so easy, instead, for refugees and other immigrants to bring family members here under the family reunification policies, as in the case of Najim al-Ali, who successfully brought in 15 family members, when New Zealanders, such as Dean Kenny, returning here with their families are being treated like criminals in their own country?

Hon Paul Swain: Of course, the refugee reunification of families policy was supported when the leader of the party that member belongs to was the Treasurer. It seems inexcusable to me that New Zealand First now wants to make political points out of this situation, when it supported those kinds of policies as part of a National-led Government.

MORE PAIN FOR SWAIN[345]

Rt Hon Winston Peters: In respect of the work of the Refugee Status Appeals Authority, why was the Minister so scathing about the concept of a flying squad to investigate properly the number of illegal aliens in this country, yet he had to admit at the select committee hearing this morning that he has set up – since last week – just such a 35-person squad; and when will he say: "Sorry, Winston. You were right in the first place."?

Hon Paul Swain: I raise a point of order, Madam Speaker. That member knows, unless he was out for a fag, that I made no such comment at the select committee this morning. I ask that he withdraw that comment.

Rt Hon Winston Peters: Madam Speaker, you know full well that he cannot mention someone not being present at a select committee, or in the House. That is his first offence. The second one is repeating the awful porky he told the media in the first place – that he did not believe in the need for a flying squad. And now he has got one –

Hon Paul Swain: What was said at the select committee is that there has been a border investigation branch since about 1998. There was a fraud unit established, and additional resources have been put into it. What we absolutely reject are the kinds of dawn raids that were part of National Party policy, and that are the kind of thing that that member wants to set up – horseback riders going up and down the country, acting as if they are something out of The Lord of the Rings. We are not having that, and we will not have that, under a Labour-led Government.

Rt Hon Winston Peters: I raise a point of order, Madam Speaker. Will

---

345 Hansard, Questions of the Day, 8 June 2005

you please arrange for him to get a Valium before he answers questions? He cannot rant and rave like that. If he wants to rant and rave like that, he should admit that the only time there were dawn raids was under a Labour Government, between 1972 and 1975. No wonder he feels guilty about it!

THE TONGAN RUGBY TEAM[346]

Rt Hon Winston Peters: Where is the Tongan rugby team?

Hon Dr Michael Cullen: I think the current Tongan rugby team is in Tonga.

Rt Hon Winston Peters: I raise a point of order, Madam Speaker. I did not ask about the Tongan national team. I asked about the team that the Immigration Service lost 2 years ago and still cannot find.

Madam Speaker: That is a point of information more than a point of order.

Rt Hon Winston Peters: Where is the Tongan rugby team that went missing 2 years ago?

Hon Dr Michael Cullen: I do not know. Its members may well be canvassing for the New Zealand First party by now.

EXPLAINING HIS COURT RECORD[347]

Rt Hon Winston Peters: The other party to the case decided to take the matter all the way to the Court of Appeal on the basis that it was a very serious case, and that it required a much higher court to decide. The Court of Appeal said to that very worthy MP that it thought a District Court could decide that issue on a case or action such as a strike out. The Court of Appeal told a member of Parliament to go back to the District Court, where he was bound to have his case struck out. But down at the District Court something went wrong, and the other man won. So the poor member of Parliament had to go to the High Court on appeal. He won half the case. Round about then, the money ran out. About seven other legal cases were going on at the same time, so members can see what I mean.

Darren Hughes: How many did the member win?

Rt Hon Winston Peters: I won every one of them. With this one here I got only halfway, because I could not afford to go back to the Court of Appeal, where I am certain I would have got justice. In fact, one might say that, like Cassius Clay, I am about 21 and nought. That is a serious contender!

---

346 Hansard, Questions of the Day, 17 May 2005
347 Hansard, Privileges Committee, 11 May 2005

UNDERAGE DRINKING[348]
Craig Mcnair (NZ First): New Zealand First members support this bill. I start by saying that New Zealand First has been the only party to be totally consistent in voicing its absolute opposition to the lowering of the drinking age, with all New Zealand First MPs having voted against the lowering of the drinking age back in 1999. New Zealand First has led the way on this issue not only by voting against the lowering of the drinking age but also by our leader, Winston Peters, introducing the Local Government (Prohibition of Liquor in Public Places) Amendment Bill back in 2001 so that councils could take control of their streets. It has worked.

LABOUR WEAK ON CRIME[349]
Ron Mark (NZ First): John Albert Thomas Clarke committed crimes in December 1996. In 1997 he was charged with violently attacking a woman in her home. He had tried to rape her, he had threatened to kill her, and he had beaten her with his fists and then with a tennis racquet. He was committed for trial and given bail. On 20 September 1997 he was charged with rape, kidnap, unlawful sexual connection, threatening to kill, and injuring with intent to cause grievous bodily harm to a 15-year-old girl. He had strangled her until she nearly passed out, threatened to drive her off the top of a cliff in Lyttelton in the back of his car, and told her he would bash her to death with a crowbar from his boot. And he admitted all those charges. He had done all that while he was on bail.

On 25 September 1997, although he was sentenced to a total of – I had it wrong; I said he was sentenced to what was essentially 38 years' jail, but a quick tally shows that it was 44 years. Let me make it clear. Clarke received 3 years' imprisonment for threatening to kill, 3 years for indecent assault, and 2 years for injuring with intent. He was sentenced to 6 years' imprisonment for abduction, 3 years for threatening to kill, 5 years for injuring with intent again, and 11 years each for each of the sexual violation charges, but with all terms to be served concurrently. Clearly the judge knew how dangerous this man was.

But then we come to December 2004 when, although Clarke had served only 7 years in prison, under this Government and its policies we saw him

---
348 Hansard, Sale of Liquor, 11 May 2005
349 Hansard, General Debate, 9 March 2005

released on home detention to Cardijn House in Addington, Christchurch. The staff at Cardijn House, a group of social support workers led by a 76-year-old supervisor, were given no details whatsoever of Clarke's past offending. They have subsequently said that had they known about it, they would have refused to have him there. On 26 January the Parole Board heard Clarke's parole application. Just 8 weeks after being put on home detention, he was paroled. On 18 February 2005 a complaint was made to the Sydenham police against Clarke, alleging that he had duped two of the female staff in the Cardijn House facility into having sexual relationships with him, that he had tried to do the same with a third woman who had gone to Cardijn House to seek assistance from the support staff, and that he had gone on to threaten to kill and to take revenge on all three of those women. He subsequently threatened the children of one of the women, who had rejected his advances.

John Albert Thomas Clarke is a high-risk sexual offender. He shows no remorse. He is proud of his past; he boasts of it. On being placed in home detention, he immediately engaged in acts of conning innocent women into relationships and then, when he did not get his way, he threatened to kill and rape them all, and he threatened children. Clarke continues to associate with known paedophiles. Clark was released by the Parole Board after serving only 7 years of his sentence. The report that the Parole Board obviously received from the Department of Corrections was inaccurate at best, and a whitewash or absolutely pure fiction at worst. Those responsible for that report – not the Parole Board – are the Minister, the Department of Corrections, and the much-vaunted integrated offender management system that they are so proud of – a system that continually fails, continually lets people down, and continually jeopardises the safety and well-being of New Zealanders, as it has done in this case.

No disclosure was made to the staff of Cardijn House as to this man's past. I understand that there was disclosure to a priest who recommended that he go there, but no disclosure at all was made to the female staff of that place or, indeed, to the 76-year-old woman who ran it. Why not? Because this politically correct Government will not allow such disclosure about people who are placed on home detention. Indeed, Mr Rick Barker stood up and told this House one day there were no violent offenders on home detention. How does that Minister feel today? He is soft on crime, Labour is politically correct, and the people who pay the price for that are people like "victim C", a young, innocent woman who was conned and duped and whose children were threatened.

LAUGHING AT RAPE VICTIMS[350]
Ron Mark (NZ First): Today I wish to raise in the House, once again, the question of John Albert Thomas Clarke.
Jill Pettis: Oh!
Ron Mark: There goes the chief Government whip, a female who thinks that revelations about a man who raped a 15-year-old schoolgirl are boring. I tell that member that the subsequent molestation of three more women by that man, since he was placed on home detention and on parole, is not a boring matter to those victims. This Government, Jill Pettis, and Trevor Mallard, who is trying to interject, must take responsibility and be accountable for the situation. Last week I told the House that this man had been sentenced to a total of 44 years in jail.
Jill Pettis: You're obsessed!
Ron Mark: I want it on the record that Jill Pettis is laughing about this man. That is why these sorts of people – people like Mr Jarden, who raped two schoolgirls – are out on our streets or released into home detention. I ask the member whether that is something else to laugh about. Is that a joke, too? She should try telling that to the parents of those girls.

This question has to be asked: who put Mr Clarke on home detention? How could that possibly happen? How can the Minister of Corrections say that Mr Clarke completed his home detention successfully, when there are now three new victims who have said that Mr Clarke was smoking marijuana, drinking, and was alone with children, consorting and associating with them – thereby breaching the three conditions that were part of his release? This Government is becoming legendary for being blind to, deaf to, and totally disinterested in the pleas of victims.

I ask Jill Pettis – on behalf of a young mother who is now on the run, who is somewhere in New Zealand, hopping from plane to plane and from home to home, fearful that this man, Mr Clarke, will be released back into the community, because that is what she has been told – why the police will not be charging him with threatening to kill? The Department of Corrections said that he had completed his home detention successfully.

---
350 Hansard, General Debate, 16 March 2005

Rubbish! He was alone with children, whereas a specific condition of his home detention was that he was not allowed to be alone with children. And Jill Pettis, a member of the Government, laughs. Everyone in the gallery saw her laugh. It is a joke to her.

MORE INTERESTED IN TRAFFIC TICKETS[351]

Rt Hon Winston Peters: Would the Minister be concerned to hear that on the date and time in question, a call was made over the police radio requesting back-up for an incident involving suspicious persons believed to be armed, and that that call was ignored by an officer in a traffic patrol car within a kilometre of the incident, who was instead content to continue to write out a traffic ticket for a former policeman who heard the conversation over the police radio; and is that not just further proof of the Minister's ring-fencing traffic patrol cars in order to ignore emergencies?

111 CALLS GO UNRESPONDED[352]

Ron Mark (NZ First) to the Minister of Police: Did he ascertain from the police review into Christchurch 111 calls why a Christchurch dispatcher alleged he or she could not contact three traffic units to send to an abduction and an assault on 4 July because they were logged "out of service" and not listening to their radios?

Hon George Hawkins (Minister of Police): The police have investigated all the allegations made by the member, and after listening to the tapes and talking to the staff involved, the police found that the claims made by Ron Mark were "factually incorrect". I prefer to believe the police.

Ron Mark: Does the Minister agree that this press release issued by police headquarters spin doctors yesterday is not worth the paper it is written on, given that the people involved were not even interviewed as part of the Minister's so-called review of the incident?

Rt Hon Winston Peters: Why did the Minister just tell the House that the police were not able to go beyond the press statement and documents released by Ron Mark because certain items had been blacked out, thereby not giving the police a chance to find out what personnel they should investigate; and how does he reconcile that with the statement of

---
351 Hansard, Questions for Oral Answer, 10 March 2005
352 Hansard, Questions of the Day, 17 February 2005

8 February that despite Ron Mark blacking the names out, the police got to those people – how does he reconcile those two statements?

Hon George Hawkins: What was identified very clearly was what the event was, which was not clear when the member originally had the information before the House.

Ron Mark: Can the Minister then explain why it is that on 4 July 2004, at the time that the incident occurred – when the staff involved in the incident and senior traffic officers were discussing it, both in writing and verbally – the assurances and explanations that the communications staff received at that time by email bore no resemblance to the miraculous revelations that we are now getting out of police headquarters; is this simply a whitewash, a cover-up, or a scam?

Mr Speaker: The Minister can answer one of those questions.

Hon George Hawkins: I still prefer to believe the police rather than that member.

Hon Tony Ryall: My question asked for the explanation of the contradiction in the House caused when the Minister said he was advised by the police that they could identify the events – that is what he said not 4 minutes ago – whereas in the House on 8 February he said that the police could identify the sources. That is the reason why Mr Mark is querying the Minister's original answer today.

Mr Speaker: I listened to the Minister's reply, and he certainly addressed that.

Rt Hon Winston Peters: I raise a point of order, Mr Speaker. I hate to raise this, but my colleague came to the House today because his reputation was on the line. A ministerial statement had gone out, stating that he was wrong. He knows that the key sources were not interviewed by the police prior to the release of that fallacious press statement. He came here with one purpose: to ask the Minister why the sources had not been interviewed.

We have had countless points of order and supplementary questions on this matter, and the Minister has clearly not told the House the truth at all. There is a wide variance between what the Minister said on 8 February and what he has said today. His defence today was that the police could not interview the sources, because Mr Mark had blacked out the names of the sources on the emails that he had released to the press. That is what he said by way of his first line of defence. We now know categorically, from the Minister's own statement, that that is not the truth. We are now at the end of the substantive question, and we are no further down the track with regard to getting an honest answer from the Minister.

THE TAMIHERE INTERVIEW[353]

Rodney Hide: Notwithstanding the Prime Minister's claim about excessive alcohol, what is her response to John Tamihere's claim in the interview that this Labour Government is run by anti-family homosexuals and trade unionists who do nothing but plot and plan and double-cross their coalition partners?

Rt Hon Helen Clark: I suggest the member gets some new glasses and examines the quality of our front bench.

Dr Don Brash: Has the Prime Minister seen Mr Tamihere's reference to "ministerial klingons" and to the Hon Steve Maharey and others as "very smarmy, very clever, but no substance", and does she understand that many New Zealanders are very grateful to Mr Tamihere for providing those revealing insights into her ministerial colleagues, which were gained from his privileged vantage point in her Cabinet in recent years?

Rt Hon Helen Clark: Yes, I have seen the statements. I note that Mr Tamihere referred to a number of his colleagues as very clever, unlike Brian Connell's reference to the Leader of the Opposition as "stupid".

Rt Hon Winston Peters: Can the Prime Minister please reconcile these two events: Lianne Dalziel being told to go home for allegedly not telling the truth, and John Tamihere being told to go home for irrefutably telling the truth?

Rt Hon Helen Clark: In recent months I have been in the House when members of the Opposition have refused to believe that anything Mr Tamihere says is true. I find the change of attitude very remarkable.

Rt Hon Winston Peters: Why is it wrong for a member of Parliament, whether or not that member is in the Labour Party, to point out the disturbing, manipulative, social engineering policies of her administration, and the deep disquiet that certain people have, even in the Labour Party, about the social agenda of this administration led by her, when so many of her colleagues clearly, according to Mr Tamihere, share that view – 10 he says, and 15 more on a good day – and why does that article automatically become drivel just because it embarrasses her?

---

353 Hansard, Questions of the Day, 5 April 2005

Rt Hon Helen Clark: This Government's record on families stands second to none. Members should look at the Working for Families package that is rolling out this week, whereby every family currently receiving family support can look forward to getting more support from the Labour Government.

Rt Hon Winston Peters: Why is it that John Tamihere has to be duplicitous, a liar, a tosser, a weirdo, a smarmer, or be without substance before he is allowed back into the Labour Party Cabinet?

Rt Hon Helen Clark: He does not have to be any of those things. He does have to be a team player.

SMALL PARTIES AND CONSCIENCES[354]

Rodney Hide: Can the Prime Minister confirm that, despite the United Party's vehement opposition, the Civil Union Act was passed, the Prostitution Reform Act was passed and, in fact, the entire 20 pieces of legislation that the United Future party members opposed because of their consciences were passed, and that the United Future party would make a good doormat for any political party in Government in this country?

Rt Hon Winston Peters: I raise a point of order, Madam Speaker. I seek leave for Mr Dunne to have 10 more questions so he may outline one thing he has done in the last 3 years.

Madam Speaker: That is not a point of order. Is leave seriously sought? I am sorry; the member cannot seek leave on somebody else's behalf.

THE SOURCE OF HIS APPRENTICE[355]

Hon Brian Donnelly: Will the Minister confirm that there would not even be a Modern Apprenticeship Training Act if it had not been for New Zealand First?

Hon Trevor Mallard: Unlike the previous questioner, I am prepared to take that member's word on that. [Interruption]

THE PRINCIPLES OF THE TREATY[356]

Pita Paraone, NZ First: The second reason that New Zealand First will not support this bill is the inclusion of the words "the principles of the Treaty

---

354   Hansard, Questions of the Day, 30 March 2005
355   Hansard, Questions of the Day, 17 March 2005
356   Hansard, Ngati Awa, 1 March 2005

of Waitangi". Although I have articulated New Zealand First's concerns on previous occasions, I think it is important to reiterate those, relevant to our doubt about the durability of the settlement. This settlement can still proceed without those words. We believe that their inclusion affects the possible durability of this settlement. I also point out to this House that it was suggested that those words – "the principles of the Treaty of Waitangi" – be included in the Foreshore and Seabed Act, and that it was at New Zealand First's insistence that they were removed.

Prebble: I listened very carefully to the remarks made by the New Zealand First member Mr Paraone, who said things that I think have a great deal of merit. How on earth can this Parliament start to define different hapū in a bill of this sort? One becomes extremely suspicious about that. I was a Minister when this treaty process first started; in fact, I was the Minister who had to do some of the original negotiations. I started from a point of not having as much knowledge as one would like, and I remember asking the officials how many iwi the Government believed there were in New Zealand. The first answer I got was that it was the same as the number of canoes, plus one iwi that came down in a ball of fire. I was later told that there were 24 iwi. Then the number went up to 48, and by the time I finished as a Minister, the Crown was recognising 120 iwi. Now it seems that the inflation of the number of iwi will become an inflation of the number of hapū. That is not an area where the Crown ought to be going, and it is certainly not something we should put into statute law.

Jim Peters, NZ First: The issue before us again is, first, that the principles of the Treaty of Waitangi are vague and undefined, and as Dr Mapp has already stated, subject to incorrect interpretation from 1987 onwards, based upon a slip by the judge of the day, amplified by misdirection by the then Labour Government, worked through the 1990s by the then National Government, and now we arrive at the situation whereby that omission, which Parliament has just declined to rectify, has implications with regard to the supposed final settlement of Ngāti Awa. Those undefined principles are the seed of potential problems in the future. They are not defined in the bill. There is no clarity or expression as to what they mean, and that gives an opportunity for others to raise matters in the future.

BEFORE SHE WAS A FUTURE AIR NEW ZEALAND LINK HIJACKER[357]

Rt Hon Winston Peters: Is he confident that Asha Ali Abdille, the refugee sickness beneficiary whom he ordered an inquiry into last year, and who has a string of criminal convictions, is not a threat to the New Zealand community; if so, why?

Hon Paul Swain: Yes, I did order an inquiry into that. There were two issues: firstly, the seriousness of the alleged crimes, which is still being investigated, and, secondly, whether she was a fit and proper person to bring in other family members. That whole policy issue is one that I have currently under review.

Rt Hon Winston Peters: Why was it, after an Official Information Act request to his office was lodged, that the reply came back with so many blanks such as that, with hardly a word on the page, that no one is any the wiser, including the blanking out of Asha Ali Abdille's criminal history, and also the department's recommendations being blanked out as to what to do with this woman who has been trying to bring 14 members of her family into this country; what on earth is going on?

WHEN IN ROME, SPEAK ROMAN[358]

Rt Hon Winston Peters (Leader – NZ First) to the Prime Minister: What impact, if any, does the understanding of the English language have on the way in which she administers her Government?

Hon Dr Michael Cullen (Deputy Prime Minister), on behalf of the Prime Minister: I believe that the Prime Minister has a reasonable understanding of the English language, sufficient at least to meet the needs of administering the Government.

Rt Hon Winston Peters: If that is the case, does she understand the English language test, which despite its failure by her administration to be administered, now has 300,000 people in this country who cannot speak English, and how on earth did that happen?

Hon Dr Michael Cullen: I am not sure whether that information or

---

357 Hansard, Questions of the Day, 1 March 2005. Abdille went on years later to hijack an Air New Zealand Link flight, and was jailed for nine years, see "Woman jailed for hijack attempt," 27 August 2010, Stuff.co.nz
358 Hansard, Questions of the Day, 10 February 2005

statistic includes those aged under 2, the great majority of whom do not speak any language, but we have had a number of immigrants from countries whose native language is not English. But of course there are a number of people I know of, not always that far from here, who claim to be native English speakers who I would not regard as functionally literate.

Rt Hon Winston Peters: Why is it that we now have a $1.2 million language line interpretation service fitted into parliamentary offices, if the Prime Minister and her colleagues had been doing their job in respect of the English language test, which despite that test now sees 300,000 people in this country who cannot speak English – how did that happen?

Rt Hon Winston Peters: Why is it that all these people coming into this country are now demanding all sorts of new language services, even to the extent that we have this service online in Parliament, when in fact they should follow the acronym of an old Chinese gentleman who said that the policy the Government should be following is "FIFO – Fit in, or fly off."?

Hon Dr Michael Cullen: Unlike the member, the Government encourages and values diversity in New Zealand's population. We know the member does not, but I do not think that is a view shared by the great majority of New Zealanders.

WOMEN MORE CONCERNED ABOUT TRAFFIC OFFENCES THAN RAPISTS – MINISTER[359]

Hon George Hawkins (Minister of Police): The document tabled by the member yesterday – table 9.6 of the New Zealand National Survey of Crime Victims – clearly states that 61.7 percent of the 3,001 women who participated in the survey were "very worried" or "fairly worried" about being involved in an accident caused by a drunk driver. That was the highest category among the 12 surveyed. I stand by my earlier statement to the House. I also remind the member that since 1999 more than 436 lives have been saved on our roads, and that impacts massively on women, children, and their families.

Hon Tony Ryall: Why is the Minister standing by his ludicrous position when even the Commissioner of Police backed away from this view on radio this morning, leaving the Minister hanging out to dry?

Hon George Hawkins: No, I am relying on the survey results that I quoted a few minutes ago. I do not rewrite surveys.

---

359 Hansard, Questions of the Day, 9 February 2005

Moana Mackey: What information can he give the House regarding the success of the police in reducing crime and reducing the road toll?

Hon George Hawkins: The statistics issued by the Commissioner of Police for the 2003-04 year show that we had the lowest crime rate for 21 years. Land Transport New Zealand states that, since 1990, road deaths have dropped 40 percent, despite a 33 percent increase in the number of vehicles on the roads and a 19 percent increase in the population. The outcome of this Government's policy is that the lives of 436 men, women, and children have been saved.

Ron Mark: Does the Minister think the family of 83-year-old Mona Morriss, who was sexually violated and murdered in her pensioner's flat last month, and the 14-year-old girl who was raped in her bedroom in south Auckland, then thrown over a 3-metre fence, in the same month, would agree with his comment that women are more concerned about speeding than they are about being attacked in their own homes; if so, why?

Stephen Franks: Why does the Minister interpret the crime victims survey to defend the police priorities in issuing speeding tickets over 11 categories of offence surveyed, when the questionnaire did not even ask about speeding, and on traffic offences asked only about drink-driving, and the numbers of women who responded were almost identical in saying they were very worried about that, and about sexual offences committed against them?

Hon George Hawkins: I am just quoting the facts from the survey.

Tariana Turia: Is rape a general duty call-out; if not, what response does the Minister have for a young woman who was raped in Hamilton 2 weeks ago, who phoned the 111 phone line and was advised that as the address she gave was not far from the police station, she could walk around there and make a statement, rather than have the police come to the house where the perpetrator was still present?

IRAENA ASHER DIED BECAUSE TRAFFIC UNITS REFUSED TO BE DIVERTED[360]

Ron Mark: How many of the 12 to 15 traffic patrols on duty in Auckland 3 months later than the incident referred to earlier in my question, on the night of Sunday, 10 October 2004 – the night Iraena Asher called 111

---
360 Hansard, Questions of the Day, 8 February 2005

fearing for her life – were diverted to come to her aid; if none, how can the Minister claim that his policy is working?

Hon George Hawkins: The member needs to put down a specific question on that and I will give him a specific answer. That point was not contained in the original question.

Ron Mark: I raise a point of order, Mr Speaker. I have brought to you in this House, on numerous occasions, difficulties we have had with even getting this Minister to answer written questions on time. Now he has the audacity, after 4 hours of being able to prepare himself for this question time, in answering an oral question, to waste our supplementary question by asking me to put it to him in writing. I ask you to ask him to answer the question.

Mr Speaker: No, I will not. The Minister gave a perfectly proper reply.

Hon Tony Ryall: The Minister has been providing members of the press gallery with a copy of the 2001 victimisation survey as evidence of his claims. I seek leave to table, table 9.6 from that report, which shows in the most worrying category that women have identified being sexually assaulted or raped as much more important than any other issue.

Document not tabled.

Ron Mark: Does he stand by his statement in the House on 2 November 2004 that all staff who are on patrol are available to attend general duties call-outs; if so, how does he reconcile that statement with an Auckland City police district strategic traffic group policy statement: "The primary task of the strategic traffic group is accident prevention patrol duty. They are not to be diverted to other tasks."; and was the Minister unaware of the police policy at the time, or was he deliberately misleading this House?

Ron Mark: I seek the leave of the House to table an email that shows quite clearly that in order to respond to a priority one call where a child was being abducted, three general duties units had to be diverted from priority two jobs they were on because the traffic highway patrol would not respond.

Document, by leave, laid on the Table of the House.

NZ FIRST IMPACT[361]

Dail Jones (NZ First): New Zealand First is very clear about what a New Zealand First Government will do as far as law and order is concerned. We will separate the traffic police from the police. We do not want our

---

361 Hansard, Appropriation Debates, 3 August 2005

main police handing out traffic tickets. We do not want our main police chasing after people who are doing 63 kilometres an hour in a built-up, residential area where they should be doing 50 kilometres an hour. The main police should be out there catching burglars, murderers, and rapists. They should have been making sure that Iraena Asher, the young woman who disappeared in the Pīhā area, was attended to – they should have called on her and made sure she was safe. That is what the police should be doing. Instead we have a disappearance that will remain one of those mysteries, and that we might still read about in 25 years' time.

New Zealand First wants to make sure that the police do policing, and we will increase the size of the New Zealand police force to achieve that. Any responsible Government would do no less, and that is what New Zealand First will do.

The other area we said we would be involved in was Treaty of Waitangi matters. It is interesting that Labour and National now support New Zealand First policy. We have a 100 percent record on that. We have now drawn the two tired old parties kicking and screaming into the 21st century, to ensure they support the policies of New Zealand First. After the next election, New Zealand First will make sure those policies are carried out.

The third area we mentioned was immigration. It is very pleasing to note that, even in Opposition, New Zealand First has been able to ensure Labour has changed its policy. We insisted that there be English language tests for migrants, and Labour has done that. We wanted changes to the skilled migrant category, and Labour has done that. New Zealand First wanted stricter health requirements for migrants, and Labour has done that. We wanted to establish an undesirables category, and Labour has done that. We wanted to put a stop to foreign nationals processing visa applications, and Labour has done that. We wanted the regulation of immigration advisers, and Labour has done that. We wanted changes to the investor category, and that has been done, too. New Zealand First has run the administration of the New Zealand Immigration Service from Opposition. Time and time again throughout the past 3 years of this administration, from 2002 to 2005, the Rt Hon Winston Peters has hammered the successive Ministers of Immigration to ensure that there are good policies as far as administration is concerned.

Unfortunately, we have no control over the number of people who come into New Zealand. On looking at the figures, I see that the smartest people in New Zealand are, clearly, Wellingtonians, because in the 18 years from 1986 to 2004 Wellington's population increased by only 15 percent. That is nice, steady growth of population in 18 years. By contrast, those of us who live in Auckland saw a population increase in that region of almost 60 percent. That is an appalling situation for Auckland. That is why I say Wellingtonians are smart. Their increase has been gentle, and can be managed. In fact, the increase in the population of the Auckland region in the last 18 years equals Wellington's entire population since day one. It is no wonder that things are so chaotic in Auckland, and that so many born and bred Aucklanders regard Auckland as a foreign city and do not go anywhere near its main streets; they are frightened and nervous to do so.

Hon Dover Samuels: Ha, ha!

Dail Jones: Mr Samuels might laugh, but it is a fact that many born and bred Aucklanders do not go down the main street any more. New Zealand First says we must have control of immigration, and we must ensure that we grant entry to immigrants with skills and knowledge of the English language. That is a priority. There should be a 5-year probation period for new immigrants.

New Zealand First will have a population policy to make sure that all New Zealanders can be involved in what happens to the future of New Zealand. I am very appreciative of the Taiwanese Association to which I and other members of Parliament spoke a little while ago. As one of its questions, it came up with the idea of a population policy. I was able to say to its members that the Rt Hon Winston Peters had already announced in his Ōrewa speech that that was what New Zealand First would be doing. We are working closely with migrant groups to ensure that everybody knows we have some sort of plan in respect of what happens to New Zealand.

As things stand at the moment, we can build as many roads as we like in Auckland, but they will never cope even with our present population, let alone with an increase of 1 million people, which is the number that some political parties want our population to increase by. I ask members if they can imagine another 450,000 people in Auckland, or another 500,000 people in 10 years' time. Labour does not say no to that, and it is quite happy to support it, because it sees it as somehow helping it to win the election. It would be an absolute disaster for Auckland. After all, I can remember when I went to Belgrade and saw all the tall apartment buildings that had been built. To a large extent, Auckland now reminds me of Belgrade in post-Tito's Yugoslavia of 1982. There are Aucklanders who are dreadfully concerned about the type of building that is being built.

In this election, New Zealand First is the only party that is concerned about the young children of New Zealand and their health. Plunket has supported New Zealand First's policy to ensure that all children up to primary school age get free health-care. Labour does not care about free health-care for young children; neither does any other party in this House. But that is New Zealand First's policy, which continues the existing policy that we had when we were in Government.

If you'd like a text searchable copy of this book, visit www.ianwishart.com and choose one of our ebook options

REVIEW COMMENTS FOR OUR STORIES

"This is a cracker of a publication. ..These articles and commentaries are always fascinating. This is a book to be treasured. Every New Zealander, born here or not, will enjoy browsing through Our Stories. And for certain, the question setters for pub quizzes the length and breadth of the country will find it an invaluable source of material." – *Iain Duffy, Daily Post*

"Anyone who enjoys history will love this book. Every day hundreds of stories are published in newspapers and magazines. Journalist Ian Wishart has collated some of the most fascinating of these forgotten stories into a book. I love these types of books that you can pick up and flick through, reading whatever catches your eye. It's a book to put by your bedside and dip into. There are editorials, letters to the editors and hundreds of historical news stories." – *Linda Hall, Bay of Plenty Times*

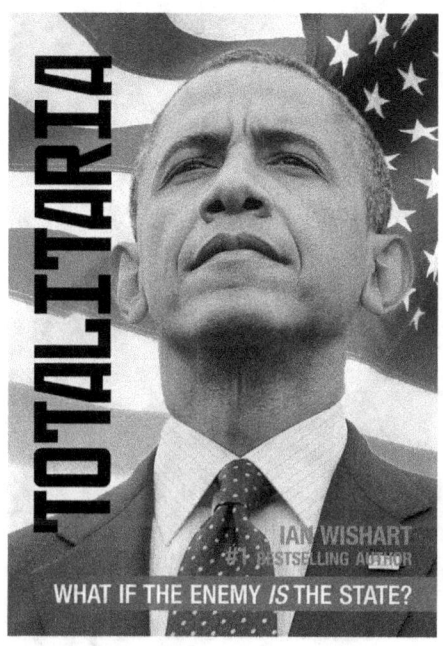

FIVE STAR REVIEWS ON AMAZON

Reading the footnotes will open your eyes. The research he has done is fantastic. The is a book to read and pass to people close to you!

Ian Wishart has clearly put a phenomenal amount time and research into this book. He has footnotes of references for nearly every statement he makes (which I truly appreciate). It is also reassuring to see how the conclusions that took me years to reach are so articulately and comprehensively laid out in print.

THE CRITICS ON THE DIVINITY CODE

"The genius of this Kiwi author is the ability to discover those ugly facts that slay the hypotheses of scientists, philosophers, historians and novelists that God does not exist and that Jesus Christ was not a person in history but a myth. Its coverage is almost encylopedic. Wishart's skill as an investigative journalist is obvious as he takes hypothesis after hypothesis and demonstrates their inadequacy...He also has a sense of humour that lightens the concentration" – *Bishop Mackey, Roman Catholic Bishop Emeritus of Auckland*

"*The Divinity Code* is one of the best 'Christian' apologetic books I have read. There are a few small details that I think shows that he is not Catholic, but it is an excellent book nevertheless. Don t miss reading it if you can. – *NZ Catholic*

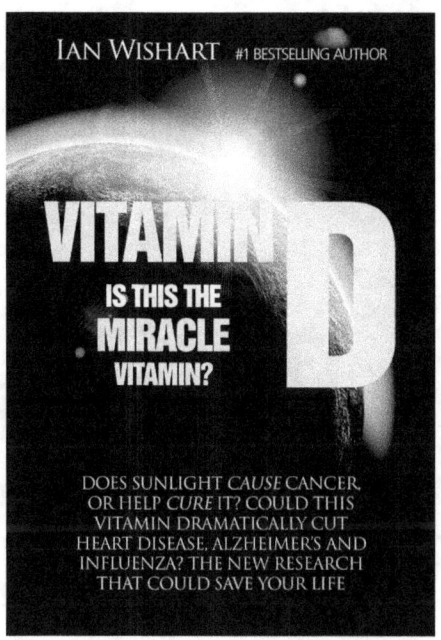

FROM THE AMAZON REVIEWS

5.0 out of 5 stars
By Dr William B. Grant, San Francisco
This book is the latest popular book on vitamin D. It covers topics of current interest including autism, cancer, erectile dysfunction, hospital-acquired infections, pregnancy, heart disease, infectious diseases, and autoimmune diseases. The research journal literature on vitamin D is growing at the rate of about 4000 papers per year yet the health system in the U.S. accepts the evidence only for falls and fractures. This book makes the case well that there are many, many beneficial effects of vitamin D. I strongly recommend this book.

5.0 out of 5 stars
By Barbara Locke
I felt this book was a great summary of the research around Vitamin D and its health effects, and the excellent referencing made it easy to read more technical research if i needed to. A very thought provoking book.

THE CRITICS ON THE GREAT DIVIDE

"*The Great Divide* is the book that somebody had to write." – *Phil Hayward*

"A page-turner that tells the story of pre-Maori history, of explorers who met a sudden death, of brave missionaries, musket wars, of the beginnings of British rule, the ins and outs of the treaty, land clashes, sovereignty wars, of the role of Christianity, and implications for today. His chatty, colloquial style could and should keep a wide range of readers on the edge of a chair…

"The chapter "Waitangi's fairytale godfathers" shreds Waitangi Tribunal arguments… Those chiefs who opposed the unity of the races under one sovereign became the Maori king movement, and the focus of the so-called Maori renaissance in the 20th century, Wishart wrote. "Their followers, however, are the ones now in charge of the Waitangi debate, the cultural gatekeepers. They are the ones who can make the majority voices from the past fall silent – their words left out of the popular history books and not quoted in universities."

So here we are in the 21st century still fighting the 19th century sovereignty war, this time using words instead of bullets. The book is a must-read." – *Mike Butler*

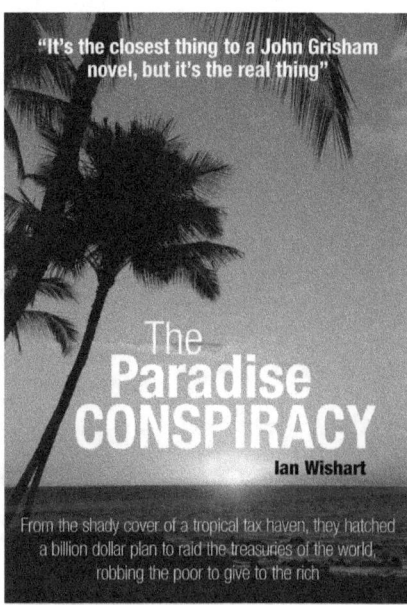